A·N·N·U·A·L E·D·I·T·I·O·N·S

Business Ethics 02/03

Fourteenth Edition

EDITOR

John E. Richardson

Pepperdine University

Dr. John E. Richardson is professor of marketing in the George L. Graziadio School of Business and Management at Pepperdine University. He is president of his own consulting firm and has consulted with organizations such as Bell and Howell, Dayton-Hudson, Epson, and the U.S. Navy, as well as with various service, nonprofit, and franchise organizations. Dr. Richardson is a member of the American Management Association, the American Marketing Association, the Society for Business Ethics, and Beta Gamma Sigma honorary business fraternity.

McGraw-Hill/Dushkin

530 Old Whitfield Street, Guilford, Connecticut 06437

Visit us on the Internet

http://www.dushkin.com

Credits

1. **Ethics, Values, and Social Responsibility in Business**
   Unit photo—© 2002 by PhotoDisc, Inc.
2. **Ethical Issues and Dilemmas in the Workplace**
   Unit photo—Courtesy of Tom Way/IBM Microelectronics.
3. **Business and Society: Contemporary Ethical, Social, and Environmental Issues**
   Unit photo—© 2002 by Sweet By & By/Cindy Brown.
4. **Ethics and Social Responsibility in the Marketplace**
   Unit photo—TRW Inc. photo.
5. **Developing the Future Ethos and Social Responsibility of Business**
   Unit photo—© 2002 by PhotoDisc, Inc.

Copyright

Cataloging in Publication Data
Main entry under title: Annual Editions: Business Ethics. 2002/2003.
1. Business Ethics—Periodicals. I. Richardson, John E., *comp.* II. Title: Business ethics.
ISBN 0–07–250700–4 658.408 ISSN 1055–5455

Fourteenth Edition

Cover image © 2002 PhotoDisc, Inc.
Printed in the United States of America 1234567890BAHBAH5432 Printed on Recycled Paper

Editors/Advisory Board

Members of the Advisory Board are instrumental in the final selection of articles for each edition of ANNUAL EDITIONS. Their review of articles for content, level, currentness, and appropriateness provides critical direction to the editor and staff. We think that you will find their careful consideration well reflected in this volume.

Staff

To the Reader

In publishing ANNUAL EDITIONS we recognize the enormous role played by the magazines, newspapers, and journals of the public press in providing current, first-rate educational information in a broad spectrum of interest areas. Many of these articles are appropriate for students, researchers, and professionals seeking accurate, current material to help bridge the gap between principles and theories and the real world. These articles, however, become more useful for study when those of lasting value are carefully collected, organized, indexed, and reproduced in a low-cost format, which provides easy and permanent access when the material is needed. That is the role played by ANNUAL EDITIONS.

Recent events have brought ethics to the forefront as a topic of discussion throughout our nation. And, undoubtedly, the area of society that is getting the closest scrutiny regarding its ethical practices is the business sector. Both the print and broadcast media have offered a constant stream of facts and opinions concerning recent unethical goings-on in the business world. Insider trading scandals on Wall Street, the marketing of unsafe products, money laundering, and questionable contracting practices are just a few examples of events that have recently tarnished the image of business.

As corporate America struggles to find its ethical identity in a business environment that grows increasingly complex, managers are confronted with some poignant questions that have definite ethical ramifications. Does a company have any obligation to help solve social problems such as poverty, pollution, and urban decay? What ethical responsibilities should a multinational corporation assume in foreign countries? What obligation does a manufacturer have to the consumer with respect to product defects and safety?

The recent Enron scandal raises important questions about the responsibility that executives have when running a publicly traded company. The fallout from the Enron bankruptcy will continue to unfold as government committees investigate how Enron, then the seventh largest company in the United States, ran its business into failure. There will undoubtedly be systemic changes in how accountants audit businesses, how executives are held to be ethically accountable, and how companies manage their investments. Not only will many practices in the business community be reassessed, but also the American government will be challenged with regard to the rules of political campaign financing.

These are just a few of the issues that make the study of business ethics important and challenging. A significant goal of *Annual Editions: Business Ethics 02/03* is to present some different perspectives on understanding basic concepts and concerns of business ethics and to provide ideas on how to incorporate these concepts into the policies and decision-making processes of businesses. The articles reprinted in this publication have been carefully chosen from a variety of public press sources to furnish current information on business ethics.

This volume contains a number of features designed to make it useful for students, researchers, and professionals. These include a *topic guide* for locating articles on specific subjects related to business ethics, the *table of contents* with summaries of each article and key concepts in italics, and a comprehensive *index.* Also included in this edition are selected *World Wide Web* sites that can be used to further explore article topics.

The articles are organized into five units. Selections that focus on similar issues are concentrated into subsections within the broader units. Each unit is preceded by an overview, which provides background for informed reading of the articles, emphasizes critical issues, and presents key points to consider that focus on major themes running through the selections.

Your comments, opinions, and recommendations about *Annual Editions: Business Ethics 02/03* will be greatly appreciated and will help shape future editions. Please take a moment to complete and return the postage-paid *article rating form* on the last page of this book. Any book can be improved, and with your help this one will continue to be.

John E. Richardson
Editor

Contents

UNIT 1
Ethics, Values, and Social Responsibility in Business

Seven selections provide an introduction to business ethics and social responsibility.

The concepts in bold italics are developed in the article. For further expansion, please refer to the Topic Guide and the Index.

UNIT 2
Ethical Issues and Dilemmas in the Workplace

Nineteen selections organized within seven subsections examine crucial employee-related issues and their ethical implications for management's decision-making practices and policies.

The concepts in bold italics are developed in the article. For further expansion, please refer to the Topic Guide and the Index.

The concepts in bold italics are developed in the article. For further expansion, please refer to the Topic Guide and the Index.

UNIT 3
Business and Society: Contemporary Ethical, Social, and Environmental Issues

Ten articles organized within three subsections provide an analysis of important ethical, social, and environmental issues affecting both domestic and global workplaces.

The concepts in bold italics are developed in the article. For further expansion, please refer to the Topic Guide and the Index.

UNIT 4
Ethics and Social Responsibility in the Marketplace

Six selections organzed within two subsections describe the practice of incorporating ethics into the marketplace.

The concepts in bold italics are developed in the article. For further expansion, please refer to the Topic Guide and the Index.

UNIT 5
Developing the Future Ethos and Social Responsibility of Business

Seven selections consider guidelines and principles for developing the future ethos and social responsibility of business.

The concepts in bold italics are developed in the article. For further expansion, please refer to the Topic Guide and the Index.

Topic Guide

This topic guide suggests how the selections in this book relate to the subjects covered in your course. You may want to use the topics listed on these pages to search the Web more easily.

On the following pages a number of Web sites have been gathered specifically for this book. They are arranged to reflect the units of this *Annual Edition.* You can link to these sites by going to the DUSHKIN ONLINE support site at *http://www.dushkin.com/online/.*

ALL THE ARTICLES THAT RELATE TO EACH TOPIC ARE LISTED BELOW THE BOLD-FACED TERM.

World Wide Web Sites

The following World Wide Web sites have been carefully researched and selected to support the articles found in this reader. The easiest way to access these selected sites is to go to our DUSHKIN ONLINE support site at *http://www.dushkin.com/online/*.

AE: Business Ethics 02/03

The following sites were available at the time of publication. Visit our Web site—we update DUSHKIN ONLINE regularly to reflect any changes.

General Sources

American Civil Liberties Union (ACLU)
http://www.aclu.org/issues/worker/campaign.html
The ACLU provides this page in its "Campaign for Fairness in the Workplace." Papers cover such privacy issues as lifestyle discrimination, drug testing, and electronic monitoring.

Center for the Study of Ethics in the Professions
http://www.iit.edu/departments/csep/
Sponsored by the Illinois Institute of Technology, this site links to a number of world business ethics centers.

Harvard Business School (HBS)
http://www.hbs.edu/educators.html
Surf through the many valuable links attached to this Educators and Research News site to preview upcoming issues of the *Harvard Business Review.*

Markkula Center
http://www.scu.edu/SCU/Centers/Ethics/
Santa Clara University's Markkula Center strives to heighten ethical awareness and to improve ethical decision making on campus and within the community. A list of published resources, links to ethical issues sites, and other data are provided.

Murray G. Bacon Center for Ethics in Business
http://www.public.iastate.edu/~BACON_CENTER/homepage.html
This Iowa State University site was developed to aid businesses to understand and come to grips with ethical dilemmas.

U.S. Department of Labor
http://www.dol.gov
Browsing through this site will lead you to a vast array of labor-related data and discussions of issues affecting employees and managers, such as the minimum wage.

U.S. Equal Employment Opportunity Commission (EEOC)
http://www.eeoc.gov
The EEOC's mission "is to ensure equality of opportunity by vigorously enforcing federal legislation prohibiting discrimination in employment." Consult this site for facts about employment discrimination, enforcement, and litigation.

Wharton Ethics Program
http://rider.wharton.upenn.edu/~ethics/#Objectives/
The Wharton School of the University of Pennsylvania provides an independently managed site that offers links to research, cases, and other business ethics centers.

UNIT 1: Ethics, Values, and Social Responsibility in Business

Association for Moral Education (AME)
http://www4.wittenberg.edu/ame/
AME is dedicated to fostering communication, cooperation, training, and research that links moral theory with educational practices. From here it is possible to connect to several sites of relevance in the study of business ethics.

Business for Social Responsibility (BSR)
http://www.bsr.org/BSRResources/Issues.cfm/
The 9 core topic areas covered by BSR are listed on this page. They cover everything from Corporate Social Responsibility to Business Ethics to Community Investment to the Environment to Governance and Accountability to Human Rights to Marketplace to Mission, Vision, Values, and finally Workplace. New information is added on a regular basis. For each topic or subtopic there is an introduction, examples of large and small company leadership practices, sample company policies, links to helping resources, and other information.

Business Policy and Strategy
http://www.aom.pace.edu/bps/bps.html
This site of the Business Policy and Strategy Division of the Academy of Management is full of information about various topics in business theory and practice.

Enron Online
http://www.enron.com/corp/
Explore the Enron Web site to find information about Enron's history, products, and services. Go to the "Press Room" section for Enron's spin on the current investigation.

Ethics Updates/Lawrence Hinman
http://ethics.acusd.edu
This site provides both simple concept definitions and complex analysis of ethics, original treatises, and sophisticated search engine capability. Subject matter covers the gamut, from ethical theory to applied ethical venues.

Institute for Business and Professional Ethics
http://www.depaul.edu/ethics/
This site is interested in research in the field of business and professional ethics. It is still under construction, so check in from time to time.

National Center for Policy Analysis
http://www.ncpa.org
This organization's archive links lead you to interesting materials on a variety of topics that affect managers, from immigration issues, to affirmative action, to regulatory policy.

Organisation and Management Theory
http://www.nbs.ntu.ac.uk/depts/hrm/list/hromt.htm
This is part of Ray Lye's Human Resource Management Resources on the Internet. It provides annotated links to an array of documents, studies, and other resources on the theory and practice of the learning organization.

Who We Are
http://enron.com/corp/
At this site, the Enron Corporation explains itself from its early history to its present day problems.

UNIT 2: Ethical Issues and Dilemmas in the

Workplace

American Psychological Association
http://www.apa.org/books/homepage.html
Search this site to find references and discussion of important ethics issues for the workplace of the 1990s, including the impact of restructuring and revitalization of businesses.

Annenberg Washington Program in Communications Policy Studies of Northwestern University
http://www.annenberg.nwu.edu/pubs/downside/
Is your employer snooping on you? Stephen Bates discusses the National Information Infrastructure (NII). View this page for issues regarding privacy rights in the workplace.

Fortune
http://www.pathfinder.com/fortune/bestcompanies/intro.html
What features make a company a desirable employer? *Fortune* magazine discusses the characteristics of the "100 Best Companies to Work For." This page leads to many other *Fortune* articles and resources and a list of the 100 best companies.

International Labour Organization (ILO)
http://www.ilo.org
ILO's home page leads you to links that describe the goals of the organization and summarizes international labor standards and human rights. Its official UN Web site locator can point you to many other useful resources.

What You Can Do in Your Workplace
http://www.connectforkids.org/info-url1564/info-url_list.htm?section=Workplace
Browse here for useful hints and guidelines about how employees, employees' families, management, and society can help a company become more family-friendly.

UNIT 3: Business and Society: Contemporary Ethical, Social, and Environmental Issues

CIBERWeb
http://ciber.centers.purdue.edu
This site of the Centers for International Business Education and Research is useful for exploring issues related to business ethics in the international marketplace.

Communications for a Sustainable Future
http://csf.colorado.edu
This site leads you to information on topics in international environmental sustainability. It features the political economics of protecting the environment.

National Immigrant Forum
http://www.immigrationforum.org
The pro-immigrant organization offers this page to examine the effects of immigration on the U.S. economy and society. Click on the links to underground and immigrant economies.

Stockholm University
http://www.psychology.su.se/units/ao/ao.html
Explore topics related to job design and other business organizational concerns through this site presented by the Division of Work and Organizational Psychology.

Sympatico: Workplace
http://sympatico.workopolis.com
This Canadian site provides an electronic network with a GripeVine for complaining about work and finding solutions to everyday work problems.

United Nations Environment Programme (UNEP)
http://www.unep.ch
Consult this UNEP site for links to topics such as the impact of trade on the environment. It will direct you to useful databases and global resource information.

United States Trade Representative (USTR)
http://www.ustr.gov
This home page of the U.S. Trade Representative provides links to many U.S. government resources for those interested in ethics in international business.

UNIT 4: Ethics and Social Responsibility in the Marketplace

Edwin B. Dean
http://mijuno.larc.nasa.gov/dfc/whatsnew.html
Read the many articles, consider the various points of view, and click on the links in this site to explore important business-related theories and issues such as cost management and living systems theory and design.

Total Quality Management Sites
http://www.nku.edu/~lindsay/qualhttp.html
This site points to a variety of interesting Internet sources to aid in the study and application of Total Quality Management principles.

U.S. Navy
http://www.navy.mil
Start at this U.S. Navy page for access to a plethora of interesting stories and analyses related to Total Quality Leadership. It addresses such concerns as how TQL can improve customer service and affect utilization of information technology.

UNIT 5: Developing the Future Ethos and Social Responsibility of Business

Sheffield University Management School
http://www.shef.ac.uk/uni/academic/I-M/mgt/research/research.html
The Current Research page of this British school will lead you to information on a broad array of real-world management issues for now and in the future.

Trinity College/Computer Science Course
http://www.cs.tcd.ie/courses/2ba6/best967/dukej/index.html
This page, Innovation in the Workplace, provides insight into what the future holds for employers and employees.

UNU/IAS Project on Global Ethos
http://www.ias.unu.edu/research_prog/governance/global_ethos.html
The United Nations University Institute of Advanced Studies (UNU/IAS) has issued this project abstract, which concerns governance and multilateralism. The main aim of the project is to initiate a process by which to generate jointly, with the involvement of actors from both state- and nonstate institutions in developed and developing countries, a global ethos that could provide or support a set of guiding principles for the emerging global community.

We highly recommend that you review our Web site for expanded information and our other product lines. We are continually updating and adding links to our Web site in order to offer you the most usable and useful information that will support and expand the value of your Annual Editions. You can reach us at: *http://www.dushkin.com/annualeditions/*.

UNIT 1

Ethics, Values, and Social Responsibility in Business

Unit Selections

1. **Thinking Ethically: A Framework for Moral Decision Making**, Manuel Velasquez, Claire Andre, Thomas Shanks, and Michael J. Meyer
2. **Managing by Values**, Ken Blanchard
3. **Defining Moments: When Managers Must Choose Between Right and Right**, Joseph L. Badaracco Jr.
4. **Doing Well by Doing Good**, *The Economist*
5. **Doing the Right Thing**, Michael Barrier
6. **Crime in the Suites**, William Greider
7. **When the Numbers Don't Add Up**, *The Economist*

Key Points to Consider

- Do you believe that corporations are more socially responsible today than they were 10 years ago? Why or why not?
- In what specific ways do you see companies practicing social responsibility? Do you think most companies are overt or covert in their social responsibility activities? Explain your answer.
- What are the economic and social implications of "management accountability" as part of the decision-making process? Does a company have any obligation to help remedy social problems such as poverty, urban decay, and pollution? Defend your response. From an organizational perspective, what do you think are the major arguments for and against social responsibility?
- Using the Enron case as your example, discuss the flaws in America's financial system that allow companies to disregard ethics, values, and social responsibility in business.

Links: www.dushkin.com/online/

These sites are annotated in the World Wide Web pages.

Association for Moral Education (AME)
http://www4.wittenberg.edu/ame/

Business for Social Responsibility (BSR)
http://www.bsr.org/BSRResources/Issues.cfm/

Business Policy and Strategy
http://www.aom.pace.edu/bps/bps.html

Enron Online
http://www.enron.com/corp/

Ethics Updates/Lawrence Hinman
http://ethics.acusd.edu

Institute for Business and Professional Ethics
http://www.depaul.edu/ethics/

National Center for Policy Analysis
http://www.ncpa.org

Organisation and Management Theory
http://www.nbs.ntu.ac.uk/depts/hrm/list/hromt.htm

Who We Are
http://enron.com/corp/

Ethical decision making in an organization does not occur in a vacuum. As individuals and as managers, we formulate our ethics (that is, the standards of "right" and "wrong" behavior that we set for ourselves) based upon family, peer, and religious influences, our past experiences, and our own unique value systems. When we make ethical decisions within the organizational context, many times there are situational factors and potential conflicts of interest that further complicate the process.

Decisions do not only have personal ramifications—they also have social consequences. Social responsibility is really ethics at the organizational level, since it refers to the obligation that an organization has to make choices and to take actions that will contribute to the good of society as well as the good of the organization. Authentic social responsibility is not initiated because of forced compliance to specific laws and regulations. In contrast to legal responsibility, social responsibility involves a voluntary response from an organization that is above and beyond what is specified by the law.

The seven selections in this unit provide an overview of the interrelationships of ethics, values, and social responsibility in business. The first two essays offer practical and insightful principles and suggestions to managers, enabling them to approach the subject of business ethics with more confidence. The next three selections point out the complexity and the significance of making ethical decisions.

Then, the subsection on Enron focuses on the enormous ethical implications of this scandal. The impacts on the ethics of accounting, on the social responsibility of the business community, on the wider issues of economic accountability, and on the politics of lobbying will be systemic and lasting. Enron's treatment of its employees and shareholders will be a lasting testament to the need for an ethical business model.

thinking ethically

A FRAMEWORK FOR MORAL DECISION MAKING

DEVELOPED BY MANUEL VELASQUEZ, CLAIRE ANDRE, THOMAS SHANKS, S.J., AND MICHAEL J. MEYER

Moral issues greet us each morning in the newspaper, confront us in the memos on our desks, nag us from our children's soccer fields, and bid us good night on the evening news. We are bombarded daily with questions about the justice of our foreign policy, the morality of medical technologies that can prolong our lives, the rights of the homeless, the fairness of our children's teachers to the diverse students in their classrooms.

Dealing with these moral issues is often perplexing. How, exactly, should we think through an ethical issue? What questions should we ask? What factors should we consider?

The first step in analyzing moral issues is obvious but not always easy: Get the facts.

The first step in analyzing moral issues is obvious but not always easy: Get the facts. Some moral issues create controversies simply because we do not bother to check the facts. This first step, although obvious, is also among the most important and the most frequently overlooked.

But having the facts is not enough. Facts by themselves only tell us what *is*; they do not tell us what *ought* to be. In addition to getting the facts, resolving an ethical issue also requires an appeal to values. Philosophers have developed five different approaches to values to deal with moral issues.

The Utilitarian Approach

Utilitarianism was conceived in the 19th century by Jeremy Bentham and John Stuart Mill to help legislators determine which laws were morally best. Both Bentham and Mill suggested that ethical actions are those that provide the greatest balance of good over evil.

To analyze an issue using the utilitarian approach, we first identify the various courses of action available to us. Second, we ask who will be affected by each action and what benefits or harms will be derived from each. And third, we choose the action that will produce the greatest benefits and the least harm. The ethical action is the one that provides the greatest good for the greatest number.

The Rights Approach

The second important approach to ethics has its roots in the philosophy of the 18th-century thinker Immanuel Kant and others like him, who focused on the individual's right to choose for herself or himself. According to these philosophers, what makes human beings different from mere things is that people have dignity based on their ability to choose freely what they will do with their lives, and they have a fundamental moral right to have these choices respected. People are not objects to be manipulated; it is a violation of human dignity to use people in ways they do not freely choose.

Of course, many different, but related, rights exist besides this basic one. These other rights (an incomplete list below) can be thought of as different aspects of the basic right to be treated as we choose.

- *The right to the truth*: We have a right to be told the truth and to be informed about matters that significantly affect our choices.
- *The right of privacy*: We have the right to do, believe, and say whatever we choose in our personal lives so long as we do not violate the rights of others.

the case of maria elena

Maria Elena has cleaned your house each week for more than a year. You agree with your friend who recommended her that she does an excellent job and is well worth the $30 cash you pay her for three hours' work. You've also come to like her, and you think she likes you, especially as her English has become better and you've been able to have some pleasant conversations.

Over the past three weeks, however, you've noticed Maria Elena becoming more and more distracted. One day, you ask her if something is wrong, and she tells you she really needs to make additional money. She hastens to say she is not asking you for a raise, becomes upset, and begins to cry. When she calms down a little, she tells you her story:

She came to the United States six years ago from Mexico with her child, Miguel, who is now 7 years old. They entered the country on a visitor's visa that has expired, and Maria Elena now uses a Social Security number she made up.

Her common-law husband, Luis, came to the United States first. He entered the country illegally, after paying smugglers $500 to hide him under piles of grass cuttings for a six-hour truck ride across the border. When he had made enough money from low-paying day jobs, he sent for Maria Elena. Using a false green card, Luis now works as a busboy for a restaurant, which withholds part of his salary for taxes. When Maria Elena comes to work at your house, she takes the bus and Luis baby-sits.

In Mexico, Maria Elena and Luis lived in a small village where it was impossible to earn more than $3 a day. Both had sixth-grade educations, common in their village. Life was difficult, but they did not decide to leave until they realized the future would be bleak for their child and for the other children they wanted to have. Luis had a cousin in San Jose who visited and told Luis and Maria Elena how well his life was going. After his visit, Luis and Maria Elena decided to come to the United States.

Luis quickly discovered, as did Maria Elena, that life in San Jose was not the way they had heard. The cousin did not tell them they would be able to afford to live only in a run-down three-room apartment with two other couples and their children. He did not tell them they would always live in fear of INS raids.

After they entered the United States, Maria Elena and Luis had a second child, Jose, who is 5 years old. The birth was difficult because she didn't use the health-care system or welfare for fear of being discovered as undocumented. But, she tells you, she is willing to put up with anything so that her children can have a better life. "All the money we make is for Miguel and Jose," she tells you. "We work hard for their education and their future."

Now, however, her mother in Mexico is dying, and Maria Elena must return home, leaving Luis and the children. She does not want to leave them because she might not be able to get back into the United States, but she is pretty sure she can find a way to return if she has enough money. That is her problem: She doesn't have enough money to make certain she can get back.

After she tells you her story, she becomes too distraught to continue talking. You now know she is an undocumented immigrant, working in your home. What is the ethical thing for you to do?

This case was developed by Tom Shanks, S.J., director of the Markkula Center for Applied Ethics. Maria Elena is a composite drawn from several real people, and her story represents some of the ethical dilemmas behind the immigration issue.

This case can be accessed through the Ethics Center home page on the World Wide Web: http://www.scu.edu/Ethics/. You can also contact us by e-mail, ethics@scu.edu, or regular mail: Markkula Center for Applied Ethics, Santa Clara University, Santa Clara, CA 95053. Our voice mail number is (408) 554-7898. We have also posted on our homepage a new case involving managed health care.

- *The right not to be injured*: We have the right not to be harmed or injured unless we freely and knowingly do something to deserve punishment or we freely and knowingly choose to risk such injuries.
- *The right to what is agreed:* We have a right to what has been promised by those with whom we have freely entered into a contract or agreement.

In deciding whether an action is moral or immoral using this second approach, then, we must ask, Does the action respect the moral rights of everyone? Actions are wrong to the extent that they violate the rights of individuals; the more serious the violation, the more wrongful the action.

The Fairness or Justice Approach

The fairness or justice approach to ethics has its roots in the teachings of the ancient Greek philosopher Aristotle, who said that "equals should be treated equally and unequals unequally." The basic moral question in this approach is: How fair is an action? Does it treat everyone in the same way, or does it show favoritism and discrimination?

Favoritism gives benefits to some people without a justifiable reason for singling them out; discrimination imposes burdens on people who are no different from those on whom burdens are not imposed. Both favoritism and discrimination are unjust and wrong.

The Common-Good Approach

This approach to ethics presents a vision of society as a community whose members are joined in the shared pursuit of values and goals they hold in common. This community comprises individuals whose own good is inextricably bound to the good of the whole.

The common good is a notion that originated more than 2,000 years ago in the writings of Plato, Aristotle, and Cicero. More recently, contemporary ethicist John Rawls defined the common good as "certain general conditions that are... equally to everyone's advantage."

In this approach, we focus on ensuring that the social policies, social systems, institutions, and environments on which we depend are beneficial to all. Examples of goods common to all include affordable health care, effective public safety, peace among nations, a just legal system, and an unpolluted environment.

Appeals to the common good urge us to view ourselves as members of the same community, reflecting on broad questions concerning the kind of society we want to become and how we are to achieve that society. While respecting and valuing the freedom of individuals to pursue their own goals, the common-good approach challenges us also to recognize and further those goals we share in common.

The Virtue Approach

The virtue approach to ethics assumes that there are certain ideals toward which we should strive, which provide for the full development of our humanity. These ideals are discovered through thoughtful reflection on what kind of people we have the potential to become.

Virtues are attitudes or character traits that enable us to be and to act in ways that develop our highest potential. They enable us to pursue the ideals we have adopted.

Honesty, courage, compassion, generosity, fidelity, integrity, fairness, self-control, and prudence are all examples of virtues.

Virtues are like habits; that is, once acquired, they become characteristic of a person. Moreover, a person who has developed virtues will be naturally disposed to act in ways consistent with moral principles. The virtuous person is the ethical person.

In dealing with an ethical problem using the virtue approach, we might ask, What kind of person should I be? What will promote the development of character within myself and my community?

Ethical Problem Solving

These five approaches suggest that once we have ascertained the facts, we should ask ourselves five questions when trying to resolve a moral issue:

- What benefits and what harms will each course of action produce, and which alternative will lead to the best overall consequences?
- What moral rights do the affected parties have, and which course of action best respects those rights?
- Which course of action treats everyone the same, except where there is a morally justifiable reason not to, and does not show favoritism or discrimination?
- Which course of action advances the common good?
- Which course of action develops moral virtues?

This method, of course, does not provide an automatic solution to moral problems. It is not meant to. The method is merely meant to help identify most of the important ethical considerations. In the end, we must deliberate on moral issues for ourselves, keeping a careful eye on both the facts and on the ethical considerations involved.

FOR FURTHER READING

Frankena, William. *Ethics*, 2nd ed. (Englewood Cliffs, N.J.: Prentice Hall, 1973).

Halberstam, Joshua. *Everyday Ethics: Inspired Solutions to Real Life Dilemmas* (New York: Penguin Books, 1993).

Martin, Michael. *Everyday Morality* (Belmont, Calif: Wadsworth, 1995).

Rachels, James. *The Elements of Moral Philosophy*, 2nd ed. (New York: McGraw-Hill, 1993).

Velasquez, Manuel. *Business Ethics: Concepts and Cases*, 3rd ed. (Englewood Cliffs, N.J.: Prentice Hall, 1992) 2–110.

This article updates several previous pieces from Issues in Ethics *by Manuel Velasquez—Dirksen Professor of Business Ethics at SCU and former Center director—and Claire Andre, associate Center director. "Thinking Ethically" is based on a framework developed by the authors in collaboration with Center Director Thomas Shanks, S.J., Presidential Professor of Ethics and the Common Good Michael J. Meyer, and others. The framework is used as the basis for many Center programs and presentations.*

Managing by Values

Where there is alignment between core values and common practices, financial results will follow.

KEN BLANCHARD

A FORTUNATE 500 COMPANY IS one determined by: the quality of life available to its employees; the quality of service provided to its customers; and the quality of its products and their placement in the marketplace. If a company excels in these things, the hard numbers of sales revenues and profitability will directly follow.

Three Precepts

In a book that I co-authored with Michael O'Connor entitled *Managing by Values*, we explain how you can become a Fortunate 500 company by learning how to define, communicate, and align your values with your practices. Unless values are prioritized, you have nothing but situational ethics where anything goes.

1. Identifying core values. Many companies claim they have a set of core values, but what they mean is a list of business beliefs that everyone would agree with, such as having integrity, making a profit, and responding to customers. Such values have meaning only when they are further defined in terms of how people actually behave and are rank-ordered to reveal priority.

For example, Disney's four core values are safety, courtesy, the show (performing your particular role well), and efficiency. If these values aren't carefully ordered, people are left to their own devices. For example, a bottom-line-oriented manager might overemphasize efficiency and thus jeopardize the three higher-ranking values.

Fortunate 500 companies first emphasize the beliefs, attitudes, and feelings that top management have about employees, customers, quality, ethics, integrity social responsibility, growth, stability, innovation, and flexibility. Organizations today must know what they stand for and on what principles they operate. Values-based behavior is a requisite for survival. Once you have a clear picture of your mission and values, you have a basis for evaluating your management practices and bringing them into alignment.

Ethics means doing the right thing by being honest, acting in a legally and socially responsible manner, being fair in our treatment of others, and acting in ways that result in feeling good about ourselves and our company.

2. Communicating core values. Make sure that your values are evident to all stakeholders-employees, customers, suppliers, stockholders, and the community. For example, if your core values are to be ethical, responsive, and profitable, you then need to look for ways to implement these values with your major stakeholders. Provide people with what you know, when you know it—especially when it is information about company finances, new products, competitive practices, and pending changes in policies. This interests most employees. Involve employees in decisions that affect them—or better yet—whenever possible let them make the decisions.

3. Aligning values and practices. Once your values have been broadly communicated, you need to assess how well these values are practiced. To be effective, values and strategies need to unite the energies of all people, especially those dealing with the company's various publics. Without some way of identifying gaps between values and behavior, a set of core values is nothing more than a wish list.

In Fortunate 500 companies, the behavior of the leaders is aligned with corporate values. Management "walks its talk." For example, if executives indicate that they value innovation and flexibility but then have an authoritarian-based bureaucracy, there is an alignment problem.

Or, if executives say that they value the full development of people's potential but then have a performance review system that forces managers to rate people on a normal distribution curve, again there is an alignment problem. Misalignment between values and practices creates an energy drain that sabotages productive behavior. Alignment liberates energy and empowers people to act congruently. That makes for loyal customers and employees and a productive environment.

Closing the Values Gap

In using our values, we have to make some hard decisions that may not, in the short run, enhance our bottom line. And yet, since ethics and relationships are our first two values, we would not be walking our talk if we acted as if we were only in business to make money.

Michael has developed two simple but powerful problem-solving tools called People-Oriented Problem Solving (POPS) and Technical-Oriented Problem Solving (TOPS). Through the use of these tools, anyone in our company can shout out "gap" if they or anyone else is being treated by someone in a way that is inconsistent with our values, or when something in our system-compensation, performance review, space use—is causing a values conflict. In the first case, POPS would come into play and, in the second case, TOPS would be appropriate.

When a gap occurs, a series of problem-solving questions are asked of the people involved in the situation to reduce the gap and get our actions back in alignment with our values. No one should get away with treating anyone in an unethical or unloving way. When all is said and done, it's all about love—who loves you and who you love. Remember, your business is important, but it's not who you are—not your reason for being.

Ken Blanchard is the author of the One-Minute Manager *series and chairman of Blanchard Training and Development; 800-728-6000.*

Defining Moments: WHEN MANAGERS MUST CHOOSE BETWEEN RIGHT and RIGHT

By Joseph L. Badaracco Jr.

THOUGHTFUL MANAGERS SOMEtimes face business problems that raise difficult, deeply personal questions. In these situations, managers find themselves wondering: Do I have to leave some of my values at home when I go to work? How much of myself—and of what I really care about—do I have to sacrifice to get ahead? When I get to the office, who am I?

Difficult questions like these are often matters of right versus right, not right versus wrong. Sometimes, a manager faces a tough problem and must choose between two ways of resolving it. Each alternative is the right thing to do, but there is no way to do both. There are three basic types of right-versus-right problems: those that raise questions about personal integrity and moral identity; conflicts between responsibilities for others and important personal values; and, perhaps the most challenging, those involving responsibilities that a company shares with other groups in society.

Most companies are now enmeshed in networks of ongoing relationships. Strategic alliances link organizations with their customers and suppliers, and even competitors. Many companies also have complicated dealings with the media, government regulators, local communities and various interest groups. These networks of relationships are also networks of managerial responsibility. Taken together, a company's business partners and stakeholders have a wide range of legitimate claims, but no company can satisfy all of them. At times, stakeholder responsibilities conflict with managers' personal and organizational obligations. When these conflicts occur, managers confront this third type of right-versus-right problem.

A particularly stark example of this occurred in the pharmaceutical industry nearly a decade ago. Late in 1988, the senior management of Paris-based Roussel-Uclaf had to decide where and how to market a new drug, called RU 486. Early tests had shown that the drug was 90 to 95 percent effective in causing a miscarriage during the first five weeks of pregnancy. The drug came to be known as "the French abortion pill," and Roussel-Uclaf and its managers found themselves at the vortex of the abortion controversy.

The chairman of Roussel-Uclaf, Edouard Sakiz, was a physician with a longstanding personal commitment to RU 486. He would make the final decisions on introducing the drug. Earlier in his career, while working as a medical researcher, Dr. Sakiz had helped develop the chemical compound on which RU 486 was based. He believed strongly that the drug could help thousands of women, particularly in poor countries, avoid injury or death from botched abortions. In the developed world, he believed, RU 486 would provide women and physicians with a valuable alternative to surgical abortions.

But Dr. Sakiz couldn't base his decision on RU 486 solely on his personal values. As the head of a company, he had other important obligations. Some were to his shareholders; from this perspective, RU 486 was a serious problem. Revenues from the drug were likely to be quite small, particularly in the early years. Yet, during this period, anti-abortion groups would mount an international boycott of products made by Roussel-Uclaf and Hoechst, the German chemical giant that was Roussel-Uclaf's largest shareholder. A successful boycott would cost the two companies far more than they would earn from RU 486. At worst, a boycott could imperil Roussel-Uclaf's survival, for it was a relatively small company with weak profits.

Like any executive, Dr. Sakiz also had responsibilities for the people in his company. He had to assess the seriousness of the threats of violence against Roussel-Uclaf and its employees.

At a personal level, Dr. Sakiz faced a version of the question, Who am I? Was he, first and foremost, a medical doctor, a scientific researcher, an advocate of women's rights, or a corporate executive with responsibilities to shareholders and employees? In addition, his decision on RU 486 would commit his company to some values rather than others, thereby answering the organizational question, Who are we?

The prospect of introducing RU 486 placed Dr. Sakiz at the center of a network of responsibilities to important groups and institutions outside Roussel-Uclaf. Among these were the French Government, which owned 36 percent of Roussel-Uclaf, and the French Ministry of Health, which closely regulated the company, thus shaping its business opportunities.

Hoechst, which owned 55 percent of Roussel-Uclaf, also made strong ethical claims on the company. Its chairman was a devout Roman Catholic, who opposed abortion on moral grounds and had repeatedly stated his position in public. Moreover, Hoechst had a mission statement committing the company to lofty goals, which was put in place partly in reaction to its role in producing a poison gas used at Auschwitz.

China was another powerful actor in the drama. It wanted access to RU 486 for population control. The moral ground for China's position was avoiding the misery and risks of starvation resulting from its surging population.

Roussel-Uclaf's network of relationships and responsibilities raised extremely difficult questions for Dr. Sakiz and his company. What, in fact, were the company's obligations to women? To the Government laboratory that helped develop the steroid molecule on which RU 486 was based? To the larger medical and research communities? Were the unborn a stakeholder group? Could Roussel-Uclaf introduce the drug both in the West, citing a woman's right to choose, and in China, where women had apparently been coerced into abortions, even near the end of their pregnancies?

Dr. Sakiz's decision would define his company's role in society and its relationships with stakeholders. Everyone was watching him intently because his actions would be decisive, for RU 486 and for the company. In addition, he would be revealing, testing and in some ways shaping his own ethics. In short, Dr. Sakiz also had to make a personal choice that would become an important part of his life and career.

In late October 1988, a month after the French Government approved RU 486, Dr. Sakiz met with the executive committee of Roussel-Uclaf. Dr. Sakiz asked for a discussion of RU 486. After several hours, he called for a vote. When he raised his own hand in favor of suspending distribution of RU 486, it was clear that the pill was doomed.

The company's decision, and Dr. Sakiz's role in it, sparked astonishment and anger. The company and its leadership, some critics charged, had doomed a promising public health tool and set an example of cowardice. Other critics suggested sarcastically that the decision was no surprise, because Roussel-Uclaf had decided, in the face of controversy during the 1960's, not to produce contraceptive pills.

Three days after Roussel-Uclaf announced that it would suspend distribution, the French Minister of Health summoned the company's vice chairman to his office and said that if it did not resume distribution, the Government would transfer the patent to a company that would. After the meeting, Roussel-Uclaf announced that it would distribute RU 486 after all.

These events suggest that the RU 486 episode was something considerably less than a profile in courage. Edouard Sakiz seemed to have protected his job by sacrificing his convictions. There was, to be sure, strong opposition to RU 486, both inside and outside the company, but Dr. Sakiz made no effort to mobilize and lead his allies. He gave up without a fight. At a defining moment for the company, Dr. Sakiz's message seemed to place political caution and returns to shareholders above research and "the service of Life," as the company's mission statement put it.

But the surprising reversal of Roussel-Uclaf's original decision caused suspicion among some observers, who began to ask whether Dr. Sakiz had figured out a way to get what he wanted with a minimum of damage to himself and his company. Indeed, some wondered if the company and the Government had choreographed the entire episode. Others noted that Government science and health officials and Roussel-Uclaf managers and researchers had worked together for years—on RU 486, on other products and on many other regulatory issues—making it easy for them to anticipate each other's reactions.

What had Dr. Sakiz accomplished? More specifically, had he protected and advanced his own position? Had he contributed to the strength and security of his company? And had he defined its role in society in a creative way?

In personal terms, Dr. Sakiz succeeded in making good on his own commitment to RU 486—Roussel-Uclaf would distribute the drug. At the same time, he protected his job against the chairman of Hoechst. Because the French Government had effectively ordered Roussel-Uclaf to distribute the drug, Hoechst would accomplish little by replacing Dr. Sakiz with an opponent of RU 486. For Roussel-Uclaf employees, the period of uncertainty and speculation was over, and the company decision was clear.

ARISTOTLE COUNSELS MODERATION AND CAUTION PRECISELY BECAUSE HE IS GIVING ADVICE FOR SITUATIONS IN WHICH IMPORTANT ETHICAL CLAIMS STAND IN OPPOSITION.

Dr. Sakiz seems to have defined Roussel-Uclaf's role in society in a remarkable, perhaps even daring way. It would be a political activist and catalyst. The company worked to stimulate and then shape media coverage; it invited its allies to mobilize after dismaying them by suspending distribution; it acceded to Government intervention that it may have encouraged or even arranged; and it tried to blur responsibility for the introduction of RU 486.

Roussel-Uclaf was committed to "the service of Life" following an original, complex and audacious strategy. Roussel-Uclaf would distribute RU 486, first in France and then elsewhere, but neither Dr. Sakiz nor his company had volunteered for martyrdom.

Clearly, there is an urgent need to find other lessons for managers who face choices like Dr. Sakiz's. The writings of Aristotle, who developed the foremost theory of human virtue, are an excellent place to find such lessons. Aristotle counsels moderation and caution precisely because he is giving advice for situations in which important ethical claims stand in opposition. He wants to discourage men and women who find tension or conflict among their duties, commitments, responsibilities and virtues from veering too sharply in one direction or another and trampling on some fundamental human values as they pursue others. This is why Stuart Hampshire has written that, for Aristotle, "balance represents a deep moral idea in a world of inescapable conflicts."

The ideal of balance provides valuable guidance for managers who must resolve right-versus-right conflicts—especially those like Edouard Sakiz's, that pit so many important values and responsibilities against each other. Aristotle's question for managers would be this: Have you done all you can to strike a balance, both morally and practically? By Aristotle's standard of balance, Dr. Sakiz performed quite well.

Joseph L. Badaracco Jr. is the John Shad Professor of Business Ethics at the Harvard Business School. He has taught courses on strategy, general management, business-government relations and business ethics in the school's M.B.A. and executive programs. Mr. Badaracco is a graduate of St. Louis University, Oxford University, where he was a Rhodes scholar, and the Harvard Business School, where he earned his M.B.A. and doctorate.

Reprinted from *strategy+business,* First Quarter 1998, pp. 4-6. Originally from *Defining Moments: When Managers Must Choose Between Right and Right,* by Joseph L. Badaracco, Jr., Boston, 1997.

Doing well by doing good

Anti-globalisation protesters see companies as unethical as well as exploitative. Firms demur, of course, but face an awkward question: Does virtue pay?

TO MANY people the very concepts of "business" and "ethics" sit uneasily together. Business ethics, to them, is an oxymoron—or, as an American journalist once put it, "a contradiction in terms, like jumbo shrimp." And yet, in America and other western countries, companies increasingly wonder what constitutes ethical corporate behaviour, and how to get their employees to observe it. Management schools teach courses on the subject to their students. Business ethics is suddenly all the rage.

Fashionable perhaps—but also vague. Protesters in Washington, DC, were this week railing against corporate immorality as well as the IMF. But plenty of people retort that companies should not be in the business of ethics at all—let alone worrying about social responsibility, morals or the environment. If society wants companies to put any of these ahead of the pursuit of shareholder value, then governments should regulate them accordingly. Thirty years ago Milton Friedman, doyen of market economics, summed up this view by arguing that "there is one and only one social responsibility of business—to use its resources and engage in activities designed to increase its profits."

Even those who think companies do have wider responsibilities argue about the best way to pursue them. Ulrich Steger, who teaches environmental management at the International Institute for Management Development in Lausanne, says that companies cannot possibly hope to pursue a single abstract set of ethical principles and should not try. No universal set of ethical principles exists; most are too woolly to be helpful; and the decisions that companies face every day rarely present themselves as ethics versus economics in any case. He says that companies should aim instead for "responsible shareholder-value optimisation": their first priority should be shareholders' long-term interests, but, within that constraint, they should seek to meet whatever social or environmental goals the public expects of them.

Certainly companies, which increasingly try to include their ethical principles in corporate codes, stumble over how to write in something about the need for profitability. Or, to put the dilemma more crudely: when money and morality clash, what should a company do? Most firms try to resolve this with the consoling belief that such clashes are more imagined than real, and that virtue will pay in the end. Yet they cannot always be right.

Indeed, companies face more ethical quandaries than ever before. Technological change brings new debates, on issues ranging from genetically modified organisms to privacy on the Internet. Globalisation brings companies into contact with other countries that do business by different rules. Competitive pressures force firms to treat their staff in ways that depart from past practice. Add unprecedented scrutiny from outside, led by non-governmental organisations (NGOs), and it is not surprising that dealing with ethical issues has become part of every manager's job.

Don't lie, don't cheat, don't steal

In America, companies have a special incentive to pursue virtue: the desire to avoid legal penalties. The first attempts to build ethical principles into the corporate bureaucracy began in the defence industry in the mid-1980s, a time when the business was awash with kickbacks and $500 screwdrivers. The first corporate-ethics office was created in 1985 by General Dynamics, which was being investigated by the government for pricing scams. Under pressure from the Defence Department, a group of 60 or so defence companies then launched an initiative to set up guidelines and compliance programmes. In 1991, federal sentencing rules extended the incentive to other industries: judges were empowered to reduce fines in cases involving companies that had rules in place to promote ethical behaviour, and to increase them for those that did not.

But the law is not the only motivator. Fear of embarrassment at the hands of NGOs and the media has given business ethics an even bigger push. Companies have learnt the hard way that they live in a CNN world, in which bad behaviour in one country can be seized on by local campaigners and beamed on the evening television news to customers back home. As non-governmental groups vie with each other for publicity and membership, big companies are especially vulnerable to hostile campaigns.

One victim was Shell, which in 1995 suffered two blows to its reputation: one from its attempted disposal of the Brent Spar oil rig in the North Sea, and the other over the company's failure to oppose the Nigerian government's execution of Ken Saro-Wiwa, a human-rights activist in a part of Nigeria where Shell had extensive operations. Since then, Shell has rewritten its business principles, created an elaborate mechanism to implement them, and worked harder to improve its relations with NGOs.

Remarkably, Shell's efforts had no clear legal or financial pressure behind them. Neither of the 1995 rows, says Robin Aram, the man in charge of Shell's policy development, did lasting damage to the company's share price or sales—although the Brent Spar spat brought a brief dip in its market share in Germany, thanks to a consumer boycott. But, he adds, "we weren't confident that there would be no long-term impact, given the growing interest of the investment community in these softer issues." And he also concedes that there was "a sense of deep discomfort from our own people." People seem happier working for organisations they regard as ethical. In a booming jobs market, that can become a powerful incentive to do the right thing.

The quest for virtue

In America there is now a veritable ethics industry, complete with consultancies, conferences, journals and "corporate conscience" awards. Accountancy firms such as PricewaterhouseCoopers offer to "audit" the ethical performance of companies. Corporate-ethics officers, who barely existed a decade ago, have become *de rigueur*, at least for big companies. The Ethics Officer Association, which began with a dozen members in 1992, has 650 today. As many as one in five big firms has a full-time office devoted to the subject. Some are mighty empires: at United Technologies, for example, Pat Gnazzo presides over an international network of 160 business-ethics officers who distribute a code of ethics, in 24 languages, to people who work for this defence and engineering giant all round the world.

For academic philosophers, once lonely and contemplative creatures, the business ethics boom has been a bonanza. They are employed by companies to run "ethics workshops" and are consulted on thorny moral questions. They also act as expert witnesses in civil lawsuits "where lawyers usually want to be able to tell the judge that their client's behaviour was reasonable. So you are usually working for the defendants. They want absolution," says Kirk Hanson, a professor at Stanford Business School.

Outside America, few companies have an ethics bureaucracy. To some extent, observes IMD's Mr Steger, this reflects the fact that the state and organised labour both still play a bigger part in corporate life. In Germany, for example, workers' councils often deal with issues such as sexual equality, race relations and workers' rights, all of which might be seen as ethical issues in America.

In developing a formal ethics policy, companies usually begin by trying to sum up their philosophy in a code. That alone can raise awkward questions. The chairman of a large British firm recalls how his company secretary (general counsel) decided to draft an ethics code with appropriately lofty standards. "You do realise", said the chairman, "that if we publish this, we will be expected to follow it. Otherwise our staff and customers may ask questions." Dismayed, the lawyer went off to produce something more closely attuned to reality.

Not surprisingly, codes are often too broad to capture the ethical issues that actually confront companies, which range from handling their own staff to big global questions of policy on the environment, bribery and human rights. Some companies use the Internet to try to add precision to general injunctions. Boeing, for instance, tries to guide staff through the whole gamut of moral quandaries, offering an online quiz (with answers) on how to deal with everything from staff who fiddle their expenses on business trips to suppliers who ask for kickbacks.

The best corporate codes, says Robert Solomon of the University of Texas, are those that describe the way everybody in the company already behaves and feels. The worst are those where senior executives mandate a list of principles—especially if they then fail to "walk the talk" themselves. However, he says, "companies debate their values for many months, but they always turn out to have similar lists." There is usually something about integrity; something about respect for the individual; and something about honouring the customer.

The ethical issues that actually create most problems in companies often seem rather mundane to outsiders. Such as? "When an individual who is a wonderful producer and brings in multiple dollars doesn't adhere to the company's values," suggests Mr Gnazzo of United Technologies: in other words, when a company has to decide whether to sack an employee who is productive but naughty. "When an employee who you know is about to be let go is buying a new house, and you're honour-bound not to say anything," says Mr Solomon. "Or, what do you do when your boss lies to you? That's a big one."

Issues such as trust and human relations become harder to handle as companies intrude into the lives of their employees. A company with thousands of employees in South-East Asia has been firing employees who have AIDS, but giving them no explanation. It now wonders whether this is ethical. Several companies in America scan their employees' e-mail for unpleasant or disloyal material, or test them to see if they have been taking drugs. Is that right?

Even more complicated are issues driven by conflicts of interest. Edward Petry, head of the Ethics Officer Association, says the most recent issue taxing his members comes from the fad for Internet flotations. If a company is spinning off a booming e-commerce division, which employees should be allowed on to the lucrative "friends-and-family" list of share buyers?

Indeed, the revolution in communications technologies has created all sorts of new ethical dilemmas—just as technological change in medicine spurred interest in medical ethics in the 1970s. Because it is mainly businesses that develop and spread new technologies, businesses also tend to face the first questions about how to use them. So companies stumble into such questions as data protection and customer privacy. They know more than ever before about their customers' tastes, but few have a clear view on what uses of that knowledge are unethical.

Foreigners are different

Some of the most publicised debates about corporate ethics have been driven by globalisation. When companies operate abroad, they run up against all sorts of new moral issues. And one big problem is that ethical standards differ among countries.

Reams of research, says Denis Collins in an article for the *Journal of Business Ethics*, have been devoted to comparing ethical sensitivities of people from different countries. As most of this work has been North American, it is perhaps not surprising that it concluded that American business people are more "ethically sensitive" than their counterparts from Greece, Hong Kong, Taiwan, New Zealand, Ukraine and Britain. They were more sensitive than Australians about lavish entertainment and conflicts of interest; than French and Germans over corporate social responsibility; than Chinese in matters of bribery and confidential information; and than Singaporeans on software piracy. Given such moral superiority, it is surprising that American companies seem to turn up in ethical scandals at least as often as those from other rich countries.

Many companies first confronted the moral dilemmas of globalisation when they had to decide whether to meet only local environmental standards, even if these were lower than ones back home. This debate came to public attention with the Bhopal disaster in 1984, when an explosion at a Union Carbide plant in India killed at least 8,000 people. Most large multinationals now have global minimum standards for health, safety and the environment.

These may, however, be hard to enforce. BP Amoco describes in a recent environmental and social report a huge joint venture in inland China. "Concerns remain around the cultural and regulatory differences in risk assessment and open reporting of safety incidents," the report admits. "For instance, deference to older and more senior members of staff has occasionally inhibited open challenging of unsafe practices." BP Amoco thinks it better to stay in the venture and try to raise standards. But Shell claims to have withdrawn from one joint venture because it was dissatisfied with its partner's approach. Most companies rarely talk about these cases, creating the suspicion that such withdrawals are rare.

Bribery and corruption have also been thorny issues. American companies have been bound since 1977 by the Foreign Corrupt Practices Act. Now all OECD countries have agreed to a convention to end bribery. But many companies turn a blind eye when intermediaries make such payments. Only a few, such as Motorola, have accounting systems that try to spot kickbacks by noting differences between what the customer pays and what a vendor receives.

Some corruption is inevitable, say companies such as Shell, which work in some of the world's nastiest places. "If someone sticks a Kalashnikov through the window of your car and asks for 20 naira, we don't say that you shouldn't pay," says Mr Aram. "We say, it should be recorded." United Technologies' Mr Gnazzo takes a similar view: "We say, employees must report a gift so that everybody can see it's a gift to the company, and we can choose to refuse it. Every year we write to vendors, saying that we don't want gifts, we want good service."

Rights and wrongs

Human rights are a newer and trickier problem. Shell has written a primer on the subject, in consultation with Amnesty International. It agonises over such issues as what companies should do if they have a large investment in a country where human rights deteriorate; and whether companies should operate in countries that forbid outsiders to scrutinise their record on human rights (yes, but only if the company takes no advantage of such secrecy and is a "force for good").

The force-for-good argument also crops up when companies are accused of underpaying workers in poor countries, or of using suppliers who underpay. Such problems arise more often when there are lots of small suppliers. At Nike, a sporting-goods firm, Dusty Kidd, director of labour practices, has to deal with almost 600 supplier-factories around the world. The relationship is delicate: "They are independent businesses, but we take responsibility," says Mr Kidd. When, last year, Nike insisted on a rise in the minimum wage paid by its Indonesian suppliers, it claims to have absorbed much of the cost.

NGOs have berated firms such as Nike for failing to ensure that workers are paid a "living wage". But that can be hard, even in America. "I once asked a university president, do you pay a living wage on your campus?" recalls Mr Kidd. "He said that was different. But it isn't." In developing countries, the dilemma may be even greater: "In Vietnam, our workers are paid more than doctors. What's the social cost if a doctor leaves his practice and goes to work for us? That's starting to happen."

Stung by attacks on their behaviour in the past, companies such as Shell and Nike have begun to see it as part of their corporate mission to raise standards not just within their company, but in the countries where they work. Mr Kidd, for instance, would like Nike's factories to be places where workers' health actually improves, through better education and care, and where the status of women is raised. Such ideals would have sounded familiar to some businessmen of the 19th century: Quaker companies such as Cadbury and Rowntree, for instance, were founded on the principle that a company should improve its workers' health and education. In today's more cynical and competitive world, though, corporate virtue no longer seems a goal in its own right.

When, in the late 1980s, companies devoted lots of effort to worrying about the environment, they told themselves that being clean and green was also a route to being profitable. In the same way, they now hope that virtue will bring financial, as well as spiritual, rewards. Environmental controls can, for instance, often be installed more cheaply than companies expect. Ed Freeman, who teaches ethics at the Darden Business School at the University of Virginia, recalls how the senior executive of a big chemical company announced that he wanted "zero pollution". His engineers were horrified. Three weeks later, they returned to admit that they could end pollution and save money. "The conflict between ethics and business may be a lot less than we think," he argues.

Most academic studies of the association between responsible corporate ethics and profitability suggest that the two will often go together. Researchers have managed to show that more ethically sensitive sales staff perform better (at least in America; the opposite appears to be the case in Taiwan); that share prices decline after reports of unethical conduct; and that companies which state an ethical commitment to stakeholders in their annual reports do better financially. But proving a causal link is well-nigh impossible.

What of the growing band of ethical investors? "I don't know of a single one of these funds which looks at the effectiveness of a company's internal ethics programme," says the EOA's Mr Petry, sadly. So a defence firm scores bad marks for being in a nasty industry, but no offsetting good marks for having an elaborate compliance programme.

And then there is the impact on employees. It may be true that they like working for ethically responsible companies. But, says Stanford's Mr Hanson, "I see a lot of my graduate students leaving jobs in not-for-profits to go and work for dot.coms." Few dot.coms would know a corporate ethics code if it fell on their heads. Small firms, in particular, pay far less attention than bigger rivals to normalising ethical issues and to worrying about their social responsibilities. Yet employment is growing in small companies and falling in big ones.

There may still be two good reasons for companies to worry about their ethical reputation. One is anticipation: bad behaviour, once it stirs up a public fuss, may provoke legislation that companies will find more irksome than self-restraint. The other, more crucial, is trust. A company that is not trusted by its employees, partners and customers will suffer. In an electronic world, where businesses are geographically far from their customers, a reputation for trust may become even more important. Ultimately, though, companies may have to accept that virtue is sometimes its own reward. One of the eternal truths of morality has been that the bad do not always do badly and the good do not always do well.

Doing The Right Thing

In today's intensely competitive world, ethical business behavior isn't an outmoded luxury—it's a valuable necessity.

By Michael Barrier

"We play it straight with people," Alan Babb says, and he means it. Babb and his younger brother, Lee, own two companies in Eugene, Ore.—Delta Sand & Gravel, which produces more than a million tons of such material a year, and Delta Construction, which puts in streets and does site preparation. The two companies employ around 120 people.

Several years ago, Delta Construction hired a subcontractor—"a company that did not have good bookkeeping," Alan Babb says—to lay about $15,000 worth of concrete at one of Delta's projects.

When Babb's people realized that Delta had made more money than it expected to on that job, they checked into it, Babb says, "and we found out that we'd never paid the subcontractor"—because Delta had never received an invoice.

When Delta called to inquire about the bill, Babb says, the subcontractor said that it hadn't done the work, so Delta didn't owe it any money. "What we did," Babb says, "was send them the plans and specifications for their work; we told them the names of some of their people they had on the job; we told them how much they should bill us. So they did, and we paid them about $15,000."

To some people, doing business that way might sound like passing up found money, but Babb says: "That's just the way we work. If people overbill us, I give them a call; if people underbill us, I give them a call."

It's a way of doing business that Lee Edelstein understands. He's the CEO of TeleManagement Services, Inc., a Fort Lauderdale, Fla., company that conducts customized telemarketing programs for pharmaceutical companies that are trying to reach doctors and druggists.

"One of our major clients paid us twice for a $40,000 project," he recalls. "Somebody screwed up within their organization, and it was highly unlikely they ever would have picked it up." Deciding what to do about that overpayment required "about a three-second conversation," he says, "primarily with myself. Very clearly, that check goes back. I sent it back with an explanation that it had been paid twice in error."

The dollars involved are usually not so large, or the ethical issues so sharply defined, but such situations arise thousands of times every day in small businesses across the country.

For small-business people, the challenge is to find ways to make sure that they—and their employees—always come down as squarely on the right side as Babb and Edelstein did.

One harshly practical reason for firms to be concerned with business ethics is this: Under the U.S. Sentencing Commission's guidelines for organizational defendants, an effective ethics program can be highly important in protecting a company from criminal penalties, or at least in softening their impact, if an employee violates federal law.

"I have talked to many prosecutors," says W. Michael Hoffman, executive director of the Center for Business Ethics at Bentley College in Waltham, Mass., "and they have said that if a company can demonstrate that it has done everything it could to prevent a wayward employee from doing what he or she did, they're apt not to even prosecute the company, but to go after the employee."

Encouraging ethical behavior can thus be of great value to companies of many kinds, like those—including Delta Sand & Gravel—that are subject to environmental laws. "We have very few problems with the environmental people," Babb says, "because I believe in covering our tracks before we make them. We do our best to comply when we need to, or before we need to."

A commitment to high ethical standards is not just a way to stay out of trouble with the law, though; it's a fundamentally sound way of doing business.

"Good ethics does not always translate into good business," says Michael G. Daigneault, president of the Washington, D.C.-based Ethics Resource Center, which advises many corporations on ethical issues. "But over time, people do understand how you do business; and people do business with other people whom they trust."

One result of Delta's strong reputation, Babb says, is that vendors, knowing how reliable Delta is, are happy to give it the best possible deals. One vendor, for example, "has set us up as a distributor, so they can sell [to] us wholesale. This makes a difference."

And as far as customers are concerned, "people want us to do the work," Babb says. "They keep coming back. Occasionally we get work when we're not low bidder. It pays to play it straight; but that's what people are supposed to do."

TeleManagement Services' Edelstein recalls what happened in the wake of his returning that $40,000 check: "I learned afterward that the director of marketing for a major part of that company, in a department meeting that he had, used that as an example of the type of people they wanted to do business with. Several million dollars of work with that company later, it clearly was the right decision."

Highly ethical small-business owners can stumble, though, when it comes to encouraging strong business ethics throughout their companies.

"A lot of business owners and leaders take it for granted that everyone around them shares their values," Daigneault says. "I guarantee you that that is not the case. What is necessary is a dialogue in which the owner or leader of the business shares his or her perspective concerning appropriate conduct, the fundamental principles and standards that the company stands for—and what it won't stand for."

Even when small-business owners communicate their values, they may not realize—unless they encourage discussion of those values—how important their own example is to their employees.

When Nan DeMars, a Minneapolis-based consultant who writes a monthly column on office ethics for *The Secretary* magazine, surveyed her readers two years ago, she found them acutely aware of what they saw as their bosses' ethical lapses.

More than half of the 1,500 respondents to the survey reported experiencing verbal or emotional harassment from a boss. More concretely, 17 percent said they had notarized a document without witnessing the signature—exactly the sort of ethical fudging that a boss might regard as insignificant but that could loom large to an employee.

Sometimes, ethics may appear differently, depending on a person's vantage point within a business. In a 1994 survey of employees of businesses of all sizes by the Ethics Resource Center, the higher in a company the respondents ranked, the higher their opinion of the company's ethical performance.

The most skeptical were employees on the front lines—hourly workers in manufacturing, low-ranking supervisors, and the like. Such employees must deal with ethical issues in very specific terms:

Should they let a defective shipment go out, to the detriment of a customer, or should they call it back when they know the company is under extreme pressure to deliver—and perhaps be criticized for costing the company money?

Should they turn a blind eye when a colleague cheats on an expense report? (More than a quarter of DeMars' respondents said they had observed such falsifications.)

Most employees want to do the right thing; a business owner's task is to make it easier for them to know what's right and to make it easier for them to do it.

A formal ethics program is probably the most promising way to go about that. The Ethics Resource Center's survey found that employees of companies with strong ethics programs were much more likely to think highly of their company's ethical performance, "with the most dramatic difference seen in the more positive opinions about higher levels of management."

One of the most serious questions is whether a small business's commitment to an ethics program should embrace a written code. Daigneault thinks "it's helpful if it's written down because people take it more seriously." (To learn what's involved in writing a code of ethics, see "Should You Put It In Writing?")

Setting that question aside, there is broad agreement on some other ingredients of an effective effort to strengthen ethics in a small business. Among them:

An ethics program should distinguish between the ethical and the merely legal.

Asking whether something is legal is only the first step in determining whether it is ethical. In fact, making an activity illegal may often be society's way of ratifying its much earlier decision about what is unethical.

"Over the course of time," Daigneault says, "if ethical notions are regarded as important enough, they're promulgated into law."

Seen from that viewpoint, the rise in sexual-harassment cases, for example, may reflect less a rise in such harassment—or even in a general litigiousness—than a higher standard of behavior at more companies. The bad actors stick out more.

As widespread as DeMars' survey indicates that other kinds of harassment are, she says she thinks the situation is changing for the better. "I think [bosses] are realizing that they can't scream and yell at the people who support them," she says.

A company's leaders must support an ethics program wholeheartedly if they expect it to be taken seriously.

"It has to be genuine," Lee Edelstein says of a commitment to ethics, "or people see right through it."

Small-business owners "actually have to embody the principles they have enunciated for their employees," Daigneault says. "Employees are very watchful of the behavior of a leader, and they understand contradictions and hypocrisy quite well." But more than being ethical themselves, he says, "leaders should make it a point to catch people doing good things, and reward them."

They should also pay attention to behavior of the other kind. "One of the worst things that can happen in the culture of a small organization," Daigneault says, "is that someone is obviously doing something that everyone regards as inappropriate, and nothing happens." Employees need to know not only the rules but also that they're being enforced.

An ethics program must be a continuous effort, not a one-shot deal.

"For an ethics policy to be effective, it's got to be intrusive," said John F. Risko, CEO of Oakland, Calif.-based National Airmotive Corp., at a 1997 meeting sponsored by the Conference Board, a New York City-based national business organization that brings executives together to share practical experiences. National Airmotive, which repairs and overhauls aircraft engines, has about 500 employees.

"You have to go out of your way to mention it at a time when you wouldn't ordinarily mention it," Risko said, "to drive the point home to the employees that this is something you're committed to." You must make it clear that if an ethical problem arises, "it's not just an option to discuss it"—it's expected.

An ethics program must involve employees from the start.

Management should welcome the "intrusion" that comes from ethics consciousness in the ranks. Employee involvement—compared with the threat of government intervention or pressure from shareholders—is usually the best way to keep an ethics program energized and focused.

In words that could apply to many small businesses, Stephen I. Kasloff, ethics officer for Guardsmark, a security firm based in Memphis, Tenn., told the Conference

Should You Put It In Writing?

The experts have a short answer—"yes"—when asked whether a company should put its ethics policy in a written code.

"I would strongly encourage small businesses to have a code or credo or set of standards that they and their employees agree to abide by," says Michael G. Daigneault, president of the Ethics Resource Center in Washington, D.C. "What a code tends to do for an organization is establish a set of expectations, an understanding, a common language."

Such codes "benefit small organizations every bit as much as large organizations," Daigneault says. He even suggests bringing customers and vendors in on the formulation of the code. Be as inclusive as possible, he says.

W. Michael Hoffman, executive director of the Center for Business Ethics at Bentley College in Waltham, Mass., says that a company that thinks it doesn't need a formal code—because everyone works so closely together and everyone is so busy—is "in serious danger. You haven't set up any process where your values can be questioned, where they can be living values that are constantly involved in your business decision making."

One of the first steps a company takes in drawing up a code, Hoffman says, should be to form an ethics committee that includes the CEO and other employees from throughout the company to analyze the policies under which the firm already operates.

A company that conducts such a self-examination, Hoffman suggests, will probably uncover inconsistencies in how employees in different parts of the company are dealing with similar issues. Likewise, there may be "ethically sensitive areas" where no policy exists.

"For example," he says, "maybe there has been no real policy made in terms of gaining competitive information, and all of a sudden you realize that you've been trying to get competitive information in ways that you're not sure are consistent with your values."

Are you getting such information from a customer, perhaps, or from a disaffected employee? Do you want to continue doing that? "You need to sit down in that ethics committee, Hoffman says, "and begin to decide what kind of policy you want to operate under."

The next step, he says, is to reduce all the old policies you've gathered up, and the new ones you've formulated, "into some kind of code of conduct." Then small groups—perhaps, in a 50-employee firm, they could be made up of four or five employees each—should discuss and sharpen the code.

If employees have a say in formulating the code, Hoffman, says, "they're apt to have more buy-in, to be committed to this code. That's extremely important." To be successful, a code can't be imposed from the top, no matter how many or how few employees you have.

The code should include commonly asked questions—preferably related to the industry the company is in—that come out of the small groups, because new employees, when they read the code, will have many of the same questions.

Once a code is established, it should be re-examined continually, perhaps by a committee of employees that can recommend changes in it before it's reprinted.

When a company's leaders live up to a code, Hoffman says, "they make a code of conduct a living, breathing thing, rather than something you write up and put in a drawer."

Stories about the leaders' ethical actions can become corporate myths or legends "that solidify a true culture for a company," he says. "People try to emulate them."

However, he continues, "if a company is depending on its ethical culture's being driven by stories, without any systematic code of business conduct, there is danger. I think you need both."

Board audience: "We're a privately owned company, and we're not involved with a regulated industry, so a lot of the impetus to do the kinds of things that we do really must come from within. We want our folks to participate in our process."

To get that kind of employee buy-in, don't tell employees what their values should be but rather ask them what they are. Let their values, as well as your own, shape the company's ethical standards. You may find that your employees have a better-developed ethical sense than you have.

Likewise, you should have channels for reporting and correcting unethical behavior. "There's got to be some way for employees to report to the president or whoever's overseeing compliance with the ethical values"—and even to question the CEO's own behavior, says the Center for Business Ethics' Hoffman.

An ethics program must recognize that ethical issues are pervasive.

Issues of many kinds—involving communications or other management matters—can have a strong ethical component.

A failure to communicate clearly with the customer, for example, can be a symptom of a dangerous disregard for the customer's best interests.

In the automotive industry, says Peter Fink, owner of Certified Transmission Rebuilders, based in Omaha, Neb., "you have to spend a little time with the consumer and let them know what you're going to do and why you have to do it." It's in part to facilitate such communication that Certified emphasizes constant in-house training.

Honest communication can itself lead to ethical challenges. "The first question out of everybody's mouth," Fink says, "is, 'How much will it cost to fix it?'" —a question that he refuses to answer over the telephone.

When the customer does bring a car in, he says, "we give you the worst-case scenario and work backward; that way the '5 o'clock surprise' is that you owe me $200 less than you thought you would."

The hazard in that approach, he acknowledges, is that some people will take their cars to a shop that gives them a lower estimate—over the phone.

Ethical business behavior—honest communication—can thus mean giving up a financial advantage, but perhaps only temporarily. Fink sometimes ends up towing in cars that have wound up in a competitor's shop—where the over-the-phone estimate turns out to have been much too low.

Edelstein of TeleManagement Services also must deal with customers whose expectations are unrealistic "on the high side," he says, "and I just don't want to have an unhappy client. For sure, when they're expecting 70 percent [response from a telemarketing campaign], and you know the best experience you've ever had is 45 percent, and there's nothing compelling about their program, it's our responsibility to tell them that."

Both Edelstein's company and Fink's Certified Transmission Rebuilders were state honorees last year in the Blue Chip Enterprise Initiative. The program recognizes small firms that have met challenges and emerged stronger as a result. It is sponsored by Massachusetts Mutual Life Insurance Co., known as MassMutual—The Blue Chip Company, and by the U.S. Chamber of Commerce, *Nation's Business*, and "First Business," the Chamber's weekday morning television news program.

Even when a small business hasn't adopted a formal ethics program, a companywide commitment to ethical practices can have an impact that may not be within the reach of even the most ethical large corporation.

Because ethical decisions at a small business don't have to be filtered through a corporate bureaucracy for approval, the people at small companies are uniquely well-equipped to clothe the concept of business ethics in what Hoffman calls "a human dimension, a social dimension." Ethics at such small firms cease being an abstraction and instead become people showing concern for one another in a business setting.

Small businesses are almost by definition vulnerable; setbacks that might not faze a mismanaged big business can put a small firm out of business in weeks or months. A commitment to ethical practices can translate that vulnerability into a companywide determination not to take advantage of others who may be either temporarily or permanently in a similar position.

Probably no one feels more vulnerable, for instance, than the automotively unlettered customer facing the prospect of major repair work. Fink has built Certified Transmission Rebuilders on giving customers the assurance that they're not paying for repairs they don't need.

Fink, who has about 140 employees at 10 retail locations in four states, purposely does not pay his diagnosticians on commission, he says, "because we don't want that to influence their decision."

He asks customers whose transmissions have been replaced to bring their cars back for a second examination within 15 days (an arbitrary time limit that's intended just to encourage them to return; Certified will recheck the car free whenever it's brought back in).

"We do a follow-up on it, which is very expensive and time-consuming, to make sure it's right," Fink says. "It's tough to tell a customer it's not working right when they don't even realize it's not, but we'll do that." If Certified has to redo any of its work, it will provide a rental car—as well as do the additional work—without charge.

Many other small firms offer customer service that is comparably ethical at its core. Dolores White, who is the fourth generation of her family to run E. E. Ward Transfer and Storage Co., in Columbus, Ohio, says that the 15-employee moving company has stayed in business as long as it has—since 1881—"because of our reputation."

Years ago, when her grandfather was running the company, "he was highly respected in the community because he had such a warm personal touch with everyone," she says. "This is what we've tried to inspire in our men: Do the best job, and be concerned with our customers."

Many times, she says, "the moves are not pleasant ones: some are the result of divorces or deaths. We do a lot of moves where senior citizens are leaving their homes and going off to retirement centers, and our men work well with them, they're very patient with them, and try to help them as much as possible. A lot of retirement homes refer them to us."

That same concern for the vulnerable aged is evident in what Gwenith Hulsey says about the residents of Agape Manor and village, her assisted-living facility in Hazel Green, Ala., "We work very, very closely with the families," she says. "We keep them informed, and we want them involved."

Agape, which also was a 1997 state honoree in the Blue Chip program, holds two or three events a year aimed at bringing together families, residents, and staff members.

"Sometimes people run out of money," she says. "In that situation, we've worked with the families to help them continue to stay with us. We find out what the families can contribute, over Social Security, and then we just write off part of their bill. You care for them, and you don't want to disrupt their lives because of money. It's hard to move someone who's 98 years old."

In Hulsey's case, her concern for Agape's residents and their families has been repaid with their concern for Agape itself. She recalls a situation when a resident fell at Agape, broke a hip, and ultimately wound up at a rehabilitation facility. "I don't know what happened there," Hulsey says, "but the family was very disturbed.

"They talked to an attorney about suing, and the attorney suggested they start with where she fell." As the resident's daughter told Hulsey, she rejected the idea because she had seen for herself the concern that Hulsey and Agape's employees felt for her mother.

"Most human beings have memories," says Delta Sand & Gravel's Alan Babb in what could be a motto for a small-business ethics program. "We would rather they have good memories of us than bad memories."

Article 6

CRIME IN THE SUITES

WILLIAM GREIDER

The collapse of Enron has swiftly morphed into a go-to-jail financial scandal, laden with the heavy breathing of political fixers, but Enron makes visible a more profound scandal—the failure of market orthodoxy itself. Enron, accompanied by a supporting cast from banking, accounting and Washington politics, is a virtual piñata of corrupt practices and betrayed obligations to investors, taxpayers and voters. But these matters ought not to surprise anyone, because they have been familiar, recurring outrages during the recent reign of high-flying Wall Street. This time, the distinctive scale may make it harder to brush them aside. "There are many more Enrons out there," a well-placed Washington lawyer confided. He knows because he has represented a couple of them.

The rot in America's financial system is structural and systemic. It consists of lying, cheating and stealing on a grand scale, but most offenses seem depersonalized because the transactions are so complex and remote from ordinary human criminality. The various cops-and-robbers investigations now under way will provide the story line for coming months, but the heart of the matter lies deeper than individual venality. In this era of deregulation and laissez-faire ideology, the essential premise has been that market forces discipline and punish the errant players more effectively than government does. To produce greater efficiency and innovation, government was told to back off, and it largely has. "Transparency" became the exalted buzzword. The market discipline would be exercised by investors acting on honest information supplied by the banks and brokerages holding their money, "independent" corporate directors and outside auditors, and regular disclosure reports required by the Securities and Exchange Commission and other regulatory agencies. The Enron story makes a sick joke of all these safeguards.

But the rot consists of more than greed and ignorance. The evolving new forms of finance and banking, joined with the permissive culture in Washington, produced an exotic structural nightmare in which some firms are regulated and supervised while others are not. They converge, however, with *kereitzu*-style back-scratching in the business of lending and investing other people's money. The results are profoundly conflicted loyalties in banks and financial firms—who have fiduciary obligations to the citizens who give them money to invest. Banks and brokerages often cannot tell the truth to retail customers, depositors or investors without potentially injuring the corporate clients that provide huge commissions and profits from investment deals. Sometimes bankers cannot even tell the truth to themselves because they have put their own capital (or government-insured deposits) at risk in the deals. These and other deformities will not be cleaned up overnight (if at all, given the bipartisan political subservience to Wall Street interests). But Enron ought to be seen as the casebook for fundamental reform.

The people bilked in Enron's sudden implosion were not only the 12,000 employees whose 401(k) savings disappeared while Enron insiders were smartly cashing out more than $1 billion of their own shares. The other losers are working people across America. Enron was effectively owned by them. On June 30, before the CEO abruptly resigned and the stock price began its terminal decline, 64 percent of Enron's 744 million shares were owned by institutional investors, mainly pension funds but also mutual funds in which families have individual accounts. At midyear, the company was valued at $36.5 billion, having fallen from $70 billion in less than six months. The share price is now close to zero. Either way you figure it, ordinary Americans—the beneficial owners of pension funds—lost $25–$50 billion because they were told lies by the people and firms they trusted to protect their interests.

The corporate transgressions could not have occurred if supposedly independent watchdogs had not failed to execute their obligations.

This is a shocking but not a new development. Global Crossing went from $60 a share to pennies (as with Enron, the market had said it was worth more than General Motors). CEO Gary Winnick cashed out early for $600 million, but the insiders did not share the bad news with other shareholders. Workers at telephone companies bought by Global Crossing had been compelled to accept its stock in their retirement plans. (Winnick bought a $60 million home in Bel Air, said to be the highest-priced single-family dwelling in America.) Lucent's stock price tanked with similar consequences for employees and shareholders, while executives sold $12 million in shares back to the failing company. (After running Lucent into the ground, CEO Richard McGinn left with an $11.3 million severance package.) There are many Enrons, as the lawyer said.

The disorder writ large by the Enron story is this regular plundering of ordinary Americans, who are saving on their own or who have accepted deferred wages in the form of future retirement benefits. Major pension funds can and do sue for damages when they are defrauded, but this is obviously an impotent form of discipline. Labor Department officials have known the vulnerable spots in pension-fund protection for many years and regularly sent corrective amendments to Congress—ignored under both parties. In the financial world, the larceny is effectively decriminalized—culprits typically settle in cash with fines or settlements, without admitting guilt but promising not to do it again. If jailtime deters garden-variety crime, maybe it would be useful therapy for corporate and financial behavior.

The most important reform that could flow from these disasters is legislation that gives employees, union and nonunion, a voice and role in supervising their own pension funds as well as the growing 401(k) plans. In Enron's case, the employees who were not wiped out were sheet-metal workers at subsidiaries acquired by Enron whose union locals insisted on keeping their own separately managed pension funds. Labor-managed pension funds, with holdings of about $400 billion, are dwarfed by corporate-controlled funds, in which the future beneficiaries are frequently manipulated to enhance the company's bottom line. Yet pension funds supervised jointly by unions and management give better average benefits and broader coverage (despite a few scandals of their own). If pension boards included people whose own money is at stake, it could be a powerful enforcer of responsible behavior.

The corporate transgressions could not have occurred if the supposedly independent watchdogs in the system had not failed to execute their obligations. Wendy Gramm, wife of Senator Phil, the leading Congressional patron of banking's privileges, is an "independent" director of Enron and supposedly speaks for the broader interests of other stakeholders, from the employees to outside shareholders. Instead, she sold early too. With notable exceptions, the "independent" directors on most corporate boards are a well-known sham—typically handpicked by the CEO and loyal to him, even while serving on the executive compensation committees that ratify bloated CEO pay packages. The poster boy for this charade is Michael Eisner of Disney. As CEO, he must answer to a board of directors that includes the principal of his kids' elementary school, actor Sidney Poitier, the architect who designed Eisner's Aspen home and a university president whose school got a $1 million donation from Eisner. As Robert A.G. Monks and Nell Minow, leading critics of corporate governance, asked in one of their books: "Who is watching the watchers?"

Do not count on "independent" auditors, as Arthur Andersen vividly demonstrated at Enron. While previous scandals did not involve massive document-shredding, Andersen's behavior is actually typical among the Big Five accounting firms that monopolize commercial/financial auditing worldwide. Andersen already faces SEC investigation for its role in "Chainsaw Al" Dunlap's butchery of Sunbeam and has paid $110 million to settle Sunbeam investors' damage suits. A decade ago Andersen fronted for Charles Keating's notorious Lincoln Savings & Loan, which bilked the elderly and then collapsed at taxpayer expense—despite a prestigious seal of approval from Alan Greenspan (Keating went to prison; Greenspan became Federal Reserve Chairman). But why pick on Arthur Andersen? Ernst & Young paid out even more for "recklessly misrepresenting" the profit claims of Cendant Corporation—$335 million to the New York and California public-employee pension funds. Cendant itself has paid out $2.8 billion to injured investors, but hopes to recover some money by suing Ernst & Young. PriceWaterhouseCoopers handled the books at Lucent, accused of inflating profits by $679 million in 2000 and prompting yet another SEC investigation.

The corruption of customary auditing—and the fact that an industry-sponsored board sets the arcane accounting tricks for determining whether profits are real or fictitious—is driven partly by the Big Five's dual role as consultants and auditors. First they help a company set its business strategy, then they examine the books to see if management is telling the truth. This egregious conflict of interest should have been prohibited long ago, but the scandal has reached a ripeness that now calls for a more radical solution—the creation of public auditors, hired by government, paid by insurance fees levied on industry and completely insulated from private interests or politics. Actually, this isn't a very radical idea, since the government already exercises the same close scrutiny and supervision over commercial banks. Because that banking sector lost its primary role in lending during the past two decades, the same public auditing and supervisory protections should be extended to cover the unregulated money-market firms and funds that have displaced the bankers. Enron is unregulated, though it functioned like a giant financial house. So is GE Capital, a money pool much larger than all but a few commercial banks. Mutual funds and hedge funds are essentially free of government scrutiny. So are the exotic financial derivatives that Enron sold and that led to shocking breakdowns like the bankruptcy of Orange County, California.

The government failed too, mainly by going limp in its due diligence but also by withdrawing responsibility through legislative deregulation. The one brave exception was Arthur Levitt, Clinton's SEC commissioner, who gamely raised some of these questions, but without much effect because he was hammered by the industry and its Congressional cheerleaders. Corrupt accountants and investment bankers now have a friendlier commissioner at the SEC—lawyer Harvey Pitt, whose firm has represented Arthur Andersen, each of the Big Five and Ivan Boesky, whose fraud case was settled for $100 million. Pitt blames Arthur Levitt's inquiries for upsetting the accounting industry's self-regulation. Given his connections, Pitt should not just recuse himself from the Enron case—a crisis of legitimacy for the SEC—he should be compelled to resign. Similarly sympathetic cops are scattered throughout the regulatory agencies. At the Federal Reserve, a new governor, Mark Olson, headed "regulatory consulting" in Ernst & Young's Washington office. Another new Fed governor, Memphis banker Susan Bies, has been an active opponent of strengthening derivatives regulation.

But the heart of the scandal resides in New York, not Washington. The major houses of Wall Street play a double game with their customers—doing investment deals with companies in their private offices while their stock analysts are out front whipping up enthusiasm for the same companies' stocks. Think of Goldman Sachs still advising a "buy" on Enron shares last fall, even as the company abruptly revealed a $1.2 billion erasure in shareholder equity. Goldman earned $69 million from Enron underwriting in recent years, the leader among the $323 million Enron paid Wall Street firms. Think of the young Henry Blodget, now famous as Merrill Lynch's never-say-sell tout for the same Nasdaq clients whose fees helped fuel Blodget's $5-million-a-year income (Merrill has begun settling investor lawsuits in cash). Think of Mary Meeker at Morgan Stanley Dean Witter, dubbed the "Queen of the Net" for pumping up Internet firms while Morgan Stanley was taking in $480 million in fees on Internet IPOs. The conflict is not exactly new but has reached staggering dimensions. The brokers whose stock tips you can trust are the ones who don't offer any.

The larger and far more dangerous conflict of interest lies in the convergence of government-insured commercial banks and the investment banks, because this marriage has the potential not only to burn investors but to shake the financial system and entire economy. If the newly created and top-heavy mega-banks get in trouble, their friends in power may arrange another cozy government bailout for those it deems "too big to fail." The banking convergence, slyly under way for years, was formally legalized in the 1999 repeal of Glass-Steagall, the New Deal law that separated the two sectors to eliminate the very kind of self-dealing that the Enron case suggests may be threatening again. We don't yet know how much damage has been done to the banking system, but its losses seem to grow with each new revelation. JP Morgan Chase and Citigroup provided billions to Enron while also stage-managing its huge investment deals around the world and arranging a fire-sale buyout by Dynegy that failed (Morgan also played financial backstop for Enron's various kinds of trading transactions). Instead of backing off and demanding more prudent management, these two banks lent additional billions during Enron's final days, perhaps trying to save their own positions (we don't yet know). Instead of warning other banks of the rising dangers, Chase and Citi led the happy talk. Both have syndicated many billions in bank loans to other commercial banks—a rich fee-generating business that allows them to pass the risks on to others (federal regulators report that the volume of "adversely classified" syndicated loans has risen to 8 percent, tripling the problem loans since 1998).

Gentlemanly solicitude for big boys who get in trouble connects Washington with Wall Street and spans both political parties.

These facts may help explain why former Treasury Secretary Robert Rubin, now of Citigroup, called an old friend at Treasury and suggested federal intervention. Rubin's bank has a large and growing hole in its own loan portfolio. Could Treasury please pressure the credit-rating agencies, Rubin asked, not to downgrade Enron? Though he styles himself as a high-minded public servant, Rubin was trying to save his own ass. Indeed, he called the very Treasury official who, as an officer of the New York Federal Reserve back in 1998, had engineered the cozy bailout of Long Term Capital Management—the failing hedge fund that Citigroup, Merrill and other major financial houses had financed. Gentlemanly solicitude for big boys who get in trouble connects Washington with Wall Street and spans both political parties.

In this new world of laissez-faire, when things go blooey, the government itself is exposed to risk alongside hapless investors—if the commercial banks are lending federally insured deposits along with their own investment plays or are exercising what amounts to an equity position in the failed management. This is allegedly forbidden by "firewalls" within the mega-banks, but when a banker gets in deep enough trouble, he may be tempted to use the creative accounting needed to slip around firewalls. "A bank that has equity shares in a company that goes south can no longer make neutral, objective judgments about when to cut off credit," said Tom Schlesinger, executive director of the Financial Markets Center. "The rationale for repealing Glass-Steagall was that it would create more diversified banks and therefore more stability. What I see in these mega-banks is not diversification but more concentration of risk, which puts the taxpayers on the hook. It also creates a financial sector much less responsive to the real needs of the economy."

The fallacies of our era are on the table now, visible for all to see, but the follies are unlikely to be challenged promptly—not without great political agitation. The other obvious deformity exposed by Enron is the insidious corruption of democracy by political money. The routine buying of politicians, federal regulators and laws does not constitute a go-to-jail scandal since it all appears to be legal. But we do have a strong new brief for enacting campaign finance reform that is real. The market ideology has produced the best government that money can buy. The looting is unlikely to end so long as democracy is for sale.

William Greider is The Nation*'s national affairs correspondent.*

Article 7

Special report: The trouble with accounting

When the numbers don't add up

LONDON, NEW YORK AND SAN FRANCISCO

To be efficient, markets need reliable information. Enron shows the extent to which they are not getting it

RARELY has an accounting scam had such wide repercussions. As the fog surrounding Enron's accounts slowly lifts, investors are beginning to see what a mountain of muck it concealed. As a result, they have turned resolutely against companies with opaque accounts—from American blue chips such as General Electric to Elan, an Irish pharmaceuticals group whose share price halved on February 4th when it confessed to the deleterious effect of some hitherto undisclosed assets on its 2001 earnings.

External auditors have come under heavy suspicion. Andersen, Enron's auditor until the energy company filed for bankruptcy in December, is now the weakest link in a profession forced on to the defensive. And the failure of companies' internal audit committees to spot the transgressions has raised doubts about the effectiveness of "independent" non-executive directors.

More importantly, the very tools of the auditors' trade—the accounting standards by which they measure a company's performance—are increasingly being questioned. What can be done to restore faith in accounts and accountants?

Accountants themselves have begun belatedly to clean up their act. This week Paul Volcker, a former chairman of the Federal Reserve and now chairman of the foundation that governs the International Accounting Standards Board (IASB), a body which oversees the harmonisation of accounting rules worldwide, agreed to chair a committee set up by Andersen to recommend reforms. Andersen has promised to implement whatever the committee recommends.

Auditor, audit thyself

One recommendation is likely to be a split of its auditing and consulting businesses. The conflict between the two has been controversial for some time. In 2000, Andersen earned more from Enron from non-audit services ($27m) than it did from auditing ($25m). A report submitted to Enron's board on February 2nd revealed details of further conflicts of interest between the two businesses. For example, Andersen earned $5.7m in 2000 by providing non-audit services relating to LJM and Chewco, two of the numerous "special purpose entities" (SPEs) that are at the heart of Enron's attempt to hide its true financial condition from investors.

Last week, PricewaterhouseCoopers, another of the big five firms which dominate the auditing of large quoted companies in America and Europe, brought forward the spin-off of its consulting arm. And this week Deloitte Touche Tohmatsu, the biggest international firm, said it too would separate its audit and consulting businesses, a route already followed in the last two years by KPMG and Ernst & Young (see chart). James Copeland, Deloitte's chief executive, says that the firm has not yet decided how to go about the separation, but it will have a plan ready by the end of May. Andersen, the fifth member of the big five, says it has begun to avoid doing non-audit work for audit clients as part of its post-Enron reforms.

These moves are not altruistic. Many clients are considering following the lead given by Unilever and Walt Disney. Both companies have announced, post-Enron, that they will not give any more consulting work to their auditors. Harvey Pitt, the chairman of the Securities and Exchange Commission (SEC), does not—unlike his predecessor, Arthur Levitt—think a formal ban is necessary, but says that "if Congress goes for it, I'll support it." Britain's financial markets regulator, the Financial Services Authority (FSA), is contemplating a ban on firms carrying out consulting work for their audit clients.

Mr Levitt, who was chairman of the SEC from 1993–2000, campaigned to ban accounting firms from selling services such as consulting to their audit clients. At the time, Mr Pitt was on the other side of the fence. As a lawyer, he represented Ernst & Young and PricewaterhouseCoopers "as they negotiated appropriate independence rules with the SEC", as he puts it.

Intense lobbying by accounting firms at the time forced Mr Levitt to agree a compromise whereby the firms would merely disclose each year how much they had earned from selling non-audit services to each firm that they audited. It showed that companies such as Motorola, Gap and Raytheon paid their auditors more than ten times as much for consulting as for auditing. At the time, Deloitte Touche Tohmatsu was the most fiercely opposed to the ban of all the big accounting firms. And this week it was unrepentant. The decision to separate auditing and consulting, said Mr Copeland, was made "very, very reluctantly. We do not believe this is a superior answer for auditing."

Board stiffs

The Enron affair has also highlighted the failure of companies' internal audit committees (a subset of their board) to police their auditors properly. It is not yet clear why Enron's audit committee failed so completely, but questions are being raised about the conflicts of interest of some of its members.

Enron made substantial donations to the political campaigns of Phil Gramm, the senator husband of Wendy Gramm, the audit committee's chairman, as well as to a charity supported by Mrs Gramm. Lord Wakeham, a former British energy minister who was on the audit committee and who had a consulting contract with Enron, stepped aside last week from his job as chairman of the Press Complaints Commission, Britain's media watchdog.

The FSA has set out the responsibilities of the chairmen of British banks' audit committees, and made it clear that in the event of an audit failure, the chairman will be held responsible. At the Halifax, a large British bank, the audit committee's head now spends two days a week on his audit duties, and is paid commensurately. (A typical board member in America would consider two days a month to be a burden.) More pay and more time are certainly needed for audit committees to be effective. More important, though, is an independent frame of mind, and most boards tend to crush that rather than encourage it.

In the absence of adequate internal policemen, what other system of auditing the auditors might be effective? Nobody takes seriously the current peer review process, in which each of the big five firms gives a clean bill of health to another. Nor was America's Public Oversight Board, a private-sector body of five veteran executives from outside the industry, much use. Its members resigned last month after Mr Pitt proposed (without first consulting them) a vague new body to oversee the profession. One answer might be for a company's auditor to be chosen by a regulator, such as the SEC, or by a body like Britain's Audit Commission, which already chooses the auditors of local authorities' accounts.

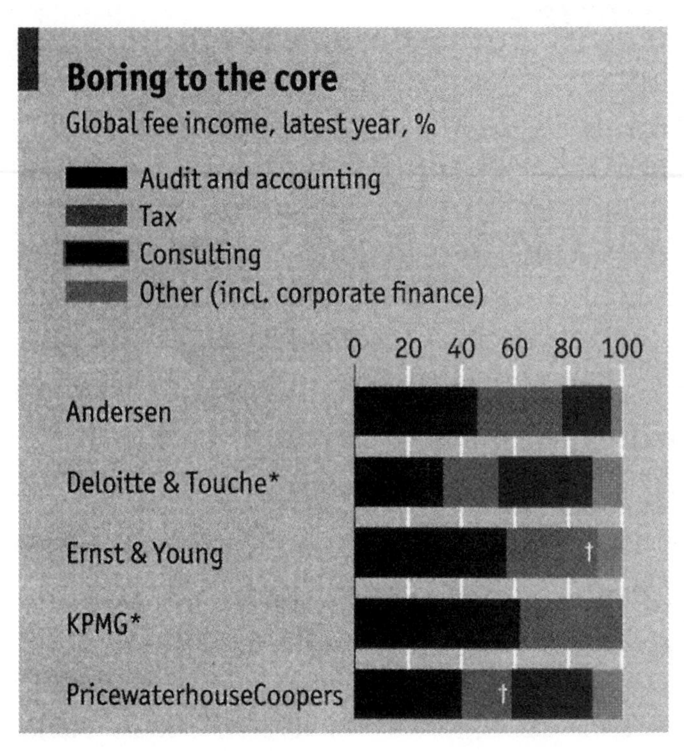

*US only †Including legal work
Source: *International Accounting Bulletin*

Raising standards

The biggest accounting issue raised by Enron, however, is over accounting standards, the rules determining how companies should draw up their accounts. In America, these are set by the Financial Accounting Standards Board (FASB), a bunch of accountants who have drawn up a body of "generally accepted accounting principles" (GAAP). Other countries do things differently, and some follow the rules laid down by the IASB.

Mr Pitt says that he is supportive of the IASB and its idea of a single set of accounting standards for the world. Nevertheless, foreign companies wanting to list on the New York Stock Exchange still have to provide a reconciliation of their accounts with GAAP. Mr Pitt warns that any weakening of GAAP in order to converge with international rules is out of the question.

David Cairns, a former head of the IASB, thinks that after Enron America may accept that standards issued by other people can be as good or better than its own. Take, for example, the treatment of Enron's SPEs. For 20 years FASB failed to respond to requests to clarify the treatment of these. As a consequence, companies were allowed to leave very material items out of their accounts. International accounting rules on SPEs, as laid out by the IASB, are tougher and would, if applied properly, have forced Enron and its auditors to include them in the firm's accounts.

Mr Pitt has told the FASB to come up with a new standard for SPEs by the end of this year. But he wants to go much further and shake up the FASB itself which, he says, "is not performing satisfactorily". "It does not set out enough principles, and those that it does take too long." The recent appointment of Bob Herdman, formerly a senior executive at Ernst & Young, as chief economist at the SEC is encouraging more companies to seek the SEC's advice on what accounting rules they should follow.

Broadly, there are two main approaches to rule-setting. One is to define precisely how to deal with each and any situation. The other is to spell out rough principles and let auditors decide how to apply them. America has typically gone for precise rules rather than broad principles. Post-Enron, many people (including Mr Pitt) believe that this draws a road map for avoidance. If the rule says that above 10% an item should be shown, then those with something to hide go for 9.9%.

Areas where the accounting rules are still dangerously murky include:

- Off-balance-sheet activities. Companies use a variety of permitted devices besides SPEs to push either assets or liabilities off their balance sheets. These include leasing and securitisation. For example, an airline can own no planes in accounting terms, yet have long-term leases on them that are all but the same as ownership.
- Employee share options. These are clearly a cost of employment, yet they are not included in costs when calculating profits. The FASB had to back away from changing this after intense lobbying by companies, accountants and politicians. The IASB is currently under similar pressure as it considers the same issue.
- Derivatives. Assets are traditionally valued at historic cost (what they were bought for), but this makes little sense for financial instruments that swing wildly in value from day to day. There has been some progress towards valuing derivatives in real time ("marking to market"), but there is still a long way to go. One particular problem lies in the treatment of hedging, where a derivative is used to offset exposure to a real asset on a balance sheet which is not marked to market.
- Intangible assets. These account for an increasing proportion of companies' total assets, but they are largely excluded from

balance sheets—whether they are relatively simple to value (like patents and licences) or fuzzier (like brands and goodwill).

• Revenue recognition. Companies have considerable discretion over when they book a profit or set aside reserves against a future loss. Global Crossing, for example, a recently bankrupted telecoms company audited by Andersen, leased capacity to other telecoms carriers and treated this as immediate revenue. At the same time, it leased capacity from other providers and treated this as a capital expense, amortising it over time. Likewise, Enron was able to record profits for a joint venture with Blockbuster Video that never actually got off the ground.

The manipulation of expenses presents a particular challenge because the arguments for doing it are often strong, even though the result can be misleading. A company called Pre-Paid Legal Services was forced by the SEC to restate (as expenses) some sales commissions which it had treated as assets. Richard Sloan, a professor at the University of Michigan, says such a practice can be justified because upfront costs are often incurred to create future revenue streams, to which they should be related in time. In the mid-1990s, Waste Management became notorious for the way in which it treated all sorts of routine expenses as the costs of acquiring contracts, costs that could thus be deferred for years. For a long time, that was how America Online treated the cost of acquiring its subscribers.

Another common way of distorting accounts is by "channel stuffing". Companies such as Sunbeam, Lucent and Xerox's Latin American division attempted to meet ambitious quarterly goals in the late 1990s by reporting products as sold when they had merely been placed in a warehouse or on a retailer's shelf. Once there, they acted as an impediment to future sales and often had to be dumped later at low prices. That, in turn, forced the companies to restate their earlier profits.

High jinks in high tech

Confusing the picture even further has been the growing use of non-standard "pro-forma" accounting—particularly popular with the high-tech industry. Not content with creating a new economy, it has set about creating accounting rules to go with it. More than in any other sector, high-tech firms are calculating earnings not just by applying GAAP, but by using homemade formulas to exclude "special expenses"—a method that invariably makes the numbers look a lot better.

On February 4th, for example, Priceline.com, an online travel agency, reported a pro-forma net income of $3.3m, a sum that converted under GAAP rules into a loss of $1.3m. SGI, a computer maker, recently announced a "profit" of $400,000 after leaving out consulting fees of $10m for installing a new software system.

Amazon is often criticised for its confusing accounting practices. The online retailer surprised analysts in January by announcing a $5m net profit in its latest quarter, calculated under GAAP rules. In its press release about the figures, the company mentioned two other profits: "pro-forma operating profit" (of $59m) and "pro-forma net profit" (of $35m). The first number excludes stock options, amortisation of goodwill and restructuring costs; the second ignores things such as currency gains and losses, and something called the "cumulative effect of change in accounting principle".

Many in the IT industry argue that pro-forma figures give a more accurate picture of a company's prospects than the official GAAP numbers, which include many non-cash and one-off charges. But their argument is weakened by the random way in which companies pick-'n'-mix their formulas. Comparing pro-forma results of different companies is nigh-on impossible; it is sometimes difficult even to compare the results of one period with those of another for the same company. The market, once blind to this legerdemain, is growing wiser. The shares of Priceline.com dropped by 24% after the announcement of its profit (and simultaneous loss). Silicon Valley folk fear that, thanks to Enron, any recovery in their stocks has been postponed even further.

People problems

There are at least two other problem areas for accounting. One is the quality of accountants themselves. Richard Leftwich, a professor of accounting at the University of Chicago, says that it is difficult for the accounting profession to attract able people because the work is seen as less creative than investment banking and consulting—auditing is basically a matter of checking somebody else's figures. "The starting salary is lower in accounting than in consulting," he says, "so the quality of people attracted is lower."

Accounting firms used to argue that their consulting businesses enabled them to attract a higher calibre of auditor because many of them had an eye on moving over to become consultants. That argument has been blown apart by the long line of accounting scandals. Now that accounting firms are in the process of getting rid of their consulting arms, they may be hoping that their corporate-finance work will fill the gap. It is a growing part of their business and could be the carrot to lure able people in to auditing for a while.

Another problem is not so much that auditors have an eye out for new business within their own firm, but that they have an eye out for a better-paid job with their clients. Enron's accounts and finance departments were stuffed with former Andersen employees. And Joseph Perrone, Global Crossing's executive vice-president of finance at the time of its collapse, is a former Andersen employee who was leader of the audit team in charge of Global Crossing's accounts until he joined the company in May 2000. Strong personal ties such as these may well compromise the independence of the audit. When gamekeepers turn poachers they know very well which game to go for.

The second problem lies in the reading of accounts. Mr Pitt wants financial statements to be written in plain English, not in the current legalese. As he puts it, "the current system of disclosure is designed to avoid liability, not to inform anybody." Most controversial of all, though, he wants to end the notion that there is one (and only one) correct version of accounts. "There is no true number in accounting," he says, "and if there were, auditors would be the last people to find it."

Instead he wants to shed light on the processes of calculation that lead to the numbers in the accounts. He has already ordered auditors to identify the five assumptions that make the biggest difference, and to show how the numbers would look were different assumptions made. In this he is on the right track. Accounting will always be as much art as science. Caveat lector.

UNIT 2

Ethical Issues and Dilemmas in the Workplace

Unit Selections

Key Points to Consider

- What ethical dilemmas do managers face most frequently? What ethical dilemmas do employees face most often?
- What forms of gender and minority discrimination are most prevalent in today's workplace?
- Whistle-blowing occurs when an employee discloses illegal, immoral, or illegitimate organizational practices or activities. Under what circumstances do you believe whistle-blowing is appropriate? Why?

Links: www.dushkin.com/online/
These sites are annotated in the World Wide Web pages.

American Psychological Association
http://www.apa.org/books/homepage.html

Annenberg Washington Program in Communications Policy Studies of Northwestern University
http://www.annenberg.nwu.edu/pubs/downside/

Fortune
http://www.pathfinder.com/fortune/bestcompanies/intro.html

International Labour Organization (ILO)
http://www.ilo.org

What You Can Do in Your Workplace
http://www.connectforkids.org/info-url1564/info-url_list.htm?section=Workplace

LaRue Tone Hosmer, in *The Ethics of Management,* lucidly states that ethical problems in business are truly managerial dilemmas because they represent a conflict, or at least the possibility of a conflict, between the *economic performance* of an organization and its *social performance.* Whereas the economic performance is measured by revenues, costs, and profits, the social performance is judged by the fulfillment of obligations to persons both within and outside the organization.

Units 2 to 4 discuss some of the critical ethical dilemmas that management faces in making decisions in the workplace, in the marketplace, and within the global society. This unit focuses on the relationships and obligations of employers and employees to each other.

Organizational decision makers are ethical when they act with equity, fairness, and impartiality, treating with respect the rights of their employees. An organization's hiring and firing practices, treatment of women and minorities, allowance of employees' privacy, and wages and working conditions are areas in which it has ethical responsibilities.

The employee also has ethical obligations in his or her relationship to the employer. A conflict of interest can occur when an employee allows a gratuity or favor to sway him or her in selecting a contract or purchasing a piece of equipment, making a choice that may not be in the best interests of the organization. Other possible ethical dilemmas for employees include espionage and the betrayal of secrets (especially to competitors), the theft of equipment, and the abuse of expense accounts.

The articles in this unit are broken down into seven sections representing various types of ethical dilemmas in the workplace. The initial article in this first section discloses some sad examples of how some companies have tricked retiring employees out of their health benefits. "Electronic Communication in the Workplace—Something's Got to Give" reflects the ongoing battle over rights and privacy issues of e-mail at the office.

In the subsection entitled *Employee Crime,* three articles explore cyber crime, fraud, and workplace sabotage.

The three selections under *Sexual Treatment of Employees* take a close look at how women are treated in the workplace, examine how recent court decisions are attempting to clarify sexual harassment, and reveal why a wage gap continues to vex women.

The two readings in the *Discriminatory and Prejudicial Employment Practices* section scrutinize racism and ageism in the workplace and explore the importance of using older workers to their fullest potential.

In the next subsection, *Downsizing of the Workforce,* three articles suggest the importance of management's thinking concerning the specific reasons for considering layoffs, creative alternatives to downsizing, ways to handle terminations with dignity, and possible strategies to be used in assisting survivors of downsizings.

The selections included under the heading *Whistle-Blowing in the Organization* analyzes the ethical dilemma and possible ramifications of whistle-blowing.

The article "Intentional Integrity," which opens the last subsection of *Handling Ethical Dilemmas at Work,* discusses that while there are many things that might be legal, they might be wrong ethically. The next article underscores the urgency to pay close attention to questions of morality in the workplace. "Gold Mine or Fool's Gold?" provides a case where a new product manager faces an ethical dilemma about what to do with "proprietary and confidential" documents about his closest competitor. "Leaders as Value Shapers" delineates the importance of managers fully understanding their values as they face serious ethical dilemmas at work. "The Parable of the Sadhu" presents a real-world ethical dilemma for the reader to ponder.

CUT LOOSE

Companies Trick Retirees out of Health Benefits

by Anne-Marie Cusac

Fran Asbeck worked for IBM for thirty-two years. He retired at age fifty-six in 1994, secure in the knowledge that IBM would cover health care for himself and his wife. "The thing is, we were promised all this would be free," he says. "They said we had all the deferred money coming on down the line—a fat pension with yearly COLAs [Cost-of-Living Allowances], free lifetime health care. Those were the verbal promises made."

Two years ago, says Asbeck, IBM went back on its promises. "They just sent a letter saying, 'You've got to start paying for it'" or get less coverage, he recalls.

Asbeck, a former computer programmer who lives in Boyds, Maryland, relied on the excellent health care insurance that IBM offered. But now it's not as attractive. "Since I retired, in order to keep it at zero cost, I have had to take lower and lower levels of health insurance," he says. So Asbeck moved out of what to him was an ideal plan into IBM's preferred provider organization. He no longer gets to choose his doctors freely.

Earlier this year, Asbeck discovered that accepting a lower level of health coverage for himself and his wife wasn't going to work anymore. Worried about the risks of emergency hospitalization, he decided to start paying $80 each month.

It sounds relatively cheap as far as health insurance goes. But Asbeck says he can't afford the cost, in part because his pension has not kept up with the cost of living. That's why he's had to get another job.

"I'm just going to have to work until I'm in the box and hear the dirt hit the lid," he says.

Many IBM employees share Asbeck's plight.

The retirees were told "in department meetings, by their managers, in handbooks, that they would have free health insurance for life," says Lee Conrad, an IBM retiree who is now an organizer with Alliance@IBM, which is connected to the Communications Workers of America and based in Endicott, New York. "Now they've got to pay. This has been a real culture shock for people."

IBM defends its practice. "Back in the early '90s, the company set a limit and a cap" on the amount it would pay for retiree health care and informed the retirees that it wouldn't pay more than that, says Jana Weatherbee, a spokesperson for IBM. "That limit has been reached."

Weatherbee says she "can't speak to any verbal promises." However, she does say that the company repeatedly informed retirees in writing that, "once you reach this limit, you will start helping in the contribution for that coverage."

And the IBM insurance brochure does include this statement: "The company reserves the right, at its discretion, to amend, change, or terminate any of its benefits plans, programs, or policies, as the company requires. Nothing contained in this Enrollment Guide shall be construed as creating an expressed or implied obligation on the part of the company to maintain such benefits plans, programs, practices, or policies."

"They're covered legally," says Asbeck. But he feels betrayed. And he and other IBM retirees say they're suffering while IBM's Chairman and CEO Louis V. Gerstner Jr. is raking it in. Gerstner made $2 million in salary in 1999 and $5.25 million in bonuses, according to the company's 1999 proxy statement. The bonuses are based partly on cash flow and stock market gains. Companies can boost both by cutting retiree health benefits.

"Lou Gerstner has only been at IBM for seven years," says Conrad. "He's affecting the lives of retirees who put thirty, forty years in. They're the ones who built the company and created the wealth that Lou Gerstner is now pillaging. When you have people who are ill, on fixed income, the increased costs are going to create serious problems. That's unconscionable. How can you do this to people? IBM has their own personal piggy bank right now. And it's not their money. It's the employees' and the retirees' money."

Asbeck puts it another way: "He's getting fat on our blood."

It's not just IBM. Many other companies renege on health insurance promises made to retirees. According to a December 2000 study by William M. Mercer, Inc., a human resources and benefits firm, only 31 percent of companies with 500 or more employees now provide health care coverage to retirees under the age of sixty-five (the age that people qualify for Medicare). This is down from 35 percent in 1999 and 46 percent in 1993. The number of larger companies covering insurance for seniors ages sixty-five and older also fell, from 28 percent to 24 percent. This was the seventh year in a row that retiree insurance coverage declined.

Telephone company retirees make up probably the largest single group that has seen cuts in coverage or faced increases in monthly insurance costs, says C. William Jones, president of the Association of BellTel Retirees. The former Bell system retirees number more than one million, he says. The BellTel retirees' insurance costs have risen up to 500 percent.

"Many of the large corporations are involved," says Paul Edwards, chairman of the Coalition for Retirement Security, a grassroots organization that works on pension and retiree health insurance issues and is based in Springfield, Massachusetts. "It has become an acceptable practice. These aren't just isolated events. Just name your top corporations: IBM, GE's had some benefit reductions. We're talking millions of employees."

Michael Gordon is a D.C.-based lawyer who is working with the BellTel Retirees. In the last decade, says Gordon, five million retirees or their spouses nationwide have lost or had substantially reduced health benefits. "This is a national problem," he says. "It affects just about every retiree who has had some type of health coverage under their employers."

"We think it's a great concern," says Gerry Smolka, senior policy adviser for the Public Policy Institute of the American Association of Retired Persons. "People plan based on what they know. Health benefits are one of the things that give you financial security in retirement. It can completely erode your savings if you're not adequately covered."

Some retirees are more vulnerable than others. After age sixty-five, Medicare pays about 80 percent of medical bills, usually excluding pharmaceuticals. It can be extremely difficult for older retirees, who sometimes live on a pension that inflation has sharply reduced, to pay the remaining 20 percent.

But people who retire early, often as the result of pressure from their employers, can be in even more serious trouble. Those who are not yet eligible for Medicare may have to rely solely on their promised benefits. When their companies snip the strings, these retirees come down hard.

Some early retirees "have lost their benefits and can't get replacement insurance because they have a pre-existing condition now that is so severe no one will insure them, or because the costs are so high that they'll just eat up their pension," says Gordon. "If you're not Medicare-eligible, you're in a black hole if you've got a medical condition that requires expensive treatment and the employer pulls out the rug."

Companies have an incentive to take back retiree health benefits: They can get richer that way.

On October 25, 2000, *The Wall Street Journal* published an article entitled "Companies Transform Retiree-Medical Plans into Source of Profits." The reporter, Ellen E. Schultz, revealed that a little-known accounting rule, called the Financial Accounting Standard (FAS) 106, forced companies in the early 1990s to report the lifetime benefits they owed to future retirees as a liability.

Few companies want large liabilities on their balance sheets. So, by decreasing the amounts they owe on health insurance, they appear better off. Some companies overestimated their retiree health benefits at first. By downscaling their estimates and by cutting coverage, they improved their balance sheets.

"The kicker is that at numerous companies... the paper gains not only erased the retiree benefit expenses, but exceeded them," wrote Schultz. "And that is how benefit plans came to boost the bottom line."

"Companies that have boosted their bottom lines by this method," wrote Schultz, include R. R. Donnelly and Sons, Sears, Sunbeam, Tektronix, and Walt Disney.

One of the most egregious cases involves BWX Technologies, Inc., based in Lynchburg, Virginia. The company is a subsidiary of McDermott International, which describes itself as "a leading worldwide Energy Services Company."

In the mid-1990s, say employees, the company's naval nuclear fuel division began to push people into early retirement. "They said, 'If you retire early, you can keep your insurance,'" recalls William McKenna, a retiree from the company. But if you don't retire early, they said you'll have no insurance when you do. "About 400 people jumped on that bandwagon."

Richard Mull, a former chief electrician, says that management told him, "The most your health insurance will be for the rest of your life will be $16" per month. From 1996 through 1998, he says, "they really pressed this point. They got rid of a lot of older employees that way."

Mull left in 1997, at age sixty-two, having worked for BWX Technologies for thirty years. "I was anxious to get out of the plant," he says, mentioning a supervisor who he says died of a brain tumor thirty days after diagnosis. "They wanted to know if he'd been exposed to radiation or asbestos. Uranium 235, enriched uranium, we worked with every day. You had all these poisons around you."

When he heard about his supervisor's death, Mull decided to leave. "I said, 'I'm getting out of this place.'"

Mull got out. Then his insurance costs started to soar. In April 1998, the company segregated the retirees out from the insurance policies of the active workers. In a document entitled "Employee Information 1376" (released only to active employees, but leaked to the retirees), the company warned, "Beginning April 1, 1998, retirees enrolled in the Health Care and Life Insurance Plans will be responsible for most of the cost of those coverages."

In that document, the company explains the new charges: "The current cost of providing Health Care and Life Insurance Plans for retirees is very high and continues to increase. Changing the structure of the plans lowers the cost to the company, which helps improve the company's cash flow and its profitability."

In August 1998, Mull says he received a letter that stated the retirees would be charged between $250 and $750 per month, according to age and state of health. At that point, he says, because his health was good, his insurance costs rose to only $285 per month. By October, he says, the company had gotten rid of coverage for prescriptions and doubled the deductible for hospital visits. "They dropped about 50 percent of your coverage," says Mull.

From then on, every six months, the retirees were reassessed. "I eventually went up to $795 a month for me and my wife," says Mull. "No general, no doctor's visits, just for 70 percent hospitalization after we paid a $1,500 deductible." By April 1999, Mull says the company informed him that, at the rate he was paying, his insurance would not cover prior illnesses.

"Now, you work at a chemical or a nuclear plant for thirty years, you've got priors," he says. "I myself have mild asbestosis." Three months ago, Mull learned that he also has basal skin cancers. "The doctor said there could be a link, or there might not," he says. "I got a lot of high density radiation burns from welding."

Last July came another note from BWX Technologies' parent corporation. The premium had risen to $1,113 per month for Mull and his wife. Further, the letter said, coverage was guaranteed only if at least 85 percent of the retirees agreed to participate in the plan. "If this level of participation is not attained, it is highly likely that no alternative plan can be identified, and the company will no longer be able to provide you access to any medical coverage plan," says the document.

"People dropped their health coverage. They withdrew money from their 401(k)s, they went and got home equity loans," says McKenna, who worked for the company as a darkroom technician developing X-ray film, as a welder, and as an accountability technician. Then, after local press attention from reporter Chris Flores of the Lynchburg, Virginia, *News and Advance*, "all of a sudden, [the company] found a nice policy" for just over $600, says McKenna. Even so, he says, "After twenty, thirty years of work, it's taking your whole retirement check to pay for your health insurance."

McKenna has pulmonary illness. He says he was exposed to many hazardous chemicals and asbestos, as well as raw, unprocessed uranium. "I can no longer breathe on my own without daily doses of Prednisone and asthma medications and aerosol breathing treatments every four to six hours," he wrote to former Energy Secretary Bill Richardson on April 13, 2000, in response to Richardson's proposal to compensate sick nuclear workers.

In separate interviews, Mull and McKenna mention a recent asbestos screening organized by the retirees. "Sixty percent tested positive for lung scarring," says McKenna. "194 took the test. 150 were retirees. Our lawyer made sure the doctor read these real strict." Those that tested positive, says McKenna, "were real bad. You should have heard all the stories that retirees told about all the stuff they were exposed to."

McKenna claims that he is also in the beginning stages of asbestosis. "I went and had my test back in July. I was positive," he says. "The lady that did the lung screening said, 'They exposed you to asbestos, and now they're going to dump you in the street and take away your insurance.'"

Both Mull and McKenna now get their insurance from other sources: Mull from the Veteran's Administration, McKenna from his wife's employer.

"These are loyal, twenty-five- to thirty-year employees," says Gary Kendall, general counsel to the Virginia AFL-CIO. "The amount of insurance in some cases is equal to, or maybe even more than, their monthly pensions. Nobody can afford to carry it. Had they known that, they never would have retired."

Ron Hite, director of government and public relations for BWX Technologies, blames increasing medical costs for the surge in charges these retirees now face. "The costs are going up at just an exponential rate," he says. He also blames accounting rule FAS 106. "Companies really have no incentive to provide health care coverage," he says. But "our company tried very vigorously to keep retirees with some type of affordable insurance."

Hite says that BWX Technologies continues to contribute "a reasonable level of support" to the retirees' health care costs, but he refuses to say how much. "That's information that's proprietary," he says.

Hite also says that he cannot discuss alleged medical conditions for individual employees. "What I can tell you is we are one of the most highly regulated industries in the country," he says. "Throughout our history, we have complied with all federal and state laws."

McKenna can't get over the company's duplicity. "The bottom line is, 'We don't care about the retirees no more. We need cash flow,'" he says.

Corporations are not the only ones reneging. Unions are doing it, too. Robert Devlin was vice president of the Transportation Communications International Union for sixteen years before he retired. He is a fifty-six-year member of the union. Now he's involved with the Retired Employees Protective Association, based in River Edge, New Jersey.

"We are all retired officers or employees of a railroad union that has cut our benefits," says Devlin. "For thirty-three years, we've had health insurance, just as the railroad employees had, including cost-free insurance into retirement—not only for the rest of our lives, but to our surviving spouse. A new group of officers came in, and they decided that these old retirees are getting treated too well."

The union decided to charge retirees $100 per month, or else they would have to forfeit their insurance.

Devlin feels double-crossed. "If the railroads had done this to their employees, they would have had a strike on their hands," he says.

The union did not respond to several requests for comment.

Many retirees are outraged to learn that companies are acting legally when they do away with health benefits.

"It's a particularly nasty problem because courts have held that employers are free to end or reduce retiree health coverage almost regardless of the circumstances—whether they need to or not," says Gordon. "Even if there was an understanding when the retirees retired that these are lifetime benefits, courts have held that retirees are helpless to protect them. Every federal court in the country has had this issue litigated. It's the same problem over and over again."

The crux of the problem is that, even when companies make promises to retirees, they shield themselves with written statements claiming the right to modify or terminate the benefits at any time.

Gordon calls *GM vs. Sprague* "the most shocking case of all." About 50,000 GM employees were offered an early retirement package in the mid-1990s. The company assured them they would get the same benefits they had as employees as retirees. This, the retirees later claimed, was part of what induced them to take early retirement. Then GM backed out. The retirees went to court and eventually lost. The U.S. Supreme Court denied the case a review. "These guys are out of luck—some 50,000 of them," says Gordon.

The appellate court took a generous view of GM's side of the story. "GM's failure, if it may properly be called such, amounted to this: The company did not tell the early retirees at every possible opportunity that which it had told them many times before—namely, that the terms of the plans were subject to change," said Judge David A. Nelson in his 1998 ruling for the United States Court of Appeals for the Sixth Circuit. "There is, in our view, a world of difference between the employer's deliberate misleading of employees... and GM's failure to begin every communication to plan participants with a caveat."

But the dissent to this decision, from Chief Judge Boyce F. Martin Jr., is scathing in its evaluation of GM's behavior. "This is a classic case of corporate shortsightedness," Martin wrote. "When General Motors was flush with cash and health care costs were low, it was easy to promise employees and retirees lifetime health care. Later, when General Motors was trying to sweeten the pot for early retirees, health care was another incentive to get employees off General Motors's groaning payroll. Of course, many of the executives who promised lifetime health care to early and general retirees are probably long since gone themselves. Rather than pay off those perhaps ill-considered promises, it is easier for the current regime to say those promises never were made.... Seemingly, any reservation of rights, no matter how weakly worded or unconnected to the grant of rights, will inure a company from having to live up to its obligations in the future."

Representative John Tierney, Democrat of Massachusetts, believes retirees won't be adequately protected unless the law is changed. That's why he introduced the Emergency Retiree Health Benefits Protection Act of 2001.

"Obviously, if you don't have to show an obligation to pay out retiree health benefits, there's more cash on hand" and the company is more financially attractive, Tierney says. "Many of these companies are extraordinarily healthy financially. It has not been a hardship thing." Tierney lists several companies: "General Electric, you don't get much stronger than that. The telephone companies are surviving and doing well, for the most part. General Motors is a strong company. Sears Roebuck."

The bill, which Tierney submitted along with three other Democrats (Robert E. Andrews of New Jersey, Dale E. Kildee of Michigan, and Carolyn McCarthy of New York), would require employers to restore any post-retirement reductions or cancellations of health benefits, unless to do so would cause financial hardship. And it sets up an emergency loan guarantee of $5 billion for those employers who need financial help to give their retirees benefits.

Retirees of many corporations—including the former Bell Telephone companies, General Electric, U.S. West, SNET, Prudential, Johns Manville, the New York Transit Police, Greyhound, and Grumman Aircraft—have signed on to the legislation. Other supporters are the Institute of Electrical and Electronics Engineers and the Pension Rights Center.

But in a Republican Administration, the bill's chance of passage appears bleak, despite President Bush's pledge that health care for seniors is a top priority.

Mike Kucklinca, executive vice president of the BellTel Retirees, was a loyal employee: "I went into the company because I thought I would have job and benefit security both during my tenure and into retirement," he says. His father, a power company employee, drilled that ethic into his head, he says.

"Who would disbelieve a company that you've worked for for thirty and more years? It was like Mother Bell would take care of us. Well, she didn't. I never thought I'd be spending all this time and energy organizing to get what I and the other retirees feel we worked for all our lives. I'm going to fight until I leave this world."

Anne-Marie Cusac is Managing Editor of The Progressive.

Electronic Communication in the Workplace—Something's Got to Give

Kenneth A. Kovach, Sandra J. Conner, Tamar Livneh,
Kevin M. Scallan, and Roy L. Schwartz

Every day, millions of American workers use their e-mail and Internet systems, confident that their day's transactions are private. But nothing could be further from the truth. According to a major 1997 survey by the American Management Association, 63 percent of large and mid-sized companies acknowledged that they oversee employees through one or more electronic surveillance systems. Almost a quarter of those companies do not let their employees know they are being monitored.

The impact of e-mail has revolutionized the workplace. A poll reported by Kopp (1998) estimates that 90 percent of large companies, 64 percent of mid-sized companies, and 42 percent of small firms currently use e-mail systems. The same poll found that more than 40 million employees correspond via e-mail, and the number is expected to increase by about 20 percent each year. These statistics are indicative of the popularity of electronic communication in today's workplace. E-mail technology has facilitated more efficient interoffice communications, as well as external communications with clients, customers, and other businesses. It has also expedited personal transactions; in many instances, e-mail has effectively replaced the hand- or typewritten note and letter of memorandum.

The unique nature of e-mail as a communication media warrants special consideration regarding privacy. Although it may be used as a substitute for making a telephone call, there is a big difference between the two. The telephone call is transitory—ending when the phone is hung up—whereas an e-mail note is permanent. Moreover, e-mail can much more easily be examined by a third party without the knowledge of the communicating parties.

Employee privacy is colliding with employer rights in the ongoing battle over e-mail at the office. Who will—and should—win?

As technology becomes faster and cheaper, concerns about workplace privacy issues continue to mount. The impressive advancements in computer communications have created many new problems, and in some cases increased the severity of old ones. It is surprising that despite this growing threat to privacy, there is no legal remedy for employees should their privacy be invaded by their employer. Federal and state courts, for the most part, have upheld employer monitoring, according little or no weight to employee privacy interests—possibly because they do not understand the intrusiveness of the new monitoring technology in the workplace. Neither Congress nor state legislatures have acted to fill the void or provide comprehensive statutory protection for workers. Privacy, ostensibly one of society's most, cherished values, is gradually disappearing from the workplace. According to Fader (1998), "American laws don't protect worker privacy very well. We differ from Europe and most industrialized nations. They stringently limit the employee data companies collect, store, and disseminate. We have no such laws."

LEGAL IMPLICATIONS

The right to privacy in the employment context usually derives from the Fourth Amendment to the U.S. Constitution, which reads:

> The right of the people to be secure in their persons, houses, papers and effects, against unreasonable searches and seizures, shall not be violated, and no warrants shall issue but upon probable cause, supported by oath or affirmation, and particularly describing the place to be searched, and the persons or things to be seized.

Because the Constitution applies to actions of the state, public sector workers have the provision of appealing directly to the "reasonable expectation of privacy" standard established by the Supreme Court ruling in *Katz v. United States* (Rodriguez 1998). Private sector employees do not enjoy the same level of privacy protection because actions of private employers rarely constitute "state action," which would open the avenue of appeal directly to the Constitution. Because constitutional rights primarily protect citizens from the government, state action is required before a citizen can invoke such a right. The manner in which a government employer treats its employees is by definition a state action. The manner in which a private employer treats its employees is not. Because of this dichotomy, public sector employees enjoy far greater privacy rights than those working for private firms.

"In some cases, private sector employees have not been protected against even the most outrageous forms of employer intrusion."

For the typical private sector employee, then, the only sources of legal protection against intrusive employer surveillance are claims brought under various state statutes or the common law tort "invasion of privacy." The protection provided by these remedies varies widely from jurisdiction to jurisdiction. In some cases, private sector employees have not been protected against even the most outrageous forms of employer intrusion.

To examine the legal implications of e-mail monitoring in the workplace, it is first necessary to consider the circumstances that motivate employers to monitor their workers. One is the ease with which an employer may conduct monitoring. Yet another is the perceived need to curb misuses or abuses of an e-mail system provided and maintained by the employer. Misuse might take the form of wasted time spent sending personal messages to friends, family, or coworkers during business hours. More serious abuses could involve sending harassing messages to coworkers or revealing trade secrets to rival companies.

In the absence of constitutional protection, employees are increasingly looking to Congress and their state legislatures for statutory protection. In response to Congress's perception that abuses associated with new technologies pose a substantial risk to civil liberties, the Electronic Communications Privacy Act (ECPA) of 1986 was enacted. The ECPA amended Title III of the Omnibus Crime Control and Safe Streets Act of 1968, which merely proscribed the unauthorized *interception* of wire and oral communications. Essentially, it extended Title III's existing prohibitions against the unauthorized interception of electronic communications.

Thus, explains Kopp, Title III and the ECPA together prohibit intentional or willful interception, accession, disclosure, or use of one's oral or electronic communications. The protections extend to cover the intentional interception of communications by unauthorized individuals and third parties, as well as government agents.

However, the ECPA *does not explicitly* offer protection from employers who access or intercept the electronic communications of *their own* employees. Instead, it appears to offer protection only from the unauthorized interception from *outside parties*, or from another employee who has exceeded his authority when accessing, intercepting, or disclosing information on a private corporate system.

Although none of the provisions in the ECPA appear to limit its applicability to employer monitoring of employee e-mail, Kopp discusses three primary exceptions it does contain that may have the same practical effect: the provider exception, the ordinary course of business exception, and the consent exception.

Provider Exception. The provider exception contained in the ECPA generally exempts e-mail service providers from the ECPA prohibitions against interception or accession of e-mail communications in the workplace. A private employer will be exempt from ECPA liability *so long as it is the direct provider of the e-mail system*. This effectively reserves to employers the unrestricted right to monitor employee e-mail. However, the exception may not apply to employers that merely provide e-mail service through a common carrier such as AOL.

Ordinary Course of Business Exception. The ordinary course of business exception to the ECPA, also known as the business extension exception, states in essence that information transmitted in the ordinary course of business is excluded from the definition of "information transmitted by electronic, mechanical, or other devices," as defined in the ECPA. This exception has yet to be applied to e-mail communications in the workplace.

The Consent Exception. The consent exception to the ECPA generally applies in the event that one party to the communication has given prior consent to the interception or accession of the communication. Thus, as long as the communication is intercepted by a person who is either a party to it or has expressly consented to such interception, the prohibitions contained within the ECPA will not apply.

Common Law Torts

Because of the lack of clear constitutional or statutory protection, the primary source of employee privacy protection in the private sector workplace has been state tort law. According to Kopp, tort law recognizes four distinct torts protecting the right of privacy:

1. unreasonable intrusion upon the seclusion of another;
2. appropriation of another's name or likeness;
3. unreasonable publicity given to another's private life; or

4. publicity that unreasonably places another in a false light before the public.

The tort most closely associated with e-mail monitoring in the workplace is the "intrusion upon seclusion" tort. It holds that one who intentionally intrudes, physically or otherwise, on the solitude or seclusion of another, or another's private affairs or concerns, is subject to liability for invasion of privacy if the intrusion would be highly offensive to a reasonable person. In holding that the invasion may be "physical or otherwise," this tort could possibly be extended to protect against e-mail monitoring. It also imposes a standard of objective reasonableness. Thus, in deciding whether the intrusion is into a private matter, courts require not only that the employee have a subjective expectation of privacy, but also that the expectation be objectively reasonable.

The common law tort of invasion of privacy has been applied in two recent cases involving e-mail monitoring in the workplace, both discussed by Kopp. In *Bourke v. Nissan Motor Corp.* (1993), the plaintiffs brought action against their employer for intercepting and reviewing several personal e-mail messages. In rejecting their claim of tortious invasion of privacy, the court held that the employees did not have a reasonable expectation of privacy in their e-mail communications because they had signed a waiver stating that e-mail use was limited to company business. The court also noted that the employees were aware that other coworkers had read their e-mail messages in the past, even though they were not the intended recipients of the messages. Further, the court rejected the plaintiffs' argument that a subjective expectation of privacy existed by virtue of having personal passwords to access the e-mail system, as well as their being told to safeguard their passwords.

The most recent case to address the common law tort of invasion of privacy is *Smyth vs. Pillsbury Co.* (1996), in which an employee brought suit against his employer for wrongful discharge. The employee had been fired after company executives reviewed the contents of his e-mail messages and found them to contain offensive references toward certain company personnel. He had sent these messages to his supervisor in the knowledge that company policy held that all e-mail communications would remain private and confidential. The plaintiff argued that his termination was against public policy as a violation of his common law right to privacy. The court analyzed his claim under the definition of intrusion upon seclusion and found, first, that the plaintiff could not have a reasonable expectation of privacy in e-mail communications voluntarily made to his supervisor over the company e-mail system. Second, even if he was determined to have a reasonable expectation of privacy in the contents of his e-mail messages, the court would not consider his interception of those communications to be a substantial and highly offensive invasion of privacy, particularly since the e-mail system belonged to the company. The court concluded by adding that any privacy interest of the plaintiff was outweighed by the employer's interest in preventing inappropriate and unprofessional comments over its e-mail system.

"As the only cases so far applying common law invasion of privacy to tort e-mail monitoring, Bourke and Smyth offer a grim outlook for e-mail privacy in the workplace."

As the only cases so far applying common law invasion of privacy to tort e-mail monitoring, *Bourke* and *Smyth* offer a grim outlook for e-mail privacy in the workplace. The cases suggest that courts will provide a very narrow reading of employees' reasonable expectation of privacy. *Bourke* holds that maintaining a personal password to access the e-mail system does not give rise to an objectively reasonable expectation of privacy. *Smyth* indicates that even an employer's stated policy that employee e-mail is private and confidential will not necessarily give rise to an objectively reasonable expectation of privacy. Thus, the current state of common law with respect to e-mail monitoring clearly favors employers.

It should also be noted that a well-written e-mail policy may not only immunize an employer from liability under the ECPA, but may also immunize it from tort liability for invasion of privacy. In fact, the two cases above strongly support the proposition that a well-written e-mail policy will be sufficient to render unreasonable any expectation of privacy.

New Legislation

The weaknesses of the ECPA combined with increased employee awareness and sensitivity to privacy in the workplace have led to the proposal of new legislation to address the issue of monitoring electronic communications in the workplace. In 1991, the Privacy for Consumers and Workers Act (PCWA) was introduced in Congress, addressing issues of private-sector employee privacy and preserving employee rights. Its provisions would allow a company to monitor employees' e-mail and use the information against them to some extent. However, prior to monitoring, the company would be obligated to inform the employees of the potential, form, and scope of the monitoring, as well as what the data collected might be used for.

The original version of the PCWA failed to pass through Congress. At present, a revised version is still being debated in congressional committee. Meanwhile, the debate over private-sector workplace privacy has been stirred up. The proposal of the PCWA has served to highlight the need for further legislation—beyond the scope of the ECPA—to protect employees' rights to privacy.

BUSINESS RAMIFICATIONS

Driven by the desire to increase productivity and minimize liability, employers have adopted monitoring techniques in an effort to control all aspects of the workplace. They can provide other justifications as well for maintaining these invasive practices, such as the need to evaluate worker performance more efficiently, the need to deter or uncover employee wrongdoing and dishonesty, and even the need to limit tort liability under the respondent superior doctrine.

In 1998, U.S. industry spent half a trillion dollars on computer hardware and software, communications, and training and support. Many companies are now grappling with employees using that technology for purely personal transactions during business hours. This abuse has lowered companies' return on their technological investments. Its cost to employers can only be estimated, but all would agree it is substantial.

Examples of such employee abuse abound. Recently, Salomon Smith Barney terminated two high-ranking stock analysts for using company e-mail systems to share pornography. An analysis of computer logs by Neilsen Media Research found that employees at IBM and Apple together visited Penthouse Magazine's Web site almost 13,000 times in a single month in 1996, using up the equivalent of almost 350 eight-hour days. Another study by SurfWatch Software, a Web filtering company based in Los Altos, California, found that 24 percent of the on-line traffic at the companies surveyed was not work-related. Sites most commonly visited, reports GaroFalo (1998), were general news, sex, investments, entertainment, and sports. Thus, employers have a legitimate interest in workplace monitoring if they want to limit inappropriate use of company time and maintain or increase productivity.

When it comes to protecting themselves against liability, employers are insisting on the right to monitor communications. They rightfully cite their legitimate interest in running an efficient business and in hiring and retaining honest and productive employees who will perform their jobs in a safe manner. And they fear claims asserting a hostile workplace environment, or harassment lawsuits by workers who happen upon offensive messages. Industry leaders, including Citibank and Morgan Stanley, have been sued by employees over the content of e-mail messages. Recently, a federal court in New York held that a class action race discrimination suit seeking damages of $60 million could proceed against Morgan Stanley, a large Wall Street brokerage firm. The lawsuit stemmed in part from the alleged repeated dissemination of a racist e-mail message through the company's computer system. More and more, cases of sexual harassment and discrimination include allegations that the company e-mail systems were used to transmit inappropriate or offensive material.

Viewing the privacy component of new technology from a different angle, it is possible that increased employee privacy may result in a more efficient workplace. It sends a positive message from the employer to the employees, implicitly trusting them to be responsible for their time and productivity. Such a message could fortify the work relationship between a firm and its workers and infuse personal dignity into the workplace. In contrast, an employer who monitors the workplace daily and is privy to all internal communications may create a workplace filled with distrust. Employees who do not trust their employer have a lower incentive to be efficient, resourceful, and productive.

ETHICAL IMPLICATIONS

There are two main ethical issues regarding privacy in the workplace: employee abuse of company resources and employer abuse of workers' privacy rights. The latter hinges on the notions of human dignity and trust.

In a study reported by GaroFalo, nearly half of the 726 employees surveyed acknowledged that they had engaged in unethical actions using their employers' technology during the previous year. Further, more than one-fourth of those responding stated that they had committed at least one highly unethical or illegal act, including copying company software for home use, using office equipment to search for other jobs, accessing private computer files without permission, visiting pornographic Web sites using office equipment, or sabotaging systems or data of former employers and coworkers.

Americans' respect for privacy has helped creativity and individuality flourish. So the negative effects of reduced individual privacy rights go far beyond simple embarrassment. Loss of privacy often induces conformity to perceived societal norms in order to safeguard personal and professional interests. American culture has been built on diversity and the willingness to accept challenges that test people's creativity. Yet these traits that helped mold our country will suffer if conformity, not privacy, is considered the principle value. Perhaps worst of all, inroads into privacy inhibit personal autonomy and thus individual freedom.

Of course, in addition to the fundamental interest individuals have invested in privacy, they also have a need to obtain and maintain employment. Some employee monitoring is always necessary. Tracking productivity and attendance is done in many, if not most, organizations. It is, however, the seemingly secretive or unexpected nature of certain types of monitoring or surveillance that tend to engender most of the bad feelings that may lead to actionable invasion of privacy claims.

Employers have an obligation to respect the privacy of their employees as well as inform then of monitoring intentions and policies. In addition to buttressing a firm's right to protect its interests, implementing a formal e-mail policy would also reflect an ethical responsibility to protect employees' privacy. One approach is to create a sign-on disclaimer that defines the degree and scope of privacy allowed and reiterates the fact that e-mail is company-owned property. Moreover, employees should be informed that their e-mail communications may be monitored at any time by the company and that, by using the e-mail system, the employee is consenting to be monitored. Finally, users of the e-mail system should be told explicitly not to send inappropriate messages, or they could face disciplinary consequences, up to and including the possibility of discharge.

As workplace technology continues to improve and become more prevalent and more available to employees, so too will the opportunities for employee abuse and, concurrently, the avenues available to firms to monitor and control employee activities. Companies must, however, be cognizant of the impact such activities have on the morale of the employees, who feel that their rights are being trampled. They must also beware the possible legal ramifications of overreaching. Employers who engage in monitoring, surveillance, or searches should do so only pursuant to a well-written policy that has been distributed in advance to all employees. Moreover, any such monitoring should be reasonable in nature and strictly for business purposes.

To best address the issue of workplace privacy in light of evolving technology, new federal legislation should be enacted, balancing the rights of employees to privacy with the rights currently afforded to employers. New legislation will also serve to heighten employee awareness of companies' policies regarding the use of workplace technology. The time to embark on such a course of action was yesterday.

References

H. Chase and C.R. Ducat, *The Constitution and What It Means Today*, 13th ed. (Princeton, NJ: Princeton University Press, 1978).

B. Cole-Gomolski, "The Lethal Sting of Forgotten Mail," *Computerworld*, September 8, 1997, pp. 1, 117.

R. Dixon, "Windows Nine to Five: Smyth v. Pillsbury and the Scope of an Employee's Right of Privacy in Employer Communications," *Virginia Journal of Law and Technology*, Fall 1997, pp. 1–26.

S.S. Fader, "Want Some Privacy? Stay at Home," *Chicago Tribune*, May 28, 1998, pp. 1, 3.

W.S. Galkin, "Database Protection: Just the Facts," *The Maryland Bar Journal*, May–June 1993, p. 40.

B. GaroFalo, "Sharing a Middle Ground With Big Brother," *Connecticut Law Tribune*, May 18, 1998, p. 1.

W.S. Hubbartt, *The New Battle Over Workplace Privacy* (New York: AMACOM, 1998).

K.P. Kopp, "Electronic Communications in the Workplace: E-mail Monitoring and the Right of Privacy," *Seton Hall Constitutional Law Journal*, Summer 1998, pp. 1–30.

A. Rodriguez, "All Bark, No Byte: Employee E-Mail Privacy Rights in the Private Sector Workplace," *Emory Law Journal*, Fall 1998, p. 1439.

P. Schnaitman, "Building a Community Through Workplace E-Mail: The New Privacy Frontier," *Michigan Telecommunication and Technology Law Review*, 1998–99, p. 177.

J. Sipior, B.T. Ward, and S.M. Rainone, "Ethical Management of Employee E-Mail Privacy," *Information Systems Management*, Winter 1998, pp. 41–47.

S. Stipe, "Establish E-Mail Policy to Avoid Legal Pitfalls," *Best's Review*, July 1996, pp. 102–103.

S.E. Wilborn, "Revisiting the Public/Private Distinction: Employee Monitoring in the Workplace," *Georgia Law Review*, Spring 1998, pp. 825–887.

N. Wingfield, "More Companies Monitor Employees' E-mail," *Wall Street Journal*, December 2, 1999, p. B5.

Kenneth A. Kovach is a professor of management at George Mason University in Fairfax, Virginia. **Sandra J. Conner, Tamar Livneh, Kevin M. Scallan, and Roy L. Schwartz** are MBA students at the University of Maryland, College Park, Maryland.

CYBER CRIME

First Yahoo! Then eBay. The Net's vulnerability threatens e-commerce—and you

The scenario that no one in the computer security field likes to talk about has come to pass: The biggest e-commerce sites on the Net have been falling like dominoes. First it was Yahoo! Inc. On Feb. 6, the portal giant was shut down for three hours. Then retailer Buy.com Inc. was hit the next day, hours after going public. By that evening, eBay, Amazon.com, and CNN had gone dark. And in the morning, the mayhem continued with online broker E*Trade and others having traffic to their sites virtually choked off.

The work of some super hacker? For now, law enforcement officials don't know, or won't say. But what worries experts more than the identity of this particular culprit or outlaw group is how easily these attacks have been orchestrated and executed. Seemingly, someone could be sitting in the warmth of their home and, with a few keystrokes, disrupting electronic commerce around the globe.

DEAD HALT. Experts say it's so easy, it's creepy: The software to do this damage is simple to use and readily available at underground hacker sites throughout the Internet. A tiny program can be downloaded and then planted in computers all over the world. Then, with the push of a button, those PCs are alerted to go into action, sending a simple request for access to a site, again and again and again—indeed, scores or hundreds of times a second. Gridlock. For all the sophisticated work on firewalls, intrusion-detection systems, encryption and computer security, e-businesses are at risk from a relatively simple technique that's akin to dialing a telephone number repeatedly so that everyone else trying to get through will hear a busy signal. "We have not seen anything of this magnitude before—not only at eBay, but across so many sites," says Margaret C. Whitman, CEO of eBay.

No information on a Web site was snatched, no data corrupted, no credit-card numbers stolen—at least so far. Yet it's a deceptively diabolical trick that has temporarily halted commerce on some of the biggest Web sites, raising the question: How soft is the underbelly of the Internet? Could tricks like these jeopardize the explosive growth of the Web, where consumers and businesses are expected to transact nearly $450 billion in business this year? "It's been war out there for some time, but it's been hidden," says James Adams, co-founder of iDEFENSE, an Alexandria, Va., company that specializes in cyber threats. "Now, for the first time, there is a general awareness of our vulnerabilities and the nature of what we have wrought by running helter-skelter down the speed race of the Information Highway."

To be sure, not even the most hardened cyber sleuths are suggesting the Net is going to wither overnight from the misdeeds of these wrongdoers. But the events of recent days are delivering a shrill wake-up call to businesses that they need to spend as much time protecting their Web sites and networks as they do linking them with customers, suppliers, contractors—and you. Consider just a quick smattering of recent events: In December, 300,000 credit-card numbers were snatched from online music retailer CD Universe. In March, the Melissa virus caused an estimated $80 million in damage when it swept around the world, paralyzing e-mail systems. That same month, hackers-for-hire pleaded guilty to breaking into phone giants AT&T, GTE, and Sprint, among others, for calling card numbers that eventually made their way to organized crime gangs in Italy. According to the FBI, the phone companies were hit for an estimated $2 million.

Cyber crime is becoming one of the Net's growth businesses. The recent spate of attacks that gummed up Web sites for hours—known as "denial of service"—is only one type. Today, criminals are doing everything from stealing intellectual property and committing fraud to unleashing viruses and committing acts of cyber terrorism in which political groups or unfriendly governments nab crucial information. Indeed, the tactic used to create mayhem in the past few days is actually one of the more innocuous ones. Cyber thieves have at their fingertips a dozen dangerous tools, from "scans" that ferret out weaknesses in Web site software programs to "sniffers" that snatch passwords. All told, the FBI estimates computer losses at up to $10 billion a year.

As grim as the security picture may appear today, it could actually get worse as broadband connections catch on. Then the Web will go from being the occasional dial-up service to being "always on," much as the phone is.

HOW THIS HAPPENED TO YAHOO!, EBAY, AND E*TRADE

Disrupting the Net isn't child's play, but it isn't rocket science, either. And cleaning up the mess takes teamwork.

STEP 1 An individual or group downloads software that is readily available at scores of underground Web sites specializing in hacker tools. The software is easy to use; it's all point-and-click.

STEP 2 They break into scores of computers on the Web and plant a portion of the downloaded program, allowing the hacker to control the machine. Unfortunately, there are plenty of machines on the Net that lack the proper security to stop this.

ILLUSTRATIONS BY RAY VELLA/BW

STEP 3 They pick a target—Yahoo!, eBay, or Amazon. com—and then sit back in the privacy of their homes and instruct the computers they've hijacked to send requests for information to that site. One or two messages won't do it. But send enough at the same time and the resulting congestion clogs networks or brings computer servers and router systems to their knees. It's like constantly dialing a telephone number so that no one else can get through.

STEP 4 Responding can take hours. Tracing attackers is hard because they use fake addresses from scores of computers. But as systems administrators sift through the traffic, they can identify the general location—say, an Internet service provider. This takes a coordinated effort involving the company, its ISP, and telecom suppliers. After identifying the machines, the company writes a program to reject the requests—and prays that it doesn't get another flood of messages.

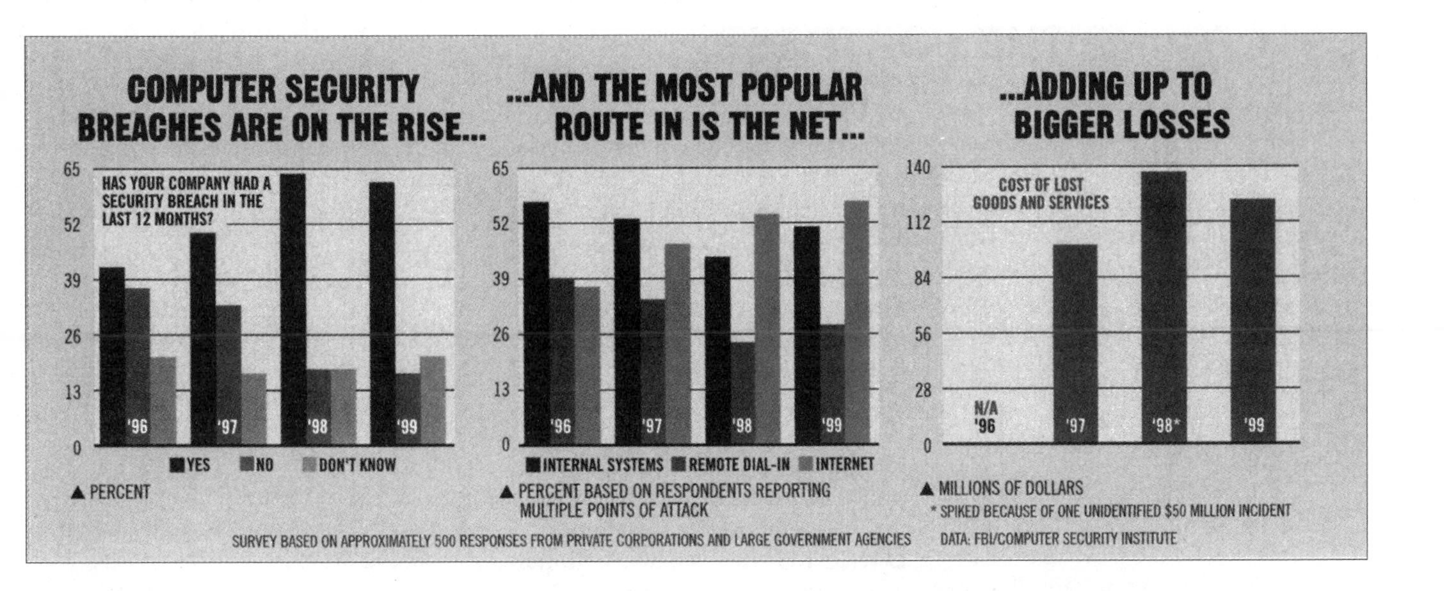

That concept may be nirvana to e-tailers, but could pose a real danger to consumers if cyber crooks can come and go into their computer systems at will. Says Bruce Schneier, chief technical officer at Counterpane Internet Security Inc. in San Jose, Calif.: "They'll keep knocking on doors until they find computers that aren't protected."

Sadly, the biggest threat is from within. Law enforcement officials estimate that up to 60% of break-ins are from employees. Take the experience of William C. Boni, a digital detective for PricewaterhouseCoopers in Los Angeles. Last year, he was called in by an entertainment company that was suspicious about an employee. The employee, it turns out, was under some financial pressure and had installed a program called Back Orifice on three of the company's servers. The program, which is widely available on the Internet, allowed him to take over those machines, gaining passwords and all the company's financial data. The employee was terminated before any damage could be done.

> "We have not seen anything of this magnitude before—not only at eBay but across so many sites. This is probably the single largest denial of service that the Internet has seen"
>
> **MARGARET C. WHITMAN**
>
> *CEO, eBay Inc.*

The dirty little secret is that computer networks offer ready points of access for disgruntled employees, spies, thieves, sociopaths, and bored teens. Once they're in a corporate network, they can lift intellectual property, destroy data, sabotage operations, even subvert a particular deal or career. "Any business on the Internet is a target as far as I'm concerned," says Paul Field, a reformed hacker who is now a security consultant.

It's point and click, then stick 'em up. Interested in a little mayhem? Security experts estimate that there are 1,900 Web sites that offer the digital tools—for free—that will let people snoop, crash computers, hijack control of a machine, or retrieve a copy of every keystroke. Steve O'Brien, vice-president for information operation assessments at Info-Ops.com, an Annapolis (Md.)-based company that provides intrusion detection services and security solutions, says the number of ways to hack into computers is rising fast. He tracks potential threats both from hacker groups and from the proliferation of programs. Once a rare find, he now discovers at least three new nasty software programs or vulnerabilities every day. And those tools aren't just for the intellectually curious. "Anyone can get them off the Internet—just point and click away," says Robert N. Weaver, a Secret Service agent in charge of the New York Area Electronic Crimes Task Force.

UNLOCKED DOORS. It's an issue that has crimefighters up in arms. At a hastily called press conference in Washington, D.C., on Feb. 9, Attorney General Janet Reno pledged to battle cyber crime. "We are committed to tracking down those responsible and bringing them to justice" and ensuring "that the Internet remains a secure place to do business," she said. But Ron Dick, chief of the Computer Investigations & Operations Section of the National Infrastructure Protection Center, pointed out that Internet security can't be assured by the government alone. Companies need to vigilantly monitor their computers to ensure that hackers don't surreptitiously install programs from which to launch attacks. "For the Internet to be a safe place, it is incumbent on everyone to remove these

STORMING THE FORTRESS

THE WEAPONS

DENIAL OF SERVICE This is becoming a common networking prank. By hammering a Web site's equipment with too many requests for information, an attacker can effectively clog the system, slowing performance or even crashing the site. This method of overloading computers is sometimes used to cover up an attack.

SCANS Widespread probes of the Internet to determine types of computers, services, and connections. That way the bad guys can take advantage of weaknesses in a particular make of computer or software program.

SNIFFER Programs that covertly search individual packets of data as they pass through the Internet, capturing passwords or the entire contents.

SPOOFING Faking an e-mail address or Web page to trick users into passing along critical information like passwords or credit-card numbers.

TROJAN HORSE A program that, unknown to the user, contains instructions that exploit a known vulnerability in some software.

BACK DOORS In case the original entry point has been detected, having a few hidden ways back makes re-entry easy—and difficult to detect.

MALICIOUS APPLETS Tiny programs, sometimes written in the popular Java computer language, that misuse your computer's resources, modify files on the hard disk, send fake e-mail, or steal passwords.

WAR DIALING Programs that automatically dial thousands of telephone numbers in search of a way in through a modem connection.

LOGIC BOMBS An instruction in a computer program that triggers a malicious act.

BUFFER OVERFLOW A technique for crashing or gaining control of a computer by sending too much data to the buffer in a computer's memory.

PASSWORD CRACKERS Software that can guess passwords.

SOCIAL ENGINEERING A tactic used to gain access to computer systems by talking unsuspecting company employees out of valuable information such as passwords.

DUMPSTER DIVING Sifting through a company's garbage to find information to help break into their computers. Sometimes the information is used to make a stab at social engineering more credible.

THE PLAYERS

WHITE-HAT HACKERS They're the good guys who get turned on the intellectual challenge of tearing apart computer systems to improve computer security.

BLACK-HAT HACKERS Joyriders on the Net. They get a kick out of crashing systems, stealing passwords, and generally wreaking as much havoc as possible.

CRACKERS Hackers for hire who break into computer systems to steal valuable information for their own financial gain.

SCRIPT BUNNIES Wannabe hackers with little technical savvy who download programs—scripts—that automate the job of breaking into computers.

INSIDERS Employees, disgruntled or otherwise, working solo or in concert with outsiders to compromise corporate systems.

tools," he says. Using them, "a 15-year-old could launch an attack."

Make that an 8-year-old, once the Internet is always on via fat broadband connections. There are currently 1.35 million homes in America with fast cable modems, according to market researcher International Data Corp. By 2003, the number will grow to 9 million, and there will be an equal or larger number of digital subscriber line (DSL) connections.

That gives hackers a broad base from which to stage an attack. When a PC is connected to a conventional phone modem, it receives a new Internet address each time the user dials onto the Net. That presents a kind of barrier to hackers hoping to break in and hijack the PC for the kind of assault that crippled eBay, Yahoo, and others. In contrast, cable and DSL modems are a welcome mat to hackers. Because these modems are always connected to the Net, they usually have fixed addresses, which can be read from e-mail messages and newsgroup postings. Home security systems known as personal firewalls are widely available for cable and DSL subscribers. But until they reach nearly 100% penetration, they won't prevent intrusions.

In the coming age of information appliances, the situation could get worse. According to many analysts, the U.S. will soon be awash in Web-browsing televisions, networked game consoles, and smart refrigerators and Web phones that download software from the Net. "These devices all have powerful processors, which could be used in an attack, and they're all connected to the Net," Schneier says.

True, broadband customers can switch off their Net connections. But as cool applications come onstream, nobody will want to do that. "There will be streaming music and video, 24-hour news, and all kinds of broadband Web collaboration," says John Corcoran, an Internet analyst with CIBC World Markets. "To take advantage of that, the door will be open 24 hours a day."

Corporations are no better off. There, security is becoming an expensive necessity. "At least 80% of a corporation's intellectual property is in digital form," says Boni. Last year, Corporate America spent $4.4 billion on sales of Internet security software, including firewalls, intrusion-detection programs, digital certificates, and authentication and authorization software, according to International Data. By 2003, those expenditures could hit $8.3 billion.

Companies are often slow to report crimes and reluctant to reclaim goods

And still computer crime keeps spreading. When the FBI and the Computer Security Institute did their third annual survey of 520 companies and institutions, more than 60% reported unauthorized use of computer systems over the past 12 months, up from 50% in 1997. And 57% of all break-ins involved the Internet, up from 45% two years ago.

As big as those numbers sound, no one really knows how pervasive cyber crime is. Almost all attacks go undetected—as many as 60%, according to security experts. What's more, of the attacks that are exposed, maybe 15% are reported to law enforcement agencies. Companies don't want the press. When Russian organized crime used hackers to break into Citibank to steal $10 million—all but $400,000 was recovered—competitors used the news in marketing campaigns against the bank.

That makes the job even tougher for law enforcement. Most companies that have been electronically attacked won't talk to the press. A big concern is loss of public trust and image—not to mention the fear of encouraging copycat hackers. Following the attacks on Feb. 8 and Feb. 9, there was a telling public silence from normally garrulous Internet executives from E*Trade to priceline. com. Those that had not been attacked yet were reluctant to speak for fear of painting a target on their site, while others wanted no more attention.

And even when the data are recovered, companies are sometimes reluctant to claim their property. Secret Service agent Bob Weaver waves a CD-ROM confiscated in a recent investigation. The disk contains intellectual property—software belonging to a large Japanese company. Weaver says he called the company, but got no response.

Thieves and hackers don't even need a computer. In many cases, the physical world is where the bad guys get the information they need for digital break-ins. Dallas FBI agent Mike Morris estimates that in at least a third of the cases he's investigated in his five years tracking computer crime, an individual has been talked out of a critical computer password. In hackerland, that's called "social engineering." Or, the attackers simply go through the garbage—dumpster diving—for important pieces of information that can help crack the computers or convince someone at the company to giving them more access.

"PAGEJACKING." One problem for law enforcement is that hackers seem to be everywhere. In some cases, they're even working for so-called computer security firms. One official recalls sitting in on the selection process for the firm that would do the Web site security software for the White House. As the company's employees set up to make their pitch, one person walked into the room and abruptly walked out. It turns out one of the people in the audience was with law enforcement, and had busted that person for hacking.

It's not just on U.S. shores that law enforcement has to battle cyber criminals. Attacks from overseas, particularly eastern European countries, are on the rise. Indeed, the problem was so bad for America Online Inc., that it cut its connection to Russia in 1996. Nabbing bad guys overseas is a particularly thorny issue. Take Aye.Net, a small Jeffersonville (Ind.)-based Internet service provider. In 1998 intruders broke into the ISP and knocked them off the Net for four days. Steve Hardin, director of systems engineering for the ISP, discovered the hackers and found messages in Russian. He reported it to the FBI, but no one has been able to track down the hackers.

As if worrying about hackers weren't enough, online fraud is also on the rise. The Federal Trade Commission, which responds to consumer complaints about bogus get-rich schemes or auction goods never delivered, says it filed 61 suits last year. How many did it have back in 1994, when the Net was in its infancy? One. So far, the actions have resulted in the collection of more than $20 million in payments to consumers and the end of schemes with annual estimated sales of over $250 million.

The FTC doesn't want to stop there. On Feb. 9, commissioners testified before a Senate panel, seeking an increase in the commission's budget, in part to fund new Internet-related policies and fight cyberfraud. The money is needed to go after ever more creative schemes. In September, for example, the FTC filed a case against individuals in Portugal and Australia who engaged in "pagejacking" and "mousetrapping" when they captured unauthorized copies of U.S.-based Web sites (including those of PaineWebber Inc. and *The Harvard Law Review*) and produced lookalike versions that were indexed by major search engines. The defendants diverted unsuspecting consumers to a sequence of porno sites that they couldn't exit. The FTC obtained a court order stopping the scheme and suspending the defendants' Web-site registrations.

All of this is not to suggest it's hopeless. Experts say the first step for companies is to secure their systems by searching for hacker programs that might be used in such attacks. They also suggest formal security policies that can be distributed to employees letting them know how often to change passwords or what to do in case of an attack. An added help: Constantly updating software with the latest versions and security patches. Down the road, techniques that can filter and trace malicious software sent over the Web may make it harder to knock businesses off the Net. Says Novell Inc. CEO Eric Schmidt:

"Security is a race between the lock makers and the lock pickers." Regulators say that cybercrime thrives because people accord the Internet far more credibility than it deserves. "You can get a lot of good information from the Internet—95% of what you do there is bona fide," says G. Philip Rutledge, deputy chief counsel of the Pennsylvania Securities Commission. "Unfortunately, that creates openings for fraud."

And other forms of mayhem. That's evident from the attacks that took down some of the biggest companies on the Net. If blackouts and other types of cyber crime are to be avoided, then Net security must be the next growth business.

By Ira Sager in New York, with Steve Hamm and Neil Gross in New York, John Carey in Washington, D.C., and Robert D. Hof in San Mateo, Calif.

Are You Teaching Your Employees to Steal?

By Gary D. Zuene, CPA

My Employees Wouldn't Embezzle: Yeah, Right

Have you taught your employees to embezzle? Yes ❑ No ❑
"Yes" is the right answer.

Here's a typical situation: You have an employee working out of town for several weeks. One evening, she has dinner and returns to the hotel room. Flipping through the TV channels, she watches a movie. What's on the hotel bill when she checks out the next day? $5. For what? A pay-per-view movie. The employee submits her expense report for the week. The hotel bill is $500. What does your accounts payable clerk do? She crosses off the $5 movie charge and reimburses the employee $495 for the hotel bill. Why? Because movies are a personal expense and against company policy.

Fraud and abuse cost the U.S. economy $400 billion a year. That translates into 6% of revenue or $9 per day, per employee.

What does the traveling employee do on the following week's expense report? Records a fake charge—for how much? Not $5. Maybe $15, $20, or more (revenge—the employee is mad) for a taxi, meal, or any expense under the maximum that doesn't require a receipt. What's the employee thinking? "I'm out here working my butt off—10 or 12 hours a day. I'm earning this company three times my salary of $65,000. I'm missing my kids' soccer games and parent-teacher meetings. And some $12-an-hour A/P clerk dings me for five bucks? She's home sleeping in her own bed, giving her kids hugs and good-night kisses."

What did you do in that two-week period? You taught the employee that in order to be treated fairly, she has to cheat—to embezzle. The following week's expense report complied with the company policy, but the policy "drives" employees to behave in a manner you don't want. Not only does the employee resent the way she was treated, but her productivity drops while she's plotting how to get repaid. Result: Your loss is much greater than $5. But since lost productivity isn't explicitly measurable, you don't even know it.

WHAT ARE EXPENSE REPORTS?

How would you like to get rid of an entire process on which you spend a ton of time but doesn't earn the company a dime and also causes other employees to call you "bean counters"?

Question: What are expense reports?

Answer: A complete waste of time.

Let me give you a personal example. I have a speakers bureau for white-collar criminals called "The Pros & The Cons." My ex-con speakers have committed frauds of up to $350 million. We're on the road a lot, so travel expenses are significant. To make their lives easier, I charge their plane fare and hotel room and tax to my American Express card (so I get the frequent flyer miles). The first year I reimbursed their miscellaneous travel expenses. They had to prepare a report. We had to foot, cross-foot, look at receipts, and finally write a check two or three weeks later. It was very time consuming and didn't make me any money. I realized reviewing expense reports was a complete waste of my time, and I wanted out of the "control business."

I analyzed this process and found that miscellaneous travel expenses (meals, tips, taxis, and so on) ran about $75 to $80 per day. So I told all my speakers that we would give them $100 per day for miscellaneous travel expenses. When I reimbursed their expenses, they would take a taxi from the airport to the hotel for $30 and have dinner at the hotel for $45. Now that they get $100 per day for these expenses, they take a $12 shuttle to the hotel. And where do you think they have dinner? At McDonalds. And here's the best part. *I don't care* how they get from the airport to the hotel or where or what they have for dinner. And my ex-cons love it. I can pay them as soon as they are done. No more filling out an expense report, then waiting two or three weeks for the check. (Ex-cons have significant cash-flow issues.)

The $100 per day is included in the Form 1099-MISC each year. It's up to the speakers to save their receipts for tax purposes. There's no magic about $100 per day. Nor does the daily reimbursement have to be the same for the entire country. It can vary by how expensive the area/city is. Notice what has happened: My speakers get paid faster, with significantly less work on both our parts. Since they eat and travel cheaper, they make more without increasing my cost. It's a win-win structure. But when employees get both a W-2 and 1099—something independent contractors don't have to worry about—the situation becomes more complex. Consult a tax expert.

FRAUD AND ABUSE ARE COSTLY

Fraud and abuse cost the U.S. economy $400 billion a year. That translates into 6% of revenue or $9 per day, per employee.[1] And relatively speaking, small companies are at a higher risk of fraud than large companies. Why? Because small companies don't have as sophisticated systems of internal controls as large companies.

And the situation is getting worse. A recent Association of Certified Fraud Examiners survey of executives found that:

- 67% said fraud is worse today than five years ago;
- 70% said fraud detection is getting better (that's encouraging);
- 75% said fraud detection resources aren't adequate; and
- Asset thefts made up 82% of the cases.

Example: The headline screams, "'Trusted' worker stole $1 million."[2] Beverly Kunkel not only was a trusted secretary who handled bookkeeping for Kendrick Mollenauer Painting, she was the wife of a lifelong friend of the company president.

"When Ford married Beverly, his second wife, we took her in like one of the family." She worked at the painting company 13 years and embezzled for 11. Kunkel was sentenced to eight to 15 years. Hired in 1985, she told the owners she had been unfairly fired from a prior job when $50,000 was missing. She admitted that theft also. When Kunkel told the owners customers were slow pays, they withdrew savings to pay bills. They also noted that Kunkel had embezzled more money in a year than they both had earned, *combined*. The company has received about $135,000 in restitution.

MY EXECUTIVES WOULDN'T STEAL

And don't think fraud and abuse are limited to lower-level employees. At a recent seminar, I asked the 200+ CFOs in attendance, "How many of you have executives that steal?" Three or four brave souls raised their hands. Then I asked, "How many of you do the company's tax return?" Everyone held a hand up. Last question: "Now, again, how many of you have executives that steal?" Everyone roared and raised their hands.

When the executive pays for the mostly personal trip to Las Vegas with company funds, it's called "tax fraud." When the bookkeeper, who hasn't had a raise in three years, writes the $5,000 check to the executive for the trip, it gives everyone in the company permission to steal. You can't expect any better ethical behavior from employees than executives exhibit.

MORAL MAJORITY:

Most people disapprove of any tax cheating. How much cheating, if any, is acceptable on your tax return? **None,** according to **87%** of the 1,000 adults polled by Roper Starch in late May. But 8% said "a little here and there," and 3% said "as much as possible." Participants weren't told the IRS had commissioned the survey because the agency wanted candid responses.[3]

NOW YOU'RE BEING SUED

The risk of this culture isn't just to the company. It can put you at risk personally. Let's assume you prepare and/or sign the company's tax return. And the return has those trips to Las Vegas for the past five years. Now the company gets into financial difficulty. It can't pay the bank loan, or the stock price declines 30%. In addition to suing the company, the plaintiffs' attorneys sue you personally. *You*. The following exchange takes place while you're on the stand trying to defend yourself:

ATTORNEY: Mr. Wilson. You were the company's chief financial officer. Is that right?

YOU: Yes.

ATTORNEY: And you have the highest standards of integrity?

YOU: That's right. (What else are you going to say?)

ATTORNEY: But yet, it's okay with you if the company's executives commit fraud and embezzle, isn't it?

YOU: No. Of course not.

ATTORNEY: Isn't this your signature on the company tax return?

YOU: Yes.

ATTORNEY: Then how do you explain this $5,000 for the CEO's personal trip to Las Vegas the past five years?

YOU: But it's only a small amount. We're a $250 million company.

ATTORNEY: So your company saved $2,500 each year in taxes. Now Mr. Wilson, who had to make up that shortfall? (Answer: the members of the jury.)

YOU: (Dumbstruck at this point and fidgeting for an answer. [No answer will get you out of trouble with the jury.])

ATTORNEY: Clearly, it's okay with you if the CEO steals a little bit. So tell me, Mr. Wilson, how much does the theft have to be before it's *not* okay with you?

What do you say at this point? Nothing. You're done. You're now protesting that the attorney backed you into a corner. No. You backed yourself into a corner by allowing deductions that are illegal. The fact that it's only $5,000 does *not* make it legal. Plaintiffs' attorneys are very good at asking questions that have no right answer, like, "Have you stopped kicking the dog yet?" Understand the risks you're taking. It's your decision.

WHEN DO PEOPLE EMBEZZLE OR ABUSE THE COMPANY?

Generally, three things have to be present before someone commits fraud or embezzles: need, opportunity, and rationalization. This is known as the "triangle of fraud." (See Figure 1.)

Figure 1: Triangle of Fraud

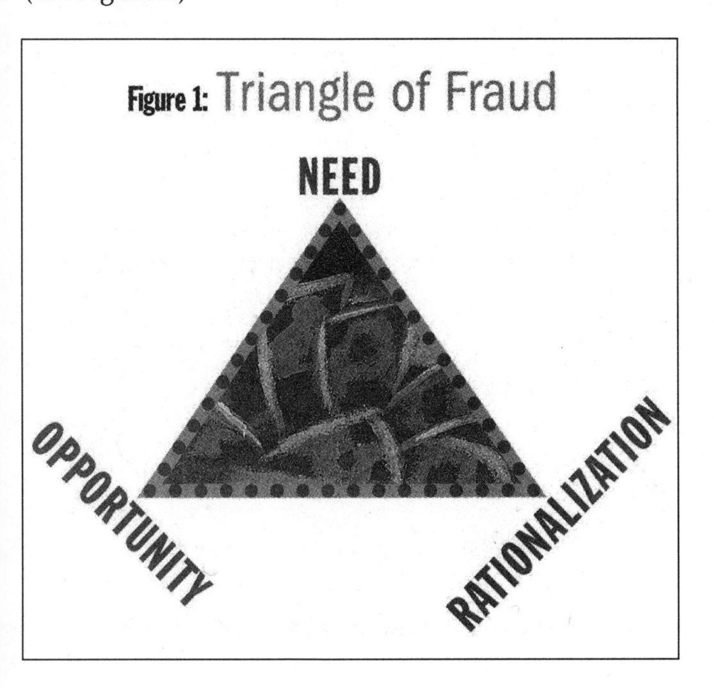

- **Need** takes two forms—direct and indirect. Direct need is stealing to fund cash needs and is often driven by an addiction—drugs, alcohol, gambling, or an extramarital affair. So the next time someone brags about an affair, warning flags should go up. Indirect need, on the other hand, is usually keeping the company afloat. This results in cooking the books to make sure the loan is obtained or renewed to buy time to fix the problem.
- **Opportunity** is defined as the perception that there's a low probability of being detected. In accounting we call this "poor internal controls."
- **Rationalization** is the employees' mental process of making the action fit within their personal code of conduct. In other words, the employees must be able to "talk themselves into the action"—"the ends justify the means."

RATIONALIZATION OFTEN RESULTS IN "SITUATIONAL FRAUD"

Employees' propensity to steal or embezzle can be described as a normal distribution. (Remember that from college?) About 5% to 10% of employees would *never*—ever—do anything wrong. About 5% to 10% of employees are always scheming. (I hope you don't have many such folks working for you.) The real problem is that 80% to 90% of employees who'll commit "situational fraud." Remember: Who are the only employees who can steal from you? Employees you trust. This isn't meant to imply you shouldn't trust your employees. It simply means you don't go soft on internal controls because you trust employees.

Here are some warning signs and risks to watch for:

- Employees who are being downsized;
- Employees who are bored and may steal for excitement;
- Employees who make an honest mistake, discover a hole in internal controls, benefit from it, and are going to "pay it back";
- Thrill seekers who like bending the rules;
- Employees who are under personal stress: money, divorce, illness (especially spouse or children);
- Employees whose financial problems suddenly disappear;
- Employees with addictions: drugs, alcohol, extramarital affairs, gambling;
- Employees who always have to be number 1 and/or can't stand *not* being the center of attention.

Who are the only employees who can steal from you? Employees you trust.

CREATE A "SELF-CORRECTING" SYSTEM

Modern CFOs know a *lot* about human behavior. Behavior *never* remains static. World-class CFOs understand that any time they change a reward, the compensation system, or the control system, people will always change their behavior to maximize the benefit to themselves.

Example: Many years ago traffic engineers set out to reduce the accident rates at intersections. They set up cameras and videotaped the traffic patterns. At that time, the green light would turn red and the red light would turn green at the same time. But that one last car tried to get through while cars with the green light had permission to go. So the engineers changed the sequence to add two or three seconds' delay (both lights are now red), giving that one last car time to go through the intersection. The accident rate declined significantly for two or three months. Then what happened? Drivers coming to an intersection with a yellow light or just-changed-to-red light realized they had several extra seconds to make it through the intersection. Instead of one car going through on the red, now it's three or four. The drivers adjusted their behavior to benefit themselves.

Change the compensation system, and employees will change their behavior. Count on it. You may solve one problem but create an even worse problem. Hockey players don't skate to where the puck is, they skate to where the puck is *going to be*. To become an indispensable member of the management team, you must anticipate how employees (and executives) will react to any changes.

MINIMIZE FRAUD

Sometimes you can minimize risks with a little creativity. For example, an owner of a small company where there's little segregation of duties can have the bank statement sent to his or her home, not to the company. To show he/she's paying attention to the statements, the owner reviews them and then asks about several items in each statement. This procedure creates the perception that a theft will probably be detected, thus reducing the "opportunity" and increasing the risk of getting caught. Minimizing the opportunity for theft and embezzlement is probably the most powerful deterrent—they might "get caught." (This would have prevented/detected Beverly Kunkel's $1 million embezzlement.)

If you're an outsider (accountant, auditor, whatever), be aware that you have to "sell" this idea from the bottom up. Few small business owners will make this change. It sends the message to the long-time employee that he or she isn't trusted anymore. Get the employee (probably a bookkeeper or controller) to ask for the change. Say, "You know, you have complete control of everything. You pay the bills, you make the bank deposits, and you reconcile the accounts. If any money is missing, who do you think Sally (the owner) will suspect? *For your own protection*, you should get Sally to look at the bank statements and initial the envelope every month. I know she's busy, but it won't take her more than five or 10 minutes."

DRIVE BEHAVIOR

Theft and embezzlement are a serious drain on company resources. Your job as CFO is to protect the company's assets. Simply assuring compliance with company policy isn't enough. World-class CFOs create self-policing or self-correcting systems. You must understand how your internal controls, compensation, and measurement systems drive behavior and structure them so people will do what you want without intervention. The job of the 21st Century CFO is to "drive" the desired behavior.

Less work. Happier employees. More profits. Anyone interested?

Notes

1. *Report to the Nation on Fraud and Abuse*, Association of Certified Fraud Examiners, 1995.
2. *The Columbus* (Ohio) *Dispatch*, April 11, 2000, p. A1.
3. *The Wall Street Journal*, September 8, 1999, p. A1.

Gary Zeune, CPA, is CEO of "The Pros & The Cons," the only speakers bureau in the U.S. for white-collar criminals. His books include The CEO's Complete Guide to Committing Frauds, Outside the Box Performance: How to Beat Your Competitors' Brains Out, *and over 35 articles on fraud and performance measures in national publications. Gary teaches fraud classes for the FBI, the U.S. Attorney, over 30 state and national CPA societies, and numerous banks and accounting firms. You can reach him at gzfraud@bigfoot.com or (614) 885-0262, or visit www.bigfoot. com/~gzfraud.*

GUERRILLA WARFARE

Disgruntled workers use sabotage to send their bosses a message.

By I. PERRIN WESTON
SPECIAL TO THE TIMES

Although employers are loath to admit it, workplace sabotage is a common and costly thorn in the side of American business.

Sabotage can manifest itself subtly or disguise itself as ineptitude, as in the case of an auto assembly line worker who deliberately leaves out a bolt, resulting in a work stoppage down the line.

Ray O'Hara, a workplace violence expert with Pinkerton Consulting & Investigations, said a necessary element of sabotage is intent. "But how do you prove intent unless it's blatant to the eye? If someone leaves a hose on all night long so that a warehouse floor is flooded, and $10,000 in products is damaged, how do you determine it was intentional unless some guy says, 'Yeah, I left that hose on because I hate the place.'"

Tinkering and tomfoolery can give way to outright warfare. When Verizon Communications employees went on strike in New York last year, police logged more than 20 suspected acts of sabotage. Two striking workers were critically burned when one of them cut into a power line he mistook for a phone line.

While hard numbers on the rate of sabotage don't exist, new studies on the sabotaging of company computer networks are revealing. A 1999 report by the San Francisco-based Computer Security Institute said 61 organizations reported a total of $21 million in losses from known incidents of internal data and network sabotage in 1998. The combined total for the previous four years of the study was $10 million.

Robert Giacalone's introduction to workplace sabotage began over drinks at a pub with a colleague one day in the early 1980s.

"He was telling me stories he'd heard from clients," said Giacalone, who is the Surtman distinguished professor of business ethics at the University of North Carolina. "I was just shocked. Some of it was very funny and some of it was very scary. All of it I saw as acts of aggression."

Giacalone, a trained psychologist and an expert on organizational behavior, has become a scholar of workplace sabotage, which he broadly defines as "an attempt, usually by employees, to damage the company."

His work has included consulting with corporations beset by sabotage and with government agencies, including the U.S. Department of Defense, the U.S. Army, the Federal Reserve Bank of Richmond and the Federal Bureau of Investigation. His research has led him to conclude that companies with chronic problems almost always invite trouble by either failing to notice or blatantly ignoring discontent among employees.

"One manufacturer I worked with had such a problem that it was like being under attack by a group of terrorists," Giacalone said. "But they could never catch the people responsible because nobody would talk. The other employees all hated the company and thought it was great."

The acts of sabotage included recalibrating machines to improperly cut metal, hunting rats with air-powered metal arrows fashioned from company materials, injecting industrial glue into the locks of executive doors and exploding a 50-gallon drum of toxic material, which forced an evacuation of the facility.

"That was so the group involved could get the first day of deer-hunting season off," said Giacalone, who interviewed factory workers on condition of anonymity. From there, the attacks began targeting a single manager.

"The guy's office chair was booby-trapped so that when he sat down it jettisoned him into the air," Giacalone said. "Amazingly, he only broke an arm."

Next, the manager's phone receiver was painted with a powerful blue dye that stained his face when he answered a call. The dye had to be removed with an acid chemical peel. Finally, the manager was walking on a lower-level tier one day when a 30-foot steel beam was dropped from above, missing him by a yard.

"That's attempted murder," Giacalone said. "The question is, how do you go from simply annoying and even costly acts of sabotage to that. The answer is that the manager in question was a vicious, mean-spirited person who was cruel and had no respect for people."

The company had received many complaints about the manager but refused to do anything about his behavior, Giacalone said. As the employees grew increasingly frustrated, acts of low-level sabotage increased.

When these signals were ignored, the sabotage grew more violent. "A message was being sent," Giacalone said. "A very strong message."

The word "sabotage," from the Flemish, literally means to jam machinery by throwing in a wooden shoe. It was a form of protest against working conditions, a way to make employers stop and listen.

When it comes to technology-dependent industries, the wooden shoe has been supplanted by electronic wrenches and the machines being jammed and destroyed are vast corporate networks.

Some high-profile sabotage cases in recent years illustrate how much damage one disgruntled employee can do.

In May, a federal jury convicted a former Omega Engineering Corp. network manager of sabotaging the network he helped create by planting a software time bomb, which he detonated after being fired. The bomb paralyzed Omega, a manufacturer of high-tech measurement and instrumentation devices used by the U.S. Navy and NASA. The company's damages exceeded $10 million.

In 1997 George Parente, a former Forbes Inc. computer technician, pleaded guilty to violating the Computer Fraud and Abuse Act for deliberately causing five of the publishing company's eight network servers to crash after his termination from a temporary position. All of the information on the affected servers was erased and no data could be restored. The sabotage forced Forbes to shut down its New York operations for two days and resulted in more than $100,000 in losses.

Internal saboteurs can do tremendous damage to an organization's computer systems and business operations, said Nancy Flynn, executive director of the ePolicy Institute and author of "The ePolicy Handbook" (Amacom, 2000).

"Lockheed Martin's system crashed for six hours one day after an employee sent 60,000 co-workers a personal e-mail with a request for an electronic receipt," Flynn said. "It was a personal message related to a national prayer day. As a result of this one e-mail, the company lost hundreds of thousands of dollars. A Microsoft rescue squad had to be flown in to repair the damage. The employee responsible was fired for sabotage."

Flynn said a company's best defense is written e-mail and Internet policies that clearly state what employees are allowed to do with the company system. She also recommends using filtering software, ongoing employee education and diligent monitoring.

"This protects the employer legally and lets employees know what violations they can expect to be terminated for," she said. "It gives notice that just because a computer is sitting on your desk, that doesn't make it your personal property."

Attorney Arthur Silbergeld, a Los Angeles-based partner with the firm Proskauer Rose and chairman of the Labor and Employment Law Section of the Los Angeles County Bar Assn., said maintaining employee hotlines or having ethical compliance officers who operate independently from the organization are also deterrents.

"Employees need someplace to take their concerns and problems," Silbergeld said. "While taking these steps won't eliminate sabotage, it will minimize it."

Computer systems aren't the only targets of sabotage. Products are also fair game. Sometimes the goal is simply to humiliate a corporation.

In 1999, a red-faced Walt Disney Co. was compelled to recall 3.4 million video releases of its classic animated children's film "The Rescuers" when a photograph of a nude female torso was discovered imbedded in two frames.

When reporters asked a Disney spokeswoman if the company knew who had tampered with the film, she would only say that it was "an internal matter."

RTMark, an Internet-based company just named one of Yahoo Internet Life's 100 Top Sites for 2000, is the merry prankster of corporate sabotage.

Staffed by volunteers, RTMark is funded by mostly anonymous investors who put money in "mutual funds," which are then used to finance various acts of sabotage against corporations to punish them for their greed.

The group's most celebrated case was the 1993 Barbie Liberation Organization caper, in which RTMark operatives switched the voice boxes on 300 Barbie and G.I Joe dolls and then restocked them on toy shelves across America.

"We are mainly interested in what we call 'tactical embarrassment,'" said New Yorker Duane Dibbley, 32, a bond ratings software programmer and RTMark volunteer. "Our goal is to harm the corporate person, which is not a living person. We want to tarnish their image."

While many cases involve an employee or former employee with a personal gripe, sabotage can spread like winter flu through an organization where the work force in general feels at odds with the boss or corporation.

"It is a normal, everyday event in any workplace where employees are discontented and don't feel like they have recourse to address problems," said Stanley Aronowitz, professor of sociology at the University of New York and director for the Center for the Study of Culture, Technology and Work. "Sabotage is a cry for voice. The problem is employers don't want to give employees a voice because it means giving up power, and the American managerial process is to give up anything but power. In this country, management has a way of thinking that if the pay is good, you should go home and shut up."

Rich Hagberg, chief executive of the Hagberg Consulting Group, a Silicon Valley-based firm that researches and consults on corporate culture, said his data confirm that employee sabotage finds fertile ground in companies "where management behaves in a way that cuts or disrupts its bond with employees."

"In the '80s and '90s, all the emphasis was placed on increasing shareholder values while employees were treated like expendable commodities," Hagberg said. "That practice has greatly damaged the relationship between employers and employees. Focusing exclusively on customers and shareholders while sacrificing workers invites sabotage, which is really an indirect expression of frustration."

Hagberg's data also suggest that employee alienation is increasing. "We are seeing more antisocial behavior and acting out," he said. "At the same time, the war for talent is getting worse. What that tells me is employers better figure out how to treat their people better if they want to attract the best talent and keep it."

The bond between employers and employees is further strained by corporations that insist on a materialist model of doing business in a postmaterialist world, Giacalone said.

"The old model said you are what you earn," Giacalone said. "But what people are saying is, 'I want a life.' All this stuff you see about downshifters giving up $200,000 jobs to take $50,000 is an indication of what's going on."

Giacalone recalls one company that was having a tough time retaining its tech people in a tight labor market. Its solution was to exceed competitive wages by 10%.

"The HR person figured this would solve the problem, but people left anyway," Giacalone said. "The scary part was they left for lower paying jobs. The HR woman said it didn't make any sense, but it does. Money is no longer a primary motivation factor."

What motivates people to stay is a work environment where they are respected, Giacalone said.

"People don't want to feel like they're working for feudal lords," he said. "They are beginning to disrespect what corporations stand for and what corporations do, largely because they feel that corporations have disrespected them. Sabotage is an outgrowth of this disrespect."

From the *Los Angeles Times*, Summer 2001, pp. 16-18.

Article 13

Legal Intelligence

Harassment Grows More COMPLEX

BY CAROLE O'BLENES

Aside from gender, harassment claims are being asserted based on other protected characteristics, including race, religion, age, disability and national origin.

Sexual harassment complaints filed with the EEOC have more than doubled since 1991, and some recent Supreme Court decisions provide new guidance to employers.

In addition to damage awards, harassment complaints carry many intangible costs, such as adverse publicity and reduced morale. Retaliation claims also are a risk.

Develop a comprehensive policy that addresses all forms of unlawful harassment, outlines procedures for reporting and investigating complaints and prevents retaliation.

Awareness of sexual harassment in the workplace has reached unprecedented levels as President Clinton's sexual encounters—Monica Lewinsky, Paula Jones and others—have made sexual harassment a common topic in the news. For employers, this heightened awareness often results in additional sexual harassment complaints as employees develop higher expectations about what behavior is appropriate and conclude that their workplaces fall short of those expectations.

In 1998, more than 15,000 sexual harassment charges were filed with the U.S. Equal Employment Opportunity Commission (EEOC), up from about 6,900 in 1991. Amounts paid out by employers charged with sexual harassment in EEOC proceedings and actions alone exploded from $7.1 million in 1990 to $49.5 million in 1997.

But unlawful workplace harassment is not limited to sexual harassment of women by men. Men also can be (and are) sexually harassed. And harassment claims are being asserted based on protected characteristics other than gender, such as race, age, religion, disability and national origin. Such recent cases include a black Muslim correction officer who claimed he was subjected to racial and religious harassment by coworkers and supervisors; a disabled employee who asserted she was ridiculed about "the disability being in her mind only"; and an Italian-American who claimed he was subjected to racist comments, slurs and jokes based on his national origin. Lifestyle issues also can lead to harassment claims, as in the case of a gay employee offended by a "born-again Christian" coworker's views on homosexuality.

RISK REDUCTION

Every employee falls into at least one of the protected categories, and many belong to several. Therefore, it's essential to prevent incidents that might lead to harassment claims and respond effectively when they do arise. This will reduce your exposure to liability and maximize workplace productivity.

The litigation costs associated with the rise in harassment complaints are enormous and increasing. As a result of the Civil Rights Act of 1991, jury trials are now available in federal harassment cases, and the remedies available to plaintiffs in such cases have expanded to include not just equitable relief, such as reinstatement and back pay, but also compensatory and punitive damages.

Last year, a federal jury awarded nearly $5.7 million to the family of a former U.S. Postal Service engineer who complained of sexual harassment prior to committing suicide. A male dude ranch wrangler was awarded $300,000 by a federal jury based on his claim that he was sexually harassed by his female supervisor. In California, the average jury verdict in employment cases in 1998 was $2.5 million. Equally important are the intangible damages associated with harassment claims, such as absenteeism, employee turnover, low morale and low productivity.

WHAT IS UNLAWFUL HARASSMENT?

The concept of unlawful harassment grew out of sexual harassment claims, but it has been applied in cases involving other protected characteristics as well. The EEOC's "Guidelines on Discrimination Because of Sex" define sexual harassment as "unwelcome sexual advances, requests for sexual favors, and other verbal or physical conduct of a sexual nature." The EEOC, commentators and courts have identified two types of harassment: "quid pro quo" and "hostile environment."

Employees who are subjected to harassment tend to assume it's because of a protected characteristic.

In two cases last summer, *Faragher v. City of Boca Raton* and *Ellerth v. Burlington Indus.*, the Supreme Court clarified the definition of sexual harassment. The court explained that quid pro quo harassment occurs when a "tangible employment action," such as termination, demotion or a significant change in assignment or benefits, results from a refusal to submit to a supervisor's sexual demands. If there is no tangible employment action, an employee may still be a victim of sexual harassment if he or she is subjected to unwelcome sexual conduct that is sufficiently severe or pervasive to unreasonably interfere with his or her work performance or create an intimidating, hostile or offensive work environment.

Quid pro quo claims are limited to the sexual harassment context. Not so for the hostile work environment standard, which the courts have applied to other types of harassment claims. Regardless of the protected characteristic relied on by the plaintiff, in these cases the courts look to the severity and pervasiveness of the alleged harassment. To prevail on a hostile environment claim, the plaintiff must also show that he or she was subjected to severe and offensive conduct *because* of his or her protected characteristic.

When a company can show that the alleged harasser treated all employees in the same negative manner—sometimes referred to as an "equal opportunity harasser"—the harassment would not be unlawful because it is not related to the plaintiff's membership in a protected class. In *Pavone v. Brown*, for example, the court held that a disabled plaintiff could not prove unlawful harassment because other, nondisabled employees complained of the same mistreat-

BRIEF CASES

THE ADA AND CORRECTIVE DEVICES

Two cases currently before the Supreme Court will resolve a difference of opinion among the courts as to whether an individual can be considered "disabled," and thus protected by the Americans with Disabilities Act (ADA), if his or her medical condition is corrected with medication or assistive devices. The two cases involve employees who were denied jobs because of medical conditions—twin pilots who are nearsighted in *Sutton v. United Airlines*, and a truck mechanic with high blood pressure in *Murphy v. United Parcel Service*. In both cases, the 10th Circuit ruled that the employees were *not* disabled because their conditions were corrected with lenses and medication, respectively.

NEW GUIDANCE ON 'REASONABLE ACCOMMODATIONS'

The EEOC issued new Guidance in February that addresses some tough questions about the reasonable accommodation requirements of the ADA. Among those questions: When must you provide an accommodation? What type is required? Under what circumstances can you claim that a requested accommodation would impose an undue hardship? According to the EEOC, once an employee indicates that her medical condition is affecting some aspect of her work, the employer is obligated to clarify her needs and identify an appropriate accommodation. Reasonable accommodations may include restructurings of some job functions, leaves of absence, modified or part-time work schedules, modified workplace policies and job reassignments.

EEOC CHALLENGES AN ENGLISH-ONLY POLICY

A federal district court recently denied an employer's motion to dismiss a lawsuit filed by the EEOC that challenges the company's brief use of an English-only policy. The employer, Synchro-Start, had established a policy requiring employees to speak only English during work hours, allegedly in response to complaints that multilingual employees were harassing and insulting coworkers in their native tongues. It rescinded the policy within nine months. The EEOC suit claims the policy discriminates on the basis of national origin because it focuses on employees whose primary language is not English. EEOC Guidelines express a presumption that English-only rules create a discriminatory environment based on national origin.

ment by the plaintiff's supervisor. But companies need to be aware that employees who are subjected to verbal abuse and other harassment tend to assume that it is because of a protected characteristic. Thus, such behavior (particularly by supervisors) presents risks of claims, litigation costs and workplace disruption even if the employer may ultimately prevail on an "equal opportunity abuser" theory.

Proof that harassment was because of a protected characteristic was the pivotal issue in a case decided by the Supreme Court last year. In *Oncale v. Sundowner Offshore Services, Inc.*, the plaintiff, a male employee alleged, among other things, that he was grabbed by his male supervisor and a male coworker who physically abused him while threatening rape. The Supreme Court concluded that a heterosexual can state a viable claim of sexual harassment against another heterosexual of the same gender (i.e., same-sex harassment), but remanded the case to the lower court to determine whether Oncale was in fact harassed *because of his sex*.

EMPLOYER LIABILITY

The Supreme Court's recent decisions in *Ellerth* and *Faragher* also clarified the circumstances under which an employer can be held liable for harassment by a supervisor. When an immediate (or successively higher) supervisor's harassment culminates in a tangible employment action, such as discharge, demotion or undesirable reassignment, the employer will be liable for the supervisor's actions.

When the harassment does not result in a tangible employment action, the employer may raise an "affirmative defense" to liability or damages. This defense is made up of two parts: First, that the employer exercised reasonable care to prevent and correct promptly any harassing behavior. Second, that the plaintiff employee unreasonably failed to take advantage of any preventive or corrective opportunities provided by the employer or to avoid harm otherwise.

The reasonableness of an employer's response also determines liability in hostile environment cases involving harassment by a coworker, nonsupervisory employee or nonemployee (such as a vendor, customer, consultant or client). For example, a local Pizza Hut franchise was held liable for $200,000 in compensatory damages plus nearly $40,000 in attorney's fees and costs because it failed to prevent two of its customers from sexually harassing a waitress. In *Lockard v. Pizza Hut, Inc.*, the waitress claimed that her manager forced her to wait on two customers who pulled her hair and sexually assaulted her. The customers had engaged in other abusive conduct in prior visits and the plaintiff had complained to her manager. A federal appeals court upheld the verdict, observing that the manager had been given notice of the harassing conduct and had unreasonably failed to remedy or prevent the harassment.

• POINTS OF POLICY

Here are the hallmarks of an effective nondiscrimination and anti-harassment policy:

- Introductory statement that expresses a commitment to a work environment that is free of discrimination and harassment.
- Equal employment opportunity statement.
- Definitions of harassment, with examples of behaviors that may constitute harassment.
- Coverage extending to all applicants, employees and third parties, such as outside vendors, consultants or customers, and to all conduct in a work-related setting—including social occasions such as client lunches and holiday parties.
- Prohibition of retaliation, enforced through disciplinary action.
- Complaint procedure designating several different "avenues of complaint" and strongly urging the reporting of all incidents.
- Assurance of a prompt investigation of complaints.
- Confidentiality maintained to the extent consistent with adequate investigation and appropriate corrective action.
- Corrective action upon a finding of misconduct, with specific examples of possible actions.

—*C.O.*

In light of the Supreme Court's recent decisions, it is critical for employers to take affirmative steps to prevent and remedy harassment. At a minimum, they should:

- Develop a written nondiscrimination and anti-harassment policy (see box).
- Ensure that the policy provides employees with effective avenues to bring complaints forward (not just through their supervisor, who may in fact be the harasser).
- Include the policy in a prominent place in an employee handbook (if there is one).
- Widely disseminate the policy (independent of the handbook) throughout the workplace on a periodic basis to make sure all employees know of its existence and understand the complaint procedure.
- Train appropriate segments of the workforce, such as senior management, managers/supervisors and complaint-receivers, to understand and apply the policy.
- Promptly respond to complaints brought under the policy by thoroughly investigating them to determine if policy violations have occurred.
- Take prompt, effective remedial action to respond to violations.

PREVENTING RETALIATION

In addition to distributing an anti-harassment policy, companies need to develop policies and procedures to prevent retaliation against individuals who file complaints of harassment or discrimination or who participate in their investigation. Charges of retaliation are on the rise, with more than 19,000 claims filed with the EEOC in 1998 alone.

Retaliation is an independent basis for employer liability under the federal discrimination laws. All too often, companies are finding that even after a discrimination or harassment claim has been dismissed for lack of evidence, the courts are ordering them to proceed to trial on claims of unlawful retaliation. This is because adverse action taken against an employee who opposes unlawful practices (by filing or threatening to file a complaint) can be considered unlawful retaliation.

For example, a federal appellate court recently reinstated a retaliation claim filed against Wal-Mart, while affirming the dismissal of the plaintiff's claims of racial harassment and discrimination. The plaintiff had alleged that within the two months after she filed a discrimination complaint with the EEOC, she was listed as a "no-show" on a scheduled day off, twice reprimanded by her manager and then given a one-day suspension. In addition, she claimed, her manager began soliciting negative statements about her from coworkers. The court held that this conduct was sufficient to support a claim of retaliation, especially because the plaintiff had not received any reprimands in the 11 months before she filed her EEOC charge.

To minimize the risk of liability for such claims, employers need to incorporate a strong prohibition against retaliation in their anti-harassment policies. They also should advise employees at all levels that retaliation will not be tolerated and will result in disciplinary action up to and including termination. Then make sure the policies are fully enforced.

After filing a charge of harassment or discrimination, employees often perceive any adverse actions as related to their complaint. Therefore, a human resources officer or other appropriate manager should carefully monitor a complainant's work environment and work with his or her supervisor to avoid even the appearance of retaliation. Further, ensure that the complainant is not shunned by his or her coworkers, and counsel managers to make a conscious effort to include complainants in appropriate workplace meetings or events.

If a complainant is a candidate for discipline for performance-related reasons, his or her manager should consult with human resources before any discipline is imposed to verify that it is warranted and consistent with comparable situations. Similarly, decisions involving raises and promotional opportunities in the complainant's department should be discussed with HR to ensure the complainant received appropriate consideration and was treated even-handedly.

Carole O'Blenes, a partner in the New York office of Proskauer Rose LLP, has practiced labor and employment law since 1976. She has represented employers in collective bargaining, arbitration, administrative proceedings and employment litigation. She also provides advice and guidance to clients on a wide range of employment and labor law matters. E-mail: coblenes@proskauer.com. Tracey I. Levy, an associate at Proskauer Rose, also contributed to this article.

Wage Gap Continues to Vex Women

The Disparity Is Growing Despite Gains in Education, Employment

By LISA GIRION
TIMES STAFF WRITER

The economic boom appears to have fattened wallets more than pocketbooks, exacerbating the persistent earnings disparity between men and women, according to two of the most recent government indicators.

Women's weekly earnings were closer to men's in 1993 than they were in 2000. When annual earnings are compared, women had their best year relative to men in 1997. By 1999, the typical woman took home $26,324, almost 28% less than the typical man's $36,476 annual income.

Economists are not sure what to make of the emerging trend, especially when American women, as a group, are better educated, take less time off after childbirth, and have access to and hold a broader array of jobs than ever before.

"It's doubly disconcerting that women are going to school and yet the pay gap is widening," said Heather Boushey, an economist at the Economic Policy Institute. "That's the question: Why is that going on?"

Although they have no way to determine how much of the pay gap can be blamed on discrimination, economists are eyeing recent employment and social shifts that they can measure. Among the likely suspects are the concentration of men in high-paying technology jobs, the recent boom in male-dominated construction employment, and the introduction into the work force of about a million former welfare mothers.

"We definitely need more research to get the true story, but I think a lot of it is the [stagnation] of the minimum wage, and the fact that men's real wages are growing again," said Heidi I. Hartmann, an economist and director of the Institute for Women's Policy Research.

"It's doubly disconcerting that women are going to school and yet the pay gap is widening. That's the question: Why is that going on?"

Heather Boushey
Economist at the Economic Policy Institute

The gender pay gap is narrowest among hourly wage earners, closing to less than 17% in 2000. One reason for that is the minimum wage is shoring up the nation's lowest-paid workers.

Hartmann said that a bill introduced in Congress last week to raise the U.S. minimum wage, as California did in January with the state minimum wage, would help close the gender pay gap. California's minimum wage is higher than the federal.

"Women are two-thirds of minimum-wage workers so if you improve the minimum wage, you disproportionately bring women up," Hartmann said.

Some economists and public policy experts criticize the pay gap as an imprecise indicator that fails to account for gender differences in education, occupation, work experience, job performance and intangibles such as career commitment and productivity.

"That number doesn't give you that," said June E. O'Neill, an economics professor at Baruch College and director of the Congressional Budget Office from 1995 to 1999. The gender gap is a reflection of "whoever happens to be working that year."

Others view the gender pay gap as a valuable trend line, a measure of the impact of public policies, market forces and personal choices on women's relative earnings. It is an important indicator, they say, of the ability of working women to support themselves and, especially with the rise in single-mother and two-income households, their families.

"I would certainly like to think that there are more opportunities now for women than there were a few years ago. Unfortunately, the statistics don't bear that out," said Alyson Reed, executive director of the National Committee on Pay Equity, a coalition of labor and civil rights groups.

"We all have the sense that things are getting better rather than worse, based on the fact that the economy has been booming," Reed said. "My speculation is that the economic boom... did not raise all boats at the same rate."

Adding to the pay gap mystery are the gains made in women's earnings in preceding decades, particularly during the 1980s. Between 1979 and 1989, the ratio

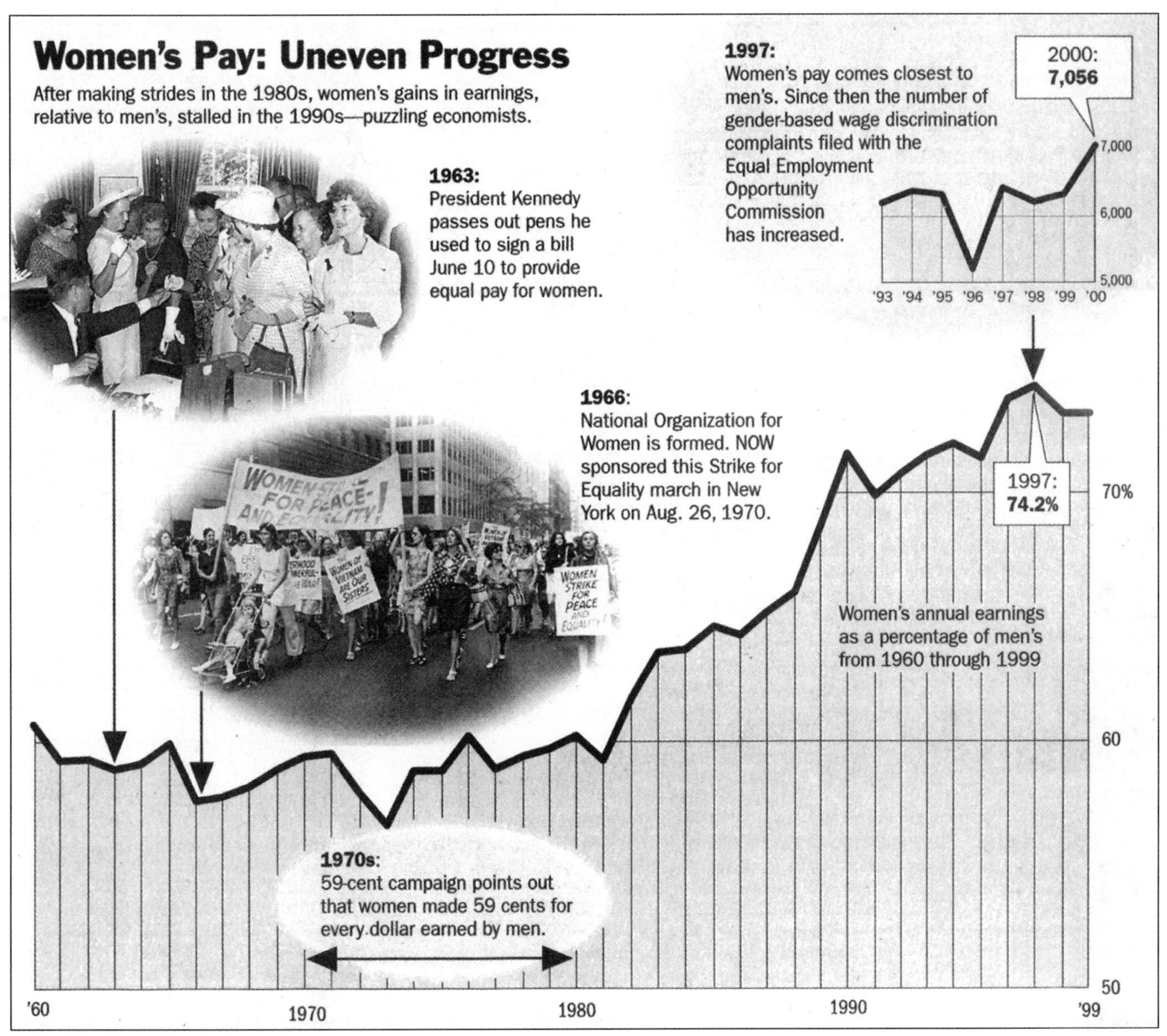

Los Angeles Times

Sources: Census Bureau, Bureau of Labor Statistics, Equal Employment Opprtunity Commission; Associated Press photos

of women's median annual earnings to men's grew from 60.2% to 71.6%. A decade later, the ratio was 72.2%.

"The big pattern is that there was a marked, rapid, sustained progress in the 1980s, and the 1990s have been more uneven," said Francine D. Blau, a professor and director of the School of Industrial and Labor Relations at Cornell University, who has written numerous books and articles on the pay gap.

Much of the earnings gains by women in the '80s were due to an increase in their job tenure, Blau said. Another factor was the decline of women as a portion of the clerical and service work force and their increase in professional and management ranks.

Women's gains, however, were only part of the 1980s pay picture, according to an analysis by the Economic Policy Institute. Almost 65% of the closing of the gender gap in the '80s was a result of the decline in men's wages as the era took its toll on male-dominated blue-collar jobs.

In the 1990s, the most dramatic departure from previous decades was the widening of the pay gap among 18- to 25-year-old workers, women and men born five years or more after President Kennedy signed the Equal Pay Act of 1963.

Young women workers had come to within 95% of their male counterparts in 1993, helping to narrow the overall gap significantly, according to recent research by Boushey, the EPI economist.

By 1999, the ratio of young women's earnings to young men's had slipped back to 92%.

"It's obviously regressive," Boushey said. "When these women turn 30, it could be worse for them than it is for women age 30 now. So it's very disconcerting."

Indeed, previous studies of the earnings gap have found that it typically widens as women enter prime child-bearing years.

Such findings are the basis of criticism of the wage gap and have led groups such as the Employment Policy Foundation to argue that the disparity owes as much to personal choice as anything else.

Young Workers Feeding the Gap

Boushey suspects changes at the top and bottom of the wage spectrum are behind the gap's growth among younger workers.

"What I found was I thought quite astounding. In 1999, young white women were less likely to be going into high-tech jobs than in 1993," Boushey said.

Indeed, during that period, the share of high-tech jobs held by white women declined 22%. Latinas' share dropped even more. Young African American women and all young men increased their share of high-tech jobs. Young white men, for example, held 60% more of these jobs in 1999 than in 1993.

Young white women who did get high-tech jobs saw their wages rise 23%, compared with 9% for their male counterparts. Young African American women in high-tech work saw wages jump 42%.

"So there are huge wage incentives here, and yet young women are not taking advantage of [them]," Boushey said. "Is it that they are feeling discriminated against, that they don't like the culture, the hours are too long, it's too entrepreneurial and they want more stability?"

There were 360,000 young workers with high-tech jobs in 1999, so their influence on the overall earnings picture would be small, Boushey said. But other reports have reflected similar disparities between men and women in high-tech fields. In May, the White House Council of Economic Advisors reported that woman held about a third of the computer science, programming and computer operating jobs, and earned about 12% less than their male counterparts.

Martin Carnoy, a Stanford University economics professor, also sees evidence that the high-tech boom could be at least partially responsible.

"I think what happened is the incomes went up in certain areas that favored men, like information technology," he said.

Boushey found another source of the widening gender gap among young low-wage workers. Here, she found the wages of African American women rose 1% between 1993 and 1999, much less than those of other groups, whose gains ranged from 5% for white women to 15% for African American men.

"I would argue that the fall in the real value of the minimum wage and welfare reform have dampened the wages of young African American women," Boushey said.

7,056 Complaints to EEOC in 2000

Another factor is discrimination, although some estimate it could account for as little as 5% of the wage gap. Even that is a big problem, said Ida L. Castro, chairwoman of the Equal Employment Opportunity Commission, whose job it is to enforce laws prohibiting pay discrimination based on sex and race.

"There are a lot of women who face that problem," Castro said. "When this country enacted the Equal Pay Act and the Civil Rights Act, it made a statement and that statement was any percentage is intolerable."

Last year there were 7,056 wage discrimination complaints made to the EEOC. Pay parity advocates said the number of complaints could be even higher if workers had a right to review confidential wage information and if the Equal Pay Act provided for compensatory and punitive damages and attorney's fees. As it stands, the act allows victims of gender-based pay discrimination to recover only back wages, which amounted to nearly $23 million in cases settled in 2000.

Castro attributed at least part of the sharp rise in complaints between 1999 and 2000 to a growing willingness among workers to share wage information as gender and racial pay inequities have become a concern for women and men.

"As families are competing in a fiercely competitive world of work, trying to retain their gains and continue to move ahead, it's no longer just a women's issue. It's a family issue," Castro said.

RACISM IN THE WORKPLACE

In an increasingly multicultural U.S., harassment of minorities is on the rise

By Aaron Bernstein

When Wayne A. Elliott was transferred in 1996 from a factory job to a warehouse at Lockheed Martin Corp.'s sprawling military-aircraft production facilities in Marietta, Ga., he says he found himself face to face with naked racism. Anti-black graffiti was scrawled on the restroom walls. His new white colleagues harassed him, Elliott recalls, as did his manager, who would yell at him, call him "boy," and tell him to "kiss my butt." He complained, but Elliot says the supervisor was no help. Instead, he assigned Elliott, now 46, to collecting parts to be boxed, which involves walking about 10 miles a day. Meanwhile, the eight whites in his job category sat at computer terminals and told him to get a move on—even though Elliott outranked them on the union seniority list.

The atmosphere got even uglier when Elliott and a few other blacks formed a small group in 1997 called Workers Against Discrimination, which led to the filing of two class actions. One day, he and the other two black men among the 30 warehouse workers found "back-to-Africa tickets" on their desks, he says, which said things like "Just sprinkle this dingy black dust on any sidewalk and piss on it, and, presto! hundreds of n-----s spring up!" They reported this, but the Lockheed security officials who responded took the three victims away in their security cars as if they were the wrongdoers, he says, and interrogated them separately.

Then, one day in 1999, according to Elliott, a hangman's noose appeared near his desk. "You're going to end up with your head in here," Elliott recalls a white co-worker threatening. Another noose appeared last November, he says. He and the other whites "hassle me all the time now, unplugging my computer so I lose work, hiding my bike or chair; it's constant," says Elliott, who gets counseling from a psychologist for the stress and says he has trouble being attentive to his two children, ages 7 and 8, when he's at home.

Lockheed spokesman Sam Grizzle says the company won't comment on any specific employee. But regarding the suits, which Lockheed is fighting, he says, "we do not tolerate, nor have we ever tolerated, harassment or discrimination of any form. We take such complaints very seriously, and we always have investigated them and taken appropriate action when needed."

The alleged incidents at Lockheed are part of an extensive pattern of charges of racial hatred in U.S. workplaces that *BusinessWeek* investigated over a two-month period. Nearly four decades after the Civil Rights Act of 1964 gave legal equality to minorities, charges of harassment at work based on race or national origin have more than doubled, to nearly 9,000 a year, since 1990, according to the Equal Employment Opportunity Commission (charts).

The problem is not confined to small Southern cities such as Marietta. In addition to high-profile suits at Lockheed, Boeing, and Texaco, dozens of other household names face complaints of racism in their workforce. Noose cases have been prosecuted in cosmopolitan San Francisco and in Detroit, with a black population among the largest in the nation.

It's true that minorities' share of the workforce grew over the decade, which could have led to a corresponding rise in clashes. Yet racial harassment charges have jumped by 100% since 1990, while minority employment grew by 36%. What's more, most charges involve multiple victims, so each year the cases add up to tens of thousands of workers—mostly blacks, but also Hispanics and Asians.

It's hard to reconcile such ugly episodes with an American culture that is more accepting of its increasing diversity than ever before. Today, immigrants from every ethnic and racial background flock to the U.S. There is a solid black middle class, and minorities are active in most walks of life, from academia

to the nightly news. When we do think about race, it's usually to grapple with more subtle and complex issues, such as whether affirmative action is still necessary to help minorities overcome past discrimination, or whether it sometimes constitutes reverse discrimination against whites.

Lockheed Martin employee Wayne Elliott says he found "back-to-Africa tickets" on his desk and was called "boy" by his manager. He complained, he says, to no avail. Then came the hangman's noose.

To some extent, the rise in harassment cases may actually reflect America's improved race relations. Because more minorities believe that society won't tolerate blatant bigotry anymore, they file EEOC charges rather than keep quiet out of despair that their complaints won't be heard, says Susan Sturm, a Columbia University law professor who studies workplace discrimination. Many cases involve allegations of harassment that endured for years.

Multimillion-dollar settlements of racial discrimination or harassment claims at such companies as Coca-Cola Co. and Boeing Co. also give victims greater hope that a remedy is available. Such suits became easier in 1991, after Congress passed a law that allowed jury trials and compensatory and punitive damages in race cases. "It's like rape, which everyone kept silent about before," says Boeing human resources chief James B. Dagnon. "Now, prominent individuals are willing to talk publicly about what happened, so there's a safer environment to speak up in."

But many experts say they are seeing a disturbing increase in incidents of harassment. Minority workers endure the oldest racial slurs in the book. They're asked if they eat "monkey meat," denigrated as inferior to whites, or find "KKK" and other intimidating graffiti on the walls at work.

Even office workers are not exempt. In May, 10 current and former black employees at Xerox Corp. offices in Houston filed harassment charges with the EEOC. One, Linda Johnson, says she has suffered racial slurs from a co-worker since 1999, when glaucoma forced her to quit the sales department and become a receptionist. Last year, a white colleague doctored a computer photo of her to make her look like a prostitute, she says. After she complained, her boss printed out the picture and hung it in his office, her charge says. "I tried to do what company procedures suggested and complain to my supervisor, then on up to human resources at headquarters," says Johnson, 47. "But they just sweep it under the rug." Xerox declined to comment on her case.

Worse yet are hangman's nooses, a potent symbol of mob lynchings in America's racial history. The EEOC has handled 25 noose cases in the past 18 months, "something that only came along every two or three years before," says Ida L. Castro, outgoing EEOC chairwoman. Management lawyers concur that racial harassment has jumped sharply. "I've seen more of these cases in the last few years than in the previous 10, and it's bad stuff," says Steve Poor, a partner at Seyfarth, Shaw, Fairweather & Geraldson, a law firm that helps companies defend harassment and discrimination suits.

Some lay the blame on blue-collar white men who think affirmative action has given minorities an unfair advantage. Their feelings may be fueled by the long-term slide in the wages of less-skilled men, which have lagged inflation since 1973. Since many whites see little evidence of discrimination anymore, the small number who harbor racist views feel more justified in lashing out at minorities, whom they perceive as getting ahead solely due to their race, says Carol M. Swain, a Vanderbilt University law professor who is writing a book about white nationalism.

SILENCE. Incidents of open racism at work occur below the national radar because all the parties have powerful incentives to keep it quiet. Plaintiffs' lawyers don't want employees to go public before a trial for fear of prejudicing their case in court. *BusinessWeek* spoke for more than a month with some lawyers before they agreed to let their clients talk. Even then, most workers refused to give their names, fearful of retaliation. Man-

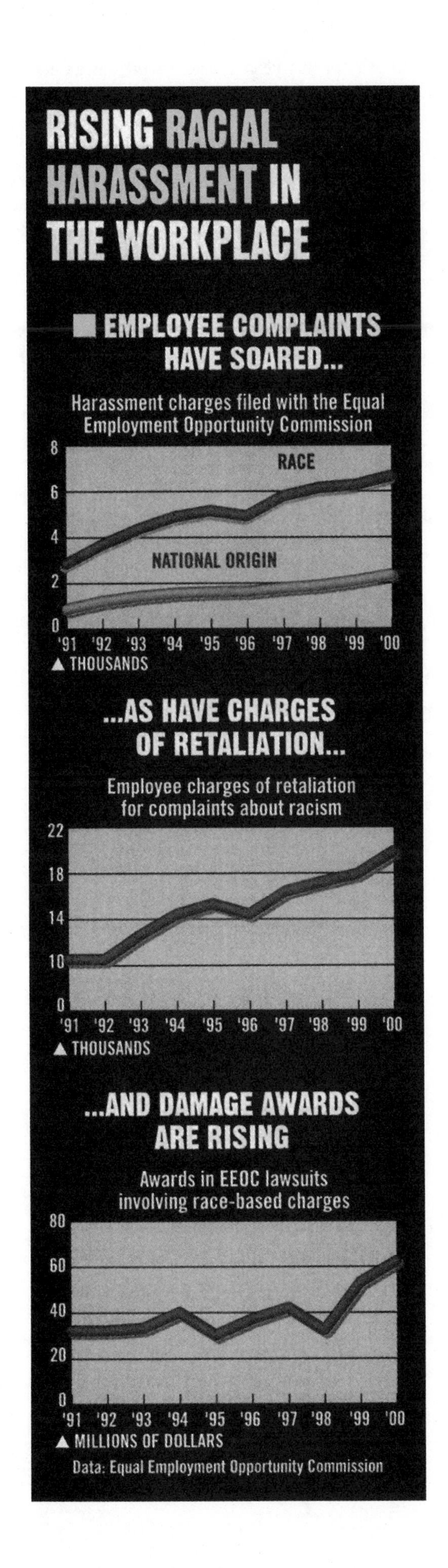

agement and plaintiffs' lawyers alike say it takes tremendous nerve to file a suit or EEOC charges, given the likelihood that coworkers or bosses will strike back. Since 1990, the number of minorities filing charges of retaliation with the EEOC after they complained about racial mistreatment has doubled, to 20,000 a year.

Companies have an even greater desire to avoid bad publicity. Many suits end when employers settle. They routinely buy employees' silence with extra damage award money.

Because racial harassment allegations can be so embarrassing, they pose a difficult challenge for companies. Some quickly go on the offensive and take steps to change. Other employers hunker down for a fight, arguing that allegations are inaccurate or exaggerated. Northwest Airlines Corp., for example, is fighting charges made by black construction workers who found a noose last July at the airline's new terminal under construction at Detroit Metro Airport. Northwest also recently settled two noose-related suits, although it denied liability. Northwest spokeswoman Kathleen M. Peach says none of the noose incidents "rise to the level of harassment. You have to ask was it a joke at a construction site? Or was it in a cargo area where a lot of ropes are used? It's not as cut-and-dried as it seems."

When Ted Gignilliat told what he knew about two nooses at Lockheed, he too became a target, he says. One anonymous caller told him he would "wind up on a slab, dead."

Some employers dismiss nooses and slurs as harmless joking. This seems to be the view taken by Lakeside Imports Inc., New Orleans' largest Toyota Motor Corp. dealer. Last August, it signed a consent decree with the EEOC to settle charges brought by six black salesmen in its 50-person used-car department. The men said that their manager, Chris Mohrman, hit and poked them with two 3 1/2-foot-long sticks with derogatory words on them that he called his "n----- sticks."

Lakeside brushed aside the incident, according to case depositions. Mohrman's manager at the time, a white man named David Oseng, had hired the black salesmen. When he heard what was going on, Oseng said in his deposition, he told the dealership's top brass. Oseng said the top two managers "told me they were tired of all the problems with the n-----s. And if we hired another n-----, [I] would be terminated."

Lakeside lawyer Ralph Zatzkis says the dealer didn't admit any guilt and denies that anything serious happened. He says the sticks, which the EEOC obtained by subpoena, did have writing on them, but "those weren't racial remarks." Zatzkis dismissed the episode as "horseplay." Mohrman and the black salesmen left Lakeside and couldn't be reached. Zatzkis says Lakeside's top managers declined to comment.

Frivolous harassment charges do occur, say experts, but they're rare. "It takes a lot of energy to raise a complaint, and you can make major mistakes assuming what the employees' motives are," warns Haven E. Cockerham, head of human resources at R.R. Donnelley & Sons Co., which is fighting a class action for alleged racial discrimination and harassment that included claims of whites donning KKK robes.

Consider Adelphia Communications Corp., a $2.9 billion cable-TV company based in Coudersport, Pa. In February, the EEOC filed suit on behalf of Glenford S. James, a 12-year veteran, and other black employees in the company's Miami office. A manager there racially harassed minorities "on a daily basis" after he took over in August, 1999, the suit says. The manager twice put a noose over James's door, it says. Once, says the complaint, the manager told an employee to "order monkey meat or whatever they eat" for James.

In a suit filed in June, James says that Adelphia didn't stop the problem until he complained to the EEOC in May, 2000. Then, the manager was terminated or resigned. Adelphia declined to comment. However, its brief in the EEOC suit admits that the manager displayed a noose and "made inappropriate statements of a racial nature." The brief says Adelphia "promptly and severely disciplined" the manager "as a result of his actions." The manager couldn't be reached.

REVENGE. Whites who stand up for co-workers also can run into trouble. Ted W. Gignilliat, a worker at the Marietta facility of Lockheed since 1965, says he was harassed so badly for speaking up about two nooses that he had to take a leave of absence. He says he was threatened, his truck was broken into, and he got anonymous phone calls at work and at home—one telling him he would "wind up on a slab, dead." In March, 2000, a psychologist told Gignilliat to stop work; he went on disability leave until May of this year. He now works as an alarm-room operator in the plant's fire station. "It's in the middle of the security office, with guards, but I feel they will retaliate against me again for stepping forward," says Gignilliat.

Usually, of course, minorities bear the brunt of revenge. Roosevelt Lewis, who delivers Wonder bread for an Interstate Bakeries Corp. bakery in San Francisco, says his white superiors have been making his life miserable ever since he and other blacks filed a race suit in 1998. A jury awarded them $132 million last year (later reduced by a judge to $32 million). Lewis says this only exacerbated the behavior. "They're trying to make you insubordinate, to create an excuse to fire you," charges Lewis. He says he has complained to higher-ups, but the hassling continues.

Jack N. Wiltrakis, Interstate's head of human resources, says the company has a hotline to headquarters in Kansas City but has received no complaints. "If they have a problem, it's incumbent on them to tell us," he says. Interstate, which has 34,000 workers in 64 bakeries around the U.S., has been sued for race problems in New York, Orlando, Indianapolis, and Richmond, Va. It has settled the two cases, denying liability, and is still fighting the others, including Lewis'. Wiltrakis says the suits haven't prompted Interstate to launch new policies.

In the end, racist behavior by employees lands at the door of corporate executives. They face a dilemma: If they admit there's a problem, the company is exposed to lawsuits and negative publicity. But denial only makes matters worse. Until more employers confront the rise of ugly racism head on, Americans will continue to see behavior they thought belonged to a more ignominious age.

With Michael Arndt in Chicago and bureau reports

Older TV Writers Press Case

Class-action lawsuit alleges that in youth-obsessed Hollywood, they're 'graylisted' after age 40. It's a potential legal bombshell that could have far-reaching ramifications.

By **LISA GIRION**
TIMES STAFF WRITER

They color over the gray, fudge birthdates, drop shows prior to 1997 from their resumes and buy trendy outfits for meetings with producers.

One sitcom veteran said that, before she attends a meeting, she goes to a salon to have her eyebrows plucked, her make-up applied and her hair blown out. That's nothing, she said, compared with her friends who try to vanquish wrinkles with collagen injections.

Aging actors trying to win parts written for ingenues?

Nope. They are writers trying to win jobs scripting lines for TV shows aimed at under-35 viewers.

In an increasingly youth-obsessed Hollywood, many writers say job offers and incomes plunge after 40. The ageism complaint has dogged the industry, particularly television, for years.

Yet in the decade or so since a documentary, "Power and Fear: The Hollywood Grey List," put the bleak outlook for older writers in the spotlight, few writers have been bold enough to go public with ageism complaints and none has taken a case to court, perhaps out of fear that whistle-blowing would extinguish any hope of working in this town again.

Until now.

In a novel and far-reaching class-action lawsuit, 28 television writers have put their names to ageism charges against more than 50 TV networks, studios, production companies and talent agencies.

"It's breathtaking in its ambition, all the people they are suing," said David Kadue, an employment lawyer with Seyfarth Shaw's Los Angeles office who represents management against discrimination claims. "This is very ambitious in alleging an industrywide practice."

The writers, including some with Emmys and credits ranging from "The Brady Bunch" to "Miami Vice," allege that the industry engages in a "graylisting" conspiracy that has intensified since the 1980s when advertisers began demanding shows for the sought-after 18-to-34 age group, whose buying habits are more susceptible to commercial influence than those of older viewers.

RICK MEYER/LOS ANGELES TIMES

Paul Levine is a writer on the television series "JAG." At age 52, he says that although he hasn't felt the sting of ageism, "from what I've been told, I'm very lucky to have a job."

The 81-page complaint, filed in federal court in Los Angeles on behalf of up to 7,000 writers, is a potential legal bombshell that attacks not just one employer, as hiring discrimination cases usually do, but an entire industry—an almost unheard-of tactic that is expected to draw the attention of lawyers and employers inside and outside the entertainment community.

Because of the high profile of the industry, the writers' case against Hollywood could affect the way employers in television and elsewhere make hiring decisions even before it is resolved, said Larry J. Shapiro, publisher of the California Employer Adviser Newsletter.

KEN HIVELY/LOS ANGELES TIMES

Martin Shapiro, whose talent agency is named as one of the defendants in the Writers Guild lawsuit, expresses surprise that agents are being targeted. He says his firm represents many writers over 40, including one of the plaintiffs.

BRIAN WALSKI/LOS ANGELES TIMES

Paul Sprenger is the lead lawyer representing the writers. He says of the far-reaching class-action case, "The statistics don't lie."

And, he said, it is expected to raise workers' awareness of age bias, an area of litigation that lawyers already expect to intensify in the next few years because most baby boomers are over 40 and now may avail themselves of the protections of the federal Age Discrimination in Employment Act.

"I think it's going to make the people… be much more careful about documenting their hiring decisions," Shapiro said.

In addition to unspecified damages, the suit seeks a remedy that could roil the industry even more than a big payout: Court supervision of network and studio hiring for five years or longer, as long as it would take to wipe out the alleged ageist exclusion of writers 40 and older.

Court supervision is not uncommon in class-action discrimination cases. The same week they filed suit on behalf of the writers, the lead law firm, Sprenger & Lang, won an $8-million settlement from CBS Inc. That lawsuit was on behalf of more than 200 women technicians working on TV stations across the country who claimed they were victims of sexual discrimination in pay and promotions. The settlement, pending court approval, also would place CBS under court supervision for four years, force operational changes and require reports on the status of women technicians.

Christine A. Littleton, a UCLA professor who teaches employment-discrimination law, said the scope of the writers' case is unusual and potentially groundbreaking.

"This could be amazing. It's a very interesting use of the class-action technique," Littleton said. "It's a real interesting case for how useful the age discrimination act is in large-scale cases as opposed to individual lawsuits where it has mostly been used. And it's also really interesting from the standpoint of the employment practices of the entertainment industry."

Some of the defendants believe the suit paints with too broad a brush.

Hugh Dodson, chief operating officer of Gersh Agency, said he was baffled that the firm was named as a defendant because it has no record of representing or being approached by any of the plaintiffs.

"We kind of feel like there is a wide net being cast here and we're being thrown into it, and we're clearly not culpable," he said.

Martin Shapiro, whose talent agency also was named, was similarly surprised that the suit targeted agents at all.

"We're employment agencies. We're employed by the talent to represent them. We don't hire them. We don't pay them. We don't make any money unless they make money," Shapiro said adding that his firm represents many writers over 40, including one of the plaintiffs.

Spelling Television employs six people older than 40, according to a statement from Chairman Aaron Spelling. "They are all executive producers as well as writers and, by the way, are doing a fantastic job for us," Spelling said in the statement. "No writers should ever be judged by their age."

Most defendants declined to comment or issued statements denying they engaged in ageism. One studio source familiar with the suit noted that a 1998 study commissioned by the Writers Guild of America West found the number of writers over 40 working in television increased slightly, from 53% to 57%, between 1991 and 1997, and said that shows the suit "cherry-picks" statistics in an effort to make the employment of older writers appear lower overall than it is.

"Anecdotally, you are going to find lots of writers not working in the Writers Guild," he said, "That's just the type of industry it is."

Paul Sprenger, a Washington, D.C.-based lawyer leading a bicoastal team representing the writers, said. "We did not cherry-pick the numbers" of writers over 40 on television shows.

"It's worse in some areas than others," he said. "But the truth is, it's what we call statistically significant in all categories and overall. The statistics don't lie."

Of the WGA's 9,500 writers, two-thirds are over 40. Yet a third or fewer over-40 writers worked on 62 of the 122 night-time TV series for which records were available, according to the suit's representation of the WGA study.

The suit also contends that television writing is unusual in that earnings fall with age because older writers are employed for briefer periods than younger writers. In 1997, for instance, median earnings for employed writers in their 30s was about $84,000, compared with $70,000 for writers in their 40s, $50,000 for writers in their 50s, and $36,000 for those in their 60s, the suit says.

The statistical disparities occur not by accident but by ageist customs, the suit says. The filing repeats alleged ageist remarks of some network executives, producers and agents. In one instance, the suit says, the late Brandon Tartikoff, who, as president of programming for NBC, allegedly "pronounced a policy of not hiring any writers over the age of 30."

The suit quotes Paul Haas, senior vice president of the talent agency International Creative Management, as saying, "Age matters. When we have someone network executives haven't heard of, they want to know how old the writer is. When we pitch somebody fresh out of college who has youth and vitality, executives like it. If there is somebody who has a bunch of credits and it appears they have been around for a while, they might not like it as much."

The suit says Haas made the comments to USA Today in 1998.

Joseph Posner, an Encino lawyer who heads the Los Angeles chapter of the National Employment Lawyers Assn., said that type of talk can be powerful evidence in an employment discrimination case.

"If I had a case where employers made those comments about their direct employees, I could almost take this to the bank," Posner said.

Shapiro, the talent agent, acknowledged that older writers have a hard go of it in Hollywood.

"I see older writers having trouble getting employment. There is no question about it, whether anybody can justify that it's age discrimination or whether there are other rationales for it," he said. "It's very disheartening to see somebody build a career and then all of a sudden to not get work, where it isn't all of a sudden they stopped doing good work."

Shapiro said he believes writing often improves with age and experience. But, he said, he does see instances where younger writers are perceived as having an edge.

"If somebody is doing a youth comedy, then they feel much more comfortable if they find a youthful writer to do it because that writer has a better feel for the people and the jargon," Shapiro said.

In the lawsuit, older writers allege that networks and studios have wrongly assumed that older writers could not script shows that appealed to the under-35 audience that advertisers desire.

"Relying on customer preferences is not going to be a defense," said Kadue, the management lawyer. "That's not a defense any more than it was a defense for Southern restaurant owners in the '60s to refuse to hire black waitresses because the customers preferred white waitresses."

The lead law firm for the writers has won two of the nation's three largest judgments on age discrimination in employment—$58.5 million against First Union Bank and $28.5 million against Ceridian Corp. Sprenger, the lead lawyer, said he has taken 15 employment-discrimination class-action suits to trial, five of them age cases.

What sets the writers' case against Hollywood apart, he said, is the apparent widespread acceptance of ageism, from talent agents to studio heads.

"They say, 'This is the greatest script I've ever seen, but you're 40 and I can't use it,'" Sprenger said.

"If they said the things that they say about older writers... about blacks, the journalists and the public would say, 'My God, what a bigot!' They say it about old people and it's just sort of accepted," he said. The older writers "say, 'I'll just try to get a younger writer to front my script.' Most people just sort of accept it and go away mad."

Feeling they had little to lose, the writers began planning the suit with Sprenger about a year ago. Since the suit was filed last month, 100 new writers have asked to join, and Sprenger is so confident of the writers' case that he expects his firm to advance them a minimum of $1 million in legal services.

The lead plaintiff, Tracy Keenan Wynn, 44, a fourth-generation member of an entertainment dynasty, won Emmys for "The Autobiography of Miss Jane Pittman" and "Tribes." He earned a substantial income from television writing for more than 25 years until about 1997 when, despite his best efforts, the work dried up and his earnings dropped to nothing, the suit says.

The loss of his livelihood has been emotionally difficult for the father of three, caused him to lose his home and forced him into bankruptcy, said Sprenger, who has instructed his clients not to discuss the case.

"His is not a unique story," Sprenger said. "People are earning $100,000 or $200,000 a year, have a mortgage and tuition obligations, and suddenly they are earning zero or close to it, and that causes severe financial crisis."

Still, many older writers are working in television. Last year at age 51, "JAG" writer Paul Levine said he believed he was the youngest rookie writer in Hollywood. The CBS show stands out for its older writing staff, including one in his 30s, another in his 40s and four in their 50s.

Levine, who had a career as a lawyer and wrote eight novels before he got the "JAG" job, said he hasn't felt the sting of ageism.

"It's never happened to me," he said. "But from what I've been told, I'm very lucky to have a job."

For a long time, Hollywood writers believed that they could sustain careers in television through age 50, but then the age ceiling seemed to drop to 40, said Adam Lapidus, a 37-year-old writer whose credits include "The Simpsons," "Full House" and "Whose the Boss?"

"I thought, 'If I can work until 50, I'm thrilled,' and suddenly it became 40, and it became scary," said Lapidus, who got his first job out of college on the strength of a script he wrote for "Golden Girls."

"Here I was, a 21-year-old male and I wrote a script about four menopausal women. I got the job because I had their voice," he said. "The point of being a good writer is you can write for anybody."

The Not-So-Fine Art Of The Layoff

Get job cuts right, and you may be able to salvage your company's future. Mess them up, and your problems are only beginning.

BY MATTHEW BOYLE

Scanning the Manhattan headquarters of Urban Box Office Network on a crisp Tuesday morning last November, Ayana Mangum felt a power similar to that possessed by the protagonist in the film *The Sixth Sense*. But Mangum's gift was slightly different: Instead of dead people, "I saw fired people," she says. Mangum had it on good authority that the ailing company was going to sack most of its staff, but she couldn't tell a soul. "Every day I got up thinking it would be my last," she recalls. Rumors escalated—even Mangum's grandmother knew about UBO's woes—but with no clear word from management, "everyone was in limbo." When the news finally hit and Mangum and 326 others lost their jobs, chaos ensued. She says of management, "They had no idea what they were doing. It was an awful, awful experience." UBO CEO Adam Kidron admits the layoff day itself was "horrendous," but insists he gave employees a week's notice that their jobs were in peril.

These days, "seeing fired people" requires no special gift—they're everywhere. Xerox, Lucent, Sara Lee, Amazon, J.C. Penney, Gateway, Nortel, Motorola, Dell, Aetna, AOL Time Warner (parent of FORTUNE's publisher), and Gillette have all announced layoffs, and the list grows by the day. In January outplacement firm Challenger Gray & Christmas tallied 142,208 announced job cuts, the highest monthly number since it began keeping track in 1993. While some dot-coms may bungle layoffs, the majority of the FORTUNE 500 plan the process with a precision that makes political conventions seem extemporaneous. "These things tend to be orchestrated particularly well," notes outplacement guru Larry Stybel.

And that could be a problem in itself: Companies have become so proficient at the science of layoffs that many have forgotten there's an art to it. Operating strictly by the book is fine for baking a cake; it's not advisable when dealing with people. "Organizations that have been through [layoffs] several times think it's business as usual," says Tom Silveri, CEO of Drake Beam Morin. "This is not a process that should be taken lightly." Herewith, then, is FORTUNE's layoff primer, in three parts.

THE PLANNING: The first thing to do, experts agree, is communicate a clear rationale for the cuts. "Employees are stakeholders, and you have to make the same justification to them that you do to investors," says Towers Perrin managing director Jeffrey Schmidt. Warning of possible layoffs may create anxiety around the water cooler, but it does give employees time to prepare themselves emotionally and financially.

At Transact Technologies, which makes receipt printers found everywhere from McDonald's to the New York Stock Exchange, 70 of its 205 employees will lose their jobs at the end of the year. But when CEO Bart Shuldman broke the news last month, no one was surprised. Shuldman had explained to employees back in December that layoffs were possible at the Wallingford, Conn., plant, which makes outdated impact printers. The company is betting instead on a new inkjet technology that requires fewer workers. "We're not going into this thing cold," he says. "If employees know what's going on, they can deal with it."

Once you've established the need for layoffs, you have to decide which positions to cut. That's anything but a one-man job. For starters, make sure division managers are involved, so that you don't end up laying off an employee with irreplaceable expertise. That could be dire. Says one Web developer who was canned at a startup financial services company: "They had no idea that the project I was leading was the corporate Website redesign," he crows. He agreed to return for three days to finish the project. But he charged a steep price: $16,000 in video equipment.

When the Ax Falls...

EMPLOYER CHECKLIST	EMPLOYEE CHECKLIST
1. Clearly explain the actions taken and the reasons for them; document everything.	1. Understand the severance agreement before you sign it. Get legal advice if necessary.
2. Prepare the managers who will deliver the message.	2. If you are over 40, you have three weeks to consider the agreement and another week to revoke it after signing.
3. Speak plainly, not in euphemisms; don't make promises.	3. Absent union rules, a company is not obligated to pay severance.
4. Emphasize that it's not personal.	4. Don't be ashamed to talk to colleagues and friends.
5. Know how layoffs will affect the demographic breakdown of the staff.	5. Take advantage of any outplacement assistance.

During the planning process it's also critical to get input from all sides—legal, human resources, finance, operations, and PR. "Doing it strictly through HR is a mistake," Silveri says. Consulting with lawyers, for example, may help keep an eye on the racial, age, and gender makeup of the staff—and avoid a discrimination suit.

Don't forget to prepare the people who will be breaking the news. The managers doing the firing need to know how to calmly convey that the decision is final, but not personal. Nearly half (46%) of the companies surveyed by HR consulting firm Lee Hecht Harrison fail to provide such training—and that can get messy. Silveri recalls a manager who was so distraught that he vomited in the bathroom before a termination meeting.

D-DAY: The day of the formal announcement is the most difficult, no matter how well choreographed. Most consultants say to make it early in the day—"The most inhumane aspect was waiting all day," remarks one victim—and early in the week. Avoid holidays, keep the meetings short, don't get personal, emphasize the business rationale, and address employee concerns. An employee's manager should break the news, not a faceless corporate axman. "It would have been easier to hear it from my boss," says a senior producer at CNN who was laid off in January. "It feels like a betrayal."

What is said is just as important. Be ready to accept responsibility. "It's easy to say the economy is going through a down cycle," says Alan Downs, a former "corporate executioner." "One of the most effective things is to say, 'We goofed.'" As for hiring burly security guards to escort people out, it may make sense to have them on hand—you never know what could happen—but they shouldn't be conspicuous.

THE AFTERMATH: Communication with "survivors" is critical, especially after the deed is done. "The worst thing managers can do is what they want to do, which is hide in the office," says Joan Caruso, managing director at the Ayers Group. And in times of duress, great communication may require more than just talking. That's why, days after Razorfish COO Jean-Philippe Maheu axed some 400 staffers, he visited some of his remaining consultants (dubbed "fish") at client Ford Motor. "I believe in communication, but I believe more in leading by example," Maheu says.

Survivors also need to know if their jobs have changed. Are they expected to do the work of those laid off? Let them know. You may also have to "re-sell" the company's vision and its future prospects. "Part of laying off people is recruiting those who stay," says Jacques Leger, managing consultant at Watson Wyatt. Remember that you will see these people again, as clients, competitors, customers—even employees. "Companies frequently forget that the person you're firing today is not going to vanish into the night," says Stybel. Layoffs, like ghosts, can haunt a company for years. If you fail to appreciate the art of the layoff, the thing that goes bump in the night may be your company's reputation.

Termination with Dignity

The Employment Roundtable

Richard Bayer, editor

Have you ever had to dismiss someone? Have you ever been dismissed yourself? How was it handled? Do you think it could have been handled better? Were you, or the employee you discharged, able to move forward and "get on with it" fairly well, or fairly quickly?

Employment separation must be handled in such a way that both the employee and the firm are empowered to move forward.

Whatever the reason for employment separation, few workplace situations are dreaded more than a face-to-face meeting to break the news that someone is being dismissed. Often the person losing the job has little idea of what is coming—and in all too many cases, the manager has little training in how to handle the situation. We must recognize the difficult business and human problems that involuntary termination presents.

Regrettably, the termination process is given far less attention than the hiring process. But there has been a trend in the last few years to correct this imbalance—simply because there is much more "built-in" turbulence in the workplace of the 1990s than there was only a few decades ago. The average American today has been in a job for only four years and, not surprisingly, expects to be in that job for only four years.

Separations resulting from mergers, downsizings, relocations, and closings are now a regular part of the business landscape. Terminations "for cause" can be on a continuum ranging from an employee's inability to adapt to a new computer system to situations in which other employees or the organization are put at risk. Although it makes great sense to handle potentially violent or otherwise dangerous situations with due caution, it makes no sense to handle all employees as if they were a threat. Companies need termination policies that apply in all but the most egregious circumstances, ensuring that:

- the goodwill toward the firm stays intact,
- the remaining employees feel secure, and
- the departing employees feel empowered.

If for no other reason than the good of the workplace itself—that is, the effect separations have on those who remain—it would be foolhardy to act as if the exit phase of employment does not deserve major attention.

Employment in this country is primarily at the pleasure of both parties. With some restrictions, firms can "hire and fire" at will. However, everyone deserves to be terminated with dignity—a term chosen advisedly. No less a body than the United Nations speaks of treating human beings with dignity, especially in critical situations. Employees are resources who contribute to productivity but, unlike facilities and equipment, they have intrinsic worth beyond their contribution.

Our goal here is to identify practices that benefit the parties involved, both employee and employer. Put yet another way, managers must understand that termination should be handled in such a way that both the employee and the organization are empowered to go forward.

Progress in this area has been uneven; our position is that American leaders need to devote more attention, energy, and dollars to refining and improving the separation process. Moreover, attention has been brought to this issue primarily because of mergers and downsizings, but termination with dignity should apply to all situations; the employee who is let go because of poor job performance is no less entitled to decent and respectful treatment consistent with the facts of each situation. Even in the case of an employee discharged for willful misconduct, the canons of decency should not be suspended.

About ***The Employment Roundtable***

Addressing Top Employment Issues

Organizations and workers alike are faced with increasingly complex employment issues today:

- What are the rights and related responsibilities of firms and workers?
- How can companies diversify?
- How should companies treat consultants (versus those on payroll)?
- How can older workers extend their careers?
- How can companies select, train, and retain "knowledge" workers?
- What should replace the old "corporate loyalty" concept?

These questions and others are often answered in sound bites or with a sensational spin to generate headlines.

However, such serious issues require balanced, in-depth study. This can be achieved by inviting the deliberation of experts from diverse perspectives. Just as war is too important to be left to the generals, analysis of vital employment issues is too important to be left solely to major corporations, think tanks, or the government. To ensure maximum insight, representatives from all these sectors should be invited to speak together and weigh in.

Beginning in December 1998, we invited experts from a variety of disciplines to gather as *The Employment Roundtable*. We are dedicated to enhancing the understanding of the top employment problems facing the United States today. Representatives come from:

- major industries (such as health care, computers, financial services, and staffing and consulting services);
- government (top directors from the Department of Labor);
- employee advocacy (The Five O'Clock Club); and
- think tanks (the Conference Board, research organizations, legal experts, academia, social ethicism, economics).

Any issue involving the optimal employment of the U.S. labor force is of potential interest to the Roundtable. As we address each issue, we expect potential solutions to emerge. Indeed, the Roundtable focuses on solving immediate organizational problems.

To safeguard the freedom of expression essential for open dialogue at the Roundtable meetings, summaries of our discussions are published without the attribution of particular remarks to particular members.

The meetings have proven most interesting and we enjoy getting together with each other. It is a privilege for each of us to associate with those who are identifying and addressing these issues.

However, our purpose is not just our own enlightenment, but advancing the common good. Therefore, we will publish white papers, essays, policy statements, and conclusions on each issue, which will be released to major organizations, the government, the press, and members of The Five O'Clock Club. This practice makes clear our purpose as an open forum whose results are available to any parties interested in U.S. employment issues.

The first of these issues, "Termination With Dignity," is presented herein.

Cordially,
Kate Wendleton, Founder, The Employment Roundtable, and President, The Five O'Clock Club

Why Should the Employer Care?

1. Termination with dignity increases a firm's ability to hire the right people. Today's labor shortage is expected to continue at least through the next decade. A company's ability to attract the best talent is influenced by its goodwill in the marketplace, which depends to some extent on how it handles terminated employees.

The workplace today is circular, not linear. Employees do not come in and stay. They come and go, intermixing with people outside who learn how they were treated. When a company lets someone go, that person touches dozens of others who can influence the company's image—and ability to hire—in the marketplace. If the company wants to compete and hire well, it must pay attention to the way it lets people go.

2. Termination with dignity is becoming a routine part of doing business in a civilized society. Not too many decades ago, few practical executives could have been persuaded that the routine cost of business included offering their employees paid vacations, health and dental insurance coverage, personal days off, matching contributions to pension plans, and so on. Over time, organizational thinking has changed, partly because of the recognition that employees are resources for which there is an increasingly competitive market.

The costs of developing and implementing dignified termination policies should be considered a part of doing business in a civilized society. Dignified termination should be seen as one of many benefits provided by an employer. The movement in past decades toward expanded and increasing employee benefits reflects an understanding of the "social contract or "social covenant"—accepted standards as to what is decent for ordinary working men and women.

The Termination Meeting

Preparedness includes:

- guidelines for management's behavior on the day of termination
- thorough training
- a carefully prepared (though flexible), positive script
- plans for taking care of separated employee(s), including quality monetary packages
- a full description of career counseling and other services ready to distribute
- a list of each employee's contributions and strong points that have been valued over the years
- thoughts regarding the method of severance payout

During the meeting, consider the following concerns:

- The employee wants to know what went wrong. People are more likely to be able to go forward if they are given an explanation.
- The employee is listening for a kind word about past performance.
- There is the matter of pride: "How will my departure be portrayed to the remaining work force?"
- There are the pragmatics: "How am I going to survive?" Have a full written summary of severance benefits available, prepared with as much care as the benefit booklets handed to new hires.
- Discuss other issues, such as professional references, so the employee can formulate a strategy to move forward.
- Allow the person to return to familiar surroundings and react with friends in order to try to proceed with some degree of normalcy for the time being. This is part of the empowering process.

One of the major components of our social covenant as fellow citizens wishing to enjoy the benefits of a vigorous economy is the understanding that we are obliged to contribute to the general well-being of society. Hence, we should have no trouble arguing for compassionate termination policies that reduce stress on families, mitigate financial hardships, and decrease the chances that discharged employees will suffer debilitating emotional crises.

3. Termination with dignity protects corporate profitability. Shareholder value will incréase and business will profit in the long run by moving vigorously in this direction. At least two arguments can be advanced here:

Organizations do not welcome negative publicity. Notoriety is not good for business. The recall of a product, scandal in the boardroom, headlines about embezzlement—or the news that 20 executives have been cut from the payroll just three months short of retirement benefits—can damage a firm's reputation. A good name is an asset not to be squandered. And firms do acquire reputations if they are bad places to work, with poor benefits or perceptions of the way people should be treated. Those that earn a reputation for decency in the way they let people go are considered attractive places for competent people to work. As termination with dignity becomes standard in the workplace, firms that fail to practice it run the risk of damaging their reputations.

The impact on the productivity of the remaining employees is an important factor. The morale of employees who survive a downsizing—or, for that matter, witness a single separation for good cause—should be of primary concern to management. Major layoffs can result in greater work loads for the remaining employees, which is cause enough for stress and hard feelings. But many other factors can also come into play. Those left behind can experience feelings of loss when familiar faces are suddenly gone, teams are broken up, and office mates have disappeared. They can be angry that "things aren't the way they used to be," and fearful that the same fate may be in store for them.

Resentment and fear can be eased if there is a general perception that the separated employees got a fair deal and that management handled the termination(s) in a decent and caring fashion. It is in management's interest that:

- people still believe "this is a good place to work";
- employee energy and focus be channeled into work and productivity; and
- venting and complaining be kept to a minimum.

Employees who have witnessed termination with dignity will be more inclined to like the firm and support its goals and mission.

There is a growing awareness in the American work force that mergers and staff reductions are now an inevitable part of the corporate landscape. This should be accompanied by a growing awareness that management will merge and cut with care for human dignity—that it is committed to making termination as painless as possible and to protecting the well-being of employees as productive resources.

HOW TO TERMINATE WITH DIGNITY: THE TERMINATION MEETING

Proper termination is a lengthy process. Many factors come into play, so it may be helpful to analyze it chronologically. To carry it off well, pay attention to:

- the extensive groundwork required first;
- the protocols and procedures to be followed when it happens; and
- the appropriate actions required in the days, weeks, or even months after a layoff or termination.

Before the Meeting

Impulse, or "letting the chips fall where they may," has no role in affirming and constructing a proper termination policy. Because preparedness is vital, termination procedures must be imbedded in written policy and, in the course of time, instilled in the culture. They must become a part of workplace protocol. In other words, this is not something to be put on the shoulders of untutored managers. The firm's guiding philosophy on the issue must be studied and mastered.

Managers must be trained. When people are going through a termination process, all parties are moving into the arena of human hurt. Great sensitivity is required. People's lives and futures are at stake, and the company's image is on the line. Accordingly, managers and HR officers must be trained to listen attentively and respond to human distress. Preparedness for this role may require, at the very least, attendance at seminars, tutoring by specially trained personnel, professional coaching on what to say and what not to say—perhaps even reliance on scripts.

Enlightened organizations have long trained managers to improve their hiring and interviewing skills, enabling them to be more astute in the selection of candidates and more aware of legal pitfalls. Who needs a manager who has not gotten the word that a female candidate cannot be asked blatantly sexist questions? The same degree of training should be given to managers for the hard task of letting people go. Who needs a manager who is too busy to care about feelings and just wants to get the unpleasant business behind him—or worse, views his task as an opportunity to settle scores? Letting people go is an extraordinarily important and sensitive task. Those entrusted with this responsibility should have the benefit of professional coaching. Smaller firms could at least give their managers selected reading material, or perhaps this article.

Develop positive scripts. We believe that carefully prepared, flexible, positive scripts are an indispensable element of the separation process. Enabling people to pick up the pieces and move on should be the goal; terminated employees who have been emotionally battered and damaged by the process may be ill-equipped to grapple with the emotional battering that may come next, such as a job search. Saying a nice word plays a critical role; the lack of kindness eats at people and erodes morale. The guiding norm, at the very least, should be "Do no harm." In a downsizing or merger situation, it is easier to assure people that this is a no-fault situation, but even here self-esteem can take a beating and positive scripts are essential.

The employee is listening for a kind word about past performance. For example:

- "George, you've been a trooper. You've helped us for 15 years and I'm sorry the company has moved in a different direction."
- "Mary, you have excellent people-relations skills and have added a lot to the group."

Be prepared to go over each employee's strong points. The manager should be prepared to review the employee's contributions and strong points that have been valued over the years. Even in a termination based on performance, prompted by the fact that acquired skills were not adequate for a particular situation, the person's assets and abilities can still be acknowledged. A termination-for-performance should not be an occasion for abuse. Financial considerations are crucial, but a generous dollar settlement usually cannot erase bitter memories of uncaring or even unkind words. The "sharp stick in the eye" is likely to be remembered long after separation money has been spent. Indeed, in those few cases in which former employees have taken legal action, the personal reasons for doing so usually have revolved around treatment during the separation process.

"The package." Preparedness also means creating plans for taking care of separated employees, and an important element in enhancing a company's reputation is the quality of "the package." This is measured by the extent to which the individuals are able to move forward professionally and personally.

Termination with dignity presupposes that "the package" will include:

- severance pay;
- professional support for the process of finding a new position (career counseling and other services); and
- in-house counseling to help the terminated employee come to an understanding of what combination of severance pay and support services is appropriate.

Many employees will be unaware of the importance of various transitional support services and inclined to dismiss them in favor of cash settlements. However, management has an obligation to evaluate separated employees individually and be prepared to guide them with sensitivity based on their needs and histories. Managers should devote considerable time and care to reviewing individual profiles and needs in order to construct separation packages of cash, career counseling, and other services in alignment with company policies, usually proportionate to the level and years of service. Preparedness means having a full, detailed, written description of the termination services and benefits ready to distribute: career counseling help, office space, education grants, health insurance continuation, and so on.

Smaller firms often cannot afford extensive packages. When choices have to be made on the basis of cost, it is usually more beneficial to provide employees with ongoing career counseling until they are reemployed (rather than, say, short-term career counseling along with expensive space and other support services).

Preparedness also requires that thought be given to the method of severance payout. Barring special requests or circumstances, paying a six-month lump sum in November or December—thereby inflating the W2 for the year—will certainly create resentment. Severance pay is rightly viewed as a limited and precious commodity; no more of it than absolutely necessary should be lost to taxes. The costs for bookkeeping and payroll services may well be greater if the payout continues for six months in the form of regular paychecks. Nevertheless, if this is in the best interest of the employee, it should be done.

Information sharing. Although there may be no way to eliminate the element of surprise, there are ways to reduce shock and humiliation in the wake of a downsizing that has been a closely guarded secret. Except in the most unusual of circumstances, there would seem to be little justification for so-called "sudden death" discharges. Horror stories abound of fired employees being asked to leave the building immediately, even being escorted from their desks to the door by security. A discharged worker is treated as a threat; a trusted employee has suddenly become a danger. This certainly creates the impression that the termination is a punishment, causing humiliation and resentment. There has perhaps been too much of an assumption on the part of some managers that this is simply the way to do it: "It's over, let's make a clean break."

"Most managers would resent an employee failing to give two weeks' notice before quitting. But the dynamics are vastly different when the separation is the employer's decision."

Management must consider the consequences in each case. Most managers would resent an employee failing to give two weeks' notice before quitting. But the dynamics are vastly different when the separation is the employer's decision. Organizations would do well to consider the positives of allowing people a "decompression" period at an appropriate time in familiar surroundings, enabling them to finish tasks, complete projects, and make arrangements for keeping in touch with coworkers. This may strike some as being highly idealistic, but carrying it off would depend heavily on how well the reason for the termination has been explained (to be discussed in more detail later).

Attention should also be given to the secrecy that usually surrounds merger negotiations or plans for downsizing. The subject is beyond the scope of this article, but it is nonetheless in need of hard analysis because of the impact on the workplace. It is more difficult to achieve termination with dignity when people have little or no warning that their jobs are about to be cut. We understand and accept the need for confidentiality at some level, but there is also the need to evaluate the impact of secrecy on the men and women of the work force.

During the Meeting

The musical *A Chorus Line* is the story of young Broadway hopefuls trying out for a new production. Near the end of the show, after all have taken their turns at dancing and singing, they stand in a line on the stage nervously facing the director. He announces, "When I call your name, please step forward." Those called do so; smiles and looks of relief cross their faces. But after calling ten people forward, the director says to them, "Thank you for coming. We appreciate your trying out, but I'm sorry we can't use you. Those who remain will receive contracts in the mail." It was a particularly cruel way to announce his selection.

The delivery. When people are being terminated, a lot depends on how they get the news—the words actually used are important—and on how the events of the day unfold. If the perception of cruelty or meanness is not avoided, there can be significant harm, not only to the employees but also to the company in the form of damaged reputation or even lawsuits. Although the overwhelming majority of legal actions brought by terminated employees are unsuccessful (employment law in this country does allow either the employer or employee to terminate the association at will), such actions do remain a nuisance. They are often emotional reactions to the hurt inflicted at the time of termination.

If 10 people are to be cut from a staff of 45, it is best that all 10 be called to a special meeting, or that their names be announced as closely together as possible. This is particularly true if all 45 people are on the same floor or in the same bullpen. The remaining 35 should be told what is happening. Sometimes management fails to think far enough ahead to see that an otherwise intolerable atmosphere will prevail. Productivity is ruined while dozens of people are waiting with dread for the phone to ring and employees are called one-by-one to "come to Personnel." If a humane policy has been adopted, people can return to their desks when they are ready, discuss events and feelings with coworkers, and sit down for a helpful session with a career counselor.

When the time for the meeting arrives, and manager and employee are face to face, termination with dignity requires addressing needs on two levels. The employee has just received life-changing news and will probably be curious about two things:

- Why has this happened to me?
- What is going to happen to me now? How will I survive this?

"Why has this happened to me?" Emotion and self-esteem are rife in this question. Company representatives should be prepared to explain, at least in a general way, why the company is cutting staff, merging, or closing. But they should also be sensitive to feelings of being singled out. "How did I end up in the group to be downsized?" This feeling may be expressed in a variety of ways—or not at all, in the turmoil of the moment—but the underlying plea is, "Please help me understand what went wrong." As discussed earlier, representatives of the organization should be prepared with positive scripts tailored to each employee. People are more likely to feel empowered if they do understand "what went wrong."

"Shock and panic can be reduced if people leave the manager's office with some sense that they are not really on the edge of disaster. They must be aware that a support system has been put in place."

Managers must also be sensitive to the matter of pride. Terminated employees will need to know how their departure will be portrayed to the remaining work force; they need to be assured that they will not come off looking like has-beens or part of a defective group that wasn't pulling its weight. Management can set the tone for the day, preserve an atmosphere of respect, and convey genuine regret that organizational necessity required hard decisions.

"What is going to happen to me now? How will I survive this?" These informational questions are typically rooted in simple panic. A fair percentage of the work force live from paycheck to paycheck. At the very most, they may have no more than a few weeks or months of savings. Some people may be in too much shock to absorb a detailed explanation of the terms of severance, but it is best to work on the assumption that survival information should be conveyed immediately.

Employees should be given full *written* summaries of separation benefits and policies. They must know what to expect in terms of:

- money;
- references;
- career counseling services;
- office space, telephone, and other support;
- health care coverage;
- 401K rollovers;
- pension rights; and
- compensation for earned vacation days.

Again, these should be prepared with as much care as the benefit booklets handed to new hires.

Shock and panic can be reduced if people leave the manager's office with some sense that they are not really on the edge of disaster. They must be aware that a support system has been put in place.

On-site liaison. HR staff should be assigned to liaise with separated workers. The primary message should be, "You have been an important and valued part of the team; we want to help you move on." This means a willingness to help people navigate life during the weeks and months that follow.

After the Meeting

References. Management should devote serious thought and research to the issue of references. Because the primary rationale for termination with dignity is to empower people and enable them to move ahead with their lives, putting in a good word for them can play a crucial role. Does maintaining a wall of silence help?

For years, conventional wisdom has held that references can translate easily into lawsuits, with the result that most companies do little more than verify dates of employment—and forbid managers to respond to requests for references. The result, of course, is that information is sought informally and travels by grapevine, increasing the chance that hearsay or rumors can damage reputations and careers.

It has been shown, however, that offering references does not put organizations at risk. Seglin (1999) reported in the *New York Times*:

> According to C. Patrick Fleener, a management professor at Seattle University, "the fear of being sued and losing is not well founded." Professor Fleener, co-author of a study of federal and state court records nationwide from 1965 to 1970 and 1985 to 1990, found only 16 defamation cases arising from reference checks. And plaintiffs prevailed in only 4 of the 16, he found.

We think it is worth the effort to reinvent strategies on references and convey good news about people to prospective employers. Even people who are fired for performance deserve to have their good points preserved in the record. "Do no harm" should apply here too.

Allowing people to return to familiar surroundings. We have already questioned the appropriateness of "sudden-death" discharges, and in describing behavior "the day of," we stress again that allowing people to return to familiar surroundings and share their reactions with friends—proceeding with some degree of normalcy for the time being—is part of the empowering process. "Clear out your desk and leave now" sends only a negative, punitive message and intensifies feelings of disorientation and loss. It certainly has a chilling effect on the morale of the surviving staff. Protocols should be in place to lessen pain and shock for all parties concerned. The overwhelming message should be: "Although today's events involve stress and a real setback, we don't want these to be worse than necessary."

Making it a reality. A thorough survey of the American employment landscape undoubtedly would reveal wide variations in termination policies. Some firms would get high marks; others have earned reputations for brutality. For the most part, we suspect that the standards advocated here are already accepted in theory by many, and even offered as written policy by some. Termination with dignity, however, is hard work, requiring a heavy commitment of money and human talent. "Writing it up" in the policy manual is one thing; true implementation is another. "Our employee manual was heavy with human concern," an executive noted in commenting on an especially bruising departmental layoff. "But to save money in the very short term, the guidelines were simply ignored."

Further study, research, and consultation among leading executives need to be undertaken to consider strategies for implementing a dignified termination process. How can ideas and ideals be translated into plans of action? In many instances we are talking about a significant change in organizational culture. As mentioned at the outset, many benefits are now taken for granted as part of the deal that American workers expect, such as insurance coverage and paid vacations. Termination with dignity should take its place as a benefit, along with others, to maximize the effectiveness of the work force and the development of employees as resources, as well as to respect human dignity.

At present, the termination process is often crippling to both companies and workers. Nothing in law or economics requires that this state of affairs be preserved. We have offered guidelines on the matter with a view to enabling companies and particularly workers to move forward empowered rather than diminished when ending employment or involuntarily departing a job.

References

Jeffrey L. Seglin, "Too Much Ado About Giving References," *New York Times*, February 21, 1999, p. D4.

Richard Bayer, co-chair of the Roundtable and article editor, is the Chief Operating Officer of the Five O'Clock Club, a national career counseling organization headquartered in Manhattan. The article is adapted from "The Five O'Clock News."

Members of The Employment Roundtable

Kate Wendleton, Founder and Ex-Officio Chair
Co-Chairs: Richard Bayer and Wendy Alfus Rothman

Steve Atamanchuk	Vice President, Human Resources, Sithe Energies
Richard Bayer, Ph.D.	Ethicist, economist, consultant on labor economics, and COO, Five O'Clock Club
Stuart Brody	Senior Counsel and Labor Attorney, Gibney, Anthony & Flaherty
Steve Cohen	Vice Dean, School of International and Public Affairs, Columbia University
Ken Goldstein	Economist, Business and Economic Analysis, The Conference Board
Mary Gorman	Director of Organization Capability, Seagram, Spirits and Wine Group
Diane Kenney	Senior Vice President, Human Resources, Warner Music Group
George Lumsby	Managing Director, Stratford Group
Patrick Oden	Managing Advisor, Ziegler Securities
Paul Orme	Executive Vice President, Business Development, ShareMax.com
Alan Richter	Founding Partner, QED Consulting
Wendy Alfus Rothman	Managing Partner, Advantage Human Resourcing
Marilyn Shea	Regional Administrator, U.S. Dept. of Labor, Employment & Training Administration
Joan Stack	Director of Human Resources, Ernst & Young LLP
Frank Thoelen	Chief Financial Officer, The A Consulting Team
Kate Wendleton	President, The Five O'Clock Club, Inc
Pearl Zuchlewski	Partner, Goodman and Zuchlewski, LLP
Consultants to the Roundtable	
Geoffrey Colvin	Editorial Director, *Fortune* Magazine
David Madison, Ph.D.	Director of National Career Counselors Guild, The Five O'Clock Club, Inc.
John Wieting	Regional Commissioner, Mid-Atlantic Region, U.S. DOL, Bureau of Labor Statistics

Contact: Richard Bayer The Employment Roundtable 300 East 40th, 6L New York, NY 10016 212-286-9332

Sorrow and Guilt: An Ethical Analysis of Layoffs

Joseph T. Gilbert
College of Business, University of Nevada, Las Vegas

Closing the office door, looking straight into an employee's face, and telling him that he no longer has a job is not an easy task. When that employee's performance has been satisfactory or even exemplary, it is even more difficult for a manager to terminate him or her. Yet, this happens hundreds of thousands of times when companies decide to reduce the size of their workforce by layoffs. From the stock market's point of view, such a decision is usually a good thing—a company's stock price often rises on the day that a layoff decision is announced. From top management's point of view, such a decision can seem to be the best, or even the only one, available to solve serious problems that the top manager must address. From the point of view of the managers or supervisors assigned to deliver the news to individuals about to be terminated, the decision often produces sorrow or guilt, or both. From the point of view of the terminated employees, shock, disbelief, and anger are among the typical reactions.

Sorrow and guilt are among the emotions associated with layoffs. Sorrow often arises as a response to suffering, whether the suffering befalls the one feeling sorry or another for whom the sorrowful person sympathizes. Guilt is usually reserved for situations involving moral issues. It typically arises when a person has done something he or she should not have done, and therefore implies some degree or moral wrong. Since layoffs cause suffering, sorrow is an appropriate emotion. Is guilt appropriate, and if so on whose part? In other words, is moral or ethical wrong involved in layoffs?

This article focuses on the decision to conduct layoffs and the subsequent decision about which employees will be laid off. Once these decisions have been reached, the managers or supervisors who conduct the interviews in which those losing their jobs receive the news are executing a strategy or decision that they usually cannot change. A manager or supervisor who felt strongly enough that the decisions were wrong could resign, but short of that their assigned role is to carry out decisions that have been made. Employees who are laid off have little choice but to leave. They can sue their former employer subsequently, but they cannot reverse the layoff decision. Financial analysts and investors who reward the decision to conduct layoffs by bidding up the price of the company's stock are reacting to the expected financial results of the decision, not to the terminations that result from it.

By concentrating our analysis on these two aspects of the subject, we deal with the key points where senior managers decide among options, and, by their decision, set a course of action with serious consequences for others (Child, 1997; McCann, 1997). We will argue that in some circumstances, laying off some employees is the ethical thing to do, and managers who fail to do so are guilty of unethical conduct. In other circumstances, no ethical defense of layoffs can be found, and managers who decide on layoffs in these circumstances are guilty of unethical acts. In a wide range of circumstances in between, there are ethical arguments for and against layoffs. For these cases, we show how ethical reasoning can be applied to assist managers in determining the morally right thing to do.

One common definition of an act with ethical or moral consequences is that such an act involves decisions freely taken that will have positive or negative consequences for others (Velasquez & Rostankowski, 1982). Layoff decisions clearly fall within this definition. Our analysis will employ the three major approaches often used in writing and teaching about managerial ethics: utilitarianism (the greatest good for the greatest number), rights and duties, and justice and fairness. The first section of this article briefly describes the most common approaches to managerial ethics as described in journal articles and books for practitioners (Arneson, Fleenor & Toh, 1997; DeGeorge, 1995). The next section reviews various reasons for layoffs, and divides them into three basic categories. The three following sections analyze the layoff decisions from these perspectives, and the final section draws conclusions about the morality of layoffs as a management tool for improving a business.

Ethical Analysis: The Basic Tools

To determine whether a decision, such as downsizing, or an action, such as laying off an employee, is ethical, managers have certain analytical techniques available to them. While these techniques are not as widely known as statistical analysis or flow charting, they are gradually becoming part of a manager's standard tool kit. Business schools are placing more emphasis on ethics, partly because of the large number of clearly unethical business practices exposed during the 1980s (Piper, Gentile & Parks, 1993; Williams, 1992).

Most business school textbooks and courses on ethics take the same basic approach to analyzing the morality or ethics (we use the words interchangeably in this article) of business decisions. The three most commonly accepted approaches draw on the work of moral philosophers dating back more than two thousand years to Plato and Aristotle. While these philosophers were not familiar with corporations or computers, they did think long and deeply about issues of morality. The fact that their writings are still read and discussed indicates that they have something worthwhile to say.

Ethics is the branch of philosophy that deals with the morality of human decisions and actions, and business ethics deals with them in a business setting. These dry-sounding definitions point to the link between the best work of some deep moral thinkers and particular decisions or actions taken by managers in a contemporary business setting.

While many people get their sense of ethics or morality from their religion, philosophy attempts to reach conclusions about right and wrong behavior without reliance on divinely inspired teaching. It asks what we as humans (rather than as Christians or Buddhists or Muslims) can conclude about the moral rightness or wrongness of our decisions and actions. Ethics also does not assume the moral correctness of laws. In other words, it is not a sufficient moral justification of an act to say that it is legal. After all, what is legal in one state or country may be illegal in another. Most people are troubled to think that the morality of their actions depends on political borders.

Utilitarianism. One approach to determining the morality of a decision or action is utilitarianism, which holds that a moral decision or action is one that results in the greatest good for the greatest number of people. The philosophers most commonly identified with this view are two nineteenth century Englishmen, Jeremy Bentham and John Stuart Mill. The assumption of this approach is that pleasure causes happiness and pain takes it away. Since pleasure and the happiness it causes are the ultimate good for humans, the act that causes the greatest pleasure or happiness for the greatest number of people is the morally good act. This view also assumes that people live in communities and must take this fact into account in deciding on the moral rightness of what they do. While this view may sound simplistic, it is often called upon in business settings to justify or condemn certain actions. We will examine the issue further, but it is common to justify layoff on the basis that terminating 500 people will save the company from bankruptcy and hence preserve the jobs of 2,500 others.

Rights and duties. A second approach to ethical analysis is to examine the issues of rights and duties. The basic position here is that individuals have rights, either as humans, as citizens of a given country or state, or as occupants of a particular position. These rights confer duties on others, and the morality of a given decision or act can be determined by an analysis of these rights and duties. The philosopher most commonly associated with this view is Immanuel Kant. While issues of rights and duties may sound more philosophical and less mathematical than that of determining the greatest good for the greatest number, it is not necessarily so. My right to personal comfort may be outweighed by your right to live. My duty to my family may be outweighed by my duty to serve my country in time of war. Once again, calculation enters into many, but not all, ethical decisions. Few people would question that humans have a basic right to life, and that random killing is morally wrong. A somewhat different question, related to layoffs, is whether workers have a right to their jobs (and, therefore, managers have a duty not to lay them off).

Justice and fairness. The third basic approach involves issues of justice and fairness. While some would treat justice and fairness as issues within the first two approaches, others maintain that they constitute a third approach. Both utilitarianism and rights and duties have been criticized for being unfair in certain cases (Scheffler, 1988). In some situations, you may not have a clear right to your job, and it may not be clear that maintaining your job serves the greatest good of the greatest number, but does not seem fair for you to be terminated when you have been performing well and earning both praises and raises. In the United States, we tend to equate justice with legality, but there are situations where an action that is legal does not seem fair or just. As with the previous two approaches, calculation sometimes enters into considerations of justice and fairness, because it may be impossible in a given situation to be fully fair to everyone involved. The philosopher whose work is most often cited on issues of justice and fairness is John Rawls (1971), a professor at Harvard University.

With this brief summary of the three most common approaches to analyzing issues of managerial ethics, we now turn to the issue of layoffs. Reductions in staff or layoffs are different from termination for cause. An employee who is fired for stealing or fighting on the job is not laid off. Layoffs are also different from reductions in staff that are accomplished by attrition (choosing not to fill vacant positions). There are a variety of reasons why managers may choose to lay-off employees. An ethical or moral analysis of layoffs requires that we identify some of these reasons.

At one extreme is the situation where a company ceases operation, either at the choice of its owners or because of bankruptcy. In this case, obviously, all employees lost their jobs, but this is not usually referred to as a layoff. A similar situation, but not as drastic, occurs when a company is in serious danger of going out of business, and reducing labor costs through layoffs is the only apparent alternative. We will refer to such situations as *layoffs to save the company*. In other situations, layoffs are a preventative measure. In such cases, managers analyze their company's competitive situation, see that it is deteriorating and that labor costs are a significant factor, and move to reduce these costs before the company reaches the life or death stage. We will refer to this category as *layoffs to improve the company*.

In still other situations, layoffs are conducted to improve an already good situation. Here it is the judgment of managers that while the company is not deteriorating, greater profits could be achieved by reducing labor costs. Such layoffs may come about in mergers or acquisitions. Here two companies become one, and frequently plants or offices are closed and their employees laid off to reduce duplication. These layoffs are also conducted to reduce labor costs, but the motivating factor (or at least the precipitating factor) is the merger or acquisition.

Another circumstance in which layoffs are conducted to improve an already good situation involves outsourcing. The theory of core competency, popular in current strategy literature (Prahalad & Hamel, 1990), suggests that a company can perform best by identifying its core competency, concentrating its efforts and its employees on performing core functions, and contracting with other companies to perform other functions. In practice, this can lead to layoffs if a company decides to stop performing certain functions and not to employ those people who formerly carried them out. We will categorize these situations (mergers, acquisitions, and outsourcing) as *layoffs to change the company*. The three categories of layoffs that we have identified (to save, to change, or to improve the company) are not mutually exclusive, but they are sufficiently different to provide a basis for further discussion.

Utilitarianism and Layoffs

On the face of it, deciding the morality of a decision or action by counting may seem strange. Yet it is an approach to decision-making that is frequent in everyday life and in the business world. Businesses in many predominantly Christian countries treat Christmas as a holiday, even though some of their employees and customers are non-Christian. All employees on a certain work shift may be required to start work at the same time even though some might prefer to start a bit earlier or later. The headwaiter who prefers to work in tanktops and cut-off jeans will soon seek other work or a different wardrobe. The greatest good of his fellow employees and the restaurant patrons will outweigh his preference for casual dress.

When a manager terminates an employee who has done nothing wrong, it can scarcely be argued that this is good for the employee. Whether the action is called downsizing, rightsizing, outplacement, or some other term, the terminated employee had a job yesterday and now does not. He or she had a regular salary, health insurance, hopes for promotion, daily social interaction with a group of fellow workers, and an identity as a salesperson or programmer or supervisor. Today these are gone, not because the employee was negligent or lazy or incompetent, but because from management's point of view, the employee was unneeded. The employee was doing a satisfactory or even a superior job in contributing to the company's success, but now has no part in the company's future. It is not surprising that laid-off employees feel that the actions of the manager who terminated them were not right.

The utilitarian argument focuses on obtaining the greatest happiness or good of the greatest number. Happiness is also the goal in other systems of ethics, dating back to Aristotle in the fourth century, B.C. This basis for deciding on moral acts makes some intuitive sense. Most people would probably agree that [it] is morally better, in general, to make people happy than to make them unhappy, to bring them pleasure rather than to bring them grief. What the utilitarian argument maintains is that it is not enough to consider the happiness or unhappiness of a single individual. Attention must be focused on the sum of happiness or grief resulting from a decision or action. Thus, the terminated employee receives pain rather than pleasure from his termination. The manager who conducts the face-to-face interview terminating the employee is likely to suffer grief rather than happiness as a result of the termination interview. If there is any moral justification for this action, it must lie in a greater sum of happiness coming to a larger number of others. An echo of this approach can be heard in the stakeholder analysis approach to issues of business strategy (Freeman, 1984; Freeman & Gilbert, 1988).

This line of reasoning is strengthened if the company, and hence the jobs of employees who are not laid off, can only be saved by reducing the labor force. If this is the case, then the happiness or pleasure of employment for all those who remain justifies the pain of those laid off and those managers who conduct the termination interviews. Further justification can be found in the happiness of stockholders, bondholders, and others who would be hurt by the company's bankruptcy. Given this situation, the utilitarian approach would clearly condone the layoffs as the moral thing to do. But how can we be sure that we are dealing with layoffs to save the company rather than to improve it.

Resolving this issue is not easy. When a company is in serious trouble, there is usually a perceived need to act quickly. Thoughtful consideration of all available alternatives is not likely to occur. Competing by price reductions only worsens a company's financial situation unless there are accompanying cost reductions. Competing by improving the present products or services, or introducing new and better ones, is often not a short-term possibility. Competing by greatly increased marketing efforts is costly, and if the company is already in financial trouble, costly solutions do not appear practical. Reducing staff can be done quickly, and there is ample precedent for such a decision (Cascio, 1993; Mabert & Schmenner, 1997). Accounting rules allow all the costs of staff reduction to be expensed in one quarter, and financial analysts usually see such one-time expenses as good for a company. While not an attractive alternative, a U.S. company in financial trouble can seek protecting by entering Chapter 11 bankruptcy, reorganizing its finances, and continuing as a going concern. As an alternative to layoffs, this solution may postpone the action, but often companies in Chapter 11 bankruptcy reduce staff as part of their reorganization before emerging from bankruptcy. So layoffs are still carried out, and the negative consequences of bankruptcy are added to the mix. In a utilitarian analysis, such a scenario is apt to result in greater unhappiness for more people (suppliers, creditors, shareholders) than would occur with layoffs alone.

In the final analysis, the only way to know for sure whether a company was in a situation of either conducting layoffs or going out of business is to wait and see. Yet it is cold comfort to managers or employees to find out after the fact that layoffs were needed to save the company and that, as a result of inaction, all jobs have been lost. Some uncertainty is inevitable regarding the question of whether the situation involves saving or improving the company. The luxury of waiting for definite answers is simply not available. Hence, we suggest a decision rule which says that if, in the judgment of senior management at the time the layoff decision is made, the situation was one of saving the company, it should be treated as such for purposes of ethical analysis.

Another possibility is that layoffs are not the only step between the present situation and a company's closing, but are seen as a way of dealing with deteriorating performance (layoffs to improve the company). In this case, it is more difficult to conclude that the unhappiness of those laid off and of managers who conduct the terminations is outweighed by a greater good for a greater number of people as a result of the company's improved performance. The unhappiness is clear, the greater good and those who benefit from it is less clear (DeMeuse, Bergmann & Vanderheiden, 1997). In this category of layoffs, the further the situation deviates from a clearcut choice between layoffs and the company's closing, the less compelling the utilitarian argument becomes. However, top managers, by their positions, are charged with the future as well as the present well-being of the company. They are responsible for being proactive as well as reactive. In a situation where layoffs now can prevent a crisis later, choosing layoffs can be the best decision for the greatest number.

In the case of layoffs to improve already adequate performance (layoffs to change the company), the decision might bring happiness to managers whose compensation is tied to company performance through stock options or bonus plans, and to stockholders if the resulting improvements in performance cause the stock price to rise. However, in many cases companies conducting layoffs to improve performance do not attain the hoped-for results (DeMeuse, Vanderheiden & Bergmann, 1977). Even if the results are achieved, unhappiness comes not only to the workers laid off and their managers, but also to many of the workers who remain. They face increased workloads and uncertainty about their own future with the company. Further, the families of those laid off also suffer pain. Workers at competing companies, observing the layoffs earned out by their rival may well suffer pain at the prospect that their own company will lay them off to maintain competitive. Thus, by a utilitarian analysis, it is by no means clear that layoffs to improve a company's position are always moral.

One further point to be noted is that in layoffs to improve the company, management is typically focused on the causal link between reducing the number of employees and improving the company's performance. In layoffs to change the company, managers may focus on the terms of a merger or acquisition agreement, or on the new company structure after a merger, or on the benefits of focusing all management attention on things that make up the company's core competencies. Managers may not give any or enough attention to the issue of layoffs, which might be seen as an administrative detail. The same basic issue needs to be considered in both kinds of layoffs (to improve and to change), but the pressure to complete a change may divert the attention of top managers in situations involving mergers and acquisitions.

The second question concerns how many and which employees are to be laid off. A utilitarian analysis emphasizes the impact of these choices (how many and who) on the results to be obtained. For the choices to be moral, the unhappiness caused must be offset by a greater sum of happiness for others resulting from the company's improved performance.

If labor costs are to be reduced sufficiently to improve competitive performance, the percentage of total employees to be laid off is likely to be impressive. As a starting point, it seems clear that enough employees must remain to produce the company's products or services in a reasonably timely manner and at a reasonably high level of quality. If timeliness or quality slip noticeably, the company's competitive position is likely to deteriorate further and financial performance will continue to worsen. In retailing and some other industries, this issue is often addressed when troubled companies close a number of outlets and lay off all employees who worked in those stores or branches.

If the reason for layoffs is to reduce labor costs, then it seems clear that laying off highly paid employees will reduce cost most. Older employees with greater seniority are normally more highly paid than newer and younger employees. A utilitarian analysis would note that older employees may suffer a greater degree of pain, since they often have a more difficult time finding new jobs than younger employees. Where negotiated contracts between labor and management prevail, unions typically negotiate as part of the contract that any layoffs occurring during the contract period will be based on reverse seniority, with the newest workers being laid off first. Another factor to be considered in a utilitarian analysis is that employees who perform their jobs best provide the most good to the company. Following this approach, the poorest performers should be laid off. However, many companies do not document performance in a way that can serve as a ground for determining layoffs on merit. Others do not choose to follow such an approach, even if they are able to.

A utilitarian approach concludes that layoffs are sometimes ethical, but some circumstances involving the desire to change a company, this approach finds that layoffs are not ethical. This approach emphasizes a consideration of human as well as financial factors and a concern for balancing the unhappiness which such actions bring to some participants with the benefits that result to others. The utilitarian approach does not assume that the company's financial situation is paramount, but does consider that greater good may come to a larger number of people, and that the unhappiness resulting from layoffs, might be morally justified by an analysis of the whole situation. It further considers that, if layoffs are to occur, the basis for deciding who will be laid off is also open to moral analysis.

Of the three approaches to ethical analysis used in this article, utilitarianism is the least abstract. Because major corporate decisions are so often based on impersonal analysis of financial considerations, the utilitarian approach adds an important perspective to those decisions.

Rights, Duties, and Layoffs

Much of philosophy deals with what it means to be human. There is general agreement that humans have a right to live, and that they have this right not because of their citizenship in one or another country, or because of their membership in a religion, or because of their occupation or position in life (Buckle, 1991). If humans have a right to live, then they have a duty not to randomly take each other's lives. In general, rights imply duties. This is obvious with a little thought. If I have a right to privacy, you have a duty not to invade my privacy. If I have a right to free speech, you have a duty not to silence me.

In addition to rights that people may have simply by reason of being human, other rights are conveyed to all or some citizens of a country. In the United States, citizens who are at least 18 and are not felons have a right to vote. Not all humans have this right, but citizens of some countries have it. Rights can also be granted to citizens of a state or province. Citizens can also have duties by virtue of their status as citizens. In time of war, it is generally agreed in many countries that citizens have a duty to perform military service, subject to considerations of age and physical conditions. This is not a mere theoretical duty; in time of war it may be a duty to die in combat.

A third group of rights consists of those a person may have by virtue of their positions in a company or agency. A supervisor may have the right to sign company checks for up to $5,000, while the chief financial officer may have the right to sign for up to $5 million. A police officer has the right to apprehend and jail a suspect, while ordinary citizens do not. These rights can be very powerful in practice. The central point is that a person has these rights not as a human or as a citizen, but by virtue of occupying a certain position.

It is important in conducting an ethical analysis to distinguish legal rights and duties from moral rights and duties. They often overlap: most people agree that random killing is both legally and morally wrong. However, they are not always identical. In the not-so-distant past, it was illegal to drive over 55 miles per hour in the U.S., but one could argue that it was not morally wrong. If legal and moral rights and duties are always identical, then a change in the legal speed limit results in a change in the moral rightness of driving at a certain speed. A further argument against identity of legal and moral rights and duties lies in the source of laws. In the U.S., federal laws that apply to all citizens are made by Congress. Many people are uneasy with the idea of Congress as their source of moral right and wrong.

The law in the U.S. as to whether an employer can terminate an employee at will (for any reason or no reason) varies from state to state (Halbert & Ingulli, 1997). Federal law prohibits termination for some reasons (age, gender, disability). In cases where a labor-management contract determines wages and conditions of work, grounds for termination are usually specific and limited. Whatever rights to a job an employee has under such agreements come from the employee's membership in a group covered by the negotiated contract. Applying a rights and duties approach to the ethical analysis of layoffs, it appears that the central question is whether an employee has a moral right to his or her job, and whether supervisors then have a corresponding moral duty not to determinate that employee until he or she forfeits that right.

Upon reflection, it is clear that an employee does not have an absolute right to retain a job. An employee who shoots his boss or is caught embezzling large amounts of money does not have a right to keep a job. A more limited question involves the right of an employee to keep a job as long as he or she is performing it satisfactorily. It is difficult to see the basis of such a right. As indicated, some rights come from our status as humans. Philosophers have argued for right to life, and to rights to truth-telling and private property, but not for a right to keep a job. With some few exceptions, U.S. employees do not have legal rights (rights as a citizen) to keep their jobs as long as they perform well. Some countries do provide such rights; others provide less legal job protection than the U.S. The third source of rights is from status in an organization, but the general status of employee does not in and of itself seem to confer the right to keep a job. Additional light is shed on this issue by considering it under our third basis of analysis, namely that of fairness and justice, in the next section.

The moral analysis of layoffs in terms of rights and duties requires an emphasis on the individual. What a manager may or may not morally do is determined by examining the rights of the individual employee. If the manager has a duty to retain the employee the duty results from the employee's right. If the manager is free to determine whether the employee keeps or loses a job, and can morally make either decision, in terms of this analysis the manager has that freedom because the employee does not have a right which constrains the manager's freedom. This part of the analysis, then, concludes that under a rights and duties approach, managers are not morally prohibited from conducting layoffs.

Managers have duties by virtue of their positions as manager. Top managers have a duty to act in the best interests of their company and its stakeholders; a wealth of literature on agency theory analyzes the manager's role as an agent for the owners or stockholders of a company (Eisenhardt, 1989). In the extreme case that characterizes our first category, where layoffs provide the only means to save the company, one could argue that top managers have a duty to do what is best for the company, and that in this case conducting layoffs is best. This approach leads to the conclusion that managers sometimes have a duty to conduct layoffs, and that failure to act on this duty would be unethical.

It is considerably less clear whether managers have a duty to conduct layoffs to improve or to change their company. Because such attempts in the past have often failed to improve performance (DeMeuse, Bergmann & Vanderheiden, 1997), it makes sense to ask whether managers have a duty to take steps that might fail. The discussion of rights and duties leads to the conclusion that managers have a right to conduct layoffs in these situations (since employees do not have an overriding right to keep their jobs); it is much harder to prove that they have a duty to do so. If they have a right to conduct layoffs to improve or change the company, then under this method of analysis, it would not be unethical to do so. Particularly in the case of layoffs to change the company, when performance is already good, it does not appear that a credible arguments can be made for a managerial duty to conduct lay-offs.

A related issue is whether an employee has a right to be treated fairly in terms of keeping a job or losing it, and what comprises such fair treatment. It is difficult to argue that an employee has no right to be treated fairly, but what constitutes fair treatment is where difficulty arises. Analysis of this issue leads to the third basic approach to determining the morality of decision.

Fairness, Justice, and Layoffs

Whether it is children complaining of their parents, baseball players complaining about an umpire's call, or employees complaining about their supervisors, disagreements about fairness and justice are commonplace. In everyday language, most people tend to equate fairness and justice, and conversely, unfairness and injustice. It seems like only a small step to say that a decision that is fair and just is also ethical or moral. As we did with rights and duties, we need to note specifically the relation between justice or fairness and the law. While they are often the same, it is possible to find examples of unjust laws and also to find examples of things not legally required that are still fair and just. In our analysis of the fairness and justice approach to ethics, then, we will not automatically assume that justice means legal justice.

A philosophical approach tries to remove the level of analysis from what an individual perceives to be fair and just, and to prescribe some rules and guidelines that can be applied across many situations. Many philosophers, beginning with Plato discuss justice as involving a sense of proportion. The just reward for a heroic deed is greater than for a minor, inconsequential action. The punishment for murder is greater than for petty theft. An unjust consequence (reward or punishment) is one that is out of proportion to the action that triggers it. Justice, in most philosophical analyses, also involves a sense of consistency. If certain actions are judged worthy of reward or punishment, each person who performs the action should, in justice, receive the same reward or punishment. This idea is sometimes expressed in the statement that those similarly situated should receive similar treatment (White, 1993: 79–129).

Perhaps the most frequently cited modern philosopher to discuss justice is John Rawls. His major work, *A Theory of Justice* (1971), analyzes justice not in terms of individual actions, but in terms of social systems. He suggests that one way to decide whether a social system is just is to ask what we would think of it if we were behind a veil of ignorance and did not know what our position was in that system. In other words, if we did not know whether we would be ruler or ruled, well-to-do or poor, talented or unskilled, would we judge the distribution of benefits and burdens, rewards and punishments, to be fair? Rawls, like philosophers, attempts to state analytic principles that can be used to judge particular cases and determine their fairness or justice.

Applying this analysis to the question of layoffs, it appears that a central question is that of the fairness to the laid-off employee. Since the employee has, by our earlier definition of the situation, performed well and done nothing to trigger termination, it does not appear that there is a proportion between the action (termination) and the preceding behavior (satisfactory performance). It also does not appear that the principle of consistency is followed, since some employees who have performed well lost their jobs, while others who have performed similarly remain employed.

An approach that is sometimes taken in the name of fairness is to lay off a certain percentage of employees "across the board." In practice, this means that each division or department or region must lay off some percentage of its employees. This does not solve the problem of fairness or consistency but merely shifts it to a lower level of decision-maker. Under this approach, the head of each unit must still decide which employees will keep their jobs and which will lose them. A disadvantage of this approach is that it disconnects layoff decisions from improving the company's performance, since it is rare that all units are equally overstaffed or equally important in their contribution to the company's overall performance.

Viewed from the perspective of the social system or the whole company, the discussion of fairness changes. In the extreme case, where failure to reduce labor costs by conducting layoffs results in the company's closing, all employees lose their jobs. If we were behind Rawls' veil of ignorance, we would certainly not choose this as a fair arrangement. Only a twisted kind of logic can defend everyone losing jobs as better than only some.

As the cause for layoffs deviates from the clearcut case where they represent the only way to avoid the company's closing, the argument from fairness when the system is viewed as a whole becomes weaker. Layoffs taken as a proactive step to forestall problems management foresees are less clearcut but still defensible. If layoffs are conducted to increase the profits of an already profitable firm, it is unlikely that a person behind Rawls' veil of ignorance would consider the system allowing this to be just.

Would it be fair and just if the employees laid off were those with the least seniority or those who, while performing adequately, did not perform as well as others who retain their jobs? From the point of view of the system, seniority or merit present arguably consistent bases for deciding who loses their job and who keeps it. We should note, however, that relative seniority is much easier to establish than relative merit in performance. From the point of view of the individual, although these approaches attain some consistency, the problem of lack of proportion remains.

Rawls would argue that we cannot lightly pass over the system point of view in analyzing moral fairness and justice. His argument here is similar to one used in another context by Ackoff (1981), who maintains that many management problems are better understood by thinking about the system of which the particular problem is a part (synthesis) rather than by breaking the problem into its constituent parts (analysis).

Grant for the sake of argument that we live in a less-than-perfect world where layoffs are necessary from time to time to preserve a company as a going concern. In this situation, if we were behind Rawls' veil of ignorance, would we approve of a system of layoffs based on either seniority or merit. In other words, is this a fair and just system?

Of the two approaches, merit would appear to be more defensible, since it ties the goal of layoffs (improved company performance) to the judgment of which individuals should suffer layoffs (those who contribute least to the company's performance). Seniority might be defensible if there is not sufficient evidence to use merit. The defense of seniority would lie in the fact that it is measurable and might be seen as a proxy for individual performance in the sense that employees with more experience will, in general, contribute more to the company's performance than those with less experience. Rawls would then ask whether we could conceive of a more fair system that was practical enough to work in the real world. If not, then by his analysis fairness and justice would be observed, and the layoff actions would be moral.

The fairness and justice approach requires an emphasis on more than just the individual, who is the center of the rights and duties approach. Questions of fairness and justice address issues of proportion and consistency, but within a narrower setting than that addressed by the utilitarian approach. Of the three methods for ethical analysis, then, utilitarianism takes the widest view, considering the greatest good of the greatest number, whoever and wherever they might be. A major criticism of this approach is that it neglects important individual concerns. The rights and duties approach, as we have noted, centers on the individual, and looks out from the individual's rights to those on whom these rights impose duties. The fairness and justice approach considers both the individual and the social system within which he or she operates. The major focus of this approach is limited to a company or agency or possibly a community.

Comments and Conclusion

We have applied the three basic theories commonly used in managerial ethics to analyze the issue of the morality of layoffs. The views of these three basic theories generally coincide. In the extreme case where layoffs are the only way to save a company, the utilitarian approach finds the decision to conduct layoffs to be moral, because the layoffs generate the greatest good for the greatest number. The rights and duties approach sees the action of layoffs in the same situation to be moral because employees do not have absolute rights to their jobs. However, this view also requires that layoffs be conducted in a fair and just manner, because employees do have a right to be treated fairly. Finally, the justice and fairness approach, does not find layoffs to be moral, because they lack proportionality between the individual's behavior (good performance) and the resulting action (termination of employment). However, when the focus is changed from fairness to each individual to fairness in the total system, layoffs are justified—at least when the alternative is that all employees lose their jobs. Since all the individuals involved are part of the system, a reasonable argument can be made that the system view is the more appropriate one to be used here. Given that layoffs are to be conducted, this approach finds seniority or merit to be moral bases for determining who will lose jobs and who will keep them.

In the opposite extreme case, where layoffs are proposed in an attempt to change a company that is already performing well and does not appear to be in danger, none of the three approaches supports the conclusion that such layoffs are ethical. In this situation, the greatest good for the greatest number is not achieved. While employees do not have rights to their jobs, managers do not have a duty to conduct such layoffs. Finally, justice and fairness are not served.

What is a manager to do in the large middle ground where the three approaches to ethical analysis do not yield clear answers? First, it is useful to note that the three approaches use different bases for deciding what is a moral act. It is clear from the history of ethics and the disputes among thoughtful individuals, that ethics is not like mathematics. It does not yield indisputable conclusions (at least, not all the time). Managers bring to their decisions their own sense of right and wrong and their own set of priorities among the three systems outlined in this article. In the last analysis, ethics is at least as much about how to think as what to think.

Yet, managers must ultimately decide whether to conduct layoffs or not. If the decision is for layoffs, they must then decide how many employees, and which ones, are to lose their jobs. Thinking through the decision in the way outlined in this article shows that ethical implications are involved in the layoff decision. Analyzing the decision and its consequences from three different perspectives brings out considerations that might otherwise have been missed. Understanding the factors involved from different perspectives presents a fuller basis for making judgments. Finally the manager must choose, even when the analysis does not provide a clear right answer.

Decision making often involves ambiguity, and top managers are selected for their ability to make decisions under uncertainty. As the cause for layoffs shifts from saving the company to improving the company (correcting performance which is deteriorating) to changing the company (mergers, acquisitions, outsourcing), each of the three ethical analyses provides less and less support for layoffs. We have outlined basic approaches to determining whether an action or decision is moral. As the moral justification of layoffs becomes less clear, the concern that managers may be acting immorally increases. The strength of the argument for "last-ditch" layoffs (reduce staff or close) carries over to cases where a worsening situation will later lead to the worse-case scenario. The weakness of the argument for layoffs when company performance is excellent and there is no apparent danger on the horizon also carries over to cases that are not quite as positive.

Managers who find themselves faced with decisions in such gray areas can apply the analytic tools outlined here. They can then make their decision knowing that they have identified the right issues and applied well-established methods for analysis. Managers who do not make such decisions, yet must carry them out, can better understand the ethical issues involved. Sorrow because of the suffering caused by layoffs may be unavoidable and appropriate. Guilt because a manager feels he or she did something morally wrong can be addressed and perhaps eliminated by the thoughtful exercise of moral judgment.

REFERENCES

Ackoff, R. (1981). *Creating the Corporate Future*, New York: John Wiley and Sons.

Aristotle, *The Nichomachean Ethics*, J. Harper, translator, Baltimore, MD: Penguin Books, 1953.

Arneson D., Fleenor C., & Toh, R.S. (1997, January–February). The ethical dimensions of airline frequent flier program, *Business Horizons* 40:1, 47–56.

Bentham, J. *An Introduction to the Principles of Morals and Legislation* (London: 1823); J.H. Burns and H.L.A. Hart, Eds. (London: Athlone Press, 1970).

Buckle, S. (1991). Natural Law, in Peter Singer, Ed., *A Companion to Ethics*, Cambridge MA: Blackwell, 161–174.

Cascio, W. (1993). Downsizing: What do we know? What have we learned? *Academy of Management Executive*, 7(1). 95–104.

Childs, J., Jr., (1997, March). Lutheran perspectives on ethical business in an age of downsizing, *Business Ethics Quarterly* 7(2). 123–131.

DeGeorge, R., *Business Ethics*, Fourth Edition, (Englewoods Cliffs, NJ: Prentice-Hall, 1995).

DeMeuse, K., Bergmann, P., & Vanderheiden. (1997, June). Corporate downsizing: Separating myth from fact, *Journal of Management Inquiry* 6(2). 168–176.

Eisenhardt, K. (1989, January). Agency theory: An assessment and review, *Academy of Management Review* 14(1). 57–74.

Freeman, R.E. (1984). *Strategic Management; A Stakeholder Approach*, Marshfield MA: Pittman.

Freeman, R.E., & Gilbert, D.R. (1988). *Corporate strategy and the search for ethics*, Englewood Cliffs, NJ: PrenticeHall.

Halbert, T. & Ingulli, E. (1997). *Law and ethics in the business environment*, Second Edition, Minneapolis/St. Paul: West Publishing.

Kant, I. (1997). *Critique of Practical Reason*, translated by L.W. Beck. Indianapolis: Bobbs-Merrill.

Mabert, V. , & Schmenner, R. (1997, July–August). Assessing the roller coaster of down-sizing, *Business Horizons*, 49(4). 45–53.

McCann, D. (1997, March). Catholic social teaching in an era of downsizing: A resource for business ethics, *Business Ethics Quarterly*, 7(2). 57–70.

Mill, J.S., *Utilitarianism* (London: 1863); in M. Warnock, Ed., Mill: *Utilitarianism and Other Writings* (Glasgow: Collins, 1962).

Piper T., Gentile, M., & Parks, S. (1993). *Can ethics be taught?* Boston MA: Harvard Business School.

Plato, *The Collected Dialogues*, E. Hamilton and H. Cairns, Eds. (New York NY: Pantheon Books, 1961).

Prahalad, C.K., & Hamel, G. (1990, May–June). The core competence of the corporation, *Harvard Business Review*. 79–91.

Rawls, J. (1971). *A theory of justice*, Cambridge, MA: Harvard University Press.

Scheffler, S. (1988). (Ed.), *Consequentialism and its critics*, New York NY: Oxford University Press.

Valesquez, M., & Rostankowski, (1982). *Ethics: Theory and practice*, Englewood Cliffs, NJ: Prentice-Hall.

White, T., (1993). *Business ethics: A philosophical reader*, New York NY: Macmillan.

Williams, G., (1992). *Ethics in modern management*, New York, NY: Quorum Books.

Dr. Gilbert teaches strategy and management ethics in the MBA program and team-teaches law, regulation, and ethics; his research has been published in a number of journals.

THE WHISTLE-BLOWER

A HERO—AND A SMOKING-GUN LETTER

Watkins' memo spoke volumes about Enron's behavior. So did higher-ups' tepid response

At last, someone in the sordid Enron Corp. scandal seems to have done the right thing. Thanks to whistle-blower Sherron S. Watkins, a no-nonsense Enron vice-president, the scope and audacity of the accounting mess is becoming all too clear. Her blunt Aug. 15 letter to Enron CEO Kenneth L. Lay warns that the company might "implode in a wave of accounting scandals." And now that her worst fears have been realized, it is also clear that Watkins' letter went far beyond highlighting a few accounting problems in a handful of off-balance-sheet partnerships. Watkins' letter lays bare for all to see the underbelly of Enron's get-rich-quick culture.

Watkins, 42, a former Arthur Andersen accountant who remains Enron's vice-president for corporate development, put her finger on the rot: top execs who, at best, appeared to close their eyes to questionable accounting maneuvers; a leadership that had lost sight of ordinary investors and the basic principles of accounting; and watchdogs—the outside auditors and lawyers whose own involvement may have left them too conflicted to query the nature of the deals. Perhaps the question shouldn't be how Enron collapsed so quickly—but why it didn't implode sooner.

Lay's response to Watkins' complaints is nearly as damning as her letter itself. Yes, he talked to her for an hour. And, yes, he ordered an outside investigation. But contrary to Watkins' advice, he appointed the company's longtime Houston law firm, Vinson & Elkins, despite the obvious conflict: V&E had worked on some of the partnerships. And Enron and V&E agreed there would be no "second-guessing" of Andersen's accounting and no "detailed analysis" of each and every transaction, according to V&E's Oct. 15 report. The inquiry was to consider only if there was new factual information that warranted a broader investigation. V&E declined comment.

Surprise: V&E concluded that a widespread investigation wasn't warranted. It simply warned that there was a "serious risk of adverse publicity and litigation." And Watkins' letter reveals the inadequacy of Lay's response in the months following CEO Jeffrey K. Skilling's sudden Aug. 14 resignation for "personal reasons." His departure triggered the letter. Lay never fully disclosed the partnerships or explained their impact to investors, even as he vowed there were no accounting issues and "no other shoe to fall." Even after Enron revealed on Oct. 16 a $1.2 billion hit to shareholder equity related to the partnerships, Lay continued to express ignorance about details of these deals and support for Chief Financial Officer Andrew S. Fastow, who managed and had stakes in certain partnerships. But on Oct. 24, Fastow was removed from his job and promptly left the company.

Watkins, an eight-year Enron veteran, is not some disgruntled naysayer who is easy to dismiss. Her lawyer, Philip H. Hilder, says she became familiar with some of the partnership dealings when she worked in June and July in Fastow's finance group. Her position allowed her to review the valuation of certain assets being sold into the partnerships, and that's when she saw "computations that just didn't jibe," says Hilder.

Former executives say the Tomball (Tex.) native was tenacious and competent. "She wasn't really an alarmist," says one

Skilling's abrupt departure will raise suspicions of accounting improprieties and valuation issues.

I am incredibly nervous that we will implode in a wave of accounting scandals. My 8 years of

I realize that we have had a lot of smart people looking at this and a lot of accountants including AA&Co. have blessed the accounting treatment. None of that will protect Enron if these transactions are ever disclosed in the bright light of day.

former Enron employee. Her mother, Shirley Klein Harrington, a former high school accounting teacher, calls her daughter "a very independent, outspoken, good Christian girl, who's going to stand up for principle whenever she can." Watkins had previously worked at Andersen in Houston and New York and then for Germany's Metallgesellschaft AG.

At those companies, she befriended Jeffrey McMahon, whom she helped recruit. Now the CFO at Enron, McMahon "complained mightily" about the Fastow partnerships to Skilling, Watkins told Lay in the letter. "Employees question our accounting propriety consistently and constantly," she claimed. McMahon didn't return calls. Skilling has denied getting any warnings about accounting.

Watkins didn't stop there. Five days after she wrote to Lay, Watkins took her concerns directly to an Andersen audit partner, according to congressional investigators. He in turn relayed her questions to senior Andersen management on the Enron account. It's not known what, if any, action they took.

Of course, Skilling and Andersen execs shouldn't have needed a letter and a phone call from Watkins to figure out something was seriously amiss. Red flags abounded. And Watkins, for one, had no trouble putting her finger on questionable accounting practices. She wondered if Enron was hiding losses in off-balance-sheet entities while booking large profits from the deals. At the same time, the outside partnerships were backed with Enron stock—a tactic sure to backfire when it was falling—and no outsiders seemed to have any capital at risk. Was Enron creating income essentially by doing deals with itself? "It sure looks to the layman on the street that we are hiding losses in a related company and will compensate that company with Enron stock in the future," she wrote.

In the end, Watkins grasped one thing that Enron's too-clever-by-half dealmakers didn't: Enron's maneuvering didn't pass the smell test. Even if Enron and its high-priced auditors and lawyers can ultimately show that they followed the letter of the law, it matters little. As Watkins herself wrote, if Enron collapses, "the business world will consider the past successes as nothing but an elaborate accounting hoax." And that seems destined to become Enron's epitaph.

By Wendy Zellner, with Stephanie Forest Anderson, in Dallas and with Laura Cohn in Washington

Blowing whistles, blowing smoke

In the halls of Congress and the columns of newspapers, all whistle-blowers are saints. But the truth is a little more complicated.

BY DAN SELIGMAN

WHISTLE-BLOWERS HAVE BEEN onstage a lot lately. A Nexis search yields 2,700 articles thus far in 1999 mentioning them. In the vast majority of these articles, it is assumed that the whistle-blower in question is a selfless protector of the public good. It is high time we examined this assumption.

One of these articles reported Al Pacino's embrace of a new script in which he plays a *60 Minutes* producer working with a tobacco industry whistle-blower. Nonfictional entries included the Microsoft internal auditor who spoke up and said the company's bookkeeping did not conform to Generally Accepted Accounting Principles. Also Predrag Markovic, said to have been fired for whistle-blowing on alleged corruption in the New York City School Construction Authority. Also assorted witnesses testifying against Columbia/HCA Healthcare for its suspected overbilling of the government in connection with Medicare reimbursements.

Perhaps the biggest media sensation of all was the saga of Jennifer Long, the IRS auditor who had earlier (September 1997) denounced what she characterized as the agency's brutality in Senate Finance Committee testimony and now (April 1999) appeared to be on the verge of getting vengefully fired for this exercise in whistle-blowing.

Whistle-blowers are ordinarily depicted as lone voices of reason, driven by idealism, courageously standing up to lawless bureaucracies, selflessly risking careers to get out the truth. This has long been the only view deemed socially acceptable in Washington. It was unmistakably on display a decade ago, when Congress passed the Whistle-Blowers Protection Act of 1989 without a single recorded nay.

This law encourages federal employees to step forward and point to fraud, waste and abuse in their agencies, and offers them considerable protection against retaliation. But that's only one highly generalized whistle-blower act. An avalanche of other federal laws on air pollution, consumer protection, occupational safety, safe drinking water, energy conservation, solid waste disposal—you name it—redundantly provide similar mixes of encouragement and protection to folks inside the agencies wishing to step up to the plate. And numerous state laws offer whistle-blower protection to both government and private sector idealists who believe their employers are doing something evil.

What's wrong with all these laws? Their failure to acknowledge the possibility that whistle-blowers are mere human beings like you and me, who go through life thinking deeply about what's best for number one. Also, the possibility that when you offer special job protection to whistle-blowers, then any human being needing job protection will suddenly have a huge incentive to blow a whistle if he can get his hands on one.

This is not to deny that some of the high-profile cases of recent months featured truly conscientious employees driven to step forward and point up outrages. The Energy Department employees who blew the whistle on the pillaging of military secrets by Chinese spies really do seem to have been performing a public service.

But some of the other cases are more nuanced. When you look at the facts more closely, you discover that the Microsoft internal auditor had been discharged for poor performance before getting into the whistle-blowing business, and the School Construction Authority official blew the whistle only after losing his job. It is hard for outsiders to judge the merits of each case, but it seems reasonable—and unsurprising—to note that a high fraction of whistle-blowing is performed by folks with personal reasons to be sore at their bosses. I recently spoke with Jeffery Trinca, a lawyer now in private practice, who in 1997 was chief of staff of the national commission to restructure the IRS, and he observed: "You have to be careful about whistleblower cases. An awful lot of the time, there's another agenda."

Then there is the case of Jennifer Long, the IRS whistle-blower. The story line pounded home by the media was that (1) she was being fired by the IRS for her prior revelations before the Finance Committee; (2) this action signified the total depravity of the IRS; and (3) Long kept her job only because Finance Committee Chairman William Roth of Delaware came riding to the rescue. My own take is that it is possible to (1) hate the IRS with a vengeance and also (2) admire tax-cutter Bill Roth, while (3) still sensing that there was a huge amount of baloney in the whistleblower story he sold the press.

From the *New York Times* to Sam Donaldson on *20/20*, the mighty American media played it the same way. The heroine was a noble IRS agent who had received top performance reviews until she blew the whistle. She said the agency fabricated evidence against taxpayers and selectively targeted poor, uneducated folks with little ability to defend themselves. She was a profile in courage—she had appeared on camera during the proceedings, while other IRS whistle-blowers testified while seated behind screens and using voice-modification equipment that left them sounding like Bugs Bunny. Intoned the *Times:* "The fact that her employers had no inhibitions about harassing her is clear evidence that the laws protecting whistle-blowers need to be strengthened."

> Take care with whistle-blowers: Even when they're right, they sometimes have an agenda of their own.

It was very hard this year to find any back talk to this party line on whistle-blowers. (One rare exception: a not-for-profit magazine called *Tax Notes*, published in Arlington, Va.) A more skeptical view might have pointed up some awkward details about the Finance Committee's presentation.

Contrary to endlessly reiterated statements in the press and on *20/20*, Jennifer Long had not received repeated rave reviews before her 1997 testimony. In fact, her work had been severely critiqued for several years, and she had reason to fear for her job. Her problems in 1996 are lengthily particularized in a race- and age-discrimination suit she brought against the IRS shortly after her testimony. Long, who is white, complained in the suit that she was being victimized by some of her black bosses in the agency—details that have gone broadly unmentioned in this year's media frenzy and were also unmentioned in her 1997 testimony, where any such allegations would, to be sure, have sent the Finance Committee script orbiting in directions uncontrollable.

Her decision to appear on camera was not an act of courage, but of prudence. It was proposed by her attorney precisely because he felt the public identification would make it harder for the agency to fire her—a judgment that turns out to have been quite shrewd.

Would Long have been a whistleblower if she hadn't received those repeated criticisms before the Finance Committee opportunity came along? Probably not. I asked her, in a recent telephone interview, whether she would have testified if the hearings had been held five years earlier, and she said no, adding: "I believed in the system then."

Big question: Were her allegations supported by the evidence? After her 1997 testimony, the IRS agreed to an examination of her charges, to be made by the Treasury Department's Office of the Inspector General. On a few issues, e.g., the tendency of the Houston office to favor managers over subordinates in disciplinary cases, the inspectors supported her views. But in most instances they found against her. After examining returns audited in Houston, they found no evidence that low-income taxpayers were being targeted, and no evidence of fabricating evidence against taxpayers.

It's a terrible thing to be defending the IRS, of all agencies. But I have to do that here.

Intentional Integrity

There are many things that might be legal or in line with policy but might be wrong ethically.

SCOTT W. VENTRELLA

INTEGRITY IS ACTING ON A PERSONAL commitment to honesty, openness, and fairness—living by and for our standards. The word "integrity" is derived from the Latin word *integer*, meaning "whole." Integrity is a centering power. It provides us with the navigational tools to guide us through the fuzzy ethical landscape.

We show integrity each time we use consistent and appropriate criteria to measure our own behavior and performance; use ethics, morals, and principles to guide our activities; do not undermine or criticize others behind their backs; acknowledge our own weaknesses; recognize others' efforts and give them credit; strive to create "win-win" outcomes with others; and do what is right, even though there may be easier, more expedient solutions.

Integrity is acting on personal commitment. It's not merely holding a moral or principled idea or position. Honesty includes truth, but should we tell the whole truth and nothing but the truth? Are there times when it is better to hold back parts of the truth? How open should we be with people?

We face many ethical dilemmas regularly. Consider the following situations: 1) Taking office supplies home for personal use; 2) Searching the Web for job opportunities on company time; 3) Going to a pornographic Web site during your lunch break; 4) Using the phone for personal use on company time; 5) Calling in sick when you are healthy; 6) Putting a personal item in your expense report as a business expense; 7) Paying somebody off because "that's the way they do business in this country"; 8) Having your assistant tell someone that you're in a meeting when you're not.

Do you consider these activities: 1) wrong—anyone caught doing this should be asked to leave the company immediately; 2) borderline—not terribly wrong, but something doesn't seem right either; or 3) totally acceptable behavior—everybody does it.

For some the choice (or decision) is a matter of interpretation. Others would say that it depends on circumstances. But for those who work in companies with established policies, the choice is clear.

While there are no easy answers to ethical dilemmas, I suggest that we adopt a "platinum standard" of ethics—truths we can turn to when we are confronted with ethical issues.

1. Question your motives. In *The Power of Ethical Management*, Norman Vincent Peale and Ken Blanchard ask: 1) Is it legal and in line with policy? If what you are doing or about to do is illegal or against policy, don't do it! 2) Is it fair to all concerned? If it's exclusionary or benefits only certain people, don't do it! And 3) "In the end, how will I feel about myself? Would I like it if my actions were broadcast for all to hear?"

2. Practice what you preach. Does your character match your actions? Do not ask others to do anything that you would not do. Know what you believe in. "We lie loudest when we lie to ourselves," noted Eric Hoffer.

3. Be your own investigative reporter. Imagine a reporter accompanies you to work and on business trips—listening to your phone conversations, sharing your mail, and observing your actions. What story would the reporter write?

4. Keep your commitments. When you say you will do something, do your associates believe you will, or do they doubt? If you make promises lightly, they will be taken lightly.

5. Learn to say "no" to things for which you have no time, talent, or sincere interest. By saying "no" to such things, you can say "yes" to what matters most.

6. Build and maintain your integrity. The two most sought-after qualities of a top executive are honesty and loyalty.

Scott W. Ventrella is principal of Positive Dynamics and author of The Power of Positive Thinking in Business: The 10 Traits for Maximum Results *(The Free Press $24) www.positivedynamics.com.*

Excuses, Excuses: Moral Slippage in the Workplace

Kevin Gibson

The 1991 Federal Sentencing Guidelines (FSG) have brought new urgency to questions of morality in the workplace. Under these guidelines, a corporation faces liability if it has demonstrated a pattern of noncompliance with a corporate code of conduct, or improper behavior. Once corporate morality was a question of sifting out "bad apples," but now more than ever we need to be concerned with the overall moral climate in a corporation.

Why do otherwise decent people deviate from what they know to be right? Naturally, some noncompliance stems from deliberate wrongdoing by particular individuals. But there are some common rationalizations to which we can all unconsciously fall prey. Once we recognize the dubious worth of these kinds of excuses, we can effectively influence the corporate moral climate.

Instituting a moral workplace has a direct bottom-line consequence. The FSG mandates multiplying a standard set of fines for a company with a history of noncompliance or lack of institutional involvement. This has sent the message that companies need to actively promote an ethical work environment. Moreover, a clear moral direction and commitment are likely to reduce lawsuits and white-collar crime, estimated at costing American business $400 billion a year.

Ethical audits of businesses tend to be concerned with whether or not a company has a code of conduct and, if so, its rates of compliance with the code. Codes are valuable in several ways. Constructive codes can give individuals some cognitive assistance in determining a reference point for judging what is ethical, especially when the person is trying to evaluate the rightness of a decision by its consequences. The modern corporation, large or small, may serve many distant markets and different constituent groups, and individuals may well be unable to gauge the full range of results of their behavior without the benefit of the "big picture."

A well-crafted code can give particular advice, instances of ideal and unacceptable behavior, and the framework to aid in making moral decisions. It can provide a wider perspective on issues and a context for corporate actions. It also has the advantage of being objective, in the sense that it gives a moral grounding that is impersonal and available to all.

Codes of conduct function well when employees are confronted with straightforward issues or legal matters, such as whether a creditor may call late at night or whether individuals may use corporate property for personal use. They are less successful, though, when the issues are vague, novel, or difficult. In these cases, the FSG requires that employees be acquainted with the principles behind the rules, so they are able to discern what to do. Ethics training, then, should deal with both the corporate code of conduct and individual moral choices.

There is a wide spectrum of "gray" cases that depend on individual moral discretion. Specific dynamics in moral reasoning may color our thinking, allowing us to be complacent or compliant in behaviors we would usually never agree with. Workplace ethics must be based on personal moral accountability rather than simple compliance with an external code.

The moral "buck" stops with real individuals rather than abstract organizations.

Very often, organizations and managers talk of ethics in terms of how to encourage and reward "the right thing to do." This constitutes a behaviorist approach suggesting that individuals are almost completely shaped by external forces. Although it is undoubtedly true that people are motivated by rewards and punishments, these mechanisms tell only part of the story. Individuals with a developed moral sense are also likely to act morally based on their ideas of conventions, social order, or larger principles. But it is also true that people have freedom of conscience and action, so we should not explain away their behavior merely by criticizing abstract, impersonal organizations. Individuals are ultimately the authors and arbiters of their actions, for better or worse, and therefore retain ultimate responsibility for what they do.

Businesses need to be concerned with the overall moral environment and the ways in which good people may unwittingly take part in morally questionable activities. Ignoring these dynamics results in significant internal losses and external sanctions. The discussion here is not exhaustive, of course, but it does address a number of common yet often unquestioned moral excuses.

FOUR TYPES OF EXCUSES

Part of figuring out how to make ethical decisions when confronted with difficult dilemmas has to do with recognizing the ways we reason about such situations. Religious, philosophical, and psychological input may be useful here. But external factors that are beyond our control may also affect the level at which we reason, and thus the ultimate decisions we make as individuals. Indeed, in the presence of some external factors, individuals may not actively reason at all, but work according to habit or obedience without a thought. Thus, if we are to encourage and implement more ethical behavior in business, it is important to consider the types of external factors that may influence our individual choices when we are faced with ethical dilemmas. Simple awareness of their existence and the ways in which they exert influence on our behaviors may be enough to lessen their power.

I Was Told to Do It

The power of authority to sway the opinions and behaviors of subordinates is one such external factor. Obedience to authority is often a simple way out of a difficult situation. Our personal values conflict, but if an authority figure commands us to make a particular response, we feel relieved of the stress of the situation because we no longer feel responsible for our actions. We dissociate ourselves from the decision and the resulting behavior because we see the cause as the authoritarian command rather than our action.

This tendency to obey authority is an integral part of the functioning of many companies. Business partners and the general public often rely on consistent and predictable activity in a firm. Employees who obey authority keep the corporate machine running smoothly and predictably. Furthermore, hierarchical structures of power often reflect disparate abilities. Most people in positions of authority have attained those positions because of expertise or superior judgment, and obedience to appropriate authority is an essential part of efficient organizational operation.

The problem, of course, is that not all of the orders that originate from authority figures are moral. Nevertheless, we often obey them, without hesitation, out of habit. Workers often simply obey without thinking. Gialdini (1984) refers to this as the "click/whirr response," in which workers "stop thinking... and start reacting." But even when we force ourselves to consider the situation we face rather than blindly obeying, we are still strongly influenced by the presence and power of authority.

Authority as a motivator is so strong that it often exerts its influence without any explicit orders. This was shown by Brief, Dukerich, and Doran (1991), who found that managers often chose to act against their own values in order to remain in line with an authority figure, even in the absence of explicit demands. The researchers set up a situation in which subjects assumed the role of managers who had to cast absentee ballots for a board meeting vote regarding an ethical dilemma faced by the company. The dilemma involved what the company should do about a drug it already produced and marketed, which was about to be banned by the FDA and had been declared less effective than other available drugs but more than twice as likely to produce detrimental side effects, including death. When the subjects were not told about the views of the chairman of the board, they voted based on their personal values. The subjects who were told of the chairman's preferences almost universally reflected his views in their votes. The authors suggest that in the face of authority we often simply cease critical assessment and become agents of a superior.

Similarly, in Stanley Milgram's famous experiment, more than half the subjects obeyed orders to administer severe electric shocks to an apparent victim who was pounding on the wall pleading for them to stop. Milgram (1974) said that the subjects were not aggressive types, and often felt very uncomfortable hurting others. Yet they conformed to the demands of an authority figure in a white coat largely because they were only functionaries and not initiators of the acts. "The individual often views authority as an impersonal force, whose dictates transcend mere human wish or desire," says Milgram. "Those in authority acquire, for some, a suprahuman character."

The implications of these findings for business ethics are highly significant. Although obedience to legitimate authority is an important part of the organization of most businesses, blind obedience to any authority, legitimate or not, morally right or wrong, is often the norm—even though this is obviously not a desirable practice.

A variant of the authority excuse is that an individual merely acted, and was not called on to make a moral assessment of what he was doing ("I only pushed the button"). Aleksandr Solzhenitsyn, in his 1970 acceptance speech for the Nobel Prize for literature, said:

> The simple step of a simple courageous man is not to take part in the lie, not to support deceit. Let the lie come into the world, even dominate the world, but not through me.

What he was saying is that *agency* matters. There may be evil in the world, but it is vitally important that we are not the ones who bring it about. Ultimately we must take personal responsibility for our acts, and cannot shrug them off as inevitable or by saying that we are mere instruments of others' will. Obeying orders as a defense of questionable actions has most often been invoked in the military, where obedience is a necessary part of the endeavor. However, as evidenced by the Nuremberg Tribunal, although individuals may be excused because of their ignorance of the illegality of the orders they are given (a private may be unaware that reprisal shootings are banned by convention, for example), claiming ignorance of the immorality of the orders is not sufficient to excuse someone from moral accountability.

Everybody's Doing It

People often use the claim "Everybody's doing it" to excuse or attempt to morally justify what otherwise appears to be an immoral action. Why, after all, should one person or one corporation be punished for what everyone else does? What kinds of assumptions underlie the "Everybody's doing it" claim?

"When the majority declared two uneven lines to be identical, many subjects were shaken by the experience of being out of step with the others, often to the point of revising their own opinions."

First, it is rarely the case that absolutely everyone is behaving uniformly. The key element in the claim is that someone may be uncertain about what to do, and looks for confirmation of his intuitions. After all, if we are completely sure of what to do, we do not need or seek outside reinforcement. The more likely case is that we are unclear about the morality of an act, and look to see what others are doing. Solomon Asch's seminal research in consensus formation suggests that because we live in groups, we have developed psychological mechanisms whereby we do not constantly question everything everyone else does. This leads to a very strong urge to conform with others even if it is counterintuitive. To illustrate, Asch (1952) put subjects among actors and had them all judge a series of lines drawn on a poster. When the majority declared two uneven lines to be identical, many subjects were shaken by the experience of being out of step with the others, often to the point of revising their own opinions.

"Morality is not a question of counting heads, and opinion polls do not reflect moral correctness."

It seems then that, especially when faced with an ambiguous situation, we seek validation by what might be called a "social comparison process." If it is common to use an office copier for personal documents and the company has no clear policy on the matter, then we may modify our intuitions based on what we perceive others to be doing. This dynamic can be of critical importance in that not only may it be used as an excuse, but in many cases people will use it to determine the ethicality of an action. At its worst, it may lead to a morality of the lowest common denominator or wholesale abandonment of individual responsibility in group settings.

What motivates us to do the actions we later try to excuse or justify with the "Everybody's doing it" claim? Two main forces seem apparent. First, we often think the practice will go on whether we participate in it or not (and by not participating we will be harmed). Second, we tell ourselves that the old adage "When in Rome, do as the Romans do" is appropriate even when what the Romans do is immoral. Let's look at these in more detail.

Conventional may not mean correct. Morality is not a question of counting heads, and opinion polls do not reflect moral correctness. The fact that most people in a company feel that mocking obese coworkers is morally acceptable will not make it morally correct. In the biblical story of Sodom and Gomorrah, Abraham returns time and again trying vainly to find someone who concurs with his moral sense. The "conventional wisdom" of what is right and wrong is certainly against Abraham in the story, but that does not mean that he *is* wrong. The lone prophet speaking against the morals of the age can quite possibly be correct, and we should not be misled or enraptured by numbers alone. Despite the advertising rhetoric, five million consumers of anything *can* be wrong in their marketing decisions. Similarly, we cannot look to others' actions as the sole arbiter of right and wrong.

"'That's just the way they operate here,' the Americans might have claimed, and quite happily gone about their business with the assistance of official bribers."

Green (1991) notes that many accountants feel pressed to stretch generally accepted accounting practices (GAAP) to their very limits in order to stay in business. If the accepted practice in accounting firms is to cast the most favorable light on the firms they audit, and that requires a stretch of the GAAP, then a firm that insists on staying well within GAAP guidelines may lose clients. One firm tightening its standards may not put an end to all the others' questionable practices, but not doing anything about it seems to give undue reverence to convention. Practices such as child labor and racial discrimination were once acceptable by prevailing standards, and if we use only convention as our moral yardstick, then we have no way of checking our own behavior. As a result, there is likely to be little moral progress.

When in Rome... What about the claim that we should "do as the Romans do," whether "Rome" is indeed a foreign country or merely the accounting circles of a big city? This problem can be seen from two perspectives. First, we may believe that we must accept different moral standards and societal practices in the name of tolerance. Thus, an American business in Rio de Janeiro before the 1997 Foreign Corrupt Practices Act may have participated in the widespread practice of bribing government officials because of a conception of bribery as a distinctly South American way of life. "That's just the way they operate here," the Americans might have claimed, and quite happily gone about their business with the assistance of official bribers. This type of motivation for the "Everybody's doing it" claim suggests that what appears to be immoral may not be immoral everywhere, in all situations. Still, moral relativism comes with problems of its own. If we wish to condemn other countries for poor human rights practices or disastrous working conditions, we must have some ground to stand on that allows us to distinguish right from wrong in their society as well as in our own. When the United Nations called for divestment from apartheid South Africa, they needed to be able to say that the apartheid policy was morally wrong. A country that chose to stay in South Africa and run its business according to apartheid laws could have tried to use the "Everybody's doing it" claim, but that would not be sufficient, even though they would be acting "as the South Africans do" while in South Africa.

Second, some businesses may use the "do as the Romans do" version of "Everybody's doing it" more as a necessity for survival than as an acceptance of an immoral practice. American firms in Brazil may pay bribes, but only grudgingly. They may consider bribery a corrupt practice, but one that is a necessary evil to remain in business in Brazil. Such a justification seems quite palatable at first glance because their intentions seem good, even if their actions are less than moral. We tend to think that having the right attitude is a large part of being moral, and we are willing to forgive those who slip up so long as they wished they could have done otherwise. But even this type of claim falls short of the needed justification, for survival need not always trump morality. If a corporation must participate in corrupt practices to survive, then perhaps it is appropriate to ask whether it ought not to be in business at all.

What about the claim that "Everybody's doing it" is an adequate excuse? An excuse is something that acknowledges that a wrong action occurred but seeks to show that the perpetrator deserves little or no responsibility for the action. Two commonly accepted excusing conditions that allow this reduction in responsibility are ignorance and the inability to do otherwise. But in the case of "Everybody's doing it," there cannot be a plea of ignorance, because we already know that everyone does it; by using this claim, we are already admitting that we have done something wrong. Moreover, the claim of inability to do otherwise requires that there could not have been withdrawal or refusal. But in the case of businesses, withdrawal or refusal is always an alternative, albeit one that might put the company's future survival at risk.

The good news is that research suggests that people will resist the urge to go along with the crowd when there are dissenting voices. It appears that if even one person publicly disagrees with an erroneous judgment by the majority of a group, individuals will then feel empowered to trust and act on their own convictions. In a corporate setting, this implies that although alignment with the culture is largely desirable, we should not demand that everyone be in lockstep. Managers need to foster an atmosphere in which various views are welcomed, encouraged, and publicly aired.

My Actions Won't Make Any Difference

Shoah, the nine-hour long documentary about the Holocaust, is unusual not only because of its length but because it has no narration. Instead, it uses just the words and voices of the interviewees throughout. Some express remorse for the ritual extermination of millions of human beings. Time and again, though, we hear phrases like "I didn't like doing it, but I didn't have any choice," or "If I hadn't done it, they would just have gotten someone else," or "I wasn't really involved; I was just a very tiny cog in a vast machine." Part of the film's power is that people who appear decent, and who no doubt think of themselves as morally fit human beings, nevertheless have engaged in horrendous acts and are able to rationalize away responsibility for their conduct.

The surprising nature of the interviewees' stance is tempered somewhat when we realize that the ethical dynamic they characterize is pervasive. As Glover (1975) notes, we all use similar reasoning from time to time in our personal and professional lives to rationalize away morally questionable actions. If this were not so, otherwise good people might end up wracked with guilt for doing morally suspect things when they feel their actions are insignificant or substitutable. The claim that "It doesn't matter morally whether I am the one who does something" is based on two related but slightly different claims. The first maintains that "My actions won't make any difference to the overall outcome." The second says that "If I don't do it, they'll just find someone else who will, so it won't make any difference in the end." Both of these kinds of rationalizations can cause otherwise decent people to engage in bad behavior.

Anything I could do would be insignificant. It is tempting to imagine that any actions we take are insignificant in the overall scheme of things. There are, after all, some five and a half billion people in the world, and even the most powerful figures, such as U.S. presidents, have their actions moderated in all sorts of ways. Why, then, should we worry about the implications of what we do?

Take voting. It is not likely that the vote you cast will be the deciding vote in a presidential election; the electoral college would have to be tied except in your state, and the outcome in your state would have to depend on just one vote. Only in that case does it seem to matter whether or not you vote. Otherwise, it will not be missed, and the system will work despite your boycott.

There are many instances in which the same sort of reasoning applies. It isn't going to make a whole lot of difference to my professional association whether I approve or disapprove of any given motion, or whether I turn up at a rally, or whether I ignore petty theft in the office. This is especially true in a large, bureaucratic corporation; the individual may seem so insignificant compared to the entire organization that his actions don't seem to amount to very much when all is said and done.

"The point is that no act is devoid of all significance, and given a sufficient number of people doing the same thing, the total effect will be consequential."

The difference is negligible. Obviously, not every case is going to be one in which the act or omission of one person makes a decisive difference. Many people will add to or detract from problems in very small ways. The mistake people make here is to think that a number divided by an infinitely large number results in zero. It doesn't; the result may be very small, but it is still discernible. The other element we must add is the way in which everyone else is acting. Again, using a mathematical formula, we have to multiply very small amounts by a large number. The point is that no act is devoid of all significance, and given a sufficient number of people doing the same thing, the total effect will be consequential.

Using an example from the philosopher Derek Parfit (1984), we can see that although individual actions may seem insignificant and inconsequential, they may have devastating results when taken as an aggregate:

> *The Harmless Torturers*. In the Bad Old Days, each torturer inflicted severe pain on one victim. Things have now changed. Each of the thousand torturers presses a button, thereby turning the switch once on each of the thousand instruments. The victims suffer the same severe pain.

> But none of the torturers makes any victim's pain perceptibly worse.... It is not enough to ask, "Will my act harm other people?" Even if the answer is No, my act may still be wrong, *because* of its effects on other people. I should ask, "Will my act be one of a set of acts that will *together* harm other people?" The answer may be Yes. And the harm to others may be great. If this is so, I may be acting *very* wrongly, like the Harmless Torturers.

Thus, although it does not seem to matter much if someone takes home a few office supplies, it would be wrong to consider that such actions had zero effect, or that they were totally inconsequential. If others see it being done, or come to think of it as acceptable behavior, then in a short time the idea may catch on and the stationery cupboard will be ravaged, despite the apparent innocence of each individual act. Even the smallest effects become very significant when enough people engage in the activity.

Rarely do workers act by themselves, and their behavior can have an exhortatory or chilling effect on others. Perhaps taking a stand on an apparently minor issue will make it easier for others to do the same. Conversely, an atmosphere of quiet compliance or complacence will foster an atmosphere that makes it more difficult for others to speak up for what they believe.

If I don't do it, someone else will. The second kind of reasoning that suggests the world is indifferent to what one does says something along the lines of "Somebody's got to do it, and if it isn't me, they'll just get someone else to come and take my place." Often this happens in a context in which events are occurring that managers or workers are uncomfortable with but realize that their continued employment could be jeopardized by speaking up. Besides, the reasoning goes, there are lots of others who would be glad to do your job and who don't share your moral qualms. You may not approve of the CEO's attitude on selling arms or using child labor in emerging economies, but you might decide it is more than your job is worth to get involved.

Clearly individuals confront a number of moral issues at work, and not all are worth risking personal welfare for. Still, some are grave enough that we should act on them, probably based on some calculation of what will bring about the maximum good in the situation. However, when the issue is framed in the usual terms of going along or being substituted, it denies the possibility that people could take an active role in countering what they see as a moral wrong.

A scientist who works on developing antipersonnel mines may be correct in thinking that if he leaves someone else will take his place. But that is not the end of the story, since he could certainly do alternative research. Let's use the analogy of a pair of balancing scales: It is true that if the scientist were to quit the job, a substitute would probably be hired; hence, the balance would remain as before. But the more accurate picture would be one in which the scientist could subsequently take a stand on the opposite side of the scales, tipping them in favor of the approach he endorses.

It's Not My Problem

Another pervasive moral excuse is that whatever is going on is outside one's realm of concern. But although there may be delimited spheres of activity in the workplace, there are times when the issue is important enough to transcend those boundaries. To illustrate, let us consider the case of Kitty Genovese. Kitty was stalked by Winston Moseley near her apartment in an area of Queens, New York, known as Kew Gardens. In the early hours of March 13, 1964, he stabbed her and she screamed for help. From the seventh floor of a nearby building someone cried, "Let that girl alone!" and Moseley broke off his assault and took shelter nearby. A few minutes later he followed Kitty to the stairwell of her building, where he stabbed her repeatedly and sexually assaulted her. She yelled loudly for as long as she could, but when the police arrived she was already dead. Thirty-eight of the neighbors interviewed by police admitted they had heard her cries but failed to do anything to help her. Some even turn off their lights so they could watch the assault in safety.

The reason the Kew Gardens case is important is because all the neighbors thought, "I might as well not help her, since someone else probably will." The neighbors engaged in substitution thinking: They thought it didn't matter whether they called the police or intervened because they were convinced that someone else was bound to do so. As it happened, collectively they did nothing, paralyzed by the belief that their individual actions would be unnecessary and ineffective because of their faulty assumptions about the likely behavior of others. In this instance, contrary to the belief of each of the witnesses, the action of any one of them could have been pivotal in saving a life.

What the case illustrates is that ultimately we are all responsible for our individual actions. Willful ignorance, abdications of responsibility, or meek compliance are not sufficient grounds for dodging the moral bullet. We cannot always count on others to do the right thing, and there will be times when we ought to be involved, even if it is inconvenient, time-consuming, or puts our jobs—or our lives—on the line.

CHANGING VIEWS OF WORKPLACE MORALITY

One view of business is that it is like a game, with separate rules for everyday behavior. This approach suggests that morally questionable activities such as bluffing, cheating, and deception are acceptable practices at work. The only constraints that apply are external, like a professional code or the law; otherwise, all is fair game. Any action that is not specifically dealt with or prohibited is considered acceptable by default, However, the spirit of the Federal Sentencing Guidelines is one of constructive prevention rather than deterrence or punishment. In that sense, employers are encouraged to have employees examine the principles and the spirit of codes and rules rather than simply complying with the letter of the law.

One effect of thinking of morality as a set of external rules is that it seems ideal, something that only saintly types could ever consistently achieve. Because we live in the real world, not the ideal one, says Davis (1990), we tend to give ourselves a slippage allowance that acknowledges our own fallibility. We leave moral perfection to those whose temperaments are naturally suited to it—the Mother Teresa figures of the world.

The difficulty with this view is that it sets up morality as an oppressive taskmaster, thwarting our own interests and desires. Little wonder that we find ourselves constantly trying to figure out ways around its pressures, or of doing the minimum required of us. We become annoyed by its demands, and attempt to get out of our moral duties by pleading helplessness in such a difficult world, or belittling personal action as ineffective.

A contrasting view suggests that morality in the workplace is an extension of our everyday morality. There are no different rules that apply uniquely in business, only different situations. Individuals, then, are integrated moral beings rather than fragmented by the demands of different roles. Morality is generated and governed internally. Consequently, awareness of the various factors and environments that foster moral lapses become of paramount importance. We cannot be content in dismissing our moral lapses as resulting from a moral bar that is set too high for us and is applicable only to a realm of naive idealists. When we conceive of morality as an expression of our own identity, as intimately part of us and the way we define ourselves in the world, then any inadvertent lapse is significant and needs to be addressed.

The dynamics of immorality in business may be pernicious. Individuals and firms may not even recognize them or their effects, especially in day-to-day operations. Therefore, it is important to mitigate them and set up structures that will help disarm their influence. There are three elements to this process:

1. Active Awareness. Awareness refers to an educated familiarity with the dynamics that can pervade moral judgment. Regular ethics awareness programs are a mitigating factor for companies under the FSG. But awareness alone is not an effective mechanism to prevent or minimize these psychological effects. Studies have shown that it is not enough to be aware of dynamics that are typically habitual and ingrained, so altering behavior requires vigilance and self-consciousness. Thus, people may institute checks or controls on their judgment processes. They may employ colleagues and associates to serve as monitors on important decisions to provide diagnostic feedback in a timely and unambiguous fashion. They may also employ explicitly normative decision-making methods, such as decision trees and other mechanisms that expose the values at work and lessen impulsive judgments.

In practical terms, this means that lectures on ethics will not suffice; training programs should have hands-on simulations, case studies, or role-playing. In the case of susceptibility to unwarranted authority, for example, employees should be made aware that most people will automatically go along with the orders of a superior even if those orders are morally questionable. This might be followed by a role play that invokes the dynamic—perhaps something as simple as a subordinate being told to allocate funds on the wrong budget line because the company has a "use it or lose it" system—and a discussion of the corporate code of conduct and individual moral responsibility.

2. Access. The second step is giving individuals access to guidance and allowing them to report unethical behavior. The FSG mandates that a high-level executive be designated to deal with ethical issues in the corporation and develop mechanisms for reporting and publicizing unacceptable practices. Codes obviously go a long way to help employees, but there will be times when it is not evident what an employee should do. Some ways of dealing with ambiguous cases are to have an ethics "hot line" that individuals can call for help, even anonymously. Companies have set up open-door policies whereby employees can drop in for advice without notice. More formally, many corporations have an ombudsman whose job it is to listen impartially to complaints or reports and deal with them fairly. These sorts of programs can offer practical advice, or act as a sounding board for employee concerns. Crucially, they offer a way for individuals to speak up without being subject to retaliation.

3. Advocacy. We should recognize the dramatic change in philosophy behind the FSG. The emphasis now is on promoting morally decent corporate citizens, which is a long way from the prior view stressing punishment of regulatory infractions. We should not take this to mean that somehow corporate responsibility has taken over individual accountability. Instead, it advocates a corporate culture with a wholesale commitment to ethical behavior. This will involve moral leadership, training, assessment, and feedback for every element in the company. It also implies that individual employees have to be attuned to the potential for both intentional and unintentional wrongdoing.

References

Solomon Asch, *Social Psychology* (New York: Prentice-Hall, 1952).

A. Brief, J. Dukerich, and L. Doran, "Resolving Ethical Dilemmas in Management: Experimental Investigations of Values, Accountability, and Choice," *Journal of Applied Social Psychology, 21,* 5 (1991): 380–396.

R. Cialdini, *Influence: How and Why People Agree to Things* (New York: Quill, 1984).

A. Davis, "Moral Theorizing and Moral Practice: Reflections on Some of the Sources of Hypocrisy," working paper, Center for Values and Social Policy, University of Colorado, Boulder, 1990.

K. Gibson and S. Goering, *Pitfalls in Practical Ethics,* unpublished report to the Business in Ethics Research Fund, 1995.

J. Glover, "It Makes No Difference Whether or Not I Do It," *Proceedings of the Aristotelian Society* (Supp.), *49* (1975): 171–190.

R.M. Green, "When Is 'Everyone's Doing It' a Moral Justification?" *Business Ethics Quarterly,* January 1991, pp. 75–94.

L. Kohlberg and R. Kramer, "Continuities and Discontinuities in Child and Adult Moral Development," *Human Development, 12* (1969): 93–120.

S. Milgram, *Obedience to Authority: An Experimental View* (New York: Harper & Row, 1974).

D. Parfit, *Reasons and Persons* (Oxford, UK: Oxford University Press, 1984).

B.F. Skinner, *Science and Human Behavior* (New York: Macmillan, 1953).

Aleksandr Solzhenitsyn, acceptance speech for Nobel Prize for Literature, 1970.

Kevin Gibson is an assistant professor of philosophy at Marquette University, Milwaukee, Wisconsin. He wishes to thank Professor Dennis Organ and the Ethics in Business Research Fund for their support and encouragement in developing this article.

What Would *You* Do?

Gold Mine or Fool's Gold?

The sheaf of competitors' documents looked fishy, but the boss said not to worry.

BY KENT WEBER

The Case

As a new product manager for a fast growing high-tech start-up, Michael Sanjiv was no stranger to high stakes and tough decisions. But on this particular 9 p.m. commute home, he was really in the slow lane, deep in thought, struggling over the information he now possessed.

Earlier that day, Michael's boss had handed him a stack of strategic documents—the private property of their closest competitor. It was a competitive intelligence gold mine: product plans, implementation processes, pricing strategies, major partner agreements, nearly 20 documents in all—most clearly marked "proprietary and confidential." Michael was dumbfounded. And he wasn't sure if the sirens he was hearing were only in his head.

"Where did you get these?" Michael asked his boss the next morning, with as much curious neutrality as he could muster. His boss told him matter-of-factly and with a hint of pride that he had taken them right off the competitor's server. "I got into a private section of their Intranet and downloaded everything that looked interesting," he said. Later, with suspicions aroused, his boss would only say he got "electronic access" via a colleague and that he personally did not have to break any passwords.

The sirens were louder now. Michael knew this would not pass the "Headline Test." If this story ever showed up in print, the company would not look good.

Michael's further research yielded few answers. There were no clear company policies or procedures that offered any real guidance. Questions abounded. Was this unethical, illegal or both? Does the answer hinge on the mere possession of stolen confidential information? Or was it important exactly how they were obtained?

Michael knew only one thing for sure. He couldn't sit back and do nothing. Back out on the commute, with sirens still sounding, Michael wondered, "What should I do?"

Seth Ross

Chief Strategy Officer, PC Guardian, San Rafael, Calif.

It is neither legal nor ethical to break into someone else's computers and steal confidential documents. Since Michael got two different stories from this boss, it seems possible a serious legal or ethical infraction has occurred. As an ethical matter, Michael probably should not use these materials to his company's benefit. As a practical matter, what appears to be a "gold mine" many only contain fool's gold. Documents may be fake or difficult to exploit. Think about McDonald's: just because you can see how they make a burger doesn't mean you have the "secret sauce."

Michael should dump the documents and evaluate whether this is an anomaly or a regular modus operandi for his new company. Given the sirens ringing, Michael's sense of fair play may not be a match for his boss's tactics or the overall culture of the company.

Pat Bryant

President of the Board, Society of Competitive Intelligence Professionals (SCIP), Alexandria, Virg.

If you are knowingly using "proprietary and confidential" information from your competitor—even if you found it on the street—you have crossed the ethical line. SCIP's "code of ethics" (www.scip.org/ci/ethics.html) provides guidelines for more than 7,000 competitive intelligence professionals, including the requirement "to fully respect all requests for confidentiality of information." The code acts as a warning sign.

Still, this kind of thing does happen. Some individuals will Fed-Ex chunks of "proprietary and confidential" competitor information to their clients or bosses, assuming they are willing recipients. If it came to me, I would Fed-Ex it right back (unused) and tell them to return it. Michael should refer his boss to SCIP's guidelines, and he could also suggest they talk to the company's legal counsel.

Kent Weber's Comments

It is striking how apparent anonymity and new tools like the Internet have increased the sheer number of situations like this one. Perhaps the top practical lesson here is a reminder of the value of proper network security.

Michael was right to be afraid of illegalities. Not knowing the documents precisely, we could not speak confidently to the prosecutorial risk, but it is true that the reach of intellectual property law has been significantly (if quietly) strengthened by President Clinton. The 1996 Espionage Act defines "trade secrets" broadly as almost any type of business information that drives independent economic value from not being generally known, and whose confidentiality has been protected by reasonable measures. Michael's company should stop this practice before a court is invited to decide what is and is not a secret.

Finally, we must support Michael for acknowledging his conscience in a tough situation. And while we might wonder what would happen if he went to the CEO, we certainly know of others who brought the truth forward and wound up being maligned. As one high-tech executive quipped, "the higher the stack of money on the table, the weirder people get."

What Actually Happened?

Michael confronted his boss privately and told him he was uncomfortable with the stolen documents. In addition to the obvious ethical and legal problems, Michael said this was a public relations nightmare waiting to happen. His boss didn't want to hear it. He insisted nothing "illegal" had been done, refused to show concern, and made it clear Michael "should not worry about it." Thereafter, Michael broached the issue with two colleagues, who seemed equally unconcerned. Not wanting to cause a stir, but clearly at odds with the judgment being exercised around him, Michael resigned quietly three days later. He sill wonders if he did exactly the right thing.

Kent Weber (kent@ethicsindex.org) has a Master's degree in Ethics from Oxford and works for a firm that advises and invests in early-stage start-ups.

All cases in What Would You Do? are real, though disguised.

Leaders as Value Shapers

Leading through vivid, living, personal example is still the best, perhaps the only, way to lead. There is power in personal example.

KEVIN FREIBERG

GREAT LEADERS UNDERSTAND that their capacities to shape values and educate through vivid, living, personal example ultimately directs the course of a firm. The way people think about customers and coworkers, the way they behave, and their impressions of right and wrong are all influenced by watching their leaders live out their values.

Every firm builds its reputation on a set of values. The question is whether the values driving the business have been haphazardly acquired or purposefully instilled, protected, and promoted. This is why leaders must embrace their role as value shapers.

Values are the emotional rules that govern people's attitudes and behaviors. They establish boundaries that influence how an organization fulfills its mission. Values are deep-seated beliefs we have about the world and how it operates. They influence outcomes and ultimately determine quality. Values provide a framework for making choices and decisions. Values are the non-negotiables, the principles for which we stand.

I see two types of values—espoused values and the values people practice. When there is alignment, leaders operate out of personal integrity—doing what they say they're going to do.

Where there is a disconnect between our espoused values and the values we practice, we find hypocrisy. Professing a belief, philosophy, or standard to which you don't hold yourself accountable is an act of pretension and insincerity. Leaders who operate out of hypocrisy breed compliance because they lack influence and must lean on positional power.

Leadership functions on the basis of trust and credibility. That's why leaders must close the gap between their espoused values and the values they practice. Leaders who live their values inspire tremendous commitment and loyalty in others. As a result, they expand their influence and their ability to effect change.

Being Faithful to Our Values

When customers, suppliers, shareholders, and employees evaluate whether or not we are faithful to the values we profess, they use the following criteria.

1. *How you spend your time.* If you want to know what an executive values watch the way he or she allocates time. We spend time on those things that are most important to us. On the busiest days of the airline industry, you'll find Herb Kelleher, Southwest Airlines' indefatigable chairman and CEO, loading bags on the tarmac, working the galleys with the flight attendants, or helping mechanics in the maintenance hangar. The way he spends his time says, "We don't hide behind titles and job descriptions; we do whatever it takes to help each other out and serve the customer."

Make a list of the top five values driving your organization. Then look at your calendar and analyze the way you allocate your time. What does your schedule say to others about what you value?

2. *How you spend your money.* Take out your checkbook and audit your expenditures. Examine the last budget you prepared. Is it consistent with what you value? The way we spend money says a lot about our priorities. If you say people are your most important assets, is that reflected in your compensation structures and your policies?

3. *Your reaction to critical incidents.* Whether it is a customer complaint or commendation, how you handle the event sends a message. When a customer asks your team to go beyond the call of duty, how do you respond? When your people do something heroic, do you celebrate and publicize their actions?

At Southwest Airlines, they celebrate the courage and competence of individuals who rise to the occasion and protect the lives of the company's valued customers.

Critical incidents do not have to be monumental in nature. When Mike Snyder, CEO of Red Robin International, picks up a candy wrapper outside of one of his restaurants, he sends a message to his people that the details count.

4. *What you reward and punish.* Do your rewards specifically reinforce the values that are driving your business? Do your incentives promote internal competition or cooperation? When one of your people takes an intelligent risk with the intent to benefit the company and fails, do you reward or punish their effort? When someone who reports to you gives you constructive feedback, how do you respond? At Southwest Airlines, people are given awards for fun and humor, sensational service, telling it like it is, creativity, and risk-taking.

5. *Questions you ask.* Do the questions you ask demonstrate your concern for your employees? Do your questions encourage people to focus on the customer or on the numbers?

The questions you ask and answer reveal a lot about what you value. When asked about the money spent on reward and recognition Herb Kelleher said, "I could cut our budget substantially by cutting recognition events, but that would be like cutting out our heart."

6. *Things you measure.* If you believe your people are your major point of differentiation, are you as rigorous about measuring their satisfaction as you are about measuring their productivity or financial results? If you believe that part of leadership is serving your internal customers, do you give those customers a chance to evaluate the quality of the services you provide? Do your team leaders go through a 360-degree feedback process, and are the results tied to their compensation structure?

As leaders we also need to remember that *our walk talks*. Everything we do and everything we choose not to do says something about what we value.

The Power of a Strong Value System

Southwest Airlines, Disney, General Electric, Federal Express, Johnson & Johnson, TDI Industries, HewlettPackard, and Merck all rank among the most admired companies in the world. They find enormous strength in their core values because strong values:

1. *Build trust and confidence.* In organizations where a strong set of shared values exists, leaders have more confidence to let go of power and authority.

2. *Foster accountability.* A strong value system creates boundaries. When the boundaries are clear, employees have more freedom and authority to act. People willingly assume responsibility and accountability when you reduce the uncertainty that comes with ill-defined boundaries.

3. *Establish a unified front.* Strong values concentrate the efforts of a team. When people are drawn together by a common set of beliefs, the values holding them together suddenly become more important than the agenda or special interests of any one individual. The result is a spirit of cohesiveness that captures the diversity of gifts and talents people bring to the team.

4. *Provide guidance in times of crisis.* In a chaotic world where people feel pressured to compromise ethics and cut corners to get results or cover up mistakes, strong values serve as a moral compass. Where there are no easy answers to difficult challenges, a strong value system can help determine the rightness of your direction.

5. *Create competitive advantage.* People want to do business with leaders who have similar values. Customers want to do business with organizations they can count on. There is a strong sense of sincerity and

authenticity in firms with clearly defined values. These companies are less likely to project a false image and make promises that they can't keep.

People who are not clear about those guiding principles for which they stand can never expect to lay a foundation for trust and credibility, let alone develop the capacity to exercise leadership. Great leaders understand that every moment of every day is a symbolic opportunity to communicate their values. They do not underestimate the power of personal example. Through their daily choices leaders carve out the character and reputation of the organization. And they provide the standard by which others calibrate their own behaviors.

Kevin Freiberg is a professional speaker and co-author of Nuts! Southwest Airlines' Personal Success, *619-624-9691.*

Article 26

The Parable of the Sadhu

After encountering a dying pilgrim on a climbing trip in the Himalayas, a businessman ponders the differences between individual and corporate ethics.

by Bowen H. McCoy

This article was originally published in the September–October 1983 issue of HBR. For its republication as an HBR Classic, Bowen H. McCoy has written the commentary "When Do We Take a Stand?" to update his observations.

Last year, as the first participant in the new six-month sabbatical program that Morgan Stanley has adopted, I enjoyed a rare opportunity to collect my thoughts as well as do some traveling. I spent the first three months in Nepal, walking 600 miles through 200 villages in the Himalayas and climbing some 120,000 vertical feet. My sole Western companion on the trip was an anthropologist who shed light on the cultural patterns of the villages that we passed through.

During the Nepal hike, something occurred that has had a powerful impact on my thinking about corporate ethics. Although some might argue that the experience has no relevance to business, it was a situation in which a basic ethical dilemma suddenly intruded into the lives of a group of individuals. How the group responded holds a lesson for all organizations, no matter how defined.

The Sadhu

The Nepal experience was more rugged than I had anticipated. Most commercial treks last two or three weeks and cover a quarter of the distance we traveled.

My friend Stephen, the anthropologist, and I were halfway through the 60-day Himalayan part of the trip when we reached the high point, an 18,000-foot pass over a crest that we'd have to traverse to reach the village of Muklinath, an ancient holy place for pilgrims.

Six years earlier, I had suffered pulmonary edema, an acute form of altitude sickness, at 16,500 feet in the vicinity of Everest base camp—so we were understandably concerned about what would happen at 18,000 feet. Moreover, the Himalayas were having their wettest spring in 20 years; hip-deep powder and ice had already driven us off one ridge. If we failed to cross the pass, I feared that the last half of our once-in-a-lifetime trip would be ruined.

The night before we would try the pass, we camped in a hut at 14,500 feet. In the photos taken at that camp, my face appears wan. The last village we'd passed through was a sturdy two-day walk below us, and I was tired.

During the late afternoon, four backpackers from New Zealand joined us, and we spent most of the night awake, anticipating the climb. Below, we could see the fires of two other parties, which turned out to be two Swiss couples and a Japanese hiking club.

To get over the steep part of the climb before the sun melted the steps cut in the ice, we departed at 3:30 A.M. The New Zealanders left first, followed by Stephen and myself, our porters and Sherpas, and then the Swiss. The Japanese lingered in their camp. The sky was clear, and we were confident that no spring storm would erupt that day to close the pass.

At 15,500 feet, it looked to me as if Stephen were shuffling and staggering a bit, which are symptoms of altitude sickness. (The initial stage of altitude sickness brings a headache and nausea. As the condition worsens, a climber may encounter difficult breathing, disorientation, aphasia, and paralysis.) I felt strong—my adrenaline was flowing—but I was very concerned about my ultimate ability to get across. A couple of our porters were also suffering from the height, and Pasang, our Sherpa sirdar (leader), was worried.

Just after daybreak, while we rested at 15,500 feet, one of the New Zealanders, who had gone ahead, came staggering down toward us with a body slung across his shoulders. He dumped the almost naked, barefoot body of an Indian holy man—a sadhu—at my feet. He had found the pilgrim lying on the ice, shivering and suffering from hypothermia. I cradled the sadhu's head and laid him out on the rocks. The New Zealander was angry. He wanted to get across the pass before the bright sun melted the snow. He said, "Look, I've done what I can. You have porters and Sherpa guides. You care for him. We're going on!" He turned and went back up the mountain to join his friends.

I took a carotid pulse and found that the sadhu was still alive. We figured he had probably visited the holy shrines at Muklinath and was on his way home. It was fruitless to question why he had chosen this desperately high route instead of the safe, heavily traveled caravan route through the Kali Gandaki gorge. Or why he was shoeless and almost naked, or how long he had been lying in the pass. The answers weren't going to solve our problem.

Stephen and the four Swiss began stripping off their outer clothing and opening their packs. The sadhu was soon clothed from head to foot. He was not able to walk, but he was very much alive. I looked down the mountain and spotted the Japanese climbers, marching up with a horse.

When I reached them, Stephen glared at me and said, "How do you feel about contributing to the death of a fellow man?"

Without a great deal of thought, I told Stephen and Pasang that I was concerned about withstanding the heights to come and wanted to get over the pass. I took off after several of our porters who had gone ahead.

On the steep part of the ascent where, if the ice steps had given way, I would have slid down about 3,000 feet, I felt vertigo. I stopped for a breather, allowing the Swiss to catch up with me. I inquired about the sadhu and Stephen. They said that the sadhu was fine and that Stephen was just behind them. I set off again for the summit.

Stephen arrived at the summit an hour after I did. Still exhilarated by victory, I ran down the slope to congratulate him. He was suffering from altitude sickness—walking 15 steps, then stopping, walking 15 steps, then stopping. Pasang accompanied him all the way up. When I reached them, Stephen glared at me and said: "How do you feel about contributing to the death of a fellow man?"

I did not completely comprehend what he meant. "Is the sadhu dead?" I inquired.

"No," replied Stephen, "but he surely will be!"

After I had gone, followed not long after by the Swiss, Stephen had remained with the sadhu. When the Japanese had arrived, Stephen had asked to use their horse to transport the sadhu down to the hut. They had refused. He had then asked Pasang to have a group of our porters carry the sadhu. Pasang had resisted the idea, saying that the porters would have to exert all their energy to get themselves over the pass. He believed they could not carry a man down 1,000 feet to the hut, reclimb the slope, and get across safely before the snow melted. Pasang had pressed Stephen not to delay any longer.

The Sherpas had carried the sadhu down to a rock in the sun at about 15,000 feet and pointed out the hut another 500 feet below. The Japanese had given him food and drink. When they had last seen him, he was listlessly throwing rocks at the Japanese party's dog, which had frightened him.

We do not know if the sadhu lived or died.

For many of the following days and evenings, Stephen and I discussed and debated our behavior toward the sadhu. Stephen is a committed Quaker with deep moral vision. He said, "I feel that what happened with the sadhu is a good example of the breakdown between the individual ethic and the corporate ethic. No one person was willing to assume ultimate responsibility for the sadhu. Each was willing to do his bit just so long as it was not too inconvenient. When it got to be a bother, everyone just passed the buck to someone else and took off. Jesus was relevant to a more individualistic stage of society, but how do we interpret his teaching today in a world filled with large, impersonal organizations and groups?"

I defended the larger group, saying, "Look, we all cared. We all gave aid and comfort. Everyone did his bit. The New Zealander carried him down below the snow line. I took his pulse and suggested we treat him for hypothermia. You and the Swiss gave him clothing and got him warmed up. The Japanese gave him food and water. The Sherpas carried him down to the sun and pointed out the easy trail toward the hut. He was well enough to throw rocks at a dog. What more could we do?"

"You have just described the typical affluent Westerner's response to a problem. Throwing money—in this case, food and sweaters—at it, but not solving the fundamentals!" Stephen retorted.

I asked, "Where is the limit of our responsibility in a situation like this?"

"What would satisfy you?" I said. "Here we are, a group of New Zealanders, Swiss, Americans, and Japanese who have never met before and who are at the apex of one of the most powerful experiences of our lives. Some years the pass is so bad no one gets over it. What right does an almost naked pilgrim who chooses the wrong trail have to disrupt our lives? Even the Sherpas had no interest in risking the trip to help him beyond a certain point."

Stephen calmly rebutted, "I wonder what the Sherpas would have done if the sadhu had been a well-dressed Nepali, or what the Japanese would have done if the sadhu had been a well-dressed Asian, or what you would have done, Buzz, if the sadhu had been a well-dressed Western woman?"

"Where, in your opinion," I asked, "is the limit of our responsibility in a situation like this? We had our own well-being to worry about. Our Sherpa guides were unwilling to jeopardize us or the porters for the sadhu. No one else on the mountain was willing to commit himself beyond certain self-imposed limits."

Stephen said, "As individual Christians or people with a Western ethical tradition, we can fulfill our obligations in such a situation only if one, the sadhu dies in our care; two, the sadhu demonstrates to us that he can undertake the two-day walk down to the village; or three, we carry the sadhu for two days down to the village and persuade someone there to care for him."

"Leaving the sadhu in the sun with food and clothing—where he demonstrated hand-eye coordination by throwing a rock at a dog—comes close to fulfilling items one and two," I answered. "And it wouldn't have made sense to take him to the village where the people appeared to be far less caring than the Sherpas, so the third condition is impractical. Are you really saying that, no matter what the implications, we should, at the drop of a hat, have changed our entire plan?"

The Individual Versus the Group Ethic

Despite my arguments, I felt and continue to feel guilt about the sadhu. I had literally walked through a classic moral dilemma without fully thinking through the consequences. My excuses for my actions include a high adrenaline flow, a superordinate goal, and a once-in-a-lifetime opportunity—common factors in corporate situations, especially stressful ones.

Real moral dilemmas are ambiguous, and many of us hike right through them, unaware that they exist. When, usually after the fact, someone makes an issue of one, we tend to resent his or her bringing it up. Often, when the full import of what we have done (or not done) hits us, we dig into a defensive position from which it is very difficult to emerge. In rare circumstances, we may contemplate what we have done from inside a prison.

Had we mountaineers been free of stress caused by the effort and the high altitude, we might have treated the sadhu differently. Yet isn't stress the real test of personal and corporate values? The instant decisions that executives make under pressure reveal the most about personal and corporate character.

As a group, we had no process for developing a consensus. We had no sense of purpose or plan.

Among the many questions that occur to me when I ponder my experience with the sadhu are: What are the practical limits of moral imagination and vision? Is there a collective or institutional ethic that differs from the ethics of the individual? At what level of effort or commitment can one discharge one's ethical responsibilities?

Not every ethical dilemma has a right solution. Reasonable people often disagree; otherwise there would be no dilemma. In a business context, however, it is essential that managers agree on a process for dealing with dilemmas.

Our experience with the sadhu offers an interesting parallel to business situations. An immediate response was mandatory. Failure to act was a decision in itself. Up on the mountain we could not resign and submit our résumés to a headhunter. In contrast to philosophy, business involves action and implementation—getting things done. Managers must come up with answers based on what they see and what they allow to influence their decision-making processes. On the mountain, none of us but Stephen realized the true dimensions of the situation we were facing.

One of our problems was that as a group we had no process for developing a consensus. We had no sense of purpose or plan. The difficulties of dealing with the sadhu were so complex that no one person could handle them. Because the group did not have a set of preconditions that could guide its action to an acceptable resolution, we reacted instinctively as individuals. The cross-cultural nature of the group added a further layer of complexity. We had no leader with whom we could all identify and in whose purpose we believed. Only Stephen was willing to take charge, but he could not gain adequate support from the group to care for the sadhu.

Some organizations do have values that transcend the personal values of their managers. Such values, which go beyond profitability, are usually revealed when the organization is under stress. People throughout the organization generally accept its values, which, because they are not presented as a rigid list of commandments, may be somewhat ambiguous. The stories people tell, rather than printed materials, transmit the organization's conceptions of what is proper behavior.

For 20 years, I have been exposed at senior levels to a variety of corporations and organizations. It is amazing how quickly an outsider can sense the tone and style of an organization and, with that, the degree of tolerated openness and freedom to challenge management.

Organizations that do not have a heritage of mutually accepted, shared values tend to become unhinged during stress, with each individual bailing out for himself or herself. In the great takeover battles we have witnessed during past years, companies that had strong cultures drew the wagons around them and fought it out, while other companies saw executives—supported by golden parachutes—bail out of the struggles.

Because corporations and their members are interdependent, for the corporation to be strong the members need to share a preconceived notion of correct behavior, a "business ethic," and think of it as a positive force, not a constraint.

As an investment banker, I am continually warned by well-meaning lawyers, clients, and associates to be wary of conflicts of interest. Yet if I were to run away from every difficult situation, I wouldn't be an effective investment banker. I have to feel my way through conflicts. An effective manager can't run from risk either; he or she has to confront risk. To feel "safe" in doing that, managers need the guidelines of an agreed-upon process and set of values within the organization.

After my three months in Nepal, I spent three months as an executive-in-residence at both the Stanford Business School and the University of California at Berkeley's Center for Ethics and Social Policy of the Graduate Theological Union. Those six months away from my job gave me time to assimilate 20 years of business experience. My thoughts turned often to the meaning of the leadership role in any large organization. Students at the seminary thought of themselves as antibusiness. But when I questioned them, they agreed that they distrusted all large organizations, including the church. They perceived all large organizations as impersonal and opposed to individual values and needs. Yet we all know of organizations in which people's values and beliefs are respected and their expressions encouraged. What makes the difference? Can we identify the difference and, as a result, manage more effectively?

WHEN DO WE TAKE A STAND?

by Bowen H. McCoy

I wrote about my experiences purposely to present an ambiguous situation. I never found out if the sadhu lived or died. I can attest, though, that the sadhu lives on in his story. He lives in the ethics classes I teach each year at business schools and churches. He lives in the classrooms of numerous business schools, where professors have taught the case to tens of thousands of students. He lives in several casebooks on ethics and on an educational video. And he lives in organizations such as the American Red Cross and AT&T, which use his story in their ethics training.

As I reflect on the sadhu now, 15 years after the fact, I first have to wonder, What actually happened on that Himalayan slope? When I first wrote about the event, I reported the experience in as much detail as I could remember, but I shaped it to the needs of a good classroom discussion. After years of reading my story, viewing it on video, and hearing others discuss it, I'm not sure I myself know what actually occurred on the mountainside that day!

I've also heard a wide variety of responses to the story. The sadhu, for example, may not have wanted our help at all—he may have been intentionally bringing on his own death as a way to holiness. Why had he taken the dangerous way over the pass instead of the caravan route through the gorge? Hindu businesspeople have told me that in trying to assist the sadhu, we were being typically arrogant Westerners imposing our cultural values on the world.

I've learned that each year along the pass, a few Nepali porters are left to freeze to death outside the tents of the unthinking tourists who hired them. A few years ago, a French group even left one of their own, a young French woman, to die there. The difficult pass seems to demonstrate a perverse version of Gresham's law of currency: The bad practices of previous travelers have driven out the values that new travelers might have followed if they were at home. Perhaps that helps to explain why our porters behaved as they did and why it was so difficult for Stephen or anyone else to establish a different approach on the spot.

Our Sherpa sirdar, Pasang, was focused on his responsibility for bringing us up the mountain safe and sound. (His livelihood and status in the Sherpa ethnic group depended on our safe return.) We were weak, our party was split, the porters were well on their way to the top with all our gear and food, and a storm would have separated us irrevocably from our logistical base.

The fact was, we had no plan for dealing with the contingency of the sadhu. There was nothing we could do to unite our multicultural group in the little time we had. An ethical dilemma had come upon us unexpectedly, an element of drama that may explain why the sadhu's story has continued to attract students.

I am often asked for help in teaching the story. I usually advise keeping the details as ambiguous as possible. A true ethical dilemma requires a decision between two hard choices. In the case of the sadhu, we had to decide how much to sacrifice ourselves to take care of a stranger. And given the constraints of our trek, we had to make a group decision, not an individual one. If a large majority of students in a class ends up thinking I'm a bad person because of my decision on the mountain, the instructor may not have given the case its due. The same is true if the majority sees no problem with the choices we made.

Any class's response depends on its setting, whether it's a business school, a church, or a corporation. I've found that younger students are more likely to see the issue as black-and-white, whereas older ones tend to see shades of gray. Some have seen a conflict between the different ethical approaches that we followed at the time. Stephen felt he had to do everything he could to save the sadhu's life, in accordance with his Christian ethic of compassion. I had a utilitarian response: do the greatest good for the greatest number. Give a burst of aid to minimize the sadhu's exposure, then continue on our way.

The basic question of the case remains, When do we take a stand? When do we allow a "sadhu" to intrude into our daily lives? Few of us can afford the time or effort to take care of every needy person we encounter. How much must we give of ourselves? And how do we prepare our organizations and institutions so they will respond appropriately in a crisis? How do we influence them if we do not agree with their points of view?

We cannot quit our jobs over every ethical dilemma, but if we continually ignore our sense of values, who do we become? As a journalist asked at a recent conference on ethics, "Which ditch are we willing to die in?" For each of us, the answer is a bit different. How we act in response to that question defines better than anything else who we are, just as, in a collective sense, our acts define our institutions. In effect, the sadhu is always there, ready to remind us of the tensions between our own goals and the claims of strangers.

The word *ethics* turns off many and confuses more. Yet the notions of shared values and an agreed-upon process for dealing with adversity and change—what many people mean when they talk about corporate culture—seem to be at the heart of the ethical issue. People who are in touch with their own core beliefs and the beliefs of others and who are sustained by them can be more comfortable living on the cutting edge. At times, taking a tough line or a decisive stand in a muddle of ambiguity is the only ethical thing to do. If a manager is indecisive about a problem and spends time trying to figure out the "good" thing to do, the enterprise may be lost.

Business ethics, then, has to do with the authenticity and integrity of the enterprise. To be ethical is to follow the business as well as the cultural goals of the corporation, its owners, its employees, and its customers. Those who cannot serve the corporate vision are not authentic businesspeople and, therefore, are not ethical in the business sense.

At this stage of my own business experience, I have a strong interest in organizational behavior. Sociologists are keenly studying what they call corporate stories, legends, and heroes as a way organizations have of transmitting value systems. Corporations such as Arco have even hired consultants to perform an audit of their corporate culture. In a company, a leader is a person who understands, interprets, and manages the corporate value system. Effective managers, therefore, are action-oriented people who resolve conflict, are tolerant of ambiguity, stress, and change, and have a strong sense of purpose for themselves and their organizations.

If all this is true, I wonder about the role of the professional manager who moves from company to company. How can he or she quickly absorb the values and culture of different organizations? Or is there, indeed, an art of management that is totally transportable? Assuming that such fungible managers do exist, is it proper for them to manipulate the values of others?

What would have happened had Stephen and I carried the sadhu for two days back to the village and become involved with the villagers in his care? In four trips to Nepal, my most interesting experience occurred in 1975 when I lived in a Sherpa home in the Khumbu for five days while recovering from altitude sickness. The high point of Stephen's trip was an invitation to participate in a family funeral ceremony in Manang. Neither experience had to do with climbing the high passes of the Himalayas. Why were we so reluctant to try the lower path, the ambiguous trail? Perhaps because we did not have a leader who could reveal the greater purpose of the trip to us.

Why didn't Stephen, with his moral vision, opt to take the sadhu under his personal care? The answer is partly because Stephen was hard-stressed physically himself and partly because, without some support system that encompassed our involuntary and episodic community on the mountain, it was beyond his individual capacity to do so.

I see the current interest in corporate culture and corporate value systems as a positive response to pessimism such as Stephen's about the decline of the role of the individual in large organizations. Individuals who operate from a thoughtful set of personal values provide the foundation for a corporate culture. A corporate tradition that encourages freedom of inquiry, supports personal values, and reinforces a focused sense of direction can fulfill the need to combine individuality with the prosperity and success of the group. Without such corporate support, the individual is lost.

That is the lesson of the sadhu. In a complex corporate situation, the individual requires and deserves the support of the group. When people cannot find such support in their organizations, they don't know how to act. If such support is forthcoming, a person has a stake in the success of the group and can add much to the process of establishing and maintaining a corporate culture. Management's challenge is to be sensitive to individual needs, to shape them, and to direct and focus them for the benefit of the group as a whole.

For each of us the sadhu lives. Should we stop what we are doing and comfort him; or should we keep trudging up toward the high pass? Should I pause to help the derelict I pass on the street each night as I walk by the Yale Club en route to Grand Central Station? Am I his brother? What is the nature of our responsibility if we consider ourselves to be ethical persons? Perhaps it is to change the values of the group so that it can, with all its resources, take the other road.

Bowen H. McCoy retired from Morgan Stanley in 1990 after 28 years of service. He is now a real estate and business counselor, a teacher and a philanthropist.

Reprinted with permission from *Harvard Business Review,* May/June 1997, pp. 54–56, 58–60, 62, 64.

UNIT 3

Business and Society: Contemporary Ethical, Social, and Environmental Issues

Unit Selections

27. **Trust in the Marketplace**, John E. Richardson and Linnea Bernard McCord
28. **Can Business Still Save the World?** Thea Singer
29. **As Leaders, Women Rule**, *Business Week*
30. **Crimes and Misdeminors**, Daniel Kadlec
31. **Virtual Morality: A New Workplace Quandary**, Michael J. McCarthy
32. **Mixed Signals**, Pamela Paul
33. **Diversity Worst Practices**, Delyte D. Frost
34. **Values in Tension: Ethics Away From Home**, Thomas Donaldson
35. **Global Standards, Local Problems**, Meryl Davids
36. **Privacy as Global Policy**, P. J. Connolly

Key Points to Consider

- How well are organizations responding to issues of work and family—flexible schedules, day care, job sharing, telecommuting?
- Is it fair to bring criminal charges against corporations and executives for unsafe products, dangerous working conditions, or industrial pollution? Why or why not?
- What ethical dilemmas is management likely to face when conducting business in foreign environments?

Links: www.dushkin.com/online/
These sites are annotated in the World Wide Web pages.

CIBERWeb
http://ciber.centers.purdue.edu

Communications for a Sustainable Future
http://csf.colorado.edu

National Immigrant Forum
http://www.immigrationforum.org

Stockholm University
http://www.psychology.su.se/units/ao/ao.html

Sympatico: Workplace
http://sympatico.workopolis.com

United Nations Environment Programme (UNEP)
http://www.unep.ch

United States Trade Representative (USTR)
http://www.ustr.gov

Both at home and abroad, there are social and environmental issues that have potential ethical consequences for management. Incidents of insider trading, deaths resulting from unsafe products or work environments, AIDS in the workplace, and the adoption of policies for involvement in the global market are a few of the issues that need to be seriously addressed by management.

This unit investigates the nature and ramifications of prominent ethical, social, and environmental issues facing management today. The unit articles are grouped into three sections. The first subsection article scrutinizes the importance of companies gaining and maintaining trust in the marketplace. The next article reveals the fate or evolution of some socially responsible pioneer companies. "As Leaders, Women Rule" points out the strengths that women have brought to the workplace. "Crimes and Misdeminors" examines the mixed reviews a teenager received for manipulating stocks.

The first two articles in the second subsection address some of the salient contemporary ethical issues that are related to the use and misuse of data on the Net and ethical privacy concerns raised by consumers. The last article in this subsection describes how some diversity practices can go amok.

The subsection *Global Ethics* concludes this unit with three readings that provide helpful insight on ethical issues and dilemmas inherent in multinational operations. They describe adapting ethical decisions to a global marketplace and offer guidelines for helping management deal with ethical issues in international markets.

TRUST IN THE MARKETPLACE

John E. Richardson and
Linnea Bernard McCord

Traditionally, ethics is defined as a set of moral values or principles or a code of conduct.

> ... Ethics, as an expression of reality, is predicated upon the assumption that there are right and wrong motives, attitudes, traits of character, and actions that are exhibited in interpersonal relationships. Respectful social interaction is considered a norm by almost everyone.
> ... the overwhelming majority of people perceive others to be ethical when they observe what is considered to be their genuine kindness, consideration, politeness, empathy, and fairness in their interpersonal relationships. When these are absent, and unkindness, inconsideration, rudeness, hardness, and injustice are present, the people exhibiting such conduct are considered unethical. A genuine consideration of others is essential to an ethical life. (Chewning, pp. 175–176).

An essential concomitant of ethics is of trust. Webster's Dictionary defines trust as "assured reliance on the character, ability, strength or truth of someone or something." Businesses are built on a foundation of trust in our free-enterprise system. When there are violations of this trust between competitors, between employer and employees, or between businesses and consumers, our economic system ceases to run smoothly. From a moral viewpoint, ethical behavior should not exist because of economic pragmatism, governmental edict, or contemporary fashionability—it should exist because it is morally appropriate and right. From an economic point of view, ethical behavior should exist because it just makes good business sense to be ethical and operate in a manner that demonstrates trustworthiness.

Robert Bruce Shaw, in *Trust in the Balance*, makes some thoughtful observations about trust within an organization. Paraphrasing his observations and applying his ideas to the marketplace as a whole:

> 1. Trust requires consumers have confidence in organizational promises or claims made to them. This means that a consumer should be able to believe that a commitment made will be met.
> 2. Trust requires integrity and consistency in following a known set of values, beliefs, and practices.
> 3. Trust requires concern for the well-being of others. This does not mean that organizational needs are not given appropriate emphasis—but it suggests the importance of understanding the impact of decisions and actions on others—i.e. consumers. (Shaw, pp. 39–40)

Companies can lose the trust of their customers by portraying their products in a deceptive or inaccurate manner. In one recent example, a Nike advertisement exhorted golfers to buy the same golf balls used by Tiger Woods. However, since Tiger Woods was using custom-made Nike golf balls not yet available to the general golfing public, the ad was, in fact, deceptive. In one of its ads, Volvo represented that Volvo cars could withstand a physical impact that, in fact, was not possible. Once a company is "caught" giving inaccurate information, even if done innocently, trust in that company is eroded.

Companies can also lose the trust of their customers when they fail to act promptly and notify their customers of problems that the company has discovered, especially where deaths may be involved. This occurred when Chrysler dragged its feet in replacing a safety latch on its Minivan (Geyelin, pp. A1, A10). More recently, Firestone and Ford had been publicly brought to task for failing to expeditiously notify American consumers of tire defects in SUVs even though the problem had occurred years earlier in other countries. In cases like these, trust might not just be eroded, it might be destroyed. It could take years of painstaking effort to rebuild trust under these circumstances, and some companies might not have the economic ability to withstand such a rebuilding process with their consumers.

A *20/20* and *New York Times* investigation on a recent *ABC 20/20* program, entitled "The Car Dealer's Secret" revealed a sad example of the violation of trust in the marketplace. The investigation divulged that many unsuspecting consumers have had hidden charges tacked on by some car dealers when purchasing a new car. According to consumer attorney Gary Klein, "It's a dirty little secret that the auto lending industry has not owned up to." (*ABC News 20/20*)

The scheme worked in the following manner. Car dealers would send a prospective buyer's application to a number of lenders, who would report to the car dealer what interest rate the lender would give to the buyer for his or her car loan. This interest rate is referred to as the "buy rate." Legally a car dealer is not required to tell the buyer what the "buy rate" is or how much the dealer is marking up the loan. If dealers did most of the loans at the buy rate, they only get a small fee. However, if they were able to convince the buyer to pay a higher rate, they made considerably more money. Lenders encouraged car dealers to charge the buyer a higher rate than the "buy rate" by agreeing to split the extra income with the dealer.

David Robertson, head of the Association of Finance and Insurance Professionals—a trade group representing finance managers—defended the practice, reflecting that it was akin to a retail markup on loans. "The dealership provides a valuable service on behalf of the customer in negotiating these loans," he said. "Because of that, the dealership should be compensated for that work." (*ABC News 20/20*)

Careful examination of the entire report, however, makes one seriously question this apologetic. Even if this practice is deemed to be legal, the critical issue is what happens to trust when the buyers discover that they have been charged an additional 1–3% of the loan without their knowledge? In some cases, consumers were led to believe that they were getting the dealer's bank rate, and in other cases, they were told that the dealer had shopped around at several banks to secure the best loan rate they could get for the buyer. While this practice may be questionable from a legal standpoint, it is clearly in ethical breach of trust with the consumer. Once discovered, the companies doing this will have the same credibility and trustworthiness problems as the other examples mentioned above.

The untrustworthiness problems of the car companies was compounded by the fact that the investigation appeared to reveal statistics showing that black customers were twice as likely as whites to have their rate marked up—and at a higher level. That evidence—included in thousands of pages of confidential documents which *20/20* and *The New York Times* obtained from a Tennessee court—revealed that some Nissan and GM dealers in Tennessee routinely marked up rates for blacks, forcing them to pay between $300 and $400 more than whites. (*ABC News 20/20*)

This is a tragic example for everyone who was affected by this markup and was the victim of this secret policy. Not only is trust destroyed, there is a huge economic cost to the general public. It is estimated that in the last four years or so, Texas car dealers have received approximately $9 billion of kickbacks from lenders, affecting 5.2 million consumers. (*ABC News 20/20*)

Let's compare these unfortunate examples of untrustworthy corporate behavior with the landmark example of Johnson & Johnson which ultimately increased its trustworthiness with consumers by the way it handled the Tylenol incident. After seven individuals, who had consumed Tylenol capsules contaminated by a third party died, Johnson & Johnson instituted a total product recall within a week costing an estimated $50 million after taxes. The company did this, not because it was responsible for causing the problem, but because it was the right thing to do. In addition, Johnson & Johnson spearheaded the development of more effective tamper-proof containers for their industry. Because of the company's swift response, consumers once again were able to trust in the Johnson & Johnson name. Although Johnson & Johnson suffered a decrease in market share at the time because of the scare, over the long term it has maintained its profitability in a highly competitive market. Certainly part of this profit success is attributable to consumers believing that Johnson & Johnson is a trustworthy company. (Robin and Reidenbach)

The e-commerce arena presents another example of the importance of marketers building a mutually valuable relationship with customers through a trust-based collaboration process. Recent research with 50 e-businesses reflects that companies which create and nurture trust find customers return to their sites repeatedly. (Dayal.... p. 64)

In the e-commerce world, six components of trust were found to be critical in developing trusting, satisfied customers:

- State-of-art reliable security measures on one's site
- Merchant legitimacy (e.g., ally one's product or service with an established brand)
- Order fulfillment (i.e. placing orders and getting merchandise efficiently and with minimal hassles)
- Tone and ambiance—handling consumers' personal information with sensitivity and iron-clad confidentiality
- Customers feeling that they are in control of the buying process
- Consumer collaboration—e.g., having chat groups to let consumers query each other about their purchases and experiences (Dayal..., pp. 64–67)

Additionally, one author noted recently that in the e-commerce world we've moved beyond brands and trademarks to "trustmarks." This author defined a trustmark as a

> ... (D)istinctive name or symbol that emotionally binds a company with the desires and aspirations of its customers. It's an emotional connection—and it's much bigger and more powerful than the uses that we traditionally associate with a trademark.... (Webber, p. 214)

Certainly if this is the case, trust—being an emotional link—is of supreme importance for a company that wants to succeed in doing business on the Internet.

It's unfortunate that while a plethora of examples of violation of trust easily come to mind, a paucity of examples "pop up" as noteworthy paradigms of organizational courage and trust in their relationship with consumers.

In conclusion, some key areas for companies to scrutinize and practice with regard to decisions that may affect trustworthiness in the marketplace might include:

- Does a company practice the Golden Rule with its customers? As a company insider, knowing what you know about the product, how willing would you be to purchase it for yourself or for a family member?
- How proud would you be if your marketing practices were made public.... shared with your friends....

or family? (Blanchard and Peale, p. 27)

- Are bottom-line concerns the sole component of your organizational decision-making process? What about human rights, the ecological/environmental impact, and other areas of social responsibility?
- Can a firm which engages in unethical business practices with customers be trusted to deal with its employees any differently? Unfortunately, frequently a willingness to violate standards of ethics is not an isolated phenomenon but permeates the culture. The result is erosion of integrity throughout a company. In such cases, trust is elusive at best. (Shaw, p. 75)
- Is your organization not only market driven, but also value-oriented? (Peters and Levering, Moskowitz, and Katz)
- Is there a strong commitment to a positive corporate culture and a clearly defined mission which is frequently and unambiguously voiced by upper-management?
- Does your organization exemplify trust by practicing a genuine relationship partnership with your customers—*before, during, and after* the initial purchase? (Strout, p. 69)

Companies which exemplify treating customers ethically are founded on a covenant of trust. There is a shared belief, confidence, and faith that the company and its people will be fair, reliable, and ethical in all its dealings. ***Total trust is the belief that a company and its people will never take opportunistic advantage of customer vulnerabilities***. (Hart and Johnson, pp. 11–13)

References

ABC News 20/20, "The Car Dealer's Secret," October 27, 2000.

Blanchard, Kenneth, and Norman Vincent Peale, *The Power of Ethical Management*, New York: William Morrow and Company, Inc., 1988.

Chewning, Richard C., *Business Ethics in a Changing Culture* (Reston, Virginia: Reston Publishing, 1984).

Dayal, Sandeep, Landesberg, Helen, and Michael Zeissner, "How to Build Trust Online," *Marketing Management*, Fall 1999, pp. 64–69.

Geyelin, Milo, "Why One Jury Dealt a Big Blow to Chrysler in Minivan-Latch Case," *Wall Street Journal*, November 19, 1997, pp. A1, A10.

Hart, Christopher W. and Michael D. Johnson, "Growing the Trust Relationship," *Marketing Management*, Spring 1999, pp. 9–19.

Hosmer, La Rue Tone, *The Ethics of Management*, second edition (Homewood, Illinois: Irwin, 1991).

Kaydo, Chad, "A Position of Power," *Sales & Marketing Management*, June 2000, pp. 104–106, 108ff.

Levering, Robert; Moskowitz, Milton; and Michael Katz, *The 100 Best Companies to Work for in America* (Reading, Mass.: Addison-Wesley, 1984).

Magnet, Myron, "Meet the New Revolutionaries," *Fortune*, February 24, 1992, pp. 94–101.

Muoio, Anna, "The Experienced Customer," *Net Company*, Fall 1999, pp. 025–027.

Peters, Thomas J. and Robert H. Waterman Jr., *In Search of Excellence* (New York: Harper & Row, 1982).

Richardson, John (ed.), *Annual Editions: Business Ethics 00/01* (Guilford, CT: McGraw-Hill/Dushkin, 2000).

_____, *Annual Editions: Marketing 00/01* (Guilford, CT: McGraw-Hill/Dushkin, 2000).

Robin, Donald P., and Erich Reidenbach, "Social Responsibility, Ethics, and Marketing Strategy: Closing the Gap Between Concept and Application," *Journal of Marketing*, Vol. 51 (January 1987), pp. 44–58.

Shaw, Robert Bruce, *Trust in the Balance*, (San Francisco: Jossey-Bass Publishers, 1997).

Strout, Erin, "Tough Customers," *Sales Marketing Management*, January 2000, pp. 63–69.

Webber, Alan M., "Trust in the Future," *Fast Company*, September 2000, pp. 209–212ff.

***Dr. John E. Richardson** is Professor of Marketing in the Graziadio School of Business and Management at Pepperdine University, Malibu, California*

***Dr. Linnea Bernard McCord** is Associate Professor of Business Law in the Graziadio School of Business and Management at Pepperdine University, Malibu, California*

CAN BUSINESS STILL SAVE THE WORLD?

The pioneers of socially responsible companies—stars like Anita Roddick and Ben Cohen—had big hearts and even bigger mouths. They hated capitalism but loved what it could help them do. Now they have followers. Sort of. Meet the new generation of activist entrepreneurs

by Thea Singer

"When we first started Ben & Jerry's, we had no intention of going into 'business'—we saw it as pretty much a lark. Then there came a time about five years ago when Jerry and I noticed that we were no longer scooping ice-cream cones behind a counter and working in the ice-cream shop, that we were bosses and administrators who were spending a lot of time on the phone and doing paperwork. When we were introduced to people and they asked, 'What do you do?' there came a point when the answer was not 'I'm a homemade ice-cream shop owner' but 'I'm a businessman.' And I had a hard time mouthing those words."

—BEN COHEN, COFOUNDER OF BEN & JERRY'S HOMEMADE INC., IN THE ARTICLE "COMING OF AGE," IN INC.'S 10TH-ANNIVERSARY ISSUE, 1989

The times they are a-changin'

CHANCES ARE, WHEN YOU HEAR THE TERM *SOCIALLY RESPONSIBLE business,* a handful of companies—and their founders—leap to mind: Ben & Jerry's Homemade (Ben Cohen, Jerry Greenfield). The Body Shop International (Anita and Gordon Roddick). Smith & Hawken (Paul Hawken). Patagonia (Yvon Chouinard). They're the (once) wild-and-crazy pioneers of a new frontier—the folks who brought us ice cream named for devotees of electric Kool-Aid and shampoo squeezed out of mud from the Atlas Mountains. At the same time they espoused "principles before profits" and a commitment to making the world—from the New York City subways to the Pentagon to the Amazon rain forest—a better place. They set up shop in the late 1970s or the 1980s, and most of them, with the help of doting media, grew fast and furiously.

But the road to success had its bumps as well. For a self-professed socially responsible company, fast growth doesn't present just the typical entrepreneurial challenges—things like maintaining product quality, keeping pace with demand, managing cash flow, and coping with sales shortfalls. It also presents special challenges, ones that come with adhering to a higher standard—that is, doing all of the above while treating employees, suppliers, and customers well, which includes being forthright in marketing claims and vendor relationships. In other words, walking the talk is the name of the game.

And that's where, for all the positive change they effected, some of the 1980s icons got into trouble in the mid 1990s. Ben & Jerry's got called on the carpet for claiming that its Rainforest Crunch ice cream was made with nuts collected by Amazon "forest peoples." In fact, to compensate for quality problems, the nut supplier, Community Products Inc. (which Cohen also owned), bought 95% of the nuts from commercial vendors. In a similar fashion, the Body Shop got skewered when a magazine article questioned its claims about animal testing, alleged that the company used petrochemicals in some of its "natural" products, and charged that its Trade Not Aid program accounted for less of its supplies than it had claimed. (The Body Shop denied all the magazine's charges.)

The people who started socially responsible companies in the '90s had the benefit of learning from their pre-

ANITA RODDICK

THE BODY SHOP INTERNATIONAL, ESTABLISHED IN 1976

Roddick, like many social-venture entrepreneurs, never dreamed she'd run a public company someday.

"I think a lot of us would have slit our wrists if we ever thought we'd be part of corporate America or England," she says. "Big business was alien to me. What I wanted to do was create a livelihood, and I think women are quite good at that—probably better than blokes. We mush up an interest and a skill, and that's a livelihood."

Roddick's company, the Body Shop, was arguably the most successful British enterprise of the 1980s and remains one of the best-known global brands to this day. But the company has taken its share of hits, both financially and emotionally.

In 1994 a journalist named Jon Entine wrote a magazine article about the Body Shop that suggested that the company was guilty of hypocritical marketing. At about the same time, the company's stock price on the London exchange plummeted amid a troubled North American expansion plan. Roddick says today that the Body Shop's problems were caused by poor hiring practices and some lousy mall leases foisted on the company by real estate brokers.

But some observers suggest that the company struggled because Anita Roddick, ever an outspoken crusader, was focused on being a social activist and was almost indifferent to her business's bottom line.

Today Roddick is still the cochairman of the Body Shop, but she says her first priority is writing. Her new book, *Business as Unusual* (Thorsons), was published in the United States in January, and she's already working on another manuscript. "I'm at a point in my life where I want to be heard," she explains. "I have knowledge, and I want to pass it on."

—*Mike Hofman*

decessors' mistakes. Which made us wonder: How did those lessons influence the way the new founders shaped their companies?

The younger entrepreneurs are quick to acknowledge their '80s counterparts as their mentors, the people who laid the groundwork for a whole new way of doing business. "They are prophets," says Wild Planet CEO Daniel Grossman. "There is no doubt." But the new breed has added its own, decidedly more pragmatic ingredients to the socially responsible business mix. "Ben and Jerry basically threw everything on the wall to see if it stuck," says Sustainable Harvest founder David Griswold. "That's not the process kind of approach that today's socially responsible businesses are taking."

The differences we uncovered between the '80s revolutionaries and today's company builders were as startling to our minds as a first taste of Ben & Jerry's "Orgasmic Flavors" of ice cream was to our palates more than two decades ago.

What you sell is important

THE PRODUCT OR SERVICE OF THE NEW COMPANIES, NOT just the mission, must be socially responsible—that is, it must advance the health and well-being of those it affects (individuals, companies, the environment), not undercut them. (See "The Young Turks," for profiles of the seven companies we've chosen to represent the new breed.) Hence: barely sweetened iced tea and totally biodegradable tea bags (Honest Tea Inc.); garden, home, and pet products made from recycled or organic materials (WorldWise Inc.); organic, shade-grown coffee with a guaranteed base price for growers (Sustainable Harvest Inc.); Web development using urban workers (CitySoft Inc.); nonsexist, nonviolent toys (Wild Planet Toys Inc.); revitalized communities and neighborhoods (Village Real Estate Services); and recycled paper products (New Leaf Paper LLC). "We want the product that we're providing to have an impact," says Seth Goldman, cofounder of Honest Tea.

Proud to be in business

MOST OF THE CURRENT BATCH OF CEOS EITHER WENT TO business school or intended to (but got sidetracked by a business opportunity). But those who didn't go that route, like New Leaf Paper cofounder Jeff Mendelsohn, understand the necessity of management expertise. "The best thing I did was hire a really good operations guy with a commitment to social responsibility, because he knows how to manage, run sales operations, and so on, better than I do," says Mendelsohn.

The young founders are businesspeople—and proud of it. "I did a lot of entrepreneurial things from a young age," boasts WorldWise CEO Aaron Lamstein. "I started one of the first computer bulletin boards in Marin County in 1980, using a TRS-80 Model 3—that's before the IBM PC." Lamstein was planning to study for both law and business degrees when his mentor swayed him in another direction by suggesting that he start a company around an environmental concept. Seth Goldman even won a business-plan competition as a student at the Yale School of Management and later started Honest Tea with one of his professors.

Several of the new socially responsible entrepreneurs, including Goldman and Sustainable Harvest's David Griswold, make a point of hiring business-school grads (or using interns from the schools) to beef up their ranks.

Paul Hawken

SMITH & HAWKEN, ESTABLISHED IN 1979

During demonstrations against the World Trade Organization summit in Seattle in 1999, Paul Hawken was among the protesters teargassed by police. In the midst of the melee, an old ally came to his rescue. "Paul was very nearly dying—choking to death with the gas—and I pulled him out of line and fed him water and vinegar" to flush his eyes, recalls the Body Shop's Anita Roddick. "I said to him, 'Fuck, here we go again. Always in the middle of the mess.'"

These days Hawken is consulting, writing, teaching, and—as in the case of the Seattle protests—marshaling the forces of antiglobalism. Hawken, who lives in Sausalito, Calif., says his political philosophy hasn't changed much since the days when he was running Smith & Hawken, writing the classic *Growing a Business*, and appearing in a 17-part PBS series based on that book. "My view then and now is that there is a powerful oligarchy in this country that most people are blind to," he says. "We are not a democracy, we are a plutocracy. This country was founded because of corporate abuse, the crown-chartered corporations that taxed without representation. Now we are still being abused by corporations, though they do it with money, power, and corrupt politicians. Until our country makes a distinction between money and governance, power and business, we will have an unjust society that preys upon itself and the world in the name of freedom, democracy, and the American way of life."

If Hawken sounds as if he doesn't like business very much, that's because he doesn't.

So if you love business, why should you bother listening to Hawken? He has a pat rebuttal. "Simple," he says. "The world of business will either be socially responsible or there won't be a world for business to be in."

—*M.H.*

"I've had business-school graduates here because I feel like the longevity of the company really depends on competing, using the rules of business," says Griswold, who'd applied to business school but kept deferring when the chance to sell the beans of Mexican coffee farmers presented itself. "Good deeds alone don't work."

That's a far cry from the likes of Ben Cohen, Anita Roddick, and Yvon Chouinard, for instance, who saw businesspeople as tools of the military-industrial complex and *profits* as a dirty word. In fact, in the '90s, when the young turks joined their elders in the Social Venture Network (SVN), an organization for entrepreneurs and investors interested in promoting social responsibility in business, the tension between the business-school contingent and the veterans was palpable. (See "Social Venture Network".)

'I came to believe that the lack of new wealth creation was really the root cause of urban problems,' says CitySoft's Nick Gleason.

"At that time Anita and Ben... certainly in their public statements, were very clear," says Wild Planet's Grossman, who first attended an SVN meeting as an intern while he was earning his M.B.A. from Stanford Business School. "They were saying, 'We would never hire an M.B.A. M.B.A.'s are poison. They think about only one bottom line. They're fixated on the notion of net profits at the expense of everything else.'" It was only later, out of necessity, that the stance softened. "Ben and Anita dropped their rhetoric about the M.B.A. thing because, frankly, through the Trojan Horse we entered, and we were there steadily for years," says Grossman.

Solid commitment to change

TODAY'S CEOS WERE DEDICATED TO THE MISSION THAT shaped their companies—or some variation of it—before they opened their doors for business. They have a history of working with nonprofits, the government, or other socially responsible endeavors. Their companies, it seems, are a natural outgrowth of their long-held values.

Daniel Grossman, who entered business school with plans to apply his hard-core business skills to the public sector or a nonprofit, served for eight years in the U.S. Foreign Service. David Griswold cofounded and ran Aztec Harvest, a sales-and-marketing outfit for coffee farmers from Mexican cooperatives that was owned by the farmers. Seth Goldman was a press secretary on Capitol Hill and marketed socially responsible mutual funds for Calvert Group. Village Real Estate Services founder Mark Deutschmann was a devotee of historic preservation.

CitySoft CEO Nick Gleason was a community and labor organizer in Oakland, Calif., and ran his own urban-development consulting company, serving nonprofits, foundations, school districts, and governments. His move to the for-profit sector evolved directly from his nonprofit experiences. "I came to believe that the lack of new wealth creation was really the root cause of urban problems," says Gleason. "Activist organizations and entrepreneurship are very similar in terms of trying to create teams, successes. Both attempt to help a group of people achieve goals in a resource-constrained environment."

THE YOUNG TURKS

COMPANY: Sustainable Harvest Inc.
HEADQUARTERS: Emeryville, Calif.
FOUNDER AND PRESIDENT: David Griswold, age 39
BUSINESS: Sourcer/importer of shade-grown, organic "relationship" coffees—that is, coffees bought from small family farms and cooperatives in Asia, Africa, and Central and South America with which the company has formed long-term relationships. The company follows "fair trade" practices, meaning it pays some growers a guaranteed minimum base price regardless of the world market price.
FOUNDED: 1996
2000 REVENUES: $2.8 million
BECAME PROFITABLE: 1998
NUMBER OF EMPLOYEES: 3

COMPANY: Honest Tea Inc.
HEADQUARTERS: Bethesda, Md.
COFOUNDER AND PRESIDENT: Seth Goldman, age 35
BUSINESS: Maker of barely sweetened bottled iced tea and fully biodegradable tea bags filled with whole tea leaves
FOUNDED: 1998
2000 REVENUES: $2 million
PROJECTED TO BECOME PROFITABLE: 2002
NUMBER OF EMPLOYEES: 12

COMPANY: Wild Planet Toys Inc.
HEADQUARTERS: San Francisco
COFOUNDER AND CEO: Daniel Grossman, age 43
BUSINESS: Designer/manufacturer of nonsexist, nonviolent, imagination-inspiring toys
FOUNDED: 1993
2000 REVENUES: $30 million
BECAME PROFITABLE: 1996
NUMBER OF EMPLOYEES: 40, including 10 in Hong Kong

COMPANY: CitySoft Inc.
HEADQUARTERS: Watertown, Mass.
COFOUNDER AND CEO: Nick Gleason, age 33
BUSINESS: Web developer with the mission of recruiting and hiring its workforce from urban neighborhoods; CitySoft does no training but does team up with tech-training centers to develop training standards.
FOUNDED: 1998
2000 REVENUES: $2 million
BECAME PROFITABLE: 1997
NUMBER OF EMPLOYEES: 50

COMPANY: WorldWise Inc.
HEADQUARTERS: San Rafael, Calif.
COFOUNDER AND CEO: Aaron Lamstein, age 33
BUSINESS: Developer/manufacturer of garden, home, and pet products made from recycled materials and sold in mass markets like Wal-Mart, Target, and the Home Depot
FOUNDED: 1990
2000 REVENUES: Under $10 million
BECAME PROFITABLE: 1996
NUMBER OF EMPLOYEES: 15 in corporate office, 45 independent manufacturing reps

COMPANY: Village Real Estate Services
HEADQUARTERS: Nashville
FOUNDER AND OWNER: Mark Deutschmann, age 43
BUSINESS: Real estate company that specializes in urban residential sales and revitalizes urban neighborhoods
FOUNDED: 1996
2000 REVENUES: $1.2 million in commissions on $92 million in sales
BECAME PROFITABLE: 1997
NUMBER OF EMPLOYEES: 10, plus 35 affiliate brokers

COMPANY: New Leaf Paper LLC
HEADQUARTERS: San Francisco
COFOUNDER AND PRESIDENT: Jeff Mendelsohn, age 34
BUSINESS: Manufacturer/distributor of recycled paper
FOUNDED: 1998
2000 REVENUES: $8 million
BECAME PROFITABLE: 1998
NUMBER OF EMPLOYEES: 10

In contrast, before the company founders of the '80s started their businesses, they were generally involved with activities removed from their companies-to-be—Anita Roddick owned a small hotel in Littlehampton, England, and was raising two young daughters; Yvon Chouinard saw mountain climbing as a calling. And they more often fell into the socially responsible world than intentionally traveled there. "The first generation went through their formative years in the '60s and didn't found their businesses with the idea that they were going to change the world, by and large," says Grossman. "Ben and Jerry kind of stumbled into making ice cream to make ends meet and then things were added as they went along."

Focusing on two bottom lines

TODAY'S CEOS ARE JUST AS DEDICATED TO BUILDING A VIABLE, profitable business as they are to hewing to a mission—and they think strategically to make both happen. So they speak of a "double bottom line."

"Part of our concept is that we must have an incredibly focused mission that includes equally environmental and social issues and economic issues—that is, making sure that we have a really solid, healthy, financially secure business," says WorldWise's Lamstein. "You can't put one in front of the other. You can't be successful if you can't do both." Says Goldman: "A commitment to socially responsible business cannot be used as an excuse to make poor business decisions. If we were to accept lower margins because of our commitment to social responsibility, then we'd be doing the broader socially responsible business movement a disservice because we wouldn't be as competitive or as attractive to investors."

GARY HIRSHBERG

STONYFIELD FARM, ESTABLISHED IN 1983

This yogurt purveyor's experience combines the idealism of the '80s pioneers with the pragmatism of the recent crop of socially responsible entrepreneurs. Before taking the grand leap into the business world, Hirshberg had worked for an ecological advocacy group called the New Alchemy Institute. "We saw Stonyfield Farm as a for-profit with a nonprofit's mission," Hirshberg recalls. "Fundamentally, we thought we could fund ourselves. I was tired of having my palm faceup at the nonprofit. I saw creating a business as breaking out of the nonprofit rut. The irony is that I spent the first 10 years of my business constantly raising money."

That first decade of entrepreneurship, which involved turning a New Hampshire dairy farm with 11 Jersey cows into a profit maker, was "horrendous," Hirshberg says today. He says Stonyfield got its act together only around 1991. Today the company sells more than $70 million worth of yogurt annually. Hirshberg is still at the helm as CEO. And his green social mission is also still front and center at the company, with environmental messages printed on the lids of millions of yogurt containers each year. The company also donates 10% of after-tax profits to fund Profits for the Planet, initiatives that "help protect or restore the earth."

Though Hirshberg is very active, he admits that the social-venture movement's "noise level" has dropped significantly in the past few years. He says that is a result of the backlash that hit colleagues like Ben Cohen and Anita Roddick. To prevent an exposé on his company, Hirshberg says, he's "almost fascistic" about monitoring what promises the company makes about its products and its activism. "I don't think we've been strident," he says. "By my nature, I guess I've always been a bit more cautious."

—M.H.

The strategic thinking that Lamstein used to get WorldWise up and running is a case in point of double-bottom-line thinking. Committed to constructing a business around environmentally responsible products, Lamstein initially devised a three-pronged model: a chain of retail stores, which would showcase WorldWise products in the context in which they'd be used; a mail-order catalog; and a research-and-development arm for creating branded products to sell wholesale.

With that model in mind, Lamstein began researching both the environmental and economic sides of the business—that is, which products the company should make, which materials and methods it should use to make them, and how it should be financed and earn revenues. Investors that he approached found the concept intriguing but couldn't understand why he wanted to spend $1 million to $2 million to start a chain of stores when he had no idea whether people wanted to buy his environmentally friendly merchandise. He took the investors' skepticism to heart. "Since I'd researched about 10,000 products, I thought, 'Why not focus on the wholesale side of the business and develop a brand that has virtually zero competition?'" Lamstein recalls.

The question then was, How do you do that? After all, environmentally friendly products were not new. Then Lamstein hit on the answer: bring products that are selling in niche markets into the mainstream. The idea was to start selling already existing products under the WorldWise brand to test which ones worked in the mass market. Once the company had gathered enough intelligence about what sold and had established some cash flow, it would develop new products of its own.

An exotic fruit-and-nut mix whose ingredients came from the Amazon rain forest was the company's first offering. Through his mentor, a seasoned businessman, Lamstein signed up Costco as a customer in 1993. "Our whole concept was that our products had to work as well as or better than others, look as good or finer, cost the same or less, and be better for the environment," says Lamstein. Because the cost-competitive piece was so important, Lamstein turned the typical start-small-and-build paradigm on its head. "We were selective about items," he says, "but we sold them in large quantities so that we could buy our materials competitively."

The mass market bit on the idea—quite literally—and WorldWise soon began developing its own products, the first of which was a charcoal starter for barbecuing that required just newspaper and no lighter fluid. Since its launch, the company has added Target, the Home Depot, and Wal-Mart to its customer list.

Control growth for the long haul

TO BE ABLE TO SUSTAIN A PROFITABLE BUSINESS AND STICK to a mission (even when times get tough), the young CEOs have to pay close attention to their companies' growth rates. In many cases they're careful not to grow too fast. "We're trying to do managed growth," says Sustainable Harvest's Griswold. "We don't want to overextend ourselves. What matters is the experience of running your company and the impact you're having on those you're working with. Size is not the most important thing; we're looking for balance as well as success." Mark Deutschmann concurs, noting that he takes on only a certain amount of business at Village Real Estate Services so that he can maintain a healthy personal life as well as stick to his values. "If we grow too fast, there's a chance we might not give enough attention to every detail and every person," he says.

BEN COHEN

BEN & JERRY'S HOMEMADE INC., ESTABLISHED IN 1978

Critics have long held that the management skills of Ben Cohen and partner Jerry Greenfield are as soft as a pint of Chunky Monkey left out on a summer afternoon. But the partners are still plugging away, 23 years after they started their ice-cream company in a converted gas station in Burlington, Vt. Today, however, their focus is almost exclusively on the company's social work, especially the foundation that they endowed with company stock in 1985. The company has donated 7.5% of pretax profits to the foundation and to Vermont community groups every year since then.

But Ben & Jerry's may face the prospect of marketing the names of two men who quit in a huff. Last spring the Anglo-Dutch conglomerate Unilever bought Ben & Jerry's for $326 million. So far, the marriage has not been a happy one for the maverick founders, who were disappointed with their new bosses' choice for a CEO. Unilever, which also sells Mentadent toothpaste and I Can't Believe It's Not Butter, installed a candidate who had previously worked for the company in Mexico; Cohen and Greenfield wanted a board member to get the top job. In November the partners threatened to quit, and their fans have set up a Web site—http://www.savebenjerry.com/—to rally support for them and to catalog their many beefs with the parent company.

The Body Shop's Anita Roddick says Cohen is sad about his eponymous company's direction, which is focused on aggressive revenue growth. "I think both Ben and I think we'd move out of our companies if they became less progressive," she says. "Ben's not interested in yet another ice cream, and I'm not interested in yet another bubble bath. We're too old just to make more money."

—M.H.

Of course, for many of the socially responsible companies, including Wild Planet Toys, reaching as wide an audience as possible is crucial if their mission is to be realized—it's important to spread the word as well as to bring in enough revenues to carry on. The companies deal with the tension between encouraging growth and staying socially responsible by using standard management techniques.

"The bigger issue is, fundamentally, What are the measures of control in the business?" says Grossman. "If you're a business that started kind of by accident—and I don't mean that in any negative way—then you don't have a kind of planning culture, and you probably don't have a culture where you think a lot about, What does it mean to have one big customer who's driving all your growth? What does it mean to have margins that are subpar for the industry? All those things that they grind into you in business school. Given those things, then, I think that among the young companies you find a greater measure of control over the path of the business. So I can look at our income statement, and I can say, 'I see some concern going forward, given the thinness of these margins,' which then directly relates to what we're able to spend on expenses, hiring, all of that stuff. So I think that just comes with the territory."

CitySoft and New Leaf Paper have tried to manage the tension between growth and goals in similar ways. Both have formed partnerships with larger companies in order to take on big projects without spreading themselves too thin. New Leaf Paper, which must cope with huge economies-of-scale issues in order to compete with the paper manufacturers that use virgin fiber, has formed alliances with various large stable companies like Old Navy Clothing, Nike, and Hewlett-Packard to ensure that its orders are of decent volume. New Leaf Paper also has set up partnerships with paper mills, both to develop and manufacture its products. CitySoft, whose revenues have jumped by 300% a year, is trying to shift from selling Web-development services to individual customers to acting as a subcontractor for larger technology integrators.

Business relationships matter

PRINCIPLES OF SOCIAL RESPONSIBILITY MUST APPLY INSIDE the company (to compensation, work hours, benefits, culture, and structure) as well as outside the business—to the best of the company's ability. Critical outside relationships include those with suppliers and customers.

Among our representative companies, benefits (aside from the traditional health insurance, vacation, and sick time) range from employee stock options (offered by four) to paid time off for volunteer work (offered by three). They all offer nonhierarchical, open structures, though they also have senior management teams. The companies' vendor relationships also reflect their social agendas. WorldWise, for instance, makes a point of using only U.S. manufacturers, which it can visit to ensure that they meet its standards; proximity to customers also means energy savings and less pollution. (In the interest of full disclosure, Lamstein notes that his company did have one item assembled in Mexico but stopped producing that product altogether when it was underpriced by competitors manufacturing in China.) Honest Tea developed a relationship with I'tchik Herbal Tea, a small woman-owned company on the Crow Reservation, in Montana, from which it buys the peppermint leaves for its First Nation tea. I'tchik gets royalties from the sales of the tea made from the peppermint, as does a Native American organization called Pretty Shield Foundation, which includes foster care among its activities.

Social Venture Network

ESTABLISHED IN 1987

Right from the start, the founders of San Francisco-based nonprofit Social Venture Network wanted a "safe harbor" where social-activist entrepreneurs could meet to commiserate, coinvest in deals, and share best practices. As part of that mission, SVN, its 400 members, and its key organizers never spoke publicly about their work. Until now.

SVN is embarking on a major overhaul. Judy Wicks, founder of White Dog Enterprises, is chairing the group's national advisory board, and Ben Cohen of Ben & Jerry's has agreed to donate $150,000 a year for three years to fund an ambitious new slate of projects. A year ago, SVN hired a new president named Chris Gallagher. Though Gallagher is only 31 years old, "if anyone can be successful in that role, Chris should be able to do it," says Stephen Williamson, the CEO of prominent juice maker and social-venture company Odwalla Inc.

Gallagher once worked as the director of strategic communications at Williamson's California juice company. "Chris and I sat shoulder to shoulder through months of very difficult times," Williamson says, referring to Odwalla's well-publicized 1996 recall of apple juice that had been contaminated with E. coli bacteria.

Gallagher says his goal is to turn the well-meaning SVN into a brawny advocacy organization. "A challenge over the years has been determining how much we should keep the spirit of fluidity of the network and how much we should also try to be a force in the world," he explains. "We're increasingly looking for a way to make an impact, to become an organization that has a public voice, and to take principled action."

—*M.H.*

Sustainable Harvest takes things even further. Given the nature of his business (it's essentially a liaison between coffee farmers, roasters, and retailers), David Griswold has been able to establish an extraordinary level of accountability with every party he does business with. He personally sources the coffee he imports, forming long-term relationships with the small family farms and cooperatives that are his growers. He's even gone so far as to break down the standard 152-pound bag of beans into 50-pound boxes made from recycled materials so that growers and roasters alike will have an easier time lifting his merchandise. "We go for a level of transparency—lay it out with your customers and suppliers," he says. "We consider what everyone needs to be profitable, looking at the other side of the fence: 'What do you need? This is what I need.'"

Wild Planet Toys also presents a comprehensive model for openness—in this case, inside the company. For starters, Wild Planet uses open-book management, which means that everyone has access to all the company's financial data, except for figures on equity ownership (though everyone does receive stock options) and salaries. "Jack Stack [president of Springfield Remanufacturing Corp. and an early proponent of open-book management] has this great motto of sharing his kingdom with everyone," says Grossman. "I don't know how widely that happened in the 1980s companies. I know that happens here. It's a very valuable tool. People don't have to whisper and wonder, 'Gee, are we really making a profit? What does our bank account look like?' Profits, margins—it's all right there."

In addition, since its inception in 1993, Wild Planet Toys has conducted annual social assessments of its inner and outer workings to make sure that the company is adhering to its stated values. Those values extend from "We believe in providing positive influences for children" to "We emphasize teamwork and make decisions as a team" to "We get involved in our community, particularly in partnerships with kids."

"I think the people who came out of the '60s were a little less democratic in terms of some of the things that they implemented," says Grossman. "I'm not judging or faulting them, but I think that their view was: 'Hey, we're leading a revolution, and the people who work for us have to understand these issues. We will help them understand those issues; we will bring them along the path. But this is the way it's going to be.' That's definitely not my style; sometimes to a fault it's not my style. It's the psychic rewards that are the most important. Not just 'Do you have a channel for dissent?' but 'Are you engaged in the company? Are you part of crafting the path to the future?'"

Nick Gleason, who spent time working on the shop floor of the airline-engine plant of Pratt & Whitney, has an eminently logical take on running a democratic company. "One of the things I learned from working in manufacturing companies is you should push decisions out to their furthest reasonable place," he says. "The CEO should make certain decisions, and certain decisions the person on the assembly line should make. The issue is what decisions should be made where. I shouldn't be running projects; the projects team should be running projects. I should be facilitating decision making around fund-raising and working with investors. And if you get too far off the appropriate decision-making roles, then you get confusion or ineffectiveness or lack of preparation."

Do the best you can at the time

IN TODAY'S SOCIALLY RESPONSIBLE BUSINESSES, UNDERSTATEMENT is the name of the game. In keeping with that sentiment, the founders hold the following guidelines in common: Don't make promises you can't keep or claims you can't stick to. Be scrupulously honest.

'All I can say is that we strive to be socially responsible,' says Wild Planet's Daniel Grossman.

Seth Goldman was very clear in explaining that the peppermint leaves he buys from I'tchik Herbal Tea are not grown on the Crow Reservation but are bought from still another source, and that he can't make claims about the labor conditions under which the company's herbs and teas are grown, because he hasn't visited the farms. Aaron Lamstein was totally up-front about the fact that he can't vouch for every condition under which workers manufacture his products, since the factories he uses are spread out across the United States, nor can he claim that all the components that accompany WorldWise's goods are recycled or organic.

"Before we go into a product agreement with anyone, we have extensive discussions—first about environmental issues, second about social issues," says Lamstein. "Tremendous numbers of components are produced for our products: the box, the label, the product itself, the instruction sheet—each could be made in a separate place. We don't visit the component manufacturers of every item. We don't have the answer to every question. Like all businesses trying to be on the cutting edge, we're learning as we go along. Our philosophy is that we need to do the best we can in as many places as we can. We also need to provide value to the customer."

Jeff Mendelsohn acknowledges that since New Leaf Paper is a rapidly growing company with only 10 employees, its priorities are developing its customer base, expanding its product line, and providing its customers with top-notch recycled papers and its employees with a fair and fulfilling work environment. "There are a number of social-responsibility issues that will become part of our agenda as we grow," says Mendelsohn. He notes that one of the mills that New Leaf Paper used recently closed its doors. "We were really sad for the employees, but we had no control over the situation," he says.

Daniel Grossman goes one step further. He doesn't even describe Wild Planet as a socially responsible company. "I'm very careful about saying, 'This is a socially responsible company,' because it's not," he says. "There are plenty of things, if you came here, if you looked at them, you could say, 'Is that responsible?' So all I can say is that we strive to be. We're public about it, and we assess our performance."

Wild Planet manufactures its toys in China, and even though it screens the factories it works with and has an office in Hong Kong, Grossman acknowledges that the company doesn't have the level of control over the manufacturing process that it would have if the toys were made in the States. "The reality is, if we're trying to create models that are sustainable, you're not going to have the control over every piece of the business, so you have to pick your places, and you have to be really clear."

In Wild Planet's early years, Grossman says, there was discussion about producing the toys in the United States. "But that would have meant that we'd end up selling probably to the top 5% of the market. And our mission was to provide these pro-social, if you will, toys to all kids, not just kids whose parents shop at FAO Schwarz. So we made that decision, we made that compromise."

Grossman applies that scrupulous honesty to matters inside Wild Planet as well. "I feel like we as businesses have obligations to our employees, and part of that obligation is to help everyone understand what the environment that we're operating in is like, to help everyone understand how our performance relates to that environment, and to make clear that the business is not a family. I think that's a setup, frankly," he says. "Sometimes people have to leave for reasons that are beyond our control. We talk about family style, but it's not a family. Anybody who's been in it knows that."

Forget the hype

FOR TODAY'S COMPANIES, SOCIAL RESPONSIBILITY IS NOT about marketing and image. In "Lost in Patagonia," a profile of the outdoor-clothing maker that appeared in *Inc.* in August 1992, Edward O. Welles wrote: "*Image* is a word that is liberally bandied about at Patagonia, and the concept serves as a key cog in the company's strategy." That's not the case in these new companies. They go about doing their socially responsible deeds quietly.

"When we first brought out our peppermint tea, our label didn't mention that we were sharing the revenues with the Crow Nation," says Goldman. "We didn't want people to think that was a gimmick." Mark Deutschmann notes that Village Real Estate Services concentrates primarily on marketing its services, not on publicizing its Village Fund, which owns 5% of the real estate business and is committed to the revitalization of urban neighborhoods.

CitySoft, too, focuses its marketing on its product and Web-development services. In fact, says Gleason, having a reputation for being socially involved could actually hurt his business. "Our whole company is focused on demonstrating the mainstream viability of urban talent, and so here's what happens if we get covered as a social story: we automatically become nonmainstream," he says. "Our goal is to have AOL want to hire us and have other companies replicate our hiring because they believe it will help them win in their business world. But if they view us as a social-service activity, not only will they be less likely to hire us and take us seriously, they'll be less likely to take the concept seriously, and they'll be less likely to do that kind of hiring themselves. Managing the messages and keeping people focused on the business is very important."

OF COURSE, DESPITE ALL THE LESSONS THAT THESE CEOs have taken to heart, it remains to be seen how their companies will fare down the road. Many of the current crop of businesses are five years old or younger and post sales from $2 million to $8 million. Ben & Jerry's, by contrast, was acquired in April 2000 by giant Unilever for $326 million and had sales last year of some $248 million.

Still, this much is clear: the socially responsible companies of today, unlike their forebears, aren't driven by a cult of personality (read: Ben Cohen, Yvon Chouinard, Paul Hawken, Anita Roddick). The very lack of name recognition among the newer CEOs we discovered in our quest proves that point. Even more important, social responsibility for the recent crop of company founders—at least at this early date—seems to be not about them nor even about their companies. It's about the mission.

Thea Singer (thea.singer@inc.com) is an associate editor at Inc.

AS LEADERS, WOMEN RULE

New studies find that female managers outshine their male counterparts in almost every measure

Twenty-five years after women first started pouring into the labor force—and trying to be more like men in every way, from wearing power suits to picking up golf clubs—new research is showing that men ought to be the ones doing more of the imitating. In fact, after years of analyzing what makes leaders most effective and figuring out who's got the Right Stuff, management gurus now know how to boost the odds of getting a great executive: Hire a female.

That's the essential finding of a growing number of comprehensive management studies conducted by consultants across the country for companies ranging from high-tech to manufacturing to consumer services. By and large, the studies show that women executives, when rated by their peers, underlings, and bosses, score higher than their male counterparts on a wide variety of measures—from producing high-quality work to goal-setting to mentoring employees. Using elaborate performance evaluations of execs, researchers found that women got higher ratings than men on almost every skill measured. Ironically, the researchers weren't looking to ferret out gender differences. They accidentally stumbled on the findings when they were compiling hundreds of routine performance evaluations and then analyzing the results.

Only 2 of the 500 top companies have female CEOs

The gender differences were often small, and men sometimes earned higher marks in some critical areas, such as strategic ability and technical analysis. But overall, female executives were judged more effective than their male counterparts. "Women are scoring higher on almost everything we look at," says Shirley Ross, an industrial psychologist who helped oversee a study performed by Hagberg Consulting Group in Foster City, Calif. Hagberg conducts in-depth performance evaluations of senior managers for its diverse clients, including technology, health care, financial-service, and consumer-goods companies. Of the 425 high-level executives evaluated, each by about 25 people, women execs won higher ratings on 42 of the 52 skills measured.

WHERE FEMALE EXECS DO BETTER: A SCORECARD

None of the studies set out to find gender differences. They stumbled on them while compiling and analyzing performance evaluations.

SKILL (EACH X-MARK DENOTES WHICH GROUP SCORED HIGHER ON THE RESPECTIVE STUDIES)	MEN	WOMEN
MOTIVATING OTHERS		✓✓✓✓✓
FOSTERING COMMUNICATION		✓✓✓*
PRODUCING HIGH-QUALITY WORK		✓✓✓✓✓
STRATEGIC PLANNING	✓✓	✓✓*
LISTENING TO OTHERS		✓✓✓✓✓
ANALYZING ISSUES	✓✓	✓✓*

*In one study, women's and men's scores in these categories were statistically even

DATA: HAGBERG CONSULTING GROUP, MANAGEMENT RESEARCH GROUP, LAWRENCE A. PFAFF, PERSONNEL DECISIONS INTERNATIONAL INC., ADVANCED TEAMWARE INC.

The growing body of new research comes at a time when talent-hungry recruiters are scrambling to find execs who can retain workers and who can excel in the smaller bureaucracies of New Economy companies. Women think through decisions better than men, are more collaborative, and seek less personal glory, says the head of IBM's Global Services Div., Douglas Elix, who hired two managers within this year—both women.

Instead of being motivated by self-interest, women are more driven by "what they can do for the company," Elix says. Adds Harvard Business School Professor Rosabeth Moss Kanter, author of the 20-year-old management classic, *Men and Women of the Corporation:* "Women get high ratings on exactly those skills needed to succeed in the global Information Age, where teamwork and partnering are so important."

Some executives now have a pro-woman hiring bias

It's no surprise, then, that some executives say they're beginning to develop a new hiring bias. If forced to choose between equally qualified male and female candidates for a top-level job, they say they often pick the woman—not because of affirmative action or any particular desire to give the female a chance but because they believe she will do a better job. "I would rather hire a woman," says Anu Shukla, who sold her Internet marketing-software company Rubric Inc. earlier this year for $390 million. "I know I'm going to get a certain quality of work, I know I'm going to get a certain dedication," she says, quickly adding that she's fully aware that not all women execs excel. Similarly, Brent Clark, CEO of Grand Rapids-based Pell Inc., the nation's largest foot-care chain, says he would choose a woman over a man, too. Women are more stable, he says, less turf-conscious, and better at "all sorts of intangibles that can help an organization."

But if women are so great, why aren't more of them running the big companies? Thousands of talented women now graduate from business schools and hold substantive middle-management jobs at major corporations—45% of all managerial posts are held by females, according to the Labor Dept. Yet only two of the nation's 500 biggest companies have female CEOs: Hewlett-Packard Co.'s Carly Fiorina and Avon Products' Andrea Jung. And of the 1,000 largest corporations, only six are run by women.

UNREWARDED. For one thing, there's still a pipeline problem: Most women get stuck in jobs that involve human resources or public relations—posts that rarely lead to the top. At the same time, female managers' strengths have long been undervalued, and their contributions in the workplace have gone largely unnoticed and unrewarded. Companies are now saying they want the skills women typically bring to the job, but such rhetoric doesn't always translate into reality. Some businesses view women only as workhorses, well-suited for demanding careers in middle management but not for prime jobs. These undercurrents of bias in Corporate America infuriate many women, who then bail out rather than navigate unsupportive terrain. "They're doing the work, but they don't make it to the top," says Lyn Andrews, president of WebMD Health, a consumer unit of WebMD Corp. in New York. Many start their own companies, while others seek a different work/family balance than many corporations offer. There are now more than 9 million women-owned businesses in the U.S., double the number 12 years ago.

The new studies offer some clues about why the cultural mismatch between women and large companies persists and why it's so critical to keep women on board. What makes the new research more compelling than other such data is that it is based on results culled from executives' actual performance evaluations rather than on opinion surveys or experiments that simulate business situations.

Because the participants had no idea that their evaluations would end up as part of a study on gender, the data are untainted, says Janet Irwin, a California management consultant who conducted one of the studies. "We were startled by the results," she says.

Irwin and her colleagues discovered that women ranked higher than men on 28 of 31 measures. Irwin was stunned by women's consistently high ratings and how the scores defied conventional wisdom. Contrary to stereotypes, women outperformed men in all kinds of intellectual areas, such as producing high-quality work, recognizing trends, and generating new ideas and acting on them. "Women's strengths are stronger than men's," says Irwin, "and their weaknesses are not as pronounced."

Bias of Experience:

"I know I'm going to get a certain quality of work," says Shukla, who recently sold her Web software company for $390 million

Several other studies showed similar patterns. Personnel Decisions International, a consulting firm in Minneapolis, looked at a huge sample—58,000 managers—and found that women outranked men in 20 of 23 areas. Larry Pfaff, a Michigan management consultant, examined evaluations from 2,482 executives from a variety of companies and found that women outperformed men on 17 of 20 measures.

Some of the researchers draw different conclusions, though, arguing that the research shows that women executives are equally effective as their male counterparts but not necessarily superior. While women score better, and the scores are statistically significant, says Susan Bebelein, executive vice-president of Personnel Decisions, those differences don't mean much in the real world. Why? Because the consulting firm has tested so many thousands of people, which can make minor differences appear more important than they really are. Women have always outscored men in such evaluations, says Bebelein, whose company began looking at gender differences in 1984. And they score highest at the most male-dominated companies because, she surmises, of the type of women who succeeds in such environments—someone who must be superior in every way.

Robert Kabacoff, a vice-president at Management Research Group in Portland, Me., also wondered if women were getting higher test scores in these studies for reasons other than gender. They might have rated higher because they weren't being compared with men holding similar jobs, he suggests. Managers of human-resources departments often get rated higher on people skills than other supervisors, for instance. If the majority of female managers in a study work in human resources, vs. only a minority of males, the results may have more to do with job than gender.

Old-School Advice:

One of managing director Kiely's ex-bosses told her: "You should be looking out for yourself, not your people"

MISUNDERSTOOD. To eliminate such potential distortions, Kabacoff conducted a differently designed study in 1998. He compared male and female managers who worked at the same companies, held similar jobs, were at the same management level, and had the same amount of supervisory experience. When he examined 1,800 supervisors in 22 management skills, he found that women outranked men on about half of the measures. Female managers were graded more effective by peers and subordinates, but bosses still judged men and women equally competent as leaders. "Men and women seem to be doing roughly equally effective jobs, but they approach their jobs differently," says Kabacoff.

Certainly, many women managers are keenly aware that they inhabit a different reality at the office than men. Nancy Hawthorne, former chief financial officer at Continental Cablevision Inc., who is now a consultant, says she often felt her bosses "wondered what the heck I was doing." At meetings, she often allowed subordinates to explain the details of ongoing projects. She felt her role was to delegate tasks to people around her to help them be more effective. "I was being traffic cop and coach and facilitator," she said. "I was always into building a department that hummed."

And sometimes, women say, they were badgered about using the very skills the research found so valuable. Sandra Kiely, managing director and chief administrative officer at National City Investment Management Co. in Cleveland, recalls that one of her bosses at National City Bank warned that her management style would hurt her career. "You should be looking out for yourself, not your people," he advised her.

Everyone knows that women have long excelled at teamwork, but getting results was one of the categories in which women earned their highest marks in these studies. Jackie Streeter, Apple Computer Inc.'s vice-president for engineering, says she has repeatedly volunteered to shift dozens of employees out of her division because she felt they would better fit into a different department—a move that she says "startled" her male colleagues. "It's not the size of your organization that counts but the size of the results you get," says Streeter, who has 350 people working for her.

Women still suffer from a lack of mentoring

Women are also more likely to disregard as a useless power trip another long-held management bugaboo: keeping information tightly controlled. "It's better to overcommunicate," says Shukla, whose Web startup, Rubric, made 65 of her 85 employees millionaires. Rather than dispensing information on a need-to-know basis, she made sure information was shared with all of her employees. She also created the CEO lunch, inviting six to eight employees at a time to discuss the business with her.

CARING WORKS. Companies can also undercut women's strengths in another, often inadvertent way: by assuming that people skills are not business skills. In fact, they are inextricable, argues Joyce Fletcher, a professor at Simmons Graduate School of Management in Boston and Author of *Disappearing Acts: Gender, Power, and Relational Practice at Work.* Employees who feel cared about by their bosses or are inspired by them often produce higher-quality work, consultants say. And supervisors who know how to deal with conflict get better results.

Women have been doing this kind of work for years, but their behavior is often devalued because their intentions are misunderstood, says Fletcher. A woman who takes the time to talk to an employee about a meeting he has missed, for instance, might simply be considered a nice person—not someone trying to make sure that the staff has enough information to make an important decision. Her business actions become invisible, since the staff attributes her behavior to just being kind.

New Business Model:

Companies assume people skills aren't business skills, says management professor Fletcher, when in fact, they're inextricable

Similarly, duties such as coaching and keeping people informed are often taken as a given. But these tasks can actually be the invisible glue that holds a company together, which, until the 360-degree feedback evaluation came along, rarely got examined. "It's like somebody doing your laundry," says Hawthorne, the former Continental Cablevision exec. "You rely on them to have clean clothes," but the work is "invisible when it's

TEACHING MEN THE RIGHT STUFF

Boys, it seems, can't afford to be boys anymore. At least not if they want to succeed as managers in the New Economy, where the old-school style of command-and-control is about as effective as getting blitzed in front of your boss at the company cocktail party.

With more and more studies showing that qualities typically associated with women are what New Economy businesses need to thrive, a new cottage industry is emerging that is taking the opposite view of Professor Henry Higgins in *My Fair Lady*: Why can't a man be more like a woman? "Men just don't have what it takes to be successful in the modern workplace," says London-based management guru James R. Traeger. "They are deskilled." Sure, the baby-faced Traeger has an ax to grind—he runs a for-men-only training program that helps guys understand the value of emotion in work relationships. Through a three-month seminar that involves intense personal scrutiny, coaching, networking, and public speaking, Traeger tries to get men to recognize and improve their abilities to communicate, build teams, and develop flexibility. "If you were to ask which of these qualities men had an upper hand at, the answer would be none," he says.

Indeed, in this vise-tight labor market, execs who are prone to scoff at such "soft skills" have found they need to listen to Traeger and his cohorts. Managers everywhere are being forced to think more about creative leadership—the kind that can steer companies across the New Economy's bumpy terrain as well as hold on to valued workers who are constantly bombarded with new job offers. "The nature of modern business requires what's more typical to the female mold of building consensus as opposed to the top-down male military model," says Millington F. McCoy, managing director at New York-based executive search firm Gould, McCoy & Chadick Inc.

After Traeger helps participants identify the gender issues, they work on communication skills, feelings, and emotional expression. "The program is about breaking down the stereotype of an aggressive, controlling, and competitive man who always wants to be right, take charge, solve problems, and also has to have the last word," says David Bancroft-Turner, founder of 3D Training & Development, a U.K.-based consulting firm, who participated in the program. "It's about learning to listen and work in harmony."

Although the U.S. hasn't yet seen this kind of men-only program, various coaching firms are similar to Traeger's. Hay Group, in Philadelphia, coaches execs to be "emotionally aware." Adapting theories from Daniel P. Goleman's book *Emotional Intelligence*, Hay Group instructs managers "to recognize the emotional hot buttons" that are "not taught in business schools," says Annie McKee, Hay's director for management-development services.

One tip that all of the seminars advocate: If you're a man, follow the lead of your female co-worker. She probably has a lot to teach you.

By Pallavi Gogoi in Chicago

WHAT CAN A GUY DO?

Tips for male managers from the female playbook

CONTROLLING BOSSES ARE BAD BOSSES So are micromanagers. Give your people the power to do their jobs.
FLEXIBILITY, NOT RIGIDITY Learn to allow your employees to sculpt their jobs. Don't finger-wag. Be open to others' opinions and build consensus.
ADMIT YOU DON'T KNOW EVERYTHING You can't solve all of your problems, but your staff probably can. Avoid hogging air time—learn to listen.

done well." Because "the guys are into glamour," says National City's Kiely, women often end up in charge of difficult and unglamorous tasks such as performance reviews.

Kiely bristles at some research that concluded that women aren't perceived as strategic or vision-oriented. Her strategy, she says, is to make people think something is their idea so she can get them to buy into a plan.

Another potential trap: Women's biggest strengths can also become their biggest weaknesses, says Vivian Eyre, a New York management consultant. By working so hard to get great results, they often take away time from building critical business alliances. "Given the opportunity to stay in their offices and make sure their report is perfect or going out of their office and talking to Joe about his business, women are more likely to do their own work," says Eyre.

What's more, she adds, women still suffer from a lack of mentoring and being kept outside informal networks of communication. Many women admit that because they spend so much time focusing on getting results, they don't think enough about strategy and vision—qualities that Harvard's Kanter says are still the most important in a top executive. "If women are seen as only gloried office facilitators but not as tough-minded risk-takers," says Kanter, "they will be held back from the CEO jobs."

In the end, it takes a lot more than competence to make it to the top. Getting the best performance evaluations in the company's history may not be nearly enough. "When you actually sit down in a selection committee to choose the CEO, lots of subtle assumptions come into play," said Deborah Merrill Sands, co-director of Simmons' Center on Gender & Organization. Companies may say they want collaborative leaders, but they still hold deep-seated beliefs that top managers need to be heroic figures. Interpersonal skills may be recognized as important, she said, but they aren't explicitly seen as corner-office skills. "We are in the process of changing our concepts of leadership," she says. "But organizations haven't evolved that much yet."

In fact, Kabacoff has just finished a new study showing how CEOs and corporate boards view upper management, and he found a clear double standard. Male CEOs and senior vice-presidents got high marks from their bosses when they were forceful and assertive and lower scores if they were cooperative and empathic. The opposite was true for women: Female CEOs got downgraded for being assertive and got better scores when they were cooperative. Kabacoff's conclusion? "At the highest levels, bosses are still evaluating people in the most stereotypical ways." That means that even though women have proven their readiness to lead companies into the future, they're not likely to get a shot until their bosses are ready to stop living in the past.

By Rochelle Sharpe in Boston

CRIMES AND MISDEMINORS

A teenager shows how easily stocks can be manipulated and how hard it is to get away with it. So why are so many hailing him as a genius?

By DANIEL KADLEC

THEY USED TO JUST LOOK LIKE KIDS, these rogue traders, boiler-room con artists and Internet scamsters possessing just enough knowledge about the stock market to fleece anyone who would listen. Now they really are kids. At 27, Nick Leeson brought down Barings bank with $1.4 billion in fraudulent trades. At 25, Gary Hoke faked a Bloomberg news report linked to a Yahoo bulletin board in a stock scam that cost investors $93,000. At 24, Rafael Shaoulian littered financial bulletin boards with unfounded hype that enabled him to sell a stock and pocket $173,000. At 23, Mark Jakob drove down the stock of Emulex with a phony Internet report. He bought with a vengeance after the decline and made $241,000 when the hoax was discovered and the stock rebounded.

Now comes Jonathan Lebed, 15, a New Jersey neophyte retracting the definition of "kid" from anyone merely young to certifiable school-age dependent. Lebed lives at home. He watches World Wrestling Federation matches. He roots for the Mets. He doesn't drive, at least not a car. But he has been in the fast lane of Wall Street swindlers for the past year, driving stocks with bogus chat-room hype that enabled him to capture $272,826 in illegal profits. Lebed settled his case with regulators last Wednesday, agreeing to disgorge the profits, plus $12,174 in interest, without admitting to any wrongdoing.

Lebed is the first minor the SEC has ever charged with securities fraud, and you may well ask, Isn't it one thing for a set of twentysomethings at work or in college to master the ole pump and dump, Net style, but quite another for a bona fide minor to get it down pat? Do we have a serious problem here?

Yes. A few of them. For starters, his antics have made Lebed something of a hero in his hometown of Cedar Grove. "I'm proud of my son," quickly proclaimed his father Gregory Lebed, a railroad worker for Amtrak who drove up to his house last week in a forest-green Mercedes SUV. Proud? Support you can understand. But mass fraud seems a strange accomplishment to crow about.

"He's like a celebrity," says Anthony Callie, a friend and classmate. "I'm sure he's got a lot of new friends." Another classmate, Nicole Basalyga, chimes in, "He outsmarted the government and made a lot of money. That's pretty cool."

Well, not really, Nicole. The government nabbed him. He had to give some of the money back, and he may still face criminal charges. That's pretty uncool. The folks at home, though, aren't thinking about any of that. This is a gilded new age in which everyone has the right to get rich, regardless of the means. Historians document periods of prosperity such as the current one. These periods almost always lead to a high incidence of scamming as the get-rich-quick mindset spreads.

Today, amid an unprecedented bull market broadly enjoyed at the dawn of the Internet, the stock market is the tool of choice—and breaking the rules becomes increasingly acceptable as the players get younger. Call it extreme capitalism. If you win, you're envied as a genius.

Another problem is the settlement. Hours after it was announced, Lebed's attorney, Kevin Marino, reportedly let the world know the disgorgement would be less than what Lebed had made. "I think it's a great idea for everyone to abide by the law," says Marino. As for regulations governing the Internet, "there's still a huge gray area out there. I believe the information industry has surpassed the regulations." To get the deal, the SEC focused on just 11 of 27 trades it had investigated. The SEC could demand restitution only from the trades covered in the settlement. Did Lebed scam the SEC too?

"All you need is a computer and a modem."

Finally, and this is the big stuff, Internet stock fraud is a growth crime. The seeming anonymity of Web postings and chat sessions has emboldened scamsters and driven down the cost of running a first-rate swindle. No longer do con artists need elaborate "boiler rooms" filled with phone banks and fast-talking stock jocks. "Historically, perpetrators had to be more sophisticated," says John Reed Stark, chief of SEC's Office of Internet Enforcement. "There were a lot more complexities to the schemes. With these manipulations, all you need is a computer and a modem to spread false information."

That's how Lebed did it. He would buy large blocks of thinly traded stocks on the NASDAQ or the over-the-counter bulletin board, moving the price up 20% or more. After the market closed and the next morning dawned, he would flood cyberspace with as many as 600 messages under different names touting the stock as one about to "take off" or, in the case of Man Sang Holdings, "the most undervalued stock in history."

Buyer Beware: The New Face of Stock Fraud

THE MOB

THE RUSE The feds say brokers, including Vinnie ("the Pork") Langella, with purported mob connections, promoted fraud

THE RESULT An FBI sweep and the arrest of 120 brokers and alleged mobsters

MARK JAKOB

THE RUSE A fake p.r. release picked up by a new Internet business distributor said Emulex would report a loss instead of a profit

THE RESULT More than $2 billion in market cap was temporarily wiped out

GARY DALE HOKE

THE RUSE On a faked page of the Bloomberg website, Hoke announced the sale of PairGain, his former employer

THE RESULT The stock soared 31%, resulting in investor losses of $93,000 when the story was refuted.

In the Man Sang case, he twice manipulated the price—once buying it at less than $2 and selling near $4, and next buying at less than $3 and selling at more than $5. Gullible chat audiences piled in, pushed up the price and then were left with big losses as the stock inevitably tanked. So cocksure of his schemes was Lebed that in some cases he entered automatic sell orders, to be triggered when the stock rose to a specific price, and then skipped off to school knowing he'd make thousands of dollars before recess. Because he is a minor, he traded through two custodial accounts in his father's name.

There's absolutely nothing new about Lebed's con. What makes it noteworthy is his age, plus the epidemic that has developed of this kind of fraud. The SEC gets 300 e-mails a day complaining about rip-offs. A quarter of its enforcement staff is dedicated to cyberspace, surfing the Net for hard sells and unrealistic investment promises.

The good news is that this stuff is easy to track down. The SEC has cracked 180 Net-fraud cases in the past five years, most of them in the past two. The charges against Lebed coincided with a nationwide fraud sweep involving 15 cases and 33 defendants. Some 70 micro-cap stocks—low volume and thinly traded—worth $1.7 billion were involved, and the total illegal profits came to $10 million. The SEC likes to bundle its cases for maximum effect. This was its fourth such sweep since the Net became a popular stomping ground for stock fraud a few years ago.

Conventional fraud investigations usually take six months to a year. But Internet fraud often wraps up in less than a week. The electronic trail is that clear—far easier to trace than the paper trail of the old economy. Last year Silicon Investor, based in Seattle and owned by Go2net, reprimanded Lebed for "violating the terms of his membership" (which can mean anything from spamming to being abusive to going "off topic" on message boards). The last time he posted a message to the site was July 17, 1999. He then apparently gave up and moved to the less regulated environment of Yahoo. What may have helped the SEC is that Silicon Investor has archived all 15 million of the messages placed on its 20,000 message boards since inception. A trail was easy to generate.

"You've got great evidence, and it's easy to find people," says the SEC's Stark. "Internet con artists may try to hide behind multiple screen aliases, but most computers leave their own electronic footprints that are relatively easy for experts to track."

For the con to work, it must be done out in the open where investors will see it and throw money at it. "You want people to find you," Stark says. "You want them to read your information." That's what makes the stock go up, but it also makes you easier to find. Lebed may have got away with his schemes for a year, but others have been identified within days. In the Emulex case in August, Jakob was targeted within hours of his phony press release. Hoke, an employee at PairGain Technologies, was nabbed just a week after his bogus release declared that PairGain was about to be bought out.

One of the amazing aspects of Lebed's story, or that of any Net fraudster, is that people act on the hype they see online. Large banks like Chase Manhattan pay millions of dollars a year in premiums to insure against a rogue trader like Leeson. Your best protection against a rogue Internet hypster is just not to listen. Most pump-and-dump schemes involve micro-cap stocks. That's your first tip-off. Often they hype them as likely to double or better in weeks. If you have questions, the SEC has a brochure, "Pump&Dump.con," with tips for avoiding scams. It's available at *www.sec.gov*.

The rash of Net fraud cases has done little to deter online investors from their passion, nor should it if they stick to investing in what they know. "Sure, there's a lot of garbage out there," says Bob Smith, a Houston oil executive. He upgraded his computer five years ago specifically to dump his broker and trade online. He checks the financial Web postings and tunes in to chat sessions on the market. But he also does his own research and notes that the hype-and-con element of Wall Street isn't just online. "Highly paid analysts hype Internet stocks with outrageous price targets, then drop their estimates," he says. "I am sure they get their firms out of a position before they drop the bomb on the rest of the investing public."

Some of the [chat room] stories might be true, but... should not be your main source of information.

—JORDAN FEIGER,
Chicago businessman

Jordan Feiger, a Chicago businessman, is another who hasn't been turned off by the scams. "When you go into a chat room, it's like picking up a copy of the Star," he says, referring to the gossipy supermarket tabloid. "Some of the stories might be true and valid, but they certainly should not be your main source of information."

By all accounts, Lebed is intelligent and likable, considered a tad geeky because of the black leather briefcase he totes to school. "He's not very active in school and stuff," notes Kristel Rice, a senior at Cedar Grove High School, where Lebed is a junior. While students knew of his interest in stock trading, he kept to himself, asking only a few to join him. "He kept quiet about it," says classmate Tom McCarthy. "He kept it personal."

Before he discovered the dark side of Net investing, he seemed on a fast track for a dream career on Wall Street. With help from his father, he began investing at the age of 12 and a year later formed an alliance, dubbed the Triple Threat, with two friends. As a team, they placed fourth among 3,500 in a national investment derby sponsored by CNBC and MCI. Lebed and his pals rolled out of bed regularly at 5 a.m. to troll for stocks on the Internet and TV.

He has railed at town-council meetings about laying high-speed cable for better Net access. He and a friend, Jared Glugeth, started a Web-based business called Promotion Solutions (*www.eprolutions.com*), which purports to help clients advertise their websites, and PRHost.com, a web-hosting service. They're a pair of go-getters. Glugeth had the foresight to use Lebed's media moment last week to hype their Web business. "I'm not here to talk about Jonathan," Glugeth told a swarm of reporters outside Lebed's house. "I'm here to talk about our company."

The press, though, wasn't biting. Soon the media wave will wash over, and Lebed and his friend will be left in anonymity again. Let's hope they have learned something.

—Reported by Edward Barnes, William Dowell, Kate Kelly and Elaine Rivera/ New York and Chris Taylor/San Francisco, with other bureaus.

Virtual Morality: A New Workplace Quandary

BY MICHAEL J. MCCARTHY
Staff reporter of THE WALL STREET JOURNAL

WHERE DO YOU DRAW THE LINE.COM? The explosion of the Internet into the workplace has empowered millions of employees, in a matter of keystrokes, to quietly commandeer company property for personal use. And ethical questions are mushrooming well beyond the propriety of workers frittering away a morning shopping online or secretly viewing pornographic Web sites.

Cautionary tales are piling up—from United Parcel Service of America Inc., which caught one employee using a UPS computer to run a personal business, to Lockheed Martin Corp., where a single e-mail heralding a religious holiday that was sent to 60,000 employees disabled company networks for more than six hours. The flood of e-mail traffic cost Lockheed Martin hundreds of thousands of dollars in lost productivity, and the employee lost his job.

Every day, companies face unexpected twists in the world of virtual morality. With the surge in day trading, is it OK for employees to log on to make a quick stock deal? How about sending out e-mails from work supporting a politician? Or using office computers to hunt for a new job? And if any of this is permissible occasionally, just when does it cross into excess?

This is a new spin on the old nuisance of employees making personal phone calls at work, but with greatly magnified possibilities. For one thing, the Web can be extremely seductive, lulling users to click screen after screen for hours at a time. Productivity can indeed suffer when dozens or hundreds of workers succumb to the temptation. What's more, unlike phone calls, electronic messages are often retrievable months or years later, and can be used as evidence in litigation against companies or individual employees.

In addition, though many workers don't realize it, when they surf the Web from work they are literally dragging their company's name along with them. Most Web sites can, and often do, trace the Internet hookups their visitors are using and identify the companies behind them. That leaves a serious potential for embarrassment if employees are visiting any number of places, from job-search sites to racist chat rooms. Caught off guard by the geometric growth of such issues, many companies have lost all hope of handling matters case by case. Some are using sophisticated software that monitors when, how and why workers are using the Internet (See "Now the Boss Knows Where You're Clicking"). Others are taking first stabs at setting boundaries.

Boeing Co., for one, seems to accept the inevitable with a policy specifically allowing employees to use faxes, e-mail and the Internet for personal reasons. But the aerospace and aircraft company also sets guidelines. Use has to be of "reasonable duration and frequency" and can't cause "embarrassment to the company." And chain letters, obscenity and political and religious solicitation are strictly barred.

Other companies are more permissive, but make it abundantly clear that employees can't expect privacy. Saying it recognizes that employees may occasionally need to use the Web or e-mail for personal reasons, Columbia/HCA Healthcare Corp. issues this warning in its "electronic communication" policy: "It is sometimes necessary for authorized personnel to access and monitor their contents." And, it adds, "in some situations, the company may be required to publicly disclose e-mail messages, even those marked private."

Attorneys have been advising companies to write such policies and alert employees that online activities will be monitored and that they can be disciplined. Such

The Wall Street Journal Workplace-Ethics Quiz

The spread of technology into the workplace has raised a variety of new ethical questions, and many old ones still linger. Compare your answers with those of other Americans. See answers at end of article.

Office Technology

1. Is is wrong to use company e-mail for personal reasons?
❑ Yes ❑ No
2. Is is wrong to use office equipment to help your children or spouse do schoolwork?
❑ Yes ❑ No
3. Is it wrong to play computer games on office equipment during the workday?
❑ Yes ❑ No
4. Is it wrong to use office equipment to do Internet shopping?
❑ Yes ❑ No
5. Is is unethical to blame an error you made on a technological glitch?
❑ Yes ❑ No
6. Is it unethical to visit pornographic Web sites using office equipment?
❑ Yes ❑ No

Gifts and Entertainment

7. What's the value at which a gift from a supplier or client becomes troubling?
❑ $25 ❑ $50 ❑ $100
8. Is a $50 gift to a boss unacceptable?
❑ Yes ❑ No
9. Is a $50 gift FROM the boss unacceptable?
❑ Yes ❑ No
10. Of gifts from suppliers: Is it OK to take a $200 pair of football tickets?
❑ Yes ❑ No
11. Is it OK to take a $120 pair of theater tickets?
❑ Yes ❑ No
12. Is it OK to take a $100 holiday food basket?
❑ Yes ❑ No
13. Is it OK to take a $25 gift certificate?
❑ Yes ❑ No
14. Can you accept a $75 prize won at a raffle at a supplier's conference?
❑ Yes ❑ No

Truth and Lies

15. Due to on-the-job pressure, have you ever abused or lied about sick days?
❑ Yes ❑ No
16. Due to on-the-job pressure, have you ever taken credit for someone else's work or idea?
❑ Yes ❑ No

Sources: Ethics Officer Association, Belmont, Mass: Ethical Leadership Group, Wilmette, Ill.; surveys sampled a cross-section of workers at large companies and nationwide

warnings make it difficult for employees to win any suit asserting that they expected their communications to be private—already an uphill claim given that the equipment belongs to the company in the first place.

Some 27% of large U.S. firms have begun checking employee e-mail, a huge jump from 15% in 1997, the American Management Association recently found. Some routinely do this to search for obscene language or images. Passed along employee to employee, those could constitute grounds for a sexual-harassment suit.

But the practice has generated controversy, particularly when workers are not forewarned. Earlier this month, California Gov. Gray Davis vetoed a measure that would have barred employers from secretly monitoring e-mail and computer files. Under the bill, companies would be allowed to do so only after they established monitoring policies and notified employees of them. Asserting that employers have a legitimate need to monitor company property, Gov. Davis said, "Every employee also understands that expense reports submitted for reimbursement are subject to employer verification as to their legitimacy and accuracy."

But even if a manager is within legal rights to peek at employee e-mail, does that make any kind of digital fishing expedition ethical? What's an employer to do, for example, if such a search of an employee's e-mail reveals that he has an undisclosed drug problem or is looking for another job?

To balance employee rights and a company's legal interests, some privacy advocates say, employers should check e-mail only after a worker is suspected of misconduct. "Just because companies own bathrooms doesn't mean they have the right to install cameras and monitor whatever goes on in there," says Marc Rotenberg, executive director of the Electronic Privacy Information Center, an advocacy group in Washington.

Against the tide, some companies and government agencies are trying to cling to "zero tolerance" policies, prohibiting any personal use of company equipment. One is Ameritech Corp., whose business code of conduct specifically states that computers and other company equipment "are to be used only to provide service to customers and for other business purposes," says a spokeswoman for the telecommunications company. The "policy ensures our employees are focused on serving customers," she adds. Reminders about the policy are sent periodically.

BellSouth was a similar hard-liner until the summer of 1998, when it caved. "We got a lot of questions from people saying they were afraid to give someone their company e-mail address for things like weekend soccer clubs," says Jerry Guthrie, the company's ethics officer. "We work long hours—we wanted to offer it as a benefit to employees."

Before BellSouth employees can log on to their computers, however, they now must click "OK" to a message warning them against misuse of e-mail and the

Internet, and alerting them that their actions can be monitored. Since the company changed the policy to allow for personal use, its security department has conducted more than 60 investigations of abuse. Some employees were suspended or fired for violations including accessing pornographic sites and spending too much time on non-business Web pages, including sports sites.

BellSouth, like many other companies, uses filtering technology to block certain sites, but even that is a chore. Since each division currently filters different sites, the company is in the process of standardizing which sites will be blocked company-wide. "Some [other] companies block sports and financial sites," says Mr. Guthrie, though BellSouth doesn't intend to. But, he says, BellSouth will probably block access to "sex sites, hate sites and gambling sites."

In May, Zona Research Inc., an Internet market researcher in Redwood City, Calif., found that fully one-third of companies screen out any sites not on an approved list. In its survey of more than 300 companies, Zona also found that 20% of companies filter sites based on the user's job and another 13% based on the time of day.

But companies trying to construct such dams are discovering leaks all the time. Gambling, adult and other controversial sites are sanitizing or disguising their address names to operate under the radar of firms monitoring and blocking Internet content. One site remained undetected to cyber-smut police until it made headlines recently. Not to be confused with 1600 Pennsylvania Avenue, www.whitehouse.com offers X-rated content.

Now the Boss Knows Where You're Clicking

By Michael J. McCarthy
Staff Reporter of The Wall Street Journal

When labor laws changed recently in England, Turner Broadcasting System Inc. worried about a pileup of overtime claims from employees in its CNN London bureau. Then the Turner computer-security group sprang into action.

The department decided to order software that could monitor every Web page every worker visits—and help pinpoint anyone wasting company time online. "If we see people were surfing the Web all day, then they don't have to be paid for that overtime," says Darren Valiance, a Turner network-security specialist, referring to the British operation. "In a perfect world, people would realize they're at work to work."

Get ready for a combustible new office issue. Advancing technology is rapidly extending electronic-eavesdropping capability to every office that uses the Internet. There is a new set of Internet-surveillance systems, with names like WEBsweeper, Disk Tracy and SecureVIEW. Some can conduct desktop-to-laptop sweeps, monitoring Web use from the mailroom to the executive suite.

Turner, a unit of Time Warner Inc., says it is planning to install software called Telemate.Net, which plumbs a company's network and churns out reports identifying and ranking its heaviest individual Internet users. It details the top sites visited across the whole company, and can do the same for particular departments, like sales or accounting.

Telemate.Net can also report Web site visits by individual employees and rank them by roughly two dozen categories, including some that most employers wouldn't be to happy about—from games, humor and pornography to cults, shopping and job-hunting. And it can instantly generate logs naming precisely who went to what sites at what times.

Telemate.Net Software Inc., an Atlanta company that went public last month, lists some blue-chip corporate clients: Arthur Andersen & Co., Maytag Corp., Philip Morris Cos. and Sears, Roebuck & Co.

Right after installing Telemate.Net in February, says Douglas Dahlberg, the information-technology manager for Wolverton & Associates Inc., he unearthed some disturbing results. Something called broadcast. com was the company's third-most-visited site. People were downloading music from the site, it turns out, using up 4% of the company's bandwidth, or Internet capacity. "When I saw that, I yanked it," says Mr. Dahlberg, who removed the so-called RealAudio capability from Wolverton's system.

Before starting Telemate.Net up, Wolverton, a civil-engineering company in Norcross, Ga., notified its three dozen employees that it would be monitoring their computer usage. "It just mustn't sink in," says Mr. Dahlberg. "I can see every little Web page you read—and still there were problems."

Indeed in April, E*Trade Group Inc., the online investment service, showed up as Wolverton's eighth-most-visited site, using up nearly 3% of overall bandwidth. That transmission capacity is a precious resource, since Wolverton's engineers routinely have to send data-heavy computer-aided-design files to clients through e-mail during the workday. In June, Mr. Dahlberg was irritated to find cnnsi.com pop up as Wolverton's No. 8 site. "Our clients should be in [the top 10], not CNN Sports," he says.

This type of electronic-file analysis hasn't been available until very recently, computer-network specialists say. The raw data have always been there, but in a form that was virtually impenetrable. From his cramped cubicle at CNN Center in Atlanta, network security specialist Mr. Vallance, a 27-year-old in black Converse high-tops, taps away at his keyboard to demonstrate one recent afternoon.

Pulling up data logs, he reveals screen after screen of enigmatic coding, individuals identified by numbers like 123.43.87.99 and other gobbledygook. A former Air Force information-security expert, Mr. Vallance knows how hard it is to scan these logs to separate routine Web site visits and e-mails from suspicious transactions. There are some easy tip-offs, though: late-night log-ons, and any lines marked "rejected" by Turner's firewalls, or devices that protect computer networks from hackers and other outsiders.

It's only 1 p.m. and Mr. Valiance guesses that these logs, just since that morning, would fill about 2,000 screens. "Trying to look through all this is impossible," he says, but scrolling through them manually is the only way he can do surveillance on employee Web usage right now.

At many companies, information technicians are called upon only after a supervisor suspects an employee is burning up hours online or visiting pornographic or other offensive pages. The computer department can quickly generate a report on an individual's transactions, and the suspicion can be rapidly borne out or disproved.

New software like Telemate.Net completely reverses that process, allowing the computer department to tip off the manager. The software systematically sorts through all employee Web site visits every day, and sorts them into categories. Any visits to amazon.com, for instance, would show up on a company report under "shopping." Visits to jobhunt.com go under "employment." By clicking on a category, a company manager can pull up "drill down" reports revealing the name of each visitor to each site, as well as what times he or she logged on to it.

Certainly there are privacy issues here. Though the company says it isn't aware of any legal challenges to its system, some overseas laws restrict what it can do. In Germany, for instance, laws forbid Telemate.Net to generate reports on Internet usage by individual employees. Mindful of privacy issues in the U.S., Telemate.Net has designed a special "VIP" function that will automatically erase the specific Web pages of anyone the computer department programs it to—the CEO, for example.

Telemate.Net's founding business 13 years ago was selling systems to help companies monitor phone usage, checking for such things as excessive personal calls. Two years ago, the company developed a sister system for the Internet. It sells Telemate.Net for $995 to $4,995 for each system a company requires. The price depends on the number of reports generated and other factors.

Several companies listed as clients in a Telemate.Net filing with the Securities and Exchange Commission had little to say on the subject. "I don't have time to run this down," said a spokesman for Maytag, the appliance maker. A Sears spokeswoman said the retailer couldn't confirm if it was a client and "didn't want to participate" in a story about monitoring employee Web use.

By policy, Philip Morris said, it won't discuss anything that might jeopardize its computer-network security. An Arthur Andersen spokeswoman said, "Our IT [information technology] folks say we don't use it much."

While marketing itself as "network intelligence for the Internet economy, Telemate.Net says it hopes its software will also be used as a tool to use the Web more productively. "Lots of companies gave employees Internet access as a perk, and now they're realizing it's an asset that has to be managed," says Vijay Balakrishnan, senior vice president, marketing.

When asked, Telemate.Net said it does indeed turn the system on itself, conducting surveillance on its 170 employees. And it has turned up some surprises. "We have a guy here—one of our top salespeople—who surfs a lot, spends an hour to an hour and a half a day working on his stock portfolio—but he's a top performer," says Morten Jensen, Telemate.Net's director, product management. "Does Jim, our VP for sales, care?" asks Mr. Jensen. "No."

How One Firm Tracks Ethics Electronically

BY MICHAEL J. MCCARTHY
Staff Reporter of THE WALL STREET JOURNAL

BETHESDA, Md.—Lockheed Martin Corp. is turning business ethics into rocket science.

While some companies worry about workers wasting time on the Web, the aerospace giant is aggressively steering them into cyberspace as part of a broad program—born of a bribery scandal—to audit, record and perfect the measurement of employee morals.

Using internal computer programs with names like Merlin and Qwizard, many of Lockheed Martin's 160,000 employees go online these days for step-by-step training on ethics and legal compliance. The system records each time an employee completes one of the sessions, which range from sexual harassment and insider trading to kickbacks and gratuities. Last month, it began alerting managers to employees who haven't yet taken required sessions.

Lockheed Martin's electronic ethics program also closely tracks alleged wrongdoing inside the company. It

Rocket Science

Lockheed keeps close tabs on how employees are disciplined for ethics violations.

	1995	1999*
Discharge	56	25
Suspension	47	14
Written reprimand	59	51
Oral reprimand	164	146
Other	60	66
Total sanctions	386	302

*Figures to June 30.

Source: Lockheed Martin

knows, for example, that it takes 30.4 days on average to complete an internal investigation of ethics violations, and that the company has fired 217 people for them since 1995. In the first six months of this year, 4.8% of its ethics allegations involved conflicts of interest, while 8.9% involved security and misuse of assets.

In short, Lockheed Martin is tackling ethical matters with a scientific precision usually associated with its F-16 fighter jets.

One big reason for these complex ethics metrics: legal defense in case the company faces charges again.

Lockheed Corp. did not have such a sophisticated program in place in 1995, when, on the eve of its merger with Martin Marietta Corp., it agreed to pay a $24.8 million fine and plead guilty to conspiring to violate U.S. antibribery laws. Lockheed admitted that it illegally paid $1 million to an Egyptian lawmaker in 1990 for helping sell its C-130 aircraft in that country.

To keep from losing government contracts, Lockheed Martin submitted to a 60-page administrative agreement that amounted to a three-year probationary period. Like clockwork, it was required to turn over to the U.S. Air Force periodic ethics reports, including details of ethical complaints made to its employee hotline and other misconduct allegations.

In its leafy, suburban office park here in the shadow of the federal government, Lockheed Martin hardly wants to jeopardize its contractor status. Fully 70% of its $26.3 billion in sales comes solely from the U.S. government. "If they debar the corporation, that's death for this company," says David T. Clous, vice president for ethics and business conduct.

What's more, the electronic ethics program could win the company lenient treatment should it be indicted in a future case. The decade-old Federal Sentencing Guidelines, which codified fines and penalties for corporate wrongdoing, also established that fines for criminal conduct could be reduced by as much as 95% if a company had concrete internal programs to detect and prevent illegal acts. But if a company couldn't produce a paper trail of proof that it had tried to prevent wrongdoing, fines and penalties could be ratcheted up by 400%.

As part of its drive to stay on the straight and narrow, Lockheed Martin also developed an ethics game, which every single employee, up to Chairman Vance D. Coffman, must play once a year. With cards and tokens, workers spend one-hour sessions packed around tables, considering how to handle ethical quandaries drawn from actual Lockheed Martin cases—from harassment to padded work schedules.

The Ethics Challenge, as it is called, has been a hit—except for one year, when the ethics department revised the game so that it no longer indicated which answers were right or wrong. The idea was to let players debate. But the indecision drove the company's exacting engineers nuts. "They had a hard time with it," says Brian Sears, an ethics officer for the aeronautics division. The game was revised again, to offer "preferred answers."

Meanwhile, the ethics department went to work developing numerous "interactive" training sessions, on security, software-license compliance and labor charging. The courses, with actors playing out hypothetical cases, were originally produced for CD-ROMs, at a cost of about $150,000 apiece.

Clicking along at a workstation, an employee usually takes about 45 minutes to complete a session. A sample question from the kickback-and-gratuity clinic:

A kickback may be in the form of:

A. Cash
B. Gift to a family member
C. Donation to a charity at your request
D. All of these (The correct answer is D.)

From the sexual-harassment segment:

Which is the best means of addressing harassment when it first occurs?

A. Ignore the harasser
B. Be direct and tell the harasser his or her behavior is unwelcome and offensive
C. Report the harasser to your manager or Human Resources
(The correct answer is B.)

To provide proof that it has been systematically teaching employees the laws appropriate to their divisions and positions, Lockheed Martin also wanted an up-to-the-minute auditing system, which would track who had taken what training session and when. Last year, turning to the power of the Web, it began using its automated Merlin system to instantly track the number of courses taken and by whom.

The company says employees have warmed up to the program, particularly since it went online and workers no longer have to check out CD-ROMs or visit special workstations to meet their training requirements. But Lockheed is realistic. "We never envision people lining up and saying, 'Rah-rah, it's time for compliance training,'" says Tracy Carter Dougherty, director of ethics communication and training.

"Computer-based training can't completely replace personalized training," says Joseph E. Murphy, an ethics and compliance specialist with Compliance Systems Legal Group in Warwick, R.I. But having a system with mandatory clinics and quizzes will help "convince a prosecutor or regulator that the company is trying to prevent and detect problems," he adds.

Indeed, Steven Shaw, the U.S. Air Force deputy general counsel who held a debarment ax over Lockheed Martin until the probationary period ended last year, says he is pleased the company is still keeping close statistical tabs on ethical conduct and compliance training. And noting that the company hasn't been indicted since the Egypt case, he adds, "To me, that says a lot about a company that large. You'll always have people who will make mistakes."

Ethics-Quiz Answers

1. 34% said personal e-mail on company computers is wrong
2. 37% said using office equipment for schoolwork is wrong
3. 49% said playing copmuter games at work is wrong
4. 54% said Internet shopping at work is wrong
5. 61% said it's unethical to blame your error on technology
6. 87% said it's unethical to visit pornographic sites at work
7. 33% said $25 is the amount at which a gift from a supplier or client becomes troubling, while 33% said $50, and 33% said $100
8. 35% said a $50 gift to the boss is unacceptable
9. 12% said a $50 gift *from* the boss is unacceptable
10. 70% said it's unacceptable to take the $200 football tickets
11. 70% said it's unacceptable to take the $120 theater tickets
12. 35% said it's unacceptable to take the $100 food basket
13. 45% said it's unacceptable to take the $25 gift certificate
14. 40% said it's unacceptable to take the $75 raffle prize
15. 11% reported they lie about sick days
16. 4% reported they take credit for the work or ideas of others

MIXED SIGNALS

WHEN IT COMES TO ISSUES OF PRIVACY, CONSUMERS ARE FRAUGHT WITH CONTRADICTIONS.

BUSINESSES OFTEN FAIL TO GRASP the contradictory nature of consumer privacy concerns. Yet the more companies understand consumer fears, and the more consumers are educated about corporate privacy practices and security provisions, the less privacy will be an issue.

BY PAMELA PAUL

By the end of summer, consumers will be awash in privacy notices from their banks, HMOs, and insurers. Thanks to the 1999 Gramm-Leach-Bliley Act, companies had until the beginning of this month to disclose how they're using consumers' personal data. The purpose of the law: to allow people more control over how their personal information is used—and with whom it's shared. The result so far: confusion, frustration, and worse—privacy panic.

Most companies realize consumers don't want them to share personal data with third parties. Yet they fail to understand why simply sending out a legalistic privacy brochure isn't enough to satisfy most consumers. More important, they fail to grasp the often-contradictory nature of consumers' privacy concerns. An exclusive poll commissioned by *American Demographics* and conducted by Market Facts in April reveals the inconsistencies between what consumers say and what they do when faced with privacy threats. Consumers may say they hate telemarketing, but they'll pony up their credit card number for the chance to win millions. They may say they're afraid of being robbed over the Internet, but they'll willingly fill out a financial background form for the opportunity to trade stocks online.

"On the one hand, consumers want companies to read their minds and give them what they want," says DeeVee Devarakonda, chief marketing officer of Quaero, a Charlotte, North Carolina-based CRM services provider. "On the other hand, that means companies have to collect information, data mine, and create profiles, which makes consumers feel like they're being tracked and exploited. If companies can get to the bottom of these contradictions and communicate to consumers well, I think both sides can benefit."

To win consumers' trust, marketers have to make sure customers understand a company's specific security provisions. They must convince the public that the special benefits reaped by giving up some privacy outweigh the cost; and they need to set a long-term policy that integrates privacy concerns into the company's overall business strategy. "Trust has become a business survival requirement," says Kristin Valente, national leader of the privacy practice at Ernst & Young.

There's no question that privacy is a major consumer issue. An October 2000 poll by the National Consumers League revealed that consumers are more worried about personal privacy than about health care, education, crime, and taxes. A January 2001 Wirthlin Worldwide poll uncovered a host of negative emotions associated with revealing personal information during business transactions. The three most common words consumers used to describe their feelings were "cautious" (92 percent), "hesitant" (81 percent), and "suspicious" (72 percent).

Such words reflect specific privacy fears. According to the *American Demographics* survey, which polled 1,024 people, consumers' No. 1 fear is that businesses or individuals will target their children—66 percent of those surveyed say they are extremely or very concerned. Another prevalent fear among consumers is that private information will somehow be used against them (58 percent). And over half of those surveyed fear that if they disclose private information, they'll be robbed or cheated, or their identity will be stolen.

GETTING PERSONAL

Women care less than men do about their food preferences, but are much more protective of body weight information.

WHICH OF THE FOLLOWING DO YOU CONSIDER PERSONAL INFORMATION?

	TOTAL	MALE	FEMALE	18-24	25-34	35-44	45-54	55-64	65+
Home address	73%	69%	78%	84%	80%	74%	74%	67%	60%
Home phone number	76%	72%	80%	79%	80%	80%	80%	69%	64%
E-mail address	67%	63%	70%	61%	74%	68%	74%	74%	45%
Credit card number	97%	96%	97%	94%	99%	99%	98%	99%	91%
Financial information	91%	89%	92%	75%	95%	96%	90%	92%	94%
Social Security number	96%	96%	97%	86%	99%	98%	97%	98%	97%
Health information	69%	69%	69%	57%	78%	69%	77%	66%	58%
Spending habits	49%	49%	48%	20%	46%	49%	51%	60%	62%
Body measurements/weight	57%	44%	69%	42%	56%	62%	64%	58%	55%
Brand preferences	19%	21%	18%	7%	18%	25%	19%	16%	24%
Product style preferences	16%	17%	15%	10%	17%	17%	17%	12%	21%
Food preferences	23%	24%	22%	9%	22%	24%	24%	22%	32%
None of the above	1%	1%	0%	4%	0%	0%	0%	0%	0%

SOURCE: APRIL 2001 AMERICAN DEMOGRAPHICS/MARKET FACTS POLL

Many of these fears are what legal scholar and privacy consultant Alan Westin calls "anti-victimization fears," because they hinge on physical or financial harm. While marketers can help assure consumers of precautions taken to address such possibilities, these fears are addressed primarily by legal action in Congress and the courts. A number of bills pending on the Hill address a host of privacy matters, including allocating authority to the FTC for privacy protection, increasing penalties against computer crimes, and tightening amendments to the Electronic Communications Privacy Act of 1986.

IN GENERAL, PEOPLE WITH HIGHER INCOMES AND MORE EDUCATION TEND TO BE MORE SENSITIVE ABOUT GUARDING THEIR PRIVACY. WOMEN ARE MORE SENSITIVE THAN MEN, SENIORS ARE MORE FEARFUL THAN THE YOUNG, AND MARRIED PEOPLE ARE MORE WARY THAN SINGLES.

"The privacy issue is very multilayered," says Rachael Shanahan, chief privacy officer for Unica, an analytical CRM provider. "Being able to separate and understand those underlying fears is important, so that marketers can address what's of real concern to their target."

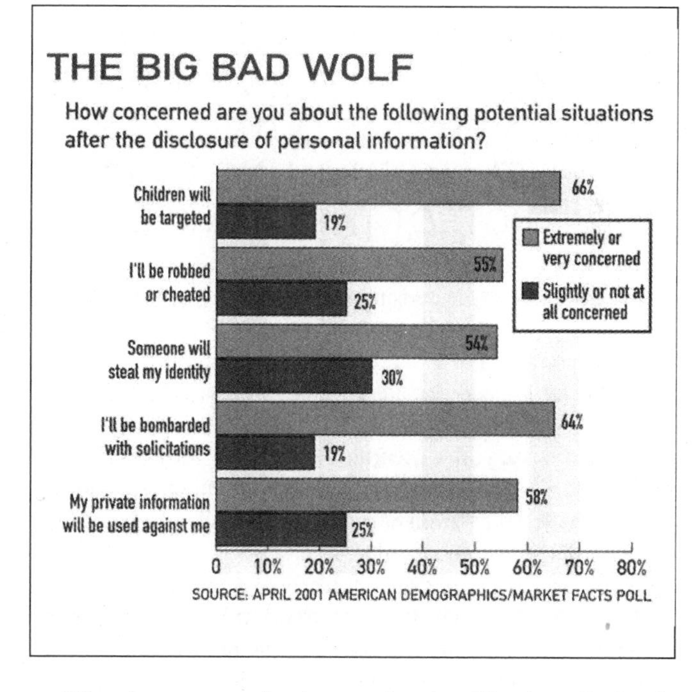

Of real concern to businesses is what Westin calls "anti-manipulation" fears ("Companies will manipulate my behavior with the information they collect.") and "anti-intrusion" fears ("Don't call me in the middle of dinnertime."). While less extreme than say, identity theft or stalking, these concerns should not be underestimated. The second most prevalent fear expressed in the *American Demographics* survey is bombardment by solicitations (64 percent are extremely or very concerned). The level of fear varies among different populations. Mark Lawrence, chief privacy officer for Compucredit, says the target group for the Aspire Visa card—people without a solid financial history, such as immigrants, college students, and those with bad credit—is less fearful of junk mail. "With our demographics, privacy isn't a big concern," Lawrence says. "I think our segment is more willing to give up private information than other groups. Part of it is that they haven't hit an annoyance threshold because they haven't been targeted by direct marketers to the same extent as other consumers."

People with higher incomes and more education tend to be more sensitive about guarding their privacy. Women are more sensitive than men, seniors are more fearful than the young, and married people are more wary than singles. "People under 30 tend to be less fearful, but you're still talking high numbers—about 58 percent—saying they're extremely or very concerned about maintaining their privacy," says Brendon Lynch, senior manager of privacy practice at PricewaterhouseCoopers. "I think marketers have to respect that consumers have individual differences, but I also believe privacy programs should be designed to accommodate the most sensitive consumer." Lee Bonds, director of customer information services at Hewlett-Packard, agrees in erring on the side of caution: "The way we're looking at it is, if you can meet the highest set of expectations, the rest of it becomes much easier. And that seems to be what a lot of companies in the technology and financial sectors are finding out."

THE FEARS EXPRESSED IN SURVEYS BY EVEN THE MOST WARY CONSUMERS FAR OUTPACE THE ACTION THEY'RE WILLING TO TAKE TO PROTECT THEIR PRIVACY.

Yet the fears expressed in surveys by even the most wary consumers far outpace the action they're willing to take to protect their privacy. For example, 70 percent of those polled by *American Demographics* are willing to press a button every time they visit a Web site or otherwise use a device to indicate a desire for privacy. But according to a March 2001 *Wall Street Journal*/Harris Interactive poll, only 54 percent of respondents claim to have taken even the relatively small step of deactivating or deleting cookies.

In general, consumers are not likely to actively protect their privacy even when steps to do so are readily available. For example, in a March 2001 Market Facts interactive poll, 60 percent of 1,823 respondents agree that the existence of a Web site privacy statement makes them feel more confident—women (65 percent) slightly more than men (56 percent). But at the same time, most consumers don't read such policy statements. According to the *Wall Street Journal*/Harris Interactive poll, a mere 4 percent read the privacy policies posted on visited Web sites every time, only 16 percent claim to read it frequently, and 40 percent admit to doing so rarely or never.

Those who don't trust companies to treat their privacy right can take matters into their own hands by installing privacy software. Microsoft is developing a new system, Platform for Privacy Preferences (P3P), which promises to allow consumers to program their own privacy standards for Internet browsing, though there are still hurdles to overcome before the software is made available. (For example, the program could severely limit information accessible to marketers.) Whether Microsoft's new system—which requires other companies to cooperate before it can be implemented—will work is unclear. Nor is it clear that consumers would be willing to use new software if it slows their browsers. In the *American Demographics* poll, only 39 percent of respondents say they would use such software if it means sacrificing speed, but even this seems high in relation to actual behavior. According to a December 2000 Harris Interactive poll, 15 percent of respondents have put software on their computers to protect private information; 10 percent have used software to surf anonymously; and 5 percent have installed software that renders online purchases anonymous.

Other signs indicate that consumer outcry over privacy is out of sync with attendant action. In an April 2000 Yankelovich poll, 79 percent of online users report that they immediately leave Web sites requiring they provide personal information before entering. But another poll by Harris Interactive has only 44 percent avoiding Web sites with lax privacy practices. Moreover, in the *Wall Street Journal*/Harris Interactive poll, only 5 percent say concerns about privacy cause them to leave a Web site or forgo an online purchase all the time; 9 percent frequently; and 47 percent claim that privacy concerns deter them rarely or never. "You might say that consumers are very conflicted," observes Unica's Shanahan.

These inconsistencies extend to offline behavior as well. In the *American Demographics* survey, 66 percent of respondents say they either have or would make a phone call to prevent telemarketing or direct mail solicitations. However such intentions don't necessarily translate into action: According to the Yankelovich survey, a comparatively small 30 percent of respondents said they had asked to have their name removed from junk mailing lists, and 24 percent requested that their phone numbers be removed.

CHIPPING AWAY AT PRIVACY CONCERNS

Creating and communicating the benefits of privacy invasion is where marketers can weigh in most effectively. Because while consumers say they want to protect their privacy, they can also be enticed to give some privacy up. According to the *American Demographics* survey, more than 1 consumer in 5 is tempted to exchange private information for cash incentives, discounts on purchases, or a free offer, such as Internet access or wireless service. Marketers can also work to persuade consumers of the myriad benefits of data collection. For example, if consumers understand that faster service, easier-to-obtain credit, cost savings, and targeted promotions are the direct result of questionnaires and cookies, they might respond better to such "invasions of privacy."

Receptivity to such benefits varies according to demographics. Interest in incentives is highest among younger con-

DEMOGRAPHICS OF PRIVACY

What Consumers Fear

Good news for marketers: According to American Demographics' survey, consumers are far less concerned about protecting their shopping habits than they are about safekeeping basic socioeconomic information. Only 19 percent consider brand preferences private, 16 percent would guard their preferred clothing styles, and 23 percent preferences in food. Concern about spending habits and brand preferences increases as one gets older (62 percent of those 65 and older consider shopping information private versus 20 percent of those 18 to 24).

Married people are more concerned about information being used against them than unmarrieds (61 percent versus 53 percent); racial minorities are more concerned than whites (69 percent and 55 percent respectively); and Northeasterners are significantly more fearful than the rest of the country.

Unmarried respondents and people without children are particularly prone to a fear of being robbed or cheated—each 5 percentage points higher than their married and child-rearing counterparts. Racial minorities, people with a high school education or less, and the unemployed are also more likely to fear such theft. As for fear of identity theft, women are more concerned than men (57 percent versus 51 percent). A high level of alarm is also seen among Southerners (57 percent), racial minorities (12 percentage points higher than whites), and the unemployed (62 percent versus 54 percent of those working full-time).

What Consumers Will Do About It

The more affluent the consumer, the more likely he is to make a phone call to protect privacy, with 76 percent of those earning more than $75,000 willing to do so versus 53 percent of those with incomes less than $25,000. Northeasterners and those with more education are also more likely to take such measures. Educated respondents would likely press a button every time they visit a Web site or otherwise use a device to indicate a desire for privacy (81 percent of those with post-grad education compared with 63 percent of those with a high school diploma or less).

Not surprisingly, willingness to pay a fee to protect privacy rises with income level. Young people are more willing than their elders; and minorities more willing than whites (37 percent and 22 percent respectively). Westerners and Northeasterners are more willing than those in other regions to fork over cash for privacy (30 percent and 27 percent respectively versus 18 percent of Midwesterners and 23 percent of Southerners).

Those least likely to take action to combat privacy threats are the retired, nearly one-third of whom indicate they are willing to do none of the above. Apathy increases with age: 34 percent of those 65 and older have done and intend to do nothing, compared with only 8 percent of those aged 18 to 24. Conversely, inaction falls with income: only 7 percent of those earning more than $75,000 intend to do nothing, compared with 18 percent of people earning under $25,000.

Conquering Consumer Fears

Most people are willing to give up some privacy—for the right price: 45 percent of consumers between the ages of 18 and 24 would exchange information for cash, compared with only 8 percent of people aged 55 to 64, and 9 percent of those over 65. Similarly, 43 percent of 18- to 24-year-olds would exchange information for a free service, compared with 13 percent of those between the ages of 55 and 64. Men, racial minorities, unmarrieds, and households without children are more likely to barter in exchange for information. The more affluent the consumer, the greater the response to cash incentives, free service, loyalty programs, and additional content or information. Consumers in the lower-income bracket are more likely to be lured by sweepstakes and discounts.

Regional differences emerged in incentive preferences. Midwesterners are the least likely to exchange private information (57 percent say that none of the above inducements would work), and Westerners most likely (only 49 percent say their privacy cannot be bought). Midwesterners are keenest on discounts and cash incentives; Westerners and Southerners favor free service first and discounts second, and Northeasterners are most compelled by cash.

—PP

sumers, which makes sense, since they've been targeted the least. "Younger, tech-savvy, better-educated consumers are also less inclined to be afraid of things like identity theft, because they actually understand how secure servers work," explains Warren Egnal, senior vice president and privacy group leader at Porter Novelli. "Part of it is just communicating to everyone else how unlikely it is, given current privacy laws and technology, that those fears could become a reality."

The more educated consumers are about a company's privacy practices and security provisions, the less of an issue privacy is to them. But to fully address consumers' privacy concerns requires a multi-pronged effort. Some companies, however, are maneuvering through consumer contradictions by integrating privacy practices into every aspect of their business and then communicating those practices to consumers. Jan Davis, president of Rocketbridge, a managed security services provider, says her approach is to provide consumers with advance notice of privacy practices, give them the choice of whether or not to participate, allow them access to their own private information once permission is given, and provide them

DANGLE A CARROT

The following would make me more likely to provide personal information:

	TOTAL	MALE	FEMALE	WHITE	NONWHITE
Free service like Internet access or wireless service	22%	26%	19%	21%	29%
Cash incentive	21%	25%	17%	20%	26%
Membership in a loyalty program	19%	21%	18%	19%	21%
Chance to win a large cash prize in a sweepstakes	15%	18%	13%	14%	20%
Access to additional content or information	17%	18%	15%	15%	25%
Discounts on purchases	22%	24%	20%	21%	30%
None of the above	53%	51%	56%	56%	41%

SOURCE: APRIL 2001 AMERICAN DEMOGRAPHICS/MARKET FACTS POLL

with incentives to participate in such programs. "The ideal of privacy is important to people," Davis explains. "But the reality is that we live in a connected society, and if you want to enjoy the benefits of that society—be it access to credit or access to information—you have to be willing to share information. If people perceive that they're getting special benefits, they're much more willing to sacrifice privacy."

At best, a balance must be struck—with clear benefits to companies and consumers. For businesses, this means weighing the kind of consumer information that yields a real return on investment versus the personal data consumers are most eager to protect. And for consumers, benefits such as discounts or promotions must be weighed against the risks of ceding private information. Once a corporate privacy policy is drafted, companies need to make sure it's enforced. Often, employing a chief privacy officer to work with marketing, communications, MIS, operations, and management is a good way to enforce such a policy. This is an increasingly popular choice for corporations that have chosen to take the lead on the privacy issue. According to Westin, who founded the Association of Corporate Privacy Officers, today's 200 to 300 chief privacy officers in America will likely grow to several thousand within a couple of years. (Germany already has 2,000 data-protection officers.)

Most important of all is that companies work with consumers, allowing them to be part of the privacy protection process, and enabling them to feel in control of their personal data as much as possible. After all, the information *does* belong to them.

DIVERSITY WORST PRACTICES

Relying on cookie-cutter replications of others' actions in diversity practice is risky business!

BY DELYTE D. FROST

FOR COMPANIES EMBARKING ON DIVERSITY INITIATIVES, a best practices search is now an accepted starting point. But is this enough? Relying on cookie-cutter replications of others' actions in diversity practice is risky business. Current diversity *best practices* research fails to establish clear standards for success; correlate results with bottom-line outcomes; collect data from all levels of organizations; and measure the impact of different corporate cultures on success.

Rather than depend on the questionable success of others, those charged with the challenging task of developing a corporate diversity program should consider and learn from the painful failures of others. Reviewing *worst practices*™ builds on the concept of learning organizations to consider what has not worked and why. Armed with this insight, new approaches will emerge.

As a beginning list, I offer these *worst practices* for diversity change efforts:

1. **Broadening the focus to include *all individual differences* when the real issues are based on innate group identities such as race, gender, sexual orientation, national identity, age and/or ability.** This general language only serves to insult employees and customers and dissipates the focus of energy on measurable outcomes. If a product were being targeted to a particular market segment, would we call that segment *all interested individuals*? And could we then measure our success in the marketplace?
2. **Using euphemisms such as *ethnic* or *culture* when we mean race... or *lifestyles* when we mean sexual**

orientations. An organization's lack of courage to name an issue with direct language signals to employees and customers a lack of comfort in addressing the real issues. This euphemistic language also signals lack of clarity or lack of commitment to the work of diversity. We must first clearly articulate the issues before we can change them.

3. **Believing that continued research on and restating of the business case for diversity will convince the dominant group of white men that diversity is the *right thing to do*.** When dominant group members resist the diversity effort this is a resistance based on emotions—not based on lack of knowledge about the business case. Resistance to diversity efforts by white men is an important dynamic that is necessary for true change. This resistance must be engaged with energy, caring, and thoughtfulness—not deflected by intellectual arguments.
4. **Senior leadership delegating the formation of a diversity philosophy and approach to those in staff positions.** True change in the culture of an organization in the area of diversity requires full leadership involvement. Top leaders must both experience and model the personal and business changes necessary for a diversity process to succeed.
5. **Focusing the change strategies and actions on the subordinate or excluded groups.** Diversity efforts fall short when they target people of color, women, gays and lesbians, the disabled and other excluded groups as the primary focus of change. While designing strategies to include a previously excluded group is important, the primary change strategies for diversity must engage the dominant organizational culture—and those who benefit from the existing practices and policies.
6. **Creating a series of activities that have no strategic link to business success will only give the appearance of true commitment.** Over time, managers and employees will become discouraged that significant time and energy is not resulting in changes in their day-to-day experience. Diversity strategies must become part of the business purpose and vision.
7. **A desire to only see the positive and/or moving to action before the current negative state has been fully understood will generally result in time, money, and energy invested in solving the wrong problem.** Many corporate cultures place such a heavy emphasis upon framing all work in the positive tone that the work needed in diversity efforts to fully describe and understand the current state—which may be blocking the inclusion of employees because of their race, gender, or sexual orientation—is often kept to a surface skim. Leadership fears that the work of the enterprise will *get stuck* in the negative; when in reality, change theory teaches us that bringing the blocking forces fully to light will ignite the energy needed to address the *real* problems.
8. **Failing to see a diversity effort as an understanding that requires knowledge and experience in the content of diversity and systems change theory can lead an organization into frustration and negative backlash.** All organizational change requires extensive knowledge and experience with planned change strategies—adding the issues of diversity to the work calls for additional depth of experience.
9. **Seeing resistance and *push back* on the diversity issues as failure has stalled many diversity efforts that were on the right track.** Unfortunately, no real change takes place in organizations without significant resistance. Resistance is the source of energy for systems change. If there is no resistance, then nothing significant is changing. Diversity strategies must include major attention to engaging and transforming—not reducing—resistance.
10. **Believing that a diversity effort can be implemented without making some employees unhappy—and, worse yet, developing a process and a plan aimed at keeping everyone happy—will surely result in failure.** When did the new accounting system meet with cheers and applause? Did all employees welcome your last change in benefits with enthusiasm? Do companies stop mergers and downsizing because employees are unhappy? Leadership must be committed to diversity strategies because they are necessary for business prosperity; and must then work with employees to change—not work to keep them satisfied with an inequitable system.
11. **Assuming that training changes behavior is a common *worst practice* in diversity.** Awareness training to shift perceptions and unarticulated assumptions is critical to change—and must be a part of an overall strategy that includes specific goals, measurement, behavior skills training and accountability. Awareness training alone will not change behavior.
12. **Leadership being influenced by individual women or people of color who personally fear change and advise the dominant leadership to avoid any controversial issues or approaches is a common *worst practice*.** Open dialogue and debate on issues of race, gender, racism, sexism, homophobia, xenophobia, and other topics on which employees have strong opinions must be a part of any successful diversity effort.
13. **Leadership making decisions for others in the organization who will be expected to implement diversity plans is a grave error.** Management and employees at all levels must be involved in diversity

planning. Those who are being asked to change know the most about what will help them change.

14. **Beginning a corporate diversity effort focused on customers and external public relations will lead to false expectations.** Priorities should be initially focused on internal culture and commitment—and once employees trust in the leadership of the corporation, they will lead the work to both customers and the public. Presenting an organization to its public as a leader of diversity before key components of the organization are committed to the change will foster the belief by employees that leadership doesn't *walk the talk.*

If your company has launched or is considering launching a diversity initiative, you know that the course ahead is into uncharted waters. A successful program compels management to question old assumptions, requires individuals to take a hard look at very personal issues, and demands profound change throughout the organization. Creating a workplace that is more humane, more inclusive, and more productive won't happen overnight. Along the way, expect to meet resistance. Listen for impassioned complaints and feel the emotional turmoil of employees locked in old prejudices and misunderstandings.

The challenge of creating an organization without oppression requires much more than consideration of what may have worked for others. It also demands careful thought about what hasn't worked. Only after analyzing the worst practices will you have a strategy that responds to and reflects the specific requirements of your organization.

Delyte D. Frost, Ph. D., is an applied behavioral scientist, who specializes in large systems change initiatives. Dr. Frost consults from her company, Cygnus Inc., and is a senior associate at Elsie Y. Cross & Associates, an organizational development firm based in Philadelphia, PA. She is available for comment by sending an email message to cygnusinc@aol.com.

Opinions expressed in this article are solely those of the author and not of the Minority Corporate Counsel Association.

From *Diversity & the Bar,* March 2001, pp. 20-22.

Values in Tension: Ethics Away from Home

When is different just different, and when is different wrong?

by Thomas Donaldson

When we leave home and cross our nation's boundaries, moral clarity often blurs. Without a backdrop of shared attitudes, and without familiar laws and judicial procedures that define standards of ethical conduct, certainty is elusive. Should a company invest in a foreign country where civil and political rights are violated? Should a company go along with a host country's discriminatory employment practices? If companies in developed countries shift facilities to developing nations that lack strict environmental and health regulations, or if those companies choose to fill management and other top-level positions in a host nation with people from the home country, whose standards should prevail?

Even the best-informed, best-intentioned executives must rethink their assumptions about business practice in foreign settings. What works in a company's home country can fail in a country with different standards of ethical conduct. Such difficulties are unavoidable for businesspeople who live and work abroad.

But how can managers resolve the problems? What are the principles that can help them work through the maze of cultural differences and establish codes of conduct for globally ethical business practice? How can companies answer the toughest question in global business ethics: What happens when a host country's ethical standards seem lower than the home country's?

Competing Answers

One answer is as old as philosophical discourse. According to cultural relativism, no culture's ethics are better than any other's; therefore there are no international rights and wrongs. If the people of Indonesia tolerate the bribery of their public officials, so what? Their attitude is no better or worse than that of people in Denmark or Singapore who refuse to offer or accept bribes. Likewise, if Belgians fail to find insider trading morally repugnant, who cares? Not enforcing insider-trading laws is no more or less ethical than enforcing such laws.

The cultural relativist's creed—When in Rome, do as the Romans do—is tempting, especially when failing to do as the locals do means forfeiting business opportunities. The inadequacy of cultural relativism, however, becomes apparent when the practices in question are more damaging than petty bribery or insider trading.

In the late 1980s, some European tanneries and pharmaceutical companies were looking for cheap waste-dumping sites. They approached virtually every country on Africa's west coast from Morocco to the Congo. Nigeria agreed to take highly toxic polychlorinated biphenyls. Unprotected local workers, wearing thongs and shorts, unloaded barrels of PCBs and placed them near a residential area. Neither the residents nor the workers knew that the barrels contained toxic waste.

We may denounce governments that permit such abuses, but many countries are unable to police transnational corporations adequately even if they want to. And in many countries, the combination of ineffective enforcement and inadequate regulations leads to behavior by unscrupulous companies that is clearly wrong. A few years ago, for example, a group of investors became interested in restoring the SS *United States*, once a luxurious ocean liner. Before the actual restoration could begin, the ship had to be stripped of its asbestos lining. A bid from a U.S. company, based on U.S. standards for asbestos removal, priced the job at more than $100 million. A company in the Ukranian city of Sevastopol offered to do the work for less than $2 million. In October 1993, the ship was towed to Sevastopol.

The Culture and Ethics of Software Piracy

Before jumping on the cultural relativism bandwagon, stop and consider the potential economic consequences of a when-in-Rome attitude toward business ethics. Take a look at the current statistics on software piracy: In the United States, pirated software is estimated to be 35% of the total software market, and industry losses are estimated at $2.3 billion per year. The piracy rate is 57% in Germany and 80% in Italy and Japan; the rates in most Asian countries are estimated to be nearly 100%.

There are similar laws against software piracy in those countries. What, then, accounts for the differences? Although a country's level of economic development plays a large part, culture, including ethical attitudes, may be a more crucial factor. The 1995 annual report of the Software Publishers Association connects software piracy directly to culture and attitude. It describes Italy and Hong Kong as having "'first world' per capita incomes, along with 'third world' rates of piracy." When asked whether one should use software without paying for it, most people, including people in Italy and Hong Kong, say no. But people in some countries regard the practice as *less* unethical than people in other countries do. Confucian culture, for example, stresses that individuals should share what they create with society. That may be, in part, what prompts the Chinese and other Asians to view the concept of intellectual property as a means for the West to monopolize its technological superiority.

What happens if ethical attitudes around the world permit large-scale software piracy? Software companies won't want to invest as much in developing new products, because they cannot expect any return on their investment in certain parts of the world. When ethics fail to support technological creativity, there are consequences that go beyond statistics—jobs are lost and livelihoods jeopardized.

Companies must do more than lobby foreign governments for tougher enforcement of piracy laws. They must cooperate with other companies and with local organizations to help citizens understand the consequences of piracy and to encourage the evolution of a different ethic toward the practice.

A cultural relativist would have no problem with that outcome, but I do. A country has the right to establish its own health and safety regulations, but in the case described above, the standards and the terms of the contract could not possibly have protected workers in Sevastopol from known health risks. Even if the contract met Ukranian standards, ethical businesspeople must object. Cultural relativism is morally blind. There are fundamental values that cross cultures, and companies must uphold them. (For an economic argument against cultural relativism, see the insert "The Culture and Ethics of Software Piracy.")

At the other end of the spectrum from cultural relativism is ethical imperialism, which directs people to do everywhere exactly as they do at home. Again, an understandably appealing approach but one that is clearly inadequate. Consider the large U.S. computer-products company that in 1993 introduced a course on sexual harassment in its Saudi Arabian facility. Under the banner of global consistency, instructors used the same approach to train Saudi Arabian managers that they had used with U.S. managers: the participants were asked to discuss a case in which a manager makes sexually explicit remarks to a new female employee over drinks in a bar. The instructors failed to consider how the exercise would work in a culture with strict conventions governing relationships between men and women. As a result, the training sessions were ludicrous. They baffled and offended the Saudi participants, and the message to avoid coercion and sexual discrimination was lost.

The theory behind ethical imperialism is absolutism, which is based on three problematic principles. Absolutists believe that there is a single list of truths, that they can be expressed only with one set of concepts, and that they call for exactly the same behavior around the world.

The first claim clashes with many people's belief that different cultural traditions must be respected. In some cultures, loyalty to a community—family, organization, or society—is the foundation of all ethical behavior. The Japanese, for example, define business ethics in terms of loyalty to their companies, their business networks, and their nation. Americans place a higher value on liberty than on loyalty; the U.S. tradition of rights emphasizes equality, fairness, and individual freedom. It is hard to conclude that truth lies on one side or the other, but an absolutist would have us select just one.

The second problem with absolutism is the presumption that people must express moral truth using only one set of concepts. For instance, some absolutists insist that the language of basic rights provide the framework for any discussion of ethics. That means, though, that entire cultural traditions must be ignored. The notion of a right evolved with the rise of democracy in post-Renaissance Europe and the United States, but the term is not found in either Confucian or Buddhist traditions. We all learn ethics in the context of our particular cultures, and the power in the principles is deeply tied to the way in which they are expressed. Internationally accepted lists of moral principles, such as the United Nations' Universal Declaration of Human Rights, draw on many cultural and religious traditions. As philosopher Michael Walzer has noted, "There is no Esperanto of global ethics."

The third problem with absolutism is the belief in a global standard of ethical behavior. Context must shape ethical practice. Very low wages, for example, may be considered unethical in rich, advanced countries, but developing nations may be acting ethically if they encourage investment and improve living standards by accepting low wages. Likewise, when people are malnourished or starving, a government may be wise to use more fertilizer in order to improve crop yields, even though that means settling for relatively high levels of thermal water pollution.

When cultures have different standards of ethical behavior—and different ways of handling unethical behavior—a company that takes an absolutist approach may find itself making a disastrous mistake. When a manager at a large U.S. specialty-products company in China caught an employee stealing, she followed the company's practice and turned the employee over to the provincial authorities, who executed him. Managers cannot operate in another culture without being aware of that culture's attitudes toward ethics.

If companies can neither adopt a host country's ethics nor extend the home country's standards, what is the answer? Even the traditional litmus test—What would people think of your actions if they were written up on the front page of the newspaper?—is an unreliable guide, for there is no international consensus on standards of business conduct.

What Do These Values Have in Common?

Non-Western	Western
Kyosei (Japanese): Living and working together for the common good.	Individual liberty
Dharma (Hindu): The fulfillment of inherited duty.	Egalitarianism
Santutthi (Buddhist): The importance of limited desires.	Political participation
Zakat (Muslim): The duty to give alms to the Muslim poor.	Human rights

Balancing the Extremes: Three Guiding Principles

Companies must help managers distinguish between practices that are merely different and those that are wrong. For relativists, nothing is sacred and nothing is wrong. For absolutists, many things that are different are wrong. Neither extreme illuminates the real world of business decision making. The answer lies somewhere in between.

When it comes to shaping ethical behavior, companies must be guided by three principles.

- Respect for core human values, which determine the absolute moral threshold for all business activities.
- Respect for local traditions.
- The belief that context matters when deciding what is right and what is wrong.

Consider those principles in action. In Japan, people doing business together often exchange gifts—sometimes expensive ones—in keeping with long-standing Japanese tradition. When U.S. and European companies started doing a lot of business in Japan, many Western businesspeople thought that the practice of gift giving might be wrong rather than simply different. To them, accepting a gift felt like accepting a bribe. As Western companies have become more familiar with Japanese traditions, however, most have come to tolerate the practice and to set different limits on gift giving in Japan than they do elsewhere.

Respecting differences is a crucial ethical practice. Research shows that management ethics differ among cultures; respecting those differences means recognizing that some cultures have obvious weaknesses—as well as hidden strengths. Managers in Hong Kong, for example, have a higher tolerance for some forms of bribery than their Western counterparts, but they have a much lower tolerance for the failure to acknowledge a subordinate's work. In some parts of the Far East, stealing credit from a subordinate is nearly an unpardonable sin.

People often equate respect for local traditions with cultural relativism. That is incorrect. Some practices are clearly wrong. Union Carbide's tragic experience in Bhopal, India, provides one example. The company's executives seriously underestimated how much on-site management involvement was needed at the Bhopal plant to compensate for the country's poor infrastructure and regulatory capabilities. In the aftermath of the disastrous gas leak, the lesson is clear: companies using sophisticated technology in a developing country must evaluate that country's ability to oversee its safe use. Since the incident at Bhopal, Union Carbide has become a leader in advising companies on using hazardous technologies safely in developing countries.

Some activities are wrong no matter where they take place. But some practices that are unethical in one setting may be acceptable in another. For instance, the chemical EDB, a soil fungicide, is banned for use in the United States. In hot climates, however, it quickly becomes harmless through exposure to intense solar radiation and high soil temperatures. As long as the chemical is monitored, companies may be able to use EDB ethically in certain parts of the world.

Defining the Ethical Threshold: Core Values

Few ethical questions are easy for managers to answer. But there are some hard truths that must guide managers' actions, a set of what I call *core human values,* which define minimum ethical standards for all companies.[1] The right to good health and the right to economic advancement and an improved standard of living are two core human values. Another is what Westerners call the Golden Rule, which is recognizable in every major religious and ethical tradition around the world. In Book 15 of his *Analects,* for instance, Confucius counsels people to maintain reciprocity, or not to do to others what they do not want done to themselves.

Although no single list would satisfy every scholar, I believe it is possible to articulate three core values that incorporate the work of scores of theologians and philosophers around the world. To be broadly relevant, these values must include elements found in both Western and non-Western cultural and religious traditions. Consider the examples of values in the insert "What Do These Values Have in Common?"

At first glance, the values expressed in the two lists seem quite different. Nonetheless, in the spirit of what philosopher John Rawls calls *overlapping consensus*, one can see that the seemingly divergent values converge at key points. Despite important differences between Western and non-Western cultural and religious traditions, both express shared attitudes about what it means to be human. First, individuals must not treat others simply as tools; in other words, they must recognize a person's value as a human being. Next, individuals and communities must treat people in ways that respect people's basic rights. Finally, members of a community must work together to support and improve the institutions on which the community depends. I call those three values *respect for human dignity, respect for basic rights*, and *good citizenship*.

Those values must be the starting point for all companies as they formulate and evaluate standards of ethical conduct at home and abroad. But they are only a starting point. Companies need much more specific guidelines, and the first step to developing those is to translate the core human values into core values for business. What does it mean, for example, for a company to respect human dignity? How can a company be a good citizen?

I believe that companies can respect human dignity by creating and sustaining a corporate culture in which employees, customers, and suppliers are treated not as means to an end but as people whose intrinsic value must be acknowledged, and by producing safe products and services in a safe workplace. Companies can respect basic rights by acting in ways that support and protect the individual rights of employees, customers, and surrounding communities, and by avoiding relationships that violate human beings' rights to health, education, safety, and an adequate standard of living. And companies can be good citizens by supporting essential social institutions, such as the economic system and the education system, and by working with host governments and other organizations to protect the environment.

The core values establish a moral compass for business practice. They can help companies identify practices that are acceptable and those that are intolerable—even if the practices are compatible with a host country's norms and laws. Dumping pollutants near people's homes and accepting inadequate standards for handling hazardous materials are two examples of actions that violate core values.

Similarly, if employing children prevents them from receiving a basic education, the practice is intolerable. Lying about product specifications in the act of selling may not affect human lives directly, but it too is intolerable because it violates the trust that is needed to sustain a corporate culture in which customers are respected.

Sometimes it is not a company's actions but those of a supplier or customer that pose problems. Take the case of the Tan family, a large supplier for Levi Strauss. The Tans were allegedly forcing 1,200 Chinese and Filipino women to work 74 hours per week in guarded compounds on the Mariana Islands. In 1992, after repeated warnings to the Tans, Levi Strauss broke off business relations with them.

Creating an Ethical Corporate Culture

The core values for business that I have enumerated can help companies begin to exercise ethical judgment and think about how to operate ethically in foreign cultures, but they are not specific enough to guide managers through actual ethical dilemmas. Levi Strauss relied on a written code of conduct when figuring out how to deal with the Tan family. The company's Global Sourcing and Operating Guidelines, formerly called the Business Partner Terms of Engagement, state that Levi Strauss will "seek to identify and utilize business partners who aspire as individuals and in the conduct of all their businesses to a set of ethical standards not incompatible with our own." Whenever intolerable business situations arise, managers should be guided by precise statements that spell out the behavior and operating practices that the company demands.

Many companies don't do anything with their codes of conduct; they simply paste them on the wall.

Ninety percent of all *Fortune* 500 companies have codes of conduct, and 70% have statements of vision and values. In Europe and the Far East, the percentages are lower but are increasing rapidly. Does that mean that most companies have what they need? Hardly. Even though most large U.S. companies have both statements of values and codes of conduct, many might be better off if they didn't. Too many companies don't do anything with the documents; they simply paste them on the wall to impress employees, customers, suppliers, and the public. As a result, the senior managers who drafted the statements lose credibility by proclaiming values and not living up to them. Companies such as Johnson & Johnson, Levi Strauss, Motorola, Texas Instruments, and Lockheed Martin, however, do a great deal to make the words meaningful. Johnson & Johnson, for example, has become well known for its Credo Challenge sessions, in which managers discuss ethics in the context of their current business problems and are invited to criticize the company's credo and make suggestions for changes. The participants' ideas are passed on to the company's senior managers. Lockheed Martin has created an innovative site on the World Wide Web and on its local network that gives employees, customers, and suppliers access to the company's ethical code and the chance to voice complaints.

If a company declared all gift giving unethical, it wouldn't be able to do business in Japan.

Codes of conduct must provide clear direction about ethical behavior when the temptation to behave unethically is strongest. The pronouncement in a code of conduct that bribery is unacceptable is useless unless accompanied by guidelines for gift giving, payments to get goods through customs, and "requests" from intermediaries who are hired to ask for bribes.

Motorola's values are stated very simply as "How we will always act: [with] constant respect for people [and] uncompromising integrity." The company's code of conduct, however, is explicit about actual business practice. With respect to bribery, for example, the code states that the "funds and assets of Motorola shall not be used, directly or indirectly, for illegal payments of any kind." It is unambiguous about what sort of payment is illegal: "the payment of a bribe to a public official or the kickback of funds to an employee of a customer...." The code goes on to prescribe specific procedures for handling commissions to intermediaries, issuing sales invoices, and disclosing confidential information in a sales transaction—all situations in which employees might have an opportunity to accept or offer bribes.

Codes of conduct must be explicit to be useful, but they must also leave room for a manager to use his or her judgment in situations requiring cultural sensitivity. Host-country employees shouldn't be forced to adopt all home-country values and renounce their own. Again, Motorola's code is exemplary. First, it gives clear direction: "Employees of Motorola will respect the laws, customs, and traditions of each country in which they operate, but will, at the same time, engage in no course of conduct which, even if legal, customary, and accepted in any such country, could be deemed to be in violation of the accepted business ethics of Motorola or the laws of the United States relating to business ethics." After laying down such absolutes, Motorola's code then makes clear when individual judgment will be necessary. For example, employees may sometimes accept certain kinds of small gifts "in rare circumstances, where the refusal to accept a gift" would injure Motorola's "legitimate business interests." Under certain circumstances, such gifts "may be accepted so long as the gift inures to the benefit of Motorola" and not "to the benefit of the Motorola employee."

Striking the appropriate balance between providing clear direction and leaving room for individual judgment makes crafting corporate values statements and ethics codes one of the hardest tasks that executives confront. The words are only a start. A company's leaders need to refer often to their organization's credo and code and must themselves be credible, committed, and consistent. If senior managers act as though ethics don't matter, the rest of the company's employees won't think they do, either.

Conflicts of Development and Conflicts of Tradition

Managers living and working abroad who are not prepared to grapple with moral ambiguity and tension should pack their bags and come home. The view that all business practices can be categorized as either ethical or unethical is too simple. As Einstein is reported to have said, "Things should be as simple as possible—but no simpler." Many business practices that are considered unethical in one setting may be ethical in another. Such activities are neither black nor white but exist in what Thomas Dunfee and I have called *moral free space.*[2] In this gray zone, there are no tight prescriptions for a company's behavior. Managers must chart their own courses—as long as they do not violate core human values.

Many activities are neither good nor bad but exist in *moral free space.*

Consider the following example. Some successful Indian companies offer employees the opportunity for one of their children to gain a job with the company once the child has completed a certain level in school. The companies honor this commitment even when other applicants are more qualified than an employee's child. The perk is extremely valuable in a country where jobs are hard to find, and it reflects the Indian culture's belief that the West has gone too far in allowing economic opportunities to break up families. Not surprisingly, the perk is among the most cherished by employees, but in most Western countries, it would be branded unacceptable nepotism. In the United States, for example, the ethical principle of equal opportunity holds that jobs should go to the applicants with the best qualifications. If a U.S. company made such promises to its employees, it would violate regulations established by the Equal Employment Opportunity Commission. Given this difference in ethical attitudes, how should U.S. managers react to Indian nepotism? Should they condemn the Indian companies, refusing to accept them as partners or suppliers until they agree to clean up their act?

Despite the obvious tension between nepotism and principles of equal opportunity, I cannot condemn the practice for Indians. In a country, such as India, that emphasizes clan and family relationships and has catastrophic levels of

The Problem with Bribery

Bribery is widespread and insidious. Managers in transnational companies routinely confront bribery even though most countries have laws against it. The fact is that officials in many developing countries wink at the practice, and the salaries of local bureaucrats are so low that many consider bribes a form of remuneration. The U.S. Foreign Corrupt Practices Act defines allowable limits on petty bribery in the form of routine payments required to move goods through customs. But demands for bribes often exceed those limits, and there is seldom a good solution.

Bribery disrupts distribution channels when goods languish on docks until local handlers are paid off, and it destroys incentives to compete on quality and cost when purchasing decisions are based on who pays what under the table. Refusing to acquiesce is often tantamount to giving business to unscrupulous companies.

I believe that even routine bribery is intolerable. Bribery undermines market efficiency and predictability, thus ultimately denying people their right to a minimal standard of living. Some degree of ethical commitment—some sense that everyone will play by the rules—is necessary for a sound economy. Without an ability to predict outcomes, who would be willing to invest?

There was a U.S. company whose shipping crates were regularly pilfered by handlers on the docks of Rio de Janeiro. The handlers would take about 10% of the contents of the crates, but the company was never sure which 10% it would be. In a partial solution, the company began sending two crates—the first with 90% of the merchandise, the second with 10%. The handlers learned to take the second crate and leave the first untouched. From the company's perspective, at least knowing which goods it would lose was an improvement.

Bribery does more than destroy predictability; it undermines essential social and economic systems. That truth is not lost on businesspeople in countries where the practice is woven into the social fabric. CEOs in India admit that their companies engage constantly in bribery, and they say that they have considerable disgust for the practice. They blame government policies in part, but Indian executives also know that their country's business practices perpetuate corrupt behavior. Anyone walking the streets of Calcutta, where it is clear that even a dramatic redistribution of wealth would still leave most of India's inhabitants in dire poverty, comes face-to-face with the devastating effects of corruption.

unemployment, the practice must be viewed in moral free space. The decision to allow a special perk for employees and their children is not necessarily wrong—at least for members of that country.

How can managers discover the limits of moral free space? That is, how can they learn to distinguish a value in tension with their own from one that is intolerable? Helping managers develop good ethical judgment requires companies to be clear about their core values and codes of conduct. But even the most explicit set of guidelines cannot always provide answers. That is especially true in the thorniest ethical dilemmas, in which the host country's ethical standards not only are different but also seem lower than the home country's. Managers must recognize that when countries have different ethical standards, there are two types of conflict that commonly arise. Each type requires its own line of reasoning.

In the first type of conflict, which I call a *conflict of relative development,* ethical standards conflict because of the countries' different levels of economic development. As mentioned before, developing countries may accept wage rates that seem inhumane to more advanced countries in order to attract investment. As economic conditions in a developing country improve, the incidence of that sort of conflict usually decreases. The second type of conflict is a *conflict of cultural tradition.* For example, Saudi Arabia, unlike most other countries, does not allow women to serve as corporate managers. Instead, women may work in only a few professions, such as education and health care. The prohibition stems from strongly held religious and cultural beliefs; any increase in the country's level of economic development, which is already quite high, is not likely to change the rules.

To resolve a conflict of relative development, a manager must ask the following question: Would the practice be acceptable at home if my country were in a similar stage of economic development? Consider the difference between wage and safety standards in the United States and in Angola, where citizens accept lower standards on both counts. If a U.S. oil company is hiring Angolans to work on an offshore Angolan oil rig, can the company pay them lower wages than it pays U.S. workers in the Gulf of Mexico? Reasonable people have to answer yes if the alternative for Angola is the loss of both the foreign investment and the jobs.

Consider, too, differences in regulatory environments. In the 1980s, the government of India fought hard to be able to import Ciba-Geigy's Entero Vioform, a drug known to be enormously effective in fighting dysentery but one that had been banned in the United States because some users experienced side effects. Although dysentery was not a big problem in the United States, in India, poor public sanitation was contributing to epidemic levels of the disease. Was it unethical to make the drug available in India after it had been banned in the United States? On the contrary, rational people should consider it unethical not to do so. Apply our test: Would the United States, at an earlier stage of development, have used this drug despite its side effects? The answer is clearly yes.

But there are many instances when the answer to similar questions is no. Sometimes a host country's standards are inadequate at any level of economic development. If a country's pollution standards are so low that working on an oil rig would considerably increase a person's risk of developing cancer, foreign oil companies must refuse to do business there. Likewise, if the dangerous side effects of a drug treatment outweigh its benefits, managers should not accept health standards that ignore the risks.

When relative economic conditions do not drive tensions, there is a more objective test for resolving ethical problems. Managers should deem a practice permissible only if they can answer no to both of the following questions: Is it possible to conduct business successfully in the host country without undertaking the practice? And Is the practice a violation of a core human value? Japanese gift giving is a perfect example of a conflict of cultural tradition. Most experienced businesspeople, Japanese and non-Japanese alike, would agree that doing business in Japan would be virtually impossible without adopting the practice. Does gift giving violate a core human value? I cannot identify one that it violates. As a result, gift giving may be permissible for foreign companies in Japan even if it conflicts with ethical attitudes at home. In fact, that conclusion is widely accepted, even by companies such as Texas Instruments and IBM, which are outspoken against bribery.

Does it follow that all nonmonetary gifts are acceptable or that bribes are generally acceptable in countries where they are common? Not at all. (See the insert "The Problem with Bribery.") What makes the routine practice of gift giving acceptable in Japan are the limits in its scope and intention. When gift giving moves outside those limits, it soon collides with core human values. For example, when Carl Kotchian, president of Lockheed in the 1970s, carried suitcases full of cash to Japanese politicians, he went beyond the norms established by Japanese tradition. That incident galvanized opinion in the United States Congress and helped lead to passage of the Foreign Corrupt Practices Act. Likewise, Roh Tae Woo went beyond the norms established by Korean cultural tradition when he accepted $635.4 million in bribes as president of the Republic of Korea between 1988 and 1993.

Guidelines for Ethical Leadership

Learning to spot intolerable practices and to exercise good judgment when ethical conflicts arise requires practice. Creating a company culture that rewards ethical behavior is essential. The following guidelines for developing a global ethical perspective among managers can help.

Treat corporate values and formal standards of conduct as absolutes. Whatever ethical standards a company chooses, it cannot waver on its principles either at home or abroad. Consider what has become part of company lore at Motorola. Around 1950, a senior executive was negotiating with officials of a South American government on a $10 million sale that would have increased the company's annual net profits by nearly 25%. As the negotiations neared completion, however, the executive walked away from the deal because the officials were asking for $1 million for "fees." CEO Robert Galvin not only supported the executive's decision but also made it clear that Motorola would neither accept the sale on any terms nor do business with those government officials again. Retold over the decades, this story demonstrating Galvin's resolve has helped cement a culture of ethics for thousands of employees at Motorola.

Design and implement conditions of engagement for suppliers and customers. Will your company do business with any customer or supplier? What if a customer or supplier uses child labor? What if it has strong links with organized crime? What if it pressures your company to break a host country's laws? Such issues are best not left for spur-of-the-moment decisions. Some companies have realized that. Sears, for instance, has developed a policy of not contracting production to companies that use prison labor or infringe on workers' rights to health and safety. And BankAmerica has specified as a condition for many of its loans to developing countries that environmental standards and human rights must be observed.

Allow foreign business units to help formulate ethical standards and interpret ethical issues. The French pharmaceutical company Rhône-Poulenc Rorer has allowed foreign subsidiaries to augment lists of corporate ethical principles with their own suggestions. Texas Instruments has paid special attention to issues of international business ethics by creating the Global Business Practices Council, which is made up of managers from countries in which the company operates. With the overarching intent to create a "global ethics strategy, locally deployed," the council's mandate is to provide ethics education and create local processes that will help managers in the company's foreign business units resolve ethical conflicts.

In host countries, support efforts to decrease institutional corruption. Individual managers will not be able to wipe out corruption in a host country, no matter how many bribes they turn down. When a host country's tax system, import and export procedures, and procurement practices favor unethical players, companies must take action.

Many companies have begun to participate in reforming host-country institutions. General Electric, for example, has taken a strong stand in India, using the media to make repeated condemnations of bribery in business and government. General Electric and others have found, however, that a single company usually cannot drive out entrenched corruption. Transparency International, an organization based in Germany, has been effective in helping coalitions of companies, government officials, and others work to reform bribery-ridden bureaucracies in Russia, Bangladesh, and elsewhere.

Exercise moral imagination. Using moral imagination means resolving tensions responsibly and creatively. Coca-Cola, for instance, has consistently turned down requests for bribes from Egyptian officials but has managed to gain political support and public trust by sponsoring a project to plant fruit trees. And take the example of Levi Strauss, which discovered in the early 1990s that two of its suppliers in Bangladesh were employing children under the age of 14—a practice that violated the company's principles but was tolerated in Bangladesh. Forcing the suppliers to fire the children would not have ensured that the children received an education, and it would have caused serious hardship for the families depending on the children's wages. In a creative arrangement, the suppliers agreed to pay the children's regular wages while they attended school and to offer each child a job at age 14. Levi Strauss, in turn, agreed to pay the children's tuition and provide books and uniforms. That arrangement allowed Levi Strauss to uphold its principles and provide long-term benefits to its host country.

Many people think of values as soft; to some they are usually unspoken. A South Seas island society uses the word *mokita*, which means, "the truth that everybody knows but nobody speaks." However difficult they are to articulate, values affect how we all behave. In a global business environment, values in tension are the rule rather than the exception. Without a company's commitment, statements of values and codes of ethics end up as empty platitudes that provide managers with no foundation for behaving ethically. Employees need and deserve more, and responsible members of the global business community can set examples for others to follow. The dark consequences of incidents such as Union Carbide's disaster in Bhopal remind us how high the stakes can be.

Notes

1. In other writings, Thomas W. Dunfee and I have used the term *hypernorm* instead of *core human value.*
2. Thomas Donaldson and Thomas W. Dunfee, "Toward a Unified Conception of Business Ethics: Integrative Social Contracts Theory," *Academy of Management Review*, April 1994; and "Integrative Social Contracts Theory: A Communitarian Conception of Economic Ethics," *Economics and Philosophy*, spring 1995.

GLOBAL STANDARDS, LOCAL PROBLEMS

"When in Rome" doesn't work anymore. More and more global firms are finding a correlation between ethical standards and economic success.

Meryl Davids

AH, THE GOOD OLD DAYS. BACK 30, 20, EVEN 10, years ago, companies could run their overseas business pretty much however they wanted. What happened in a land far away bore little consequence to the main operations. If a factory employed underage workers in Third World countries, well, that's just the way things were done over there. Giving and accepting elaborate gifts? Part of the culture. And if your subsidiary didn't adhere to the same pollution control standards as its American counterparts, it was easily justified on the grounds that environmental laws overseas weren't as strict.

But if the world shrinking to a marble has been good for American companies profiting from international operations and trade, it has also added brutal new pressures for principled behavior on a global scale. Global business ethics has now become "the ultimate dilemma for many U.S. businesses," as one business publication stated.

"The world is highly interconnected now, so American consumers increasingly know and care if a company is, say, dumping chemical waste in a river in China," says Robert MacGregor, a leader of the Caux Round Table, a group of international business leaders aiming to focus attention on global corporate responsibility. "Companies that are concerned with their reputations, and that's nearly all companies, recognize they have to focus on their global principles."

Ignoring global ethical issues can even cost you customers at home. "We have evidence that if consumers know that a company is unethical anywhere in the world, they will exercise their disapproval at the cash register," MacGregor says, not to mention the impact it has on employees and investors.

Brother, Can You Spare a Thousand?

While the heightened focus on international ethics—led by a growing charge by nonprofit organizations including Caux, the U.N., the World Bank, and others—does make it riskier to operate overseas, in many ways it is also a welcome relief to many U.S. firms. Companies here have long decried the uneven playing field created by our Foreign Corrupt Practices Act. Passed in 1977, among other things it prohibits American countries from paying bribes for expedited services. Companies from other countries, including several in Europe, however, can not only legally make those payments, but they can also deduct the money from their taxes.

With this disparity, trying to open factories or get products unloaded in countries where such payoffs are the norm has proven difficult, if not impossible, for American companies in many locales. Which areas are the most rife with problems? According to a Corruption Perception Index developed by nonprofit group Transparency International, Cameroon, Paraguay, Honduras, Tanzania, and Nigeria are seen as most corrupt (see table). While Frank Vogl, vice president of the group and a former World Bank official, says the survey measures only perceptions (of ordinary citizens, business leaders, and experts), "countries that are seen to have high levels of corruption almost certainly do have them." Russia, too, falls near the bottom of the scale, as does China, a situation many believe has contributed to these countries' current economic woes.

"The rogue capitalism in Russia, and the cronyism and lack of transparency in Asia, aren't good for business there—or here," MacGregor says. "Principled business is not just a theoretical notion; it has pragmatic implica-

The Transparency International 1998 Corruption Perceptions Index

Country Rank	Country	1998 CPI Score	Standard Deviation	Surveys Used	Country Rank	Country	1998 CPI Score	Standard Deviation	Surveys Used
1	Denmark	10.0	0.7	9	44	Zimbabwe	4.2	2.2	6
2	Finland	9.6	0.5	9	45	Malawi	4.1	0.6	4
3	Sweden	9.5	0.5	9	46	Brazil	4.0	0.4	9
4	New Zealand	9.4	0.7	8	47	Belarus	3.9	1.9	3
5	Iceland	9.3	0.9	6	48	Slovak Republic	3.9	1.6	5
6	Canada	9.2	0.5	9	49	Jamaica	3.8	0.4	3
7	Singapore	9.1	1.0	10	50	Morocco	3.7	1.8	3
8	Netherlands	9.0	0.7	9	51	El Salvador	3.6	2.3	3
9	Norway	9.0	0.7	9	52	China	3.5	0.7	10
10	Switzerland	8.9	0.6	10	53	Zambia	3.5	1.6	4
11	Australia	8.7	0.7	8	54	Turkey	3.4	1.0	10
12	Luxembourg	8.7	0.9	7	55	Ghana	3.3	1.0	4
13	United Kingdom	8.7	0.5	10	56	Mexico	3.3	0.6	9
14	Ireland	8.2	1.4	10	57	Philippines	3.3	1.1	10
15	Germany	7.9	0.4	10	58	Senegal	3.3	0.8	3
16	Hong Kong	7.8	1.1	12	59	Ivory Coast	3.1	1.7	4
17	Austria	7.5	0.8	9	60	Guatemala	3.1	2.5	3
18	United States	7.5	0.9	8	61	Argentina	3.0	0.6	9
19	Israel	7.1	1.4	9	62	Nicaragua	3.0	2.5	3
20	Chile	6.8	0.9	9	63	Romania	3.0	1.5	3
21	France	6.7	0.6	9	64	Thailand	3.0	0.7	11
22	Portugal	6.5	1.0	10	65	Yugoslavia	3.0	1.5	3
23	Botswana	6.1	2.2	3	66	Bulgaria	2.9	2.3	4
24	Spain	6.1	1.3	10	67	Egypt	2.9	0.6	3
25	Japan	5.8	1.6	11	68	India	2.9	0.6	12
26	Estonia	5.7	0.5	3	69	Bolivia	2.8	1.2	4
27	Costa Rica	5.6	1.6	5	70	Ukraine	2.8	1.6	6
28	Belgium	5.4	1.4	9	71	Latvia	2.7	1.9	3
29	Malaysia	5.3	0.4	11	72	Pakistan	2.7	1.4	3
30	Namibia	5.3	1.0	3	73	Uganda	2.6	0.8	4
31	Taiwan	5.3	0.7	11	74	Kenya	2.5	0.6	4
32	South Africa	5.2	0.8	10	75	Vietnam	2.5	0.5	6
33	Hungary	5.0	1.2	9	76	Russia	2.4	0.9	10
34	Mauritius	5.0	0.8	3	77	Ecuador	2.3	1.5	3
35	Tunisia	5.0	2.1	3	78	Venezuela	2.3	0.8	9
36	Greece	4.9	1.7	9	79	Colombia	2.2	0.8	9
37	Czech Republic	4.8	0.8	9	80	Indonesia	2.0	0.9	10
38	Jordan	4.7	1.1	6	81	Nigeria	1.9	0.5	5
39	Italy	4.6	0.8	10	82	Tanzania	1.9	1.1	4
40	Poland	4.6	1.6	8	83	Honduras	1.7	0.5	3
41	Peru	4.5	0.8	6	84	Paraguay	1.5	0.5	3
42	Uruguay	4.3	0.9	3	85	Cameroon	1.4	0.5	4
43	South Korea	4.2	1.2	12					

The column 1998 CPI Score relates perceptions of the degree of which corruption is seen by business people—a perfect 10.00 would be a totally corruption-free country. Standard Deviation indicates differences in the values of the sources for the 1998 index: the greater the variance, the greater the differences of perceptions of a country among the sources. The number of surveys used had to be at least 3 for a country to be included in the CPI.

tions." The belief that moral values such as openness and trust are such an integral part of successful capitalism was even held by capitalism's proud papa, Adam Smith, MacGregor says. Before writing his *Wealth of Nations*, Smith penned a treatise arguing that for capitalism to work it must be based on shared rules and common values. "When you violate those rules, the system doesn't work the way it should," MacGregor warns.

Larry Smeltzer, an ethics professor at the College of Business at Arizona State University, also sees a correlation between ethical standards and economic success. "If you look at the more progressive industrialized countries in the world—Canada, Western Europe, parts of Asia—you find a higher sense of ethics there. It goes hand in hand," Smeltzer says. By contrast, countries with low ethical gauges, such as Mexico and many African countries, have equally scant business norms. "The lack of openness and predictable business standards drives companies away," Smeltzer says. "Why would you want to do business in, say Libya, where you don't know the rules?"

Smeltzer uses the analogy of a pickup football game by some guys in a park. If you just start playing without discussing guidelines, he says, conflict is likely to result. If rules are clearly established beforehand, however, the game will run smoothly. "The need for grease payments in China tells me I'm not clear what the rules there are, so someone has to help me navigate," he says. And, Smeltzer recently wrote in an ethics paper, bribes in China given to establish connections in the government add an estimated 3% to 5% to companies' operating costs.

It was China's troubling ethics climate, in fact, that persuaded Levi Strauss & Co. to exit the market there in 1993, despite the lure of a billion potential denim-clad pairs of legs. Levi's elaborate "principled reasoning approach" demanded a thorough ethical analysis and, says, spokesperson Gavin Power, ethical issues, especially regarding workers rights, were too troubling to permit continued operations. (Having closely followed the situation there since, Levi now says it has identified several trustworthy contractors and it may soon reenter the market.) While the 1993 decision might seem financially irrational, Smeltzer believes that a close analysis shows it made good economic sense. "If the rules for business play are uncertain with respect to its citizens, how can the Chinese government provide assurances of fairness to its potential business citizens?" he reasoned in the ethics paper.

People and Pollution Woes

In addition to the issue of bribes, two other areas are increasingly coming under the hot glare of ethics-watchers: human rights and the environment. American consumers may not get too worked up over "gifts" to foreign partners or government officials, but they will quickly show their displeasure at the thought of mistreated—especially underage—workers, and toxic waste polluting pristine waters and wildernesses around the world.

Even an ethically sensitive company like Levi Strauss can find that navigating international human rights offers tough sailing. The company won great praise for its 1993 China decision, and for its handling of an incident at its Bangladesh plants in 1992. (In the latter incident, the company discovered soon after it had stepped up its campaign to monitor foreign plants that two sewing subcontractors employed young children—a norm in a country where kids without jobs frequently beg or prostitute themselves for money. Levi's cleverly solved the problem by having the contractors remove the children from the factory but continue to pay their wages on condition that they attend school full time. When they reached the local maturity age of 14, they were guaranteed back their jobs.) But even this company's ethics record has rough spots. "They treat most of their workers decently, but go to the Philippines and you will see people working 90 hours a week making Dockers," charges Charles Kernaghan, director of the nonprofit watchdog group the National Labor Committee.

Kernaghan and his group are determined to ensure that American consumers know what companies are doing overseas. His group was behind the Kathie Lee Gifford / Wal-Mart incident of 1996, when Gifford cried on air over accusations that her line was produced in sweatshops around the world employing underaged kids.

Gifford may have thought the issue would disappear when she announced that she had hired independent monitors to check conditions in factories where her line is produced, but the National Labor Committee is bent on assuring that it doesn't. The New York-based group claims some of Gifford's items are still made in sweatshops in China, where women work 84-hour weeks in unsafe factories and live 12 to a room in dirty, watched dorms. "There is a Kathie Lee and Wal-Mart Corporate Code of Conduct, but these workers have never heard of them," Kernaghan says. He also claims that Wal-Mart's campaign to assure Americans that many of its garments are made right here "is very much misleading." The NLC physically counted 105,000 private-label items in 14 stores last year and found that 83% of the items were made offshore, compared to an industry norm of 50% to 60%—a disparity Kernaghan continually points out in his numerous speeches, media contacts, and Web site.

Treating the Earth responsibly has become the third leg of the tripod on which a solid international ethics reputation now rests.

Meanwhile, treating the Earth responsibly has become the third leg of the tripod on which a solid international ethics reputation now rests. "The environment is an area of concern for companies involved with global ethics plans," says Bob Echols, manager of international

CAUX ROUND TABLE GENERAL PRINCIPLES

1. The Responsibilities of Businesses: Beyond Shareholders Toward Stakeholders. Businesses have a role to play in improving the lives of all their customers, employees, and shareholders by sharing with them the wealth they have created. Suppliers and competitors as well should expect businesses to honor their obligations in a spirit of honesty and fairness.

2. The Economic and Social Impact of Business: Toward Innovation, Justice, and World Community. Businesses established in foreign countries to develop, produce, or sell should also contribute to the social advancement of those countries by creating productive employment and helping to raise the purchasing power of their citizens. Businesses also should contribute to human rights, education, welfare, and vitalization of the countries in which they operate.

Businesses should contribute to economic and social development not only in the countries in which they operate, but also in the world community at large, through effective and prudent use of resources, free and fair competition, and emphasis upon innovation in technology, production methods, marketing, and communications.

3. Business Behavior: Beyond the Letter of Law Toward a Spirit of Trust. While accepting the legitimacy of trade secrets, businesses should recognize that sincerity, candor, truthfulness, the keeping of promises, and transparency contribute not only to their own credibility and stability but also to the smoothness and efficiency of business transactions, particularly on the international level.

4. Respect for Rules. To avoid trade frictions and to promote freer trade, equal conditions for competition, and fair and equitable treatment for all participants, businesses should respect international and domestic rules. In addition, they should recognize that some behavior, although legal, may still have adverse consequences.

5. Support for Multilateral Trade. Businesses should support the multilateral trade systems of the GATT/ World Trade Organization and similar international agreements. They should cooperate in efforts to promote the progressive and judicious liberalization of trade and to relax those domestic measures that unreasonably hinder global commerce, while giving due respect to national policy objectives.

6. Respect for the Environment. A business should protect and, where possible, improve, the environment, promote sustainable development, and prevent the wasteful use of natural resources.

7. Avoidance of Illicit Operations. A business should not participate in or condone bribery, money laundering, or other corrupt practices: Indeed, it should seek cooperation with others to eliminate them. It should not trade in arms or other materials used for terrorist activities, drug traffic, or other organized crime.

compliance at Raytheon Company, in Lexington, Mass., which is currently rolling out an ambitious worldwide plan in the 80 countries in which it does business.

Caux's MacGregor cites three reasons for the increased interest. First, American and international reporters are now likely to write about the chemical waste a company dumps far away in a river in China. Second, he says, the increasing recognition that environmental actions in one part of the world affect all others is leading business people to consider their own children and neighbors, though they live thousands of miles away from the pollution. And third, MacGregor says, there is cost. "If you are dumping waste out the back door [even in an undeveloped country], eventually you will have to spend the money cleaning it up," he says.

What To Do—And Not Do

How does a company doing business internationally navigate these ethical storm waters? According to the experts, by implementing a true ethics program with teeth, not by merely trotting out a piece of paper. And by recognizing that, despite cultural differences, certain core ethical values are held by all people around the globe.

Writing a code of ethics that clearly states what's expected of employees is a typical first step. Then you need to get input on the proposed code from foreign nationals, perhaps via committees made up of people from the various affected cultures. "Often, this is where companies begin to do it wrong," says W. Michael Hoffman, executive director of the Center for Business Ethics at Bentley College in Waltham, Massachusetts. "They take their code of ethics and translate it into foreign languages, and Joe sends it over to Juan and Hans overseas with instructions to roll it out to their divisions. But because it doesn't mesh with their culture and they don't understand why they should care, these guys don't support it." For example, Hoffman says, without a firm rationale, Japanese will not readily follow a rule that says they should not accept expensive gifts, because presents are an integral part of that society and to refuse such a gift often humiliates the giver.

How to report ethical violations is also sometimes culture-specific. "In France, Germany, and other European countries, it has been my experience that employees are very reluctant to raise an issue regarding a fellow employee," Raytheon's Echols says. Raytheon's solution is to provide numerous reporting mechanisms—ranging from phoning or faxing the corporate headquarters to speaking face-to-face with a local ethics contact, to mailing in an anonymous, postage-paid card—so the staffer can choose the one most comfortable to him. Echols is also investigating incorporating an ethics section in his company's Web site, and allowing staffers to send confidential information that way.

Once signed off on by all the affected cultures, the ethical code must then become a living document for employees. Each worker must be clear how to apply that code to everyday actions. At Minneapolis-based Honeywell Inc., which has nearly half its employees outside the U.S., senior management regularly emphasizes ethics in its regional newsletters. One such publication for the Asia-Pacific, for example, carried a message from the president that the company would prefer to lose business rather than succumb to paying a bribe. An ethics advice line encourages employees to discuss ethical decisions they are unclear about. The company, which recently rewrote its code to be less focused on the U.S. and more applicable globally, also conducts training around the world. The codes various aspects, from child labor issues to gifts and gratuities, are enumerated specifically in its code of ethics handbook.

Businesses that employ factory workers around the globe are turning to independent monitors to watch out for employee rights overseas.

More and more businesses that employ factory workers around the globe are also turning to independent monitors to watch out for employees rights overseas. The National Labor Committee favors using local religious and human-rights groups to do that job, but companies largely seem to be favoring monitoring by such auditing groups as Pricewaterhouse Coopers and Ernst & Young. Once abuses are discovered, they must be swiftly resolved. "We either work with our subcontractor to correct the problems, or if that can't be done we will and have terminated our relationship with them," Levi's Power says.

Honeywell has put teeth into its ethical principles by making adherence to the company's code a condition of employment. "Sometimes the situation is clear enough that termination is the appropriate response, and we have fired people for violating the code," says Lisa Dercks, vice president and ethics officer at Honeywell. Such consequences are important for telling employees that top management takes this topic seriously, Bentley's Hoffman says. Other companies take the opposite approach, basing employee compensation in part on adherence to ethical codes.

When drafting its code of ethics, companies must strike a balance between being sensitive to foreign cultures and their own internal sense of right and wrong. "The two extremes are ethical fanaticism, which says my way is always right, and ethical relativism, which says there are no absolutes," Hoffman says. However, there are several absolute ethical standards that everyone in the world agrees with, "and these become your core values," he says, pointing to the Caux General Principles as a good starting point for corporate discussion (see box, "Caux Round Table General Principles").

"The process that you set up to ensure that you're making solid ethical decisions is key," Hoffman says. "If you follow the process, you can be comfortable with your decision, even if other ethical companies might come to a different conclusion."

Meryl Davids, a business journalist based in Coral Springs, Fla., frequently writes for JBS.

TEST CENTER ANALYSIS

Privacy as global policy

Differing cultural and legal standards complicate policies in today's business world, but surviving means respecting customers' privacy.

By P.J. Connolly,
InfoWorld Test Center

One of the less attractive aspects of village life is a lack of privacy, and this is mirrored in the global village of the Internet. Privacy issues take on increasing importance as technology is ever more present in daily life. If a company can't assure its customers and employees that sensitive information is secure from the eyes of those who don't need to know, that company won't stay in business without mending its ways.

Privacy is arguably one of the most important areas in which society and technology will affect each other in the coming years. Companies involved internationally face obstacles when reconciling privacy customs with laws from different cultures as well as jurisdictions. The challenge for these businesses will be to find ways to implement increasingly integrated technology without running afoul of a rapidly changing set of rules.

All companies confront both ethical and legal challenges when establishing privacy policies. Ethically, businesses must remember that they are dealing with people who have a right to dignity, part of which involves a moral right to privacy, at least in Western cultures. Legally, businesses with interests in countries in which privacy standards differ from their own may have to submit to more stringent rules than competitors who haven't made the overseas investment. A company that runs afoul of government regulators can recover, but a company that loses the public's trust rarely regains it.

Ethics of privacy

Unlike other issues in which ethics and technology collide head on, privacy lacks any religious element per se. Nevertheless, some connections can be drawn between the influence in a society of ethical and religious systems that value individual dignity and the degree of privacy one can expect as a member of that society.

Technological change has often meant a waning degree of privacy, although it might be easier to view a particular technology's influence as a series of high and low points. The development of the rural telephone system in North America is an example of this phenomenon.

As telephone systems proved their value in isolated communities, one of the most cost-efficient ways to provide service was for several households to share a party line. Families expected the neighborhood snoops to listen in on calls not meant for them, and they were commonly shooed off the line. Before automatic switching and billing systems became commonplace, the switchboard operator at the local exchange knew about every long-distance call that was placed because he or she had to manually record the information.

System administrators sit in much the same position ethically as telephone operators did some 30 years ago. With the power to monitor conversations and track usage patterns, they face an ongoing conflict between the human desire to gain forbidden knowledge and the ethical discipline necessary for users to trust the system.

The one constant in any ethical approach to building a privacy policy is upholding the worth of the individual.

Privacy and the law

Privacy is one of many areas in which companies doing business across jurisdictions face challenges due to differing laws and regulations. This is becoming ever more complex in the new electronic business landscape in which companies routinely outsource functions that involve moving customer data between enterprise networks.

THE BOTTOM LINE

Enterprise privacy policies

BUSINESS CASE

Companies doing business overseas face more stringent privacy requirements than they do in the United States, and they must abide by them. Companies that don't abide by these requirements face lawsuits and governmental supervision and may be put out of business.

TECHNOLOGY CASE

In today's business world, an individual's personal data is spread across hundreds of databases. Everyone, inside IT or not, has an interest in securing privacy.

PROS

- Few companies can survive the ill will of customers and users who feel their rights are being violated
- Lawmakers and policy makers are beginning to insist on the highest level of privacy possible

CON

- Different jurisdictions have different standards for privacy protection

In the United States, privacy policies are still handled on the honor system. The Federal Trade Commission may get involved if a company's policy is deemed part of its public business, and the FTC is beginning to assume its role as a defender of consumers' privacy. Employee privacy is often left up to the laws of individual states, and privacy rights advocates have expressed concern regarding the implications of employee monitoring.

Privacy policies are getting more attention, due in part to the November elections as well as a number of well-publicized incidents. Both the Democratic and Republican parties have included "privacy planks" in their platforms, although neither has put any concrete proposals on the table. The makeup of the next Congress may well determine whether we continue on the road of self-regulation or impose through the federal government standards on how businesses handle personal data.

In Europe, a long history of governmental regulation plus a well-founded fear of official privacy violations have created a much stricter set of rules for handling personal data. Essentially, the European standard is that a business cannot pass personal information to a third party without the consent of the individual concerned.

This complicates everything from direct marketing to system backups, often due to simple ignorance of the fact that a privacy violation is technically occurring, and the implications can be serious. Although punishments usually take the form of civil penalties, businesses used to the free and easy ways of the United States don't always appreciate the seriousness of the situation until they break local laws. Fighting bureaucrats is often expensive and futile, so one solution to the problem may have to involve partitioning data along the boundaries of privacy regimes.

Another alternative is for multinational shops to adopt the standards of the strictest privacy regime as a companywide policy. The goodwill advantages of this policy might well outweigh the inconveniences. At the other extreme of the spectrum, self-regulation is not an option; some things are just too important to be left to the free market.

This was pointed out in August when it was revealed that TRUSTe, a privacy advocacy organization, had implanted a tracking code in cookies from its Web site (see "Privacy watchdog in ironic twist," www.infoworld.com/printlinks). Before that, the Toysmart case highlighted the danger of a customer database being used as an asset in a bankruptcy filing (see "Toysmart deal faces opposition," www.infoworld.com/printlinks).

Find a working solution

Doing nothing won't work for serious businesses. Even if you are just collecting data for internal marketing uses, you have an obligation to keep anything that isn't part of the public record private. If nothing else, it's what you'd want someone else to do with your information. Developing a privacy policy is actually a lot easier, however, than making one work.

Four steps to making privacy policies work

1 Know the rules. Talk to your company's attorneys, especially the foreign counsel.

2 Assess risk. Figure out who is collecting data and why, as well as how it is being used.

3 Evaluate findings. Sort out major privacy violations and work with affected departments to remain within legal bounds.

4 Check your work. Go back to the attorneys and make sure you have not increased your company's liability by accepting responsibility.

Some organizations are going as far as creating a position of CPO (chief privacy officer), who reports to the CIO or CEO. Although some of these new positions stem from settlements of privacy-infringement disputes, there is no

DEVELOPING A PRIVACY POLICY

Most companies already have privacy policies in place, although they don't refer to them as such. They are often developed by a human resources department as part of the guidelines protecting confidential employee information. Unfortunately, the same culture that honors the privacy of employee data is often eager to treat confidential customer data with utter disregard for privacy concerns.

If you are in a position to change this, several challenges confront you, but your task is not hopeless. When establishing a privacy policy, you should follow a few basic steps.

The first thing you should do is talk to your company's lawyers. Figure out what laws and regulations you're already supposed to be following. Find out what the penalties are for not complying. If you have operations across state or national jurisdictions, what differences exist in the laws, and how have the courts interpreted the laws?

Next, you have to apply what you've learned from counsel to your operations. For example, is your company's customer data moving from one set of privacy laws to another because one system is in Los Angeles and the other in Paris? This can affect everything from mail merges to host backups, so be sure to keep asking, "What else is there?"

Worse, you may face very real constraints on what to do with data. For example, European regulators have complained about companies moving customer files to nations such as the United States that have more relaxed privacy standards.

This means that you have a lot of digging to do to figure out how your company is collecting data, what is being collected and why, and finally, what happens to the data. Don't be surprised if you learn that your massive corporation runs a bunch of "guerrilla" databases that IT officially knows nothing about.

Don't try to be Joe Friday when you're doing your research. Most of what you are going to discover in the way of potential privacy violations is just that—potential instead of actual. You are much better off coming across as an educator rather than an enforcer.

Once you figure out where your company stands in regard to the law, take your list of potential problems and determine the risk factor for each item. For example, a mailing list that consists simply of names and addresses is much less likely to cause trouble than, for example, a list of names, addresses, and Social Security numbers.

After you have completed this triage, advised the appropriate managers, and written your company's new policy, go back to the lawyers. Make sure you are not overdoing it and exposing yourself to a lawsuit because your policy is unenforceable or too aggressive.

question that a need exists in most businesses for someone with the authority to say no to sales and marketing and the ability to explain why using the data hurts the company more than not using it does.

No matter how you go about it, privacy is a business issue, and protecting customer and employee privacy is just as important as protecting financial data, trade secrets, or the payroll. Companies that fail to realize this may not be able to compete in the world of e-business. That's no secret.

Senior Analyst P.J. Connolly (pj_connolly@infoworld.com) has plenty to hide and 14 years of experience with securing company data.

UNIT 4

Ethics and Social Responsibility in the Marketplace

Unit Selections

Key Points to Consider

- What responsibility does an organization have to reveal product defects to consumers?
- Given the competitiveness of the business arena, is it possible for marketing personnel to behave ethically and both survive and prosper? Explain. Give suggestions that could be incorporated into the marketing strategy for firms that want to be both ethical and successful.
- Name some organizations where you feel genuinely valued as a customer. What are the characteristics of these organizations that distinguish them from their competitors? Explain.
- Which area of marketing strategy is most subject to public scrutiny in regard to ethics—product, pricing, place, or promotion? Why? Give some examples of unethical techniques or strategies involving each of these four areas.

Links: www.dushkin.com/online/

These sites are annotated in the World Wide Web pages.

Edwin B. Dean
http://mijuno.larc.nasa.gov/dfc/whatsnew.html

Total Quality Management Sites
http://www.nku.edu/~lindsay/qualhttp.html

U.S. Navy
http://www.navy.mil

From a consumer viewpoint, the marketplace is the "proof of the pudding" or the place where the "rubber meets the road" for business ethics. In other words, what the company has promulgated about the virtues of its product or service has little meaning if the company's actual marketing practices and its treatment of the consumer contradict its claims.

At its core, marketing has a very noble and moral purpose: to satisfy human needs and wants and to help people through the exchange process. Marketing involves the coordination of the variables of product, price, place, and promotion to effectively and efficiently address the needs of consumers. Unfortunately, at times the unethical marketing practices of some firms have cast a shadow of suspicion over marketing in general. Because marketing is the aspect of business that is most visible to the public, it has perhaps taken a disproportionate share of the criticism directed toward the free-enterprise system.

This unit takes a careful look at the strategic process and practice of incorporating ethics into the marketplace. The first subsection, *Marketing Strategy and Ethics,* contains three articles describing how marketing strategy and ethics can be integrated in the marketplace. The first article provides a perspective on ways companies are discovering the value of ethics. Then, "The Perils of Doing the Right Thing" describes the difficulties some companies have encountered when attempting to do the right thing. "Too Close for Comfort" closes this subsection by revealing the responsibilities and problems of a company gathering too much personal data about its customers.

In the second section, *Ethical Practices in the Marketplace,* the first article delineates the importance of having an organizational culture that encourages and supports sound ethical behavior and socially responsible business practices. The next selection examines how a new start-up company can make ethics a distinguishing mark of its culture. "The 100 Best Corporate Citizens" reflects a ranking of some of America's most profitable and socially responsible public companies.

Companies Are Discovering the VALUE OF ETHICS

Employees "motivated by strong moral and religious values are less likely to behave opportunistically and, as a result, are more productive and thus more profitable."

by Norman E. Bowie

Most discussion of business ethics focuses on ethics as a constraint on profit. From this view, ethics and profit are related inversely: the more ethical a business is, the less profitable it is; the more profitable, the less ethical. Certainly, there are times when doing the morally correct thing will reduce profits. Not using an "agent" to provide bribes when doing business abroad is one example. Nonetheless, the traditional characterization of an inverse relationship between ethics and profits is only part of the story at best. A more balanced view points out that there frequently is a positive relation between ethics and profits; normally, ethics enhances the bottom line, rather than diminishing it.

The best news is that the conventional cynical view about business ethics provides a money-making opportunity and can be the source of a competitive advantage. Other things being equal, a firm known for its high ethical standards can have an above-average profit. An auto repair shop known for its honesty is a busy and prosperous one.

Ethical behavior contributes to the bottom line by reducing the cost of business transactions, establishing trust among stakeholders, increasing the likelihood of successful teamwork, and preserving the social capital necessary for doing business.

First, an ethical firm reduces the cost of business transactions. For instance, most economic exchanges have a period of time between the payment for a good or service and delivery, or, conversely, a period of time between the delivery of a good or service and payment for it. This time gap can stand in the way of a profitable transaction. Perhaps the supplier will not deliver or the vendor will fail to pay. A small supplier is offered a large contract by a major manufacturer. Although one might think that the small supplier would be overjoyed by such an arrangement, it should be cautious. It can be held hostage by the much larger manufacturer, which can delay payment for the product or demand other concessions.

Recently, a number of large firms in the U.S. unilaterally announced an increase in the time that they would settle their accounts. Obviously, this fact makes future suppliers more reluctant to do business with these firms. The major manufacturer with a reputation for prompt payment will get the small supplier to provide the quality product. The major manufacturer that lacks a reputation for prompt payment will not.

Yet another illustration concerns the acceptability of checks as a means of payment. A seafood shop in Ocean City, Md., had the following notice posted on the wall: "We will not accept checks and here is why." Below the notice was a row of checks stamped "Insufficient funds." That seafood shop no longer would do business with those who wanted to pay by check.

There are vast regional differences in the acceptability of checks as a means of payment. In the Upper Midwest, they are accepted routinely. In most grocery stores and in some other businesses, the customer even may make the check out for an amount larger than the purchase and thus get both the purchase and some cash. On the East Coast, checks are not accepted routinely as a means of payment. Instead, credit cards are. Since most credit card sales represent additional costs, merchants in the Upper Midwest have lower costs of doing business than those merchants in other parts of the country.

Employee and customer theft is a major problem for business, as are shirking on the job and a declining work ethic. A culture of drug abuse exacerbates the problem. Business incurs great costs in dealing with these issues. Elaborate security systems are put into place. Employees are asked to submit to "honesty tests" and expensive drug screening.

Yet, businesspeople, along with most everyone else, recognize differences in the propensity of individuals to steal, take drugs, or shirk their responsibilities on the job. Again on a statistical basis, there are regional differences. During the 1980s, firms moved to the Upper Midwest despite the harsh climate and high taxes to take advantage of a workforce that had a high work ethic. Recently, the shift has been to Utah, a state with a large percentage of Mormons—a highly religious group that has a strong work ethic. Such examples are not limited to the U.S. In Budapest, Hungary, a large number of managers prefer to hire only those under the age of 30 because these younger employees are less likely to be infected by the bad work habits that existed under communism.

What these examples show is that those motivated by strong moral and religious values are less likely to behave opportunistically and, thus, will be more productive and more profitable. Employees and customers with the right values need less monitoring and fewer honesty and drug tests. Consequently, employers will try to hire people who statistically are more likely to be honest.

Ethical behavior builds trust, which increases the likelihood of profit. As a company builds trust, customers, employees, and suppliers are less likely to behave opportunistically. A reputation for trust will attract like-minded customers, employees, and suppliers. Thus, trust is reinforcing in a kind of virtuous circle.

Moreover, a firm characterized by high trust stakeholder relationships is likely to have competitive advantages. If trust is defined as keeping one's word and not taking undue advantage (behaving opportunistically) when one has the capability of doing so, the competitive advantage gained by a trusting organization will be clear.

Human resource management will be very different in a trusting organization. The essential point is that trusting relationships change the nature of monitoring. In nontrusting relationships, the supervisor functions as a policeman; in trusting relationships, as a mentor, the way a professor functions with a doctoral student or a coach develops a young pitcher. The kind of monitoring a mentor does is very different from that which a policeman does. A mentoring relationship allows qualitative criteria and uses fewer quantitative measures, is less frequent, and requires less in the way of detail.

Lately, there has been much discussion about teamwork and about eliminating layers of management. Workers are to be "empowered"—*i.e.*, given more responsibility and discretion as the layers of management control wither away. If teamwork and empowerment are not to be empty rhetoric, the nature of supervision must be more of a mentoring than a policing type. Greater trust will be a key element in any cost savings that result from eliminating layers of management and the empowerment of employee teams.

Trust also reduces the amount of bias in forecasts and overstatement of need in budgetary requests. Nearly every person in a business organization has experience with the budget game: A number of budgetary units report to a higher authority that sets the budget for each unit. The authority asks what each of the units need. Each unit knows that there are not sufficient funds to meet all the needs; therefore, the requests of each unit will not be granted fully. Each unit then overstates its need so that the failure to meet the requests will not cause as much pain. As a result, the central authority engages in long costly negotiations with each unit to arrive at a figure that is fairly close to what each unit would have expected to receive. Transaction costs could have been reduced greatly if the information to the central budget authority had reflected true need more accurately. If the various units could agree to make accurate requests and trust one another to keep their promises, these traditional transaction costs could be slashed.

A more trusting organization could help American manufacturing enterprises overcome two disadvantages. Traditionally, the engineering team that designs a product does its work separately. Those who manufacture the product have little, if anything, to say about its design. As a result, some problems with a prototype do not appear until the manufacturing stage. Much time is lost as the prototype is redesigned to meet the requirements of mass production.

The sales unit of a firm and the manufacturing unit often work at cross-purposes. The sales force has incentives to sell as much of a product as it can. Indeed, the commission system is what provides the incentive. However, if quality is to be maintained and backlogged orders are to be kept to a minimum, sales must not exceed the ability of the manufacturing process to produce the goods in question. Given the commission system, there is no incentive for the sales staff to take these limitations into account and to cooperate with manufacturing to secure the optimal amount of sales at any given time.

As the result of Japanese competition, these defects have been recognized, and American companies have realized that there must be greater cooperation among units within the firm. Trust among the units and a supportive compensation scheme are required for greater cooperation. To build that trust, managers need to speak differently about other units in the firm than they do about its competitors. The unit that manufactures the product is not the enemy of the salesperson. Failure to understand that distinction undermines the trust needed to achieve a competitive advantage.

What holds true within a firm will continue to do so as various companies enter into joint ventures. With such cooperation among firms from different countries becoming increasingly common and successful, one would expect to see more joint ventures between corporations that have higher levels of trust. The rationale for this is fairly clear. If one member of the joint venture fails to keep its contract, behaves opportunistically, or provides a shoddy product or service, all parties will suffer. The unhappy customer will blame all alike. Thus, a trustworthy partner is the best partner in a business sense. Picking a moral partner may be the most important decision to be made when setting up a joint venture.

Finally, trust is needed for successful research and development. The rationale for this contention is based on the knowledge of the environment needed for creative thought, particularly scientific research. Some corporations have adopted a competitive strategy of introducing new products at such a rate that goods created in the last few years account for a certain percentage of the firm's sales. Such companies refuse to rest on their laurels.

How can such a strategy be achieved? There is considerable evidence that creative people are most productive in an environment with minimal monitoring and control. It is counterproductive to have laboratory scientists filling out weekly reports asking them what they discovered that week. Providing research scientists with the freedom and independence necessary to stimulate creative thinking requires a great deal of trust on the part of management. Firms with a culture of trust are likely to be more adaptive and innovative.

Yet another benefit of ethical behavior is that it provides a solution to what theorists call collective action problems. A collective action problem occurs when an obvious public good can not be achieved because it is not in the self-interest of any individual who is a part of the problem to take steps to resolve it. Thus, large cities throughout the world suffer from traffic congestion. All would benefit if many more people used public transportation. For any individual, though, the reduction in congestion resulting from his or her taking the bus is very small, while the inconvenience, especially given its imperceptible effect on congestion, is large. Therefore, this individual, and every other automobile owner, will tend to drive and traffic congestion will remain horrible.

There are many ways of tackling a collective action problem. One traditional means is to provide incentive so that the cost-benefit ratio is reversed. For instance, instituting tolls for cars that greatly increase the cost of driving to work would force drivers onto the bus or train.

Collective action problems exist in business as well. Assume that, in certain situations, the production of a good or service requires a team effort and that the individual contribution of each team member can not be isolated and measured. Any team member who acts in a purely self-interested manner would free ride off the others. This free-riding phenomenon explains why many hard-working students complain bitterly about group projects that are graded on the productivity of the group.

Indeed, if enough members free ride, the gain in potential productivity from teamwork would be lost. In such situations, the benefits of group activity are optimized only when there is no free riding. For that to occur, each member of the group must make a commitment not to free ride. This commitment is most likely in a moral community where the members are bound together by common values and mutual respect.

Social capital

A final benefit of ethical corporate behavior is that it preserves the social capital that makes a free market possible. A market system does not operate in a vacuum, but coexists with many other institutions in society, including the family, the church, and the political, criminal justice, and educational systems. Each of these institutions contributes toward making capitalism possible: The court system enforces contracts; the political system provides monetary stability; and the educational system trains future employees and prepares them for the workforce.

Corporate misconduct raises the cost and reduces the amount of social capital. The more businesspeople try to avoid the terms of their agreement, the greater the number of disputes that end up in court. More and more umpires are needed. When the environment is despoiled or misleading advertising occurs, the public demands more regulation. Increased governmental activity adds to the cost of government.

A market system needs moral capital as well. If capitalism is to be successful, there must be both within society and within capitalism a widespread acceptance of certain moral norms, such as truth-telling, bill-paying, and fair play. When these norms are perceived as being violated, a vicious circle begins. If other people will not play by the rules, then each person reasons there is no longer gain from following the rules. As more and more people abandon these moral forms, the social capital that makes market activity possible is depleted.

A major concern about Russia is whether the criminal element has gotten such a hold on business activity that capitalism becomes impossible. What some commentators refer to as "wild capitalism" is doomed to failure. Once again, ethical behavior contributes to the bottom line, but in this case to the bottom line of capitalism itself, rather than to the bottom line of an individual firm.

Some may object to this analysis. They might say that businesspeople should do the right thing because it is right, rather than because such actions contribute to the bottom line.

Philosophers are familiar with the hedonic paradox: "The more you consciously seek happiness, the less likely you are to find it." If you do not believe this, just get up some morning and resolve that every act will be done in order to achieve happiness. You soon will be miserable. Happiness is the result of successful achievement, but is not itself something you try to achieve. According to Aristotle, self-realization is what you try to achieve, and happiness is the result of achieving it.

Perhaps, to some extent, profits are like that. If your focus on them is excessive, you are less likely to achieve them. The conventional wisdom is that managers should focus on the bottom line. There is an obsession in America with quarterly reports—one that forces managers to focus on the short run, rather than the long run. If corporations took the moral point of view, they would focus on meeting the needs of their stakeholders. For instance, they might focus on providing secure work for employees and quality products for customers. If they did that, profits likely would follow.

Second, employees are very suspicious of management's motives when new concepts like empowerment or quality circles are introduced. If the employees think that these ideas are being implemented to increase profits, they often will attempt to sabotage them, even if the workers would be better off. Thus, quality circles and empowerment only can succeed if all those affected believe such practices are being introduced for the right reasons.

Third, media reports of corporate good works frequently are greeted with public scorn because the public is suspicious of the corporation's motives. "They are just trying to buy good will" is a phrase that is heard often. Corporate executives who really do act from ethical motives are frustrated when their motives are questioned. Yet, it is hard for the public to determine motives, which is why reputation, corporate character, and a record of altruistic acts are important. If Johnson & Johnson proclaims moral motives for what the pharmaceutical company does, it tends to be believed. The public remembers how Johnson & Johnson handled the Tylenol poisonings. Not only did the firm do the right thing—pulling the product from the market and repackaging it in a more secure manner—it did so for the right reason. Moreover, Johnson & Johnson profited as a result.

What of the future? All capitalist systems are not alike. Japanese capitalism differs from German capitalism and both differ from the American version. Which will be most successful in the next century? The answer depends on many factors. One is ethics because, as has been shown, ethical behavior can lower costs, increase productivity, and preserve the social capital that makes capitalism possible. It is in our national interest to ensure that American capitalism is a leader in ethics as well as in product development and cheap capital.

Dr. Bowie is Elmer L. Andersen Chair in Corporate Responsibility, University of Minnesota, Minneapolis.

The Perils of Doing the Right Thing

By Andrew W. Singer

At a May 11 press conference, Ford Motor Co. released its first-ever "corporate citizenship" report. In the 98-page document, titled "Connecting With Society," the company acknowledged serious concerns about its highly profitable sport utility vehicles. Not only do SUVs pollute the air and guzzle gas at rates far higher than conventional automobiles, the report conceded, they may be hazardous to other drivers.

Ford's was an unusual announcement. SUVs, after all, contribute about half of the company's earnings. The public's taste for these vehicles has shown no sign of waning. And even though they're three times as likely as cars to kill the other driver in a crash, the government has yet to declare these vehicles inherently unsafe.

What, then, was the company doing announcing that it had problems with these immensely popular, high-margin vehicles?

The front page of the next day's *New York Times* noted that Ford scion and chairman William Clay Ford Jr., whose family controls 40 percent of the company's voting shares, "has been active in environmental causes since his days at prep school and at Princeton" and was now worried "that car makers could get reputations like those of tobacco companies" if they ignored these problems. (The company did *not* pledge to stop producing SUVs, however.)

The company has been lauded for its candor. Veteran automobile-industry analyst Mary Ann Keller, now an executive with Priceline.com Inc., calls the announcement a "welcome instance of leadership." Norman Bowie, Dixons Professor of Business Ethics and Social Responsibility at London Business School, describes Ford's decision as "significant and courageous."

What makes the company's action noteworthy is that it carries real risks. According to Bowie, the biggest danger is a "backlash" among current and prospective SUV owners, who could begin to think the cars dangerous.

"Public tastes are fickle," says Brock Yates, editor-at-large of *Car and Driver*. "No one anticipated the surge in interest in SUVs, and like all fads it could disappear." And credit agency Standard & Poor's has warned that "[t]he automaker's stability could be affected if the sport-utility market slumped."

Before one proclaims a new era of social responsibility, then—as some did in the wake of the Ford press conference—one would do well to pause. Good corporate citizenship is praiseworthy, of course. But it isn't always easy. Indeed, if one looks at the experiences of other companies once acclaimed as "leaders," it is a decidedly mixed history. For all their high promise and initial acclaim, many firms later emerged scarred and chastened, victims of public derision, consumer boycotts, shareholder rebellion, and even bankruptcy.

If Ford does follow through on its exemplary course, it might do well to consider some of the lessons learned by other companies—often the hard way:

Lesson No. 1: Make sure what you are doing is really leadership— and not just self-adulation.

When asked about Ford's quandary—financial dependence on a product that carries potential environmental and safety problems—Bentley College business ethicist W. Michael Hoffman responds, "You can be ethical, and smart too."

Hoffman recalls a story recounted at a 1977 Bentley ethics conference, about a small paper company located on a polluted

New England stream. At a celebration of the first Earth Day, the mill's owner "got religion." He spent $2.5 million in an effort to clean up the company's effluent and, several months later, went broke, since he couldn't compete with other paper companies that didn't follow his example. He was unrepentant, though, "encased in a kind of angelic halo as he spoke of the necessity of clean water and sacrificing material things for spiritual ends." When it was pointed out that the water was no cleaner overall, he said, "Well, that's those other 17 fellows upstream."

"He went out of business, and he put 500 people out of work," Hoffman says. "But he felt ethically pure. That's just crazy." He describes the mill owner's attempt to "do it on his own" as a typically individualistic, American response.

Ford Motor could behave like the mill owner—act alone—and simply stop making SUVs. But that could be financially disastrous. "Ford's executives can do other things," Hoffman continues. "If they are truly concerned about a product but know they can't disarm unilaterally, then they have to work diligently within their industry and with government."

Cornell University economist Robert H. Frank says that the fact that Ford is concerned "is a positive thing." But this is "a collective-action problem," he says. "It's not a matter of Ford breaking any law." The solution Frank suggests: William Clay Ford should sit down with the U.S. secretary of transportation and work something out; a possible solution might involve instituting new passenger-vehicle taxes based on weight, emission levels, and fuel economy.

In late July, Ford took another step, announcing that it had decided to increase the fuel economy of its SUVs by 25 percent over the next five years. Its main competitor, General Motors, bristled: Vice chairman Harry Pearce expressed annoyance at Ford's claim of being "somehow the environmental leader." GM, he insisted, is and will be far superior to Ford in the area of fuel economy. On the other hand, the company is proceeding with full production of the 7,000-plus-pound Hummer, a version of the Humvee, a military transport made famous in the Gulf War.

Lesson No. 2: Be prepared to be attacked by virtue of your virtue.

H.B. Fuller Co., a Minneapolis-based adhesives manufacturer, enjoyed a reputation as one of America's most socially responsible companies. It endowed a chair in the study of business ethics at the University of Minnesota and established a charitable foundation dedicated to the environment, the arts, and social programs. Minnesotans regarded longtime president Elmer L. Andersen so highly that they elected him governor in 1960.

But beginning in the late 1980s, the company was dogged by reports that one of its adhesives, Resistol, had become the drug of choice for glue-sniffing street kids in Central America.

H.B. Fuller seemed unprepared for the furor that arose over the abuse of one of its products. "It's a social problem. It's not a product problem," the company argued. Still, it pulled the product off retail shelves in Guatemala and Honduras.

That didn't stop activists from protesting Fuller's continued marketing of Resistol to industrial customers, and to retailers in neighboring countries. Activists picketed annual shareholder meetings and brought wrongful-death suits against the company. "At risk are millions of dollars and the reputations of the company's top leaders," noted the Minneapolis *Star Tribune*.

How could such a well-regarded company become ensnared in such a circumstance? After all, Fuller's competitors were manufacturing and marketing glue in Latin America at the time, and impoverished street kids were abusing their products too. "But no one expected much of those companies," says Bowie. Social critics mostly gave them a free pass.

Unfortunately, "If you do something ethical, and then market it, and there's a little failure, you get hammered," says Bowie, who adds that company leaders were perhaps not as "proactive as they should have been."

Michael G. Daigneault, president of the nonprofit Ethics Resource Center in Washington, D.C., observes, "There are risks inherent in being perceived as, or fostering the perception of being, an exceptionally ethical or socially responsible organization. People will hold you to that standard."

This isn't to say that such a reputation is not positive. But it can backfire, particularly if a company is "overzealous" in promoting itself in this area. Daigneault says that companies that have made absolute statements—like Wal-Mart Stores Inc. claiming that all of its products are made in the United States, or Tom's of Maine Inc. insisting that all of its products are "natural"—have sometimes invited criticism. "The irony," he says, "is that a lot of these organizations have the best intentions, and many actually walk the talk—99 percent of the time." But the 1 percent of the time that they slip up, someone will be waiting for them.

Lesson No. 3: Expect to have your motives questioned and your leadership credentials challenged.

"The only thing good without qualification is a good will," wrote Immanuel Kant. In business, however, it's often difficult to distinguish goodwill from economic self-interest.

Consider the case of Smith & Wesson, the nation's largest handgun manufacturer. In March, the company entered into an agreement with federal, state, and local governments to restrict the sale of handguns. The company agreed to sell only to "authorized dealers and distributors" that would conform to a code of conduct. Among other things, this required dealers to conduct background checks on buyers at gun shows, and it put some restrictions on multiple gun sales. No other gun manufacturer signed the agreement.

On some fronts, Smith & Wesson was celebrated for its commitment. President Clinton observed that "it took a lot of courage" for the company to sign the agreement in the face of industry resistance. Housing and Urban Development secretary Andrew Cuomo described the settlement as "the most important announcement" during his tenure at HUD, and added, "The principles of the agreement will provide a framework for a new, enlightened gun policy for this nation."

Target of Criticism

"No loaded firearms or live ammunition beyond this point," reads the sign on the front door of Smith & Wesson's headquarters in Springfield, Mass.—a reminder that this is not your average business. Nor was there anything quite ordinary about the industry reaction to the firearms manufacturer's decision to accept some restrictions on its handgun sales.

Smith & Wesson CEO Edward Shultz says he wasn't surprised by the response to the firm's March 17 settlement announcement. "When you take this sort of step, you don't do it without a lot of thought. Certainly, it would have been easier to go with the crowd."

The National Rifle Association denounced Smith & Wesson, the nation's largest gun maker, for surrendering to the Clinton administration. NRA president Charlton Heston asserted that Smith & Wesson's British owner, Tomkins PLC, places less value on the Second Amendment right to bear arms than Americans do. The attorney general of Connecticut warned of "extreme elements that want to punish [Smith & Wesson] or retaliate against it for doing the right thing."

Why such a strong reaction? "We're dealing with the most anti-gun administration in recent history," says Shultz. The fact that S&W is even talking to the Clinton administration "irritates folks."

Still, Shultz says, he hadn't counted on the breadth of the detractors. The majority of S&W customers agree with the company's actions, he asserts. But its move seems to have "had an impact on anyone who owns a firearm." It's as if an automaker had installed safety air bags before any of its competitors and "it angered not just its customers but anyone who owned a car."

Shultz says he understands the emotions of the critics. As a boy in eastern Iowa, he "grew up with guns as a part of [his] daily life. But my head says that the world is changing and we will have to get in harmony with it."

Lawsuits against gun makers—who are being held partly responsible for bloodshed like that which rocked Columbine High School last year—will continue for the next five to 10 years, he predicts. "When you have the federal government after you, and the states, and lots of the cities, it's hard to say that all these people are wrong and you're right."

Will the company be stronger in the long run for signing the agreement? "Our belief was that if we didn't make this decision, we would go out of business," due to ceaseless, costly litigation. "This way, we can still prosper."

Significantly, perhaps, when New York became the first state to take the firearms-manufacturing industry to court in late June, Smith & Wesson was not named in the lawsuit. Local governments have since dropped S&W from lawsuits, too. Meanwhile, though, "The rest of the industry has held fast," noted *The New York Times*. No other gun maker signed the agreement, which requires manufacturers to take steps such as installing safety locks on guns.

Shultz has been working in the consumer-goods sector for 37 years, the last nine of which he has spent in the firearms industry. "I came from the outside to make a change here" because the company was in some financial trouble in 1992. At that time, "I never dreamed of the things that we face today in the legal and political arena."

He says that what S&W is doing is viewed as a huge compromise because it's voluntary, rather than mandated by laws and regulations. Inevitably, though, the firearms industry has to go through change. "Change is expensive, it's painful, and it involves some risk," he says.

"I've spent most of my career dealing with conflicts relating to change," Shultz says. "If I retire, it will probably be from one change too many."

—**A.W.S.**

Reaction was somewhat less approving in other quarters, however. The National Rifle Association and the National Shooting Sports Foundation (NSSF) denounced Smith & Wesson for "selling out" the industry and called for an immediate boycott of the company's products. (See "Target of Criticism.")

Still, Smith & Wesson CEO Edward Shultz says he's comfortable with his decision. Standards of social responsibility change, he says: "We can't operate as we did in 1935 or 1955 or 1975 and still be described as responsible." In 1955, a customer could order a gun out of a catalog, and the weapon would be delivered to that person's house. "Today, that would be viewed as totally irresponsible," he says.

"From a pure business standpoint, it makes sense to find a solution," Shultz continues. "To understand what's going on, you have to get in a conversation with the people trying to put you out of business," like anti-handgun groups. It also made sense to "settle," given the numbers of lawsuits being brought against the firearms industry in the wake of the Columbine shooting and other acts of carnage. "Rather than go out of business paying for lawsuits, if we go out of business, it will be because customers refuse to buy our products," he says.

Opposition to the company's position proved more lasting and damaging than anticipated. Some dealers refused to sell S&W products, incensed by the code of conduct that the manufacturer imposed on them. In June, Smith & Wesson announced that it was suspending firearms manufacturing at two New England factories for three weeks. It acknowledged that a contributing factor was "the reaction of some consumers to the agreement Smith & Wesson signed with federal, state and local government entities."

"I don't think they anticipated the severity of the response," says Robert Delfay, president and CEO of the NSSF, the largest firearms-industry trade group. Many members saw it as an infringement of their Second Amendment right to bear arms.

Also, inevitably, some critics saw the firm's actions as a matter of sheer expediency. "I don't view what Smith & Wesson did as leadership," Delfay says. "We think it was capitulation to strong-arm tactics by government officials." As he sees it, the gun makers showing real leadership are those that haven't "capitulated to government blackmail."

"Was that a decision of conscience?" asks ethicist Mark Pastin, president of the Council of Ethics Organizations in Alexandria, Va., of the S&W action. "Or a response to what the market demands of the company?"

Consultant Eileen Shapiro, author of *The Seven Deadly Sins of Business*, insists that Smith & Wesson's decision *did* represent a leadership position, because it involved real action: "They did something that matched their rhetoric."

It's not exceptional that some ambiguity attends the gun maker's action. Few business actions, after all, are ethically "pure." Most are a kind of double helix: one strand virtue, the other economic self-interest. It is almost impossible to disentangle the two.

Shapiro, for one, disputes that Ford Motor took any leadership position with its May announcement. Ford isn't redeploying any of its assets. It will still build SUVs. Moreover, she says, "This guy [William Ford] actually drives an SUV!"

A week after the Ford press conference, automobile-industry watcher Brock Yates said, "Internally, we're hearing a lot of concern and confusion. It's seen as a hollow gesture. The grandest gesture would have been to cancel the Excursion, which has become a paradigm for SUV evil."

In sum, even when a company takes a socially responsible stance, it should still expect to have its moral bona fides questioned. Ed Shultz speaks from experience: "Leadership is never very popular, particularly if decisions are made to change and to move forward."

Lesson No. 4: Circumstances beyond your control—including public hysteria—can undermine your position.

In the early 1990s, chemicals manufacturer Monsanto Co. placed a big bet on an exciting new business: sustainable agriculture. It committed its resources to developing seemingly miraculous genetically altered crops—cotton that could be grown without pesticides, tomatoes altered to ripen slowly, potatoes that were insect-resistant.

"Monsanto is in a unique position to contribute to the global future," gushed prominent biodiversity advocate Peter Raven at a "global forum" in 1995. "Because of your skills, your dedication, and your understanding, you are equal to the challenge."

The first breakthrough had come two years earlier, in November 1993. After nine years of investigation, the FDA approved the use of Monsanto's bovine growth hormone (marketed under the name of Posilac), which when injected into a cow's pituitary gland increased milk output by 25 percent.

Monsanto spent $1 billion to develop Posilac, with Wall Street's approval. Posilac, after all, was the first of perhaps dozens of genetically altered agricultural products to be introduced in years ahead. The profits anticipated would fill company coffers.

The company's CEO, Robert B. Shapiro, was acclaimed as a visionary. "Bob Shapiro displayed enormous vision in committing the company to sustainable business practices" that neither deplete the world of resources nor damage the environment, noted Robert H. Dunn, president of Business for Social Responsibility, a San Francisco-based membership organization.

Only a few years later, however, things had gone terribly wrong with Monsanto's new direction. A wave of protesters had arisen to campaign against Posilac, and foreign governments were beginning to pay attention. In 1998, a British researcher declared on television that eating genetically modified (GM) potatoes could stunt rats' growth. A Cornell University study contended that pollen from GM corn harmed butterflies.

Europe resisted the U.S.-dominated GM crop business; supermarket chains rejected foods containing GM ingredients. France, citing the precautionary principle, ordered the destruction of hundreds of hectares of rapeseed that had been accidentally planted with seeds containing GM material. Brazil sent out police to burn GM crops. U.S. food processors, such as Archer Daniels Midland Co., advised suppliers to segregate GM from non-GM crops.

Environmentalists turned on Monsanto. Greenpeace told the European Union that it "cannot continue to let GMOs [genetically modified organisms] contaminate our food and environment."

All of this battered the company's share price. Early this year, one analyst noted that "investors have valued Monsanto's $5 billion-a-year agricultural-business unit at less than zero dollars during the past week."

What happened? "In ethics, some stands look appropriate at the time," Bowie observes. But then circumstances change, or science changes, "or people get hysterical—so what looked like a good decision at one time no longer looks like a good decision."

When Bowie asked his London students this past summer why the reaction against GM foods was so severe—why the "hysteria"—they answered: "We don't trust the government." In part, this was because of the British government's belated response to the dangers of "mad cow" disease, which it long downplayed. Asks Bowie: "How could Monsanto anticipate that students wouldn't trust their government because of mad cow disease?"—and by extension, that they wouldn't believe the government when it insisted that GM foods were safe?

"You can't rationalize emotions," says one analyst who follows the company but asked not to be identified in this article.

"[Robert] Shapiro felt that the Green Movement didn't have a rational case," and so the company was reluctant to modify its position. "They should have been more sensitive to the perception of these bold moves. They didn't lay the groundwork."

Ironically, in June, the Paris-based Organization for Economic Cooperation and Development—once at the heart of the GM opposition—announced that genetically modified crops approved for human consumption are as safe as other foods. The announcement may have come a bit late, however, for Robert Shapiro and Monsanto. The company was acquired by Pharmacia & Upjohn Inc. last December—for a price considerably lower than what it could have fetched a few years earlier. Robert Shapiro was slated to be "non-executive" chairman of the merged company for 18 months, and then give way to a successor.

"In the end, Shapiro was a trailblazer," concludes the analyst. One day, the world may view positively the company's technological achievement, the medical applications, the improved yields from these crops. "There is a future, but perhaps the market wasn't ready for them."

Given the costs that some of the companies mentioned here—H.B. Fuller, Monsanto, Smith & Wesson, the New England mill owner—have paid, one might well ask: Does social responsibility pay? Does it make economic sense to take a leadership position where the environment or corporate citizenship is involved?

For years, many have asserted that good ethics is good business, Pastin observes. "But there were no examples. Now there are examples, but they are hard to interpret." There has never been systemic, credible evidence that good ethics indeed leads to good financial results, he notes.

That said, some view Ford Motor's May announcement as evidence of a new era of social responsibility. "Ford has definitely demonstrated leadership as one of the first large, global companies to file a social report as a companion to its financial report," says Dunn of Business for Social Responsibility. The company "instilled in the report a spirit of candor, acknowledging the issues it must address."

Ford has "obviously learned the lesson" of the last 20 years regarding such matters—namely, "that companies that are honest and forthright are forgiven by the public, but those that stonewall earn the public's enmity," says Booz-Allen & Hamilton leadership consultant James O'Toole, whose guess is that Ford has enough data to conclude that the safety and environmental problems regarding SUVs are real. Moreover, the automaker might have a similar problem to that of the tobacco industry: By sitting on the data, it risks lawsuits later.

By acting in an honest, straightforward manner, the companies expect to be treated accordingly by the public. "Ford is trying to establish its credentials, give itself credibility," O'Toole says. "Young William Ford is laying the foundation of trust."

"I think we're entering a new age of corporate citizenship in which candor will be rewarded," says veteran PR executive Robert Dilenschneider. "Younger people—young CEOs—are willing to stick their necks out farther than the older generation. Bill Ford is a perfect example."

Others note a certain irony here. "It's interesting that it's the Ford Motor Co. that has seen fit to come forward to talk about some safety and environmental problems with SUVs," says Bentley College's Hoffman. "Maybe it has something to do with the lessons learned from the business-ethics movement."

One of the landmark cases in that movement, after all, was the 1979 Ford Pinto case, in which the state of Indiana indicted Ford on charges of criminal homicide after a rear-ended Pinto burst into flames, killing a passenger. "It made world headlines and sent reverberations through Corporate America," Hoffman says.

Even though Ford was eventually acquitted, it "was found guilty in the court of public opinion, as well as in civil cases," particularly when it was disclosed that the company had conducted a cost-benefit analysis to determine whether it should improve safety by adding a $5.08 bladder to fuel tanks—and opted not to do so. The negative public reaction "sent a message to Corporate America," Hoffman says, "that the American public would be watching corporations more carefully in terms of their social responsibility and ethical commitment."

Given the history of other companies that took a lead in "doing the right thing," though, Ford shouldn't expect an unhindered path toward an enlightened future. There are real risks with tampering with the SUV business model: risks to the company's profits, its share price, and its reputation.

ANDREW W. SINGER is publisher and co-editor of Ethikos, *a Mamaroneck, N.Y.-based publication that examines ethical and compliance issues in business. He is writing a book on the perils of corporate leadership. His last article was a review of* When Pride Still Mattered *in the February issue.*

From *Across the Board,* October 2000, pp. 14-19.

Too Close for Comfort

WHAT YOU KNOW ABOUT YOUR CUSTOMERS MAY BE DANGEROUS. NO MARKETING TEAM OR SALES FORCE CAN AFFORD TO IGNORE TODAY'S GROUNDSWELL OF CONCERN OVER CUSTOMER PRIVACY

By Mark McMaster

Can you keep a secret?

FOR EVERY MORSEL of information you collect about your clients, the answer had better be yes. That applies to the scribbles in your salespeoples' notebooks just as much as the databases of online browsing habits, credit card numbers, and purchasing histories stored on the company network. The looming debate on consumer privacy challenges assumptions about what client information may be collected, shared, and sold, and it will soon touch every business. Large or small, online or off, companies face new responsibilities in explaining and justifying their use of personal data.

"If you lack a privacy policy and haven't educated your sales force about the ramifications of privacy law, you may be putting your company at risk legally and financially."

If you think privacy is a matter for the legal department to take care of, think again. Sales and marketing teams deal more closely with customer data than any other company unit, so if you lack a privacy policy and haven't educated your sales force about the ramifications of privacy law, you may be putting your company at risk legally and financially. "If you have personally identifiable information about customers and you misuse it, you'll find yourself on the unfriendly end of a lot of attention," says attorney Ray Everett-Church, the manager of PrivacyClue, a consulting firm in San Jose, California. "Customers do not forgive companies that misuse information."

Need proof? Look at Internet advertising powerhouse DoubleClick. Its Big Brother approach earned it an FTC inquiry, a class action suit, and a 75 percent tumble in its stock price. Likewise, GeoCities, the CVS drug store chain, and Chase Manhattan Bank have all taken legal heat and weeks of bad public relations for the release of unsuspecting consumers' identifying info. And the issue is just starting to unravel. "Anyone who thinks the privacy issue has peaked is greatly mistaken," says Jay Stanley, an e-commerce analyst at Forrester Research in Cambridge, Massachusetts. "We are in the early years of a sweeping change in attitudes that will fuel years of political battles and put once routine business practices under the microscope."

NEW TECHNOLOGIES, NEW FEARS

TODAY'S SHIFTING ATTITUDES about privacy are largely a reaction to the unprecedented opportunity for gathering consumer data on the Internet. "When you visit a Web site about baby care, and suddenly for three weeks every banner ad you see is for baby items, you start to feel like you're being watched," says Larry Ponemon, the former head of privacy practice at PricewaterhouseCoopers and the president of Guardent, a privacy management and data security firm in Waltham, Massachusetts. "Customers have learned to assume the worst," he says. Threats to privacy with innocent names like cookies and spam have entered the consumer lexicon, making Web surfers reluctant to give up information about individual preferences or identity.

As businesses track customers ever more closely with sophisticated personalization techniques and data mining technology, these fears have spread to the offline world, and consumer anxiety has produced a political response. No less than six privacy protection bills await debate in Congress, all of which would limit the ability of businesses to collect personal information about their customers. Meanwhile, the Federal Trade Commission (FTC) is using existing law to aggressively punish companies that violate consumers' rights, says Simon Lazarus, an attorney at Powell, Goldstein, Frazer & Murphy in, Washington, D.C.

A key piece of privacy legislation, the Gramm-Leach-Bliley Act, went into effect in July and requires financial institutions to provide written notice of its privacy policies and practices, and prohibits any disclosure of nonpublic personal information—such as purchase histories, birth dates, or even phone numbers—to third parties unless the consumer has the opportunity to opt out of the disclosure. Its ramifications may extend far beyond the industry it was intended to regulate, Lazarus says, extending to any company that offers credit to its customers.

B-TO-B COMPANIES AT RISK

IT'S NOT JUST business-to-consumer companies that are vulnerable. "The damages [of privacy invasion] can be more pronounced in the business-to-business world, because you're dealing with situations where information that is shared can be of serious strategic and financial significance to the victim. The damages become much greater," says Jack Vonder Heide, the president of the Technology Briefing Center, a training organization in Oakbrook Terrace, Illinois, that offers privacy training.

Vonder Heide cites the most visible example of a company strained by privacy concerns, New York-based DoubleClick, which sells its services to businesses, not consumers. DoubleClick's name has been synonymous with privacy fears since January 2000, when news broke that DoubleClick was soon to offer about 100,000 unique user profiles lifted from a dozen Web sites, complete with real-world identities and contact information gleaned from the company's recent purchase of offline consumer data seller Abacus Direct. Tracking the online behavior of these profiles would have produced a treasure trove of information for online marketers, but consumer advocates weren't pleased that advertisers would be aware of their real-world identities each time they logged onto a site affiliated with DoubleClick. Denouncing the company in the national media and threatening legal action, the words of DoubleClick's critics would scar the company for months to come.

Even more damaging, DoubleClick had unceremoniously abridged the privacy statement contained on its Web site just days before these news reports, a move that hinted at its intention to begin merging online and offline data, but offered little warning for Web users who might wish to remove their names from its lists. The popular backlash against DoubleClick shocked the company, which had a sales force focused on businesses and never saw itself as accountable to consumers themselves. "At that point, DoubleClick viewed itself as a business-to-business company—we didn't interact with consumers directly, and we didn't really have a good means of explaining how DoubleClick interacted with customers," says Jules Polonetsky, who in March 2000 was appointed DoubleClick's chief privacy officer.

Another blow was yet to come. In February 2000 the FTC opened an investigation into DoubleClick's potentially deceptive data handling practices. The company kept news of the investigation under wraps, not issuing a press release until the story was uncovered by reporters just two days before the company was to open a major stock offering. It was a mar-

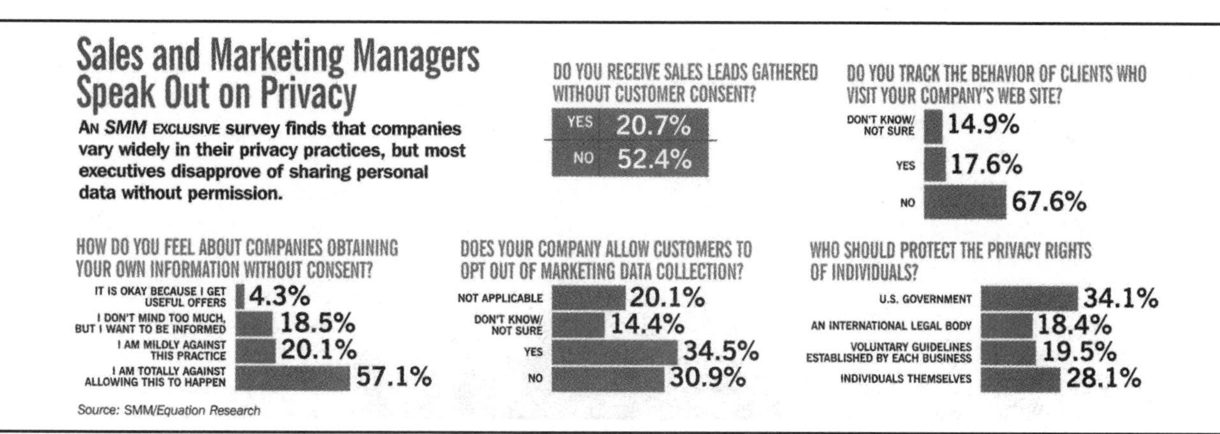

keting blunder, and over the next week, the stock fell nearly 25 percent. Unable to squeeze a return out of its sizable investment in Abacus Direct, it plunged to less than $15 a share by December 2000, after a high of $135.25 in January of that year. "It was a learning moment for the entire industry," says Nuala O'Connor, the vice president of data protection at DoubleClick. "I think DoubleClick crystallized concerns about data collection online and off. We found ourselves in the middle of a huge issue."

SALES FORCES—THE WEAKEST LINK?

SURPRISINGLY, SALESPEOPLE MAY be companies' most vulnerable point-of-contact when it comes to privacy liability. "The problem you have in a sales organization is that individual sales reps tend to be the masters of their own data," Vonder Heide says. "Salespeople have systems that range anywhere from day planners and traditional filing cabinets with paper notes, all the way up to sophisticated programs like Outlook, ACT!, and GoldMine that share data and upload it to a centralized database." Savvy salespeople slip in personal information useful in keeping up relationships with clients—perhaps the ages of a customer's children, or that a particular client is prone to overdrinking, or that Mr. Thompson's wife is battling cancer—knowledge that, in the wrong hands, could embarrass clients and encourage lawsuits. "Most companies that sell exclusively through sales organizations don't have privacy policies," Vonder Heide says. "But every sales rep should understand which customer information should be maintained, and which is appropriate to share with other parties."

Nationwide Insurance, based in Columbus, Ohio, has been grappling with the challenge of educating its salespeople about privacy for two years, says Kirk Herath, the company's chief privacy officer. "It took us half a year to determine our information practices for all of our companies and affiliates, but before we published our policies we had to educate the people on the front lines about what our privacy practices were and what their individual responsibilities were," he says.

It's not just b-to-c companies that are vulnerable. Privacy violation can be even more damaging in the business-to-business world, where leaked information can be of serious strategic significance to the victim.

Herath was particularly concerned about the company's sales force. Decades-old prospecting techniques used by insurance agents would soon become illegal under the Gramm-Leach-Bliley Act and violate Nationwide's new policies. For example, insurance agents often form partnerships with other local salespeople, such as real estate agents, car dealers, and bank representatives, passing on leads about clients new to the area and referring valuable customers. If personal information about Nationwide customers were to be shared in these exchanges, both the agents and the company itself could be sued.

"We knew our sales force would be a big source of liability," Herath says, so he developed a comprehensive training program on privacy that includes dozens of pages of practices to follow, a guide for managers on how to train agents, and a certification test for agents. The curriculum is in the early stages of implementation, and with more than 8,000 agents, including many who work at independent agencies not managed by Nationwide, achieving full compliance will take months of work.

PRACTICE MUST FOLLOW POLICY

GEOCITIES LEARNED A universal lesson in privacy law back in 1998: After you state what your policy is, you have to live up to it. The Web hosting site's registration page then contained the statement, "We will not share this information without your permission." The company nonetheless released the responses—including customers' age, education, occupation, income, and personal interests—to business partners and advertisers. In response the FTC, in its first Internet privacy enforcement action, charged GeoCities with engaging in deceptive practices. After three months of investigation, GeoCities emerged with a lucky settlement. There was no admission of wrongdoing, fine, or penalty; instead the site simply changed its privacy policy to reflect its behavior. (Federal law allows penalties of up to $11,000 per violation in such cases, Everett-Church says, and GeoCities had 2 million subscribers at the time of the FTC inquiry.) Despite emerging clean from the inquiry, GeoCities' stock fell 15 percent the day the charges were announced.

In short, any violation of a privacy policy is fraud, says Everett-Church. And this not only holds true to a company's own behavior, but its business partners' actions as well. John Blaber learned this firsthand when his company was slapped with a lawsuit for work it had done for the now-defunct Toysrus.com Web site. Blaber is the vice president of marketing for Coremetrics, a San Francisco data analysis firm that processes consumer information on Web sites. In its privacy policy, Toys "R" Us had never informed its customers that a third party was involved in collecting data, but because Coremetrics was acting as a contractor, Blaber never saw this as his concern. "The lawsuit surprised us," he says, because Coremetrics never owned the data or distributed it to an outside party. It simply recorded consumer behavior on Toysrus.com, repackaged it, and gave reports back to the company. At press time the suit was still in litigation, but Coremetrics has taken steps to avoid such problems in the future.

"As we work with clients, we step through a process of educating them," Blaber says, and the company now insists that each client notify its customers of Coremetrics' service. After his experience, Blaber suggests that in any business partnership, if any consumer data is shared, the partner must live up to the same standards set in your own company's privacy policy.

FOLLOWING THE TRAIL OF CUSTOMER DATA

WHEN BUSINESSES ARE bought or sold, or salespeople change jobs, difficult questions arise about who owns customer data and how it can be used. Sales organizations are famous for high turnover, and when reps move from company to company, they often carry along their stash of customer information. This knowledge of purchasing habits and personal facts, along with contact names and numbers, could land the rep and her former company in a lawsuit, Vonder Heide says. "The stimulus for [current and pending privacy legislation] was the growth of electronic data exchange, largely through the Internet. But the rules aren't limited to electronic methods. They cover the sharing of data in and of itself, and that sharing could be done in a word-of-mouth manner," he says.

Salespeople, who trade daily in clients' personal information, may be the weakest link in privacy protection. Few reps are kept up-to-date on corporate privacy policies.

When entire businesses are bought and sold, similar privacy quandaries emerge. CVS, a Rhode Island-based pharmacy chain, was hit with a class action lawsuit earlier this year as a result of its acquisition of 250,000 customer records from the purchase of 300 independent pharmacies. The suit was launched by an AIDS patient who felt violated by the sharing of information that clearly identified him as having the disease. Although there is no legal precedent regarding the sale of pharmacy records, Vonder Heide says there is no reason to believe that courts will not find companies liable in groundbreaking cases. "There's a certain danger now because of the litigious society we live in," he says. "You have all kinds of parties looking for test cases. If individuals feel they were wronged because their information was shared, they'll have no trouble finding a lawyer to take the case on a pro bono basis."

COMMUNICATING PRIVACY TO CUSTOMERS

WHEN IT COMES time to confront the privacy issue, many companies turn to experts like PricewaterhouseCoopers or Ernst & Young to create policies and ensure enterprisewide compliance. In 2000 PricewaterhouseCoopers completed 200 privacy audits compared with only 20 in 1999. (Among companies that already had a privacy policy in place, only 80 percent complied with their policies, Ponemon estimated while at PricewaterhouseCoopers.)

Everett-Church suggests that companies also need an internal expert who can manage privacy issues throughout the company. "Respect for customer data has to permeate a company's contacts with its customers, continually reassuring them that they are protected," he says. "That's more than just someone in the legal department slapping a privacy policy on the company Web site. Sales and marketing people must be in on the privacy story." Communication must go both ways, he adds, with salespeople and marketers receiving training on privacy policies and procedures while helping privacy officers develop rules that meet their clients' expectations.

"[Sales executives] are learning that they have to take a proactive step to explain their practices and policies so they won't be misrepresented by those who are critical of marketing and advertising," DoubleClick's Polonetsky adds. "Instead of focusing on the specifics of technologies, we need to explain simply what's taking place. As everyone understands the reality of how the technology is used, it increases consumers' comfort level."

Successful communication also benefits a brand's image. "When you've got other companies out there that aren't clued in on these issues, you can differentiate yourself by giving customers more control over their privacy," Everett-Church says. "Trust is something that is very hard to build and easy to lose, but if you incorporate it into your message, it can be a huge advantage."

That's why it's crucial that sales and marketing teams focus on matters of privacy. "They've absolutely not yet paid enough attention," Ponemon says. "The mindset of sales and marketing executives has been that privacy is the nemesis of marketing. Yes, respecting privacy creates some roadblocks and barriers. But ultimately, it's about knowing your customers and what they want and expect. It's not necessarily antagonistic."

THE MARKETING CHALLENGE

MICHAEL MIORA, a consultant with the ePrivacy Group, in Playa del Rey, California, summarizes the situation marketers face when dealing with personal information as "the privacy paradox." He says, "on the one hand, people want more privacy. They want the sites they visit to know less about them, but on the other hand, they only want information that's relevant to them to come into their mailbox."

The solution is effective marketing communication—understanding customers' concerns, addressing them in policy, and sending the right message about why your company can be trusted. Violate customers' perceptions of privacy once, and they may never come back, says Ponemon, so the time to look at your company's privacy practices is now. In the meantime, salespeople and marketers maintaining stockpiles of customer data had best keep their mouths shut.

ASSOCIATE EDITOR MARK MCMASTER CAN BE REACHED AT MMCMASTER@SALESANDMARKETING.COM

Are You Putting Your Customers' Privacy at Risk?

WITHOUT A CLEAR privacy policy, your customers may be wary of offering personal information and your sales force won't have a code of contact to adhere to. Here are what industry experts say are the four components to an airtight privacy policy:

NOTICE A clearly written and easily accessible privacy statement allows people to understand what information is being collected about them.

CHOICE Customers should be able to decline the sharing or collection of information if they so desire. A simple e-mail form or check box should be presented at the time information is gathered so that clients can decline to participate. Opt-in policies require a customer to explicitly give approval before data is shared, while less restrictive opt-out policies assume customer consent unless they otherwise give notice.

ACCESS The ability for consumers to review the data that has been collected, then correct any errors that could result in misrepresentation or shoddy marketing, is another must for companies that collect large amounts of data.

SECURITY Companies must ensure that the systems and procedures used for collecting and storing customer information are protected enough that employee error, technology problems, or data theft won't jeopardize clients' privacy. "Even if you've developed the best policy, if suddenly your Web server goes berserk and shoots out personal information all over the Internet like a garden sprinkler, then you've got bigger problems," attorney Ray Everett-Church says.

—M.M.

Managing for Organizational Integrity

By supporting ethically sound behavior, managers can strengthen the relationships and reputations their companies depend on.

Lynn Sharp Paine

Many managers think of ethics as a question of personal scruples, a confidential matter between individuals and their consciences. These executives are quick to describe any wrongdoing as an isolated incident, the work of a rogue employee. The thought that the company could bear any responsibility for an individual's misdeeds never enters their minds. Ethics, after all, has nothing to do with management.

In fact, ethics has *everything* to do with management. Rarely do the character flaws of a lone actor fully explain corporate misconduct. More typically, unethical business practice involves the tacit, if not explicit, cooperation of others and reflects the values, attitudes, beliefs, language, and behavioral patterns that define an organization's operating culture. Ethics, then, is as much an organizational as a personal issue. Managers who fail to provide proper leadership and to institute systems that facilitate ethical conduct share responsibility with those who conceive, execute, and knowingly benefit from corporate misdeeds.

Managers must acknowledge their role in shaping organizational ethics and seize this opportunity to create a climate that can strengthen the relationships and reputations on which their companies' success depends. Executives who ignore ethics run the risk of personal and corporate liability in today's increasingly tough legal environment. In addition, they deprive their organizations of the benefits available under new federal guidelines for sentencing organizations convicted of wrongdoing. These sentencing guidelines recognize for the first time the organizational and managerial roots of unlawful conduct and base fines partly on the extent to which companies have taken steps to prevent that misconduct.

Prompted by the prospect of leniency, many companies are rushing to implement compliance-based ethics programs. Designed by corporate counsel, the goal of these programs is to prevent, detect, and punish legal violations. But organizational ethics means more than avoiding illegal practice; and providing employees with a rule book will do little to address the problems underlying unlawful conduct. To foster a climate that encourages exemplary behavior, corporations need a comprehensive approach that goes beyond the often punitive legal compliance stance.

An integrity-based approach to ethics management combines a concern for the law with an emphasis on managerial responsibility for ethical behavior. Though integrity strategies may vary in design and scope, all strive to define companies' guiding values, aspirations, and patterns of thought and conduct. When integrated into the day-to-day operations of an organization, such strategies can help prevent damaging ethical lapses while tapping into powerful human impulses for moral thought and action. Then an ethical framework becomes no longer a burdensome constraint within which companies must operate, but the governing ethos of an organization.

How Organizations Shape Individuals' Behavior

The once familiar picture of ethics as individualistic, unchanging, and impervious to organizational influences has not stood up to scrutiny in recent years. Sears Auto Centers' and Beech-Nut Nutrition Corporation's experiences illustrate the role organizations play in shaping individuals' behavior—and how even sound moral fiber can fray when stretched too thin.

In 1992, Sears, Roebuck & Company was inundated with complaints about its automotive service business. Consumers and attorneys general in more than 40 states had accused the company of misleading customers and selling them unnecessary parts and services, from brake jobs to front-end alignments. It would be a mistake, however, to see this situation exclusively in terms of any one individual's moral failings. Nor did management set out to defraud Sears customers. Instead, a number of organizational factors contributed to the problematic sales practices.

In the face of declining revenues, shrinking market share, and an increasingly competitive market for undercar services, Sears management attempted to spur the performance of its auto centers by introducing new goals and incentives for employees. The company increased minimum work quotas and introduced productivity incentives for mechanics. The automotive service advisers were given product-specific sales quotas—sell so many springs, shock absorbers, alignments, or brake jobs per shift—and paid a commission based on sales. According to advisers, failure to meet quotas could lead to a transfer or a reduction in work hours. Some employees spoke of the "pressure, pressure, pressure" to bring in sales.

Under this new set of organizational pressures and incentives, with few options for meeting their sales goals legitimately, some employees' judgment understandably suffered. Management's failure to clarify the line between unnecessary service and legitimate preventive maintenance, coupled with consumer ignorance, left employees to chart their own courses through a vast gray area, subject to a wide range of interpretations. Without active management support for ethical practice and mechanisms to detect and check questionable sales methods and poor work, it is not surprising that some employees may have reacted to contextual forces by resorting to exaggeration, carelessness, or even misrepresentation.

Shortly after the allegations against Sears became public, CEO Edward Brennan acknowledged management's responsibility for putting in place compensation and goal-setting systems that "created an environment in which mistakes did occur." Although the company denied any intent to deceive consumers, senior executives eliminated commissions for service advisers and discontinued sales quotas for specific parts. They also instituted a system of unannounced shopping audits and made plans to expand the internal monitoring of service. In settling the pending lawsuits, Sears offered coupons to customers who had bought certain auto services between 1990 and 1992. The total cost of the settlement, including potential customer refunds, was an estimated $60 million.

Contextual forces can also influence the behavior of top management, as a former CEO of Beech-Nut Nutrition Corporation discovered. In the early 1980s, only two years after joining the company, the CEO found evidence suggesting that the apple juice concentrate, supplied by the company's vendors for use in Beech-Nut's "100% pure" apple juice, contained nothing more than sugar water and chemicals. The CEO could have destroyed the bogus inventory and withdrawn the juice from grocers' shelves, but he was under extraordinary pressure to turn the ailing company around. Eliminating the inventory would have killed any hope of turning even the meager $700,000 profit promised to Beech-Nut's then parent, Nestlé.

A number of people in the corporation, it turned out, had doubted the purity of the juice for several years before the CEO arrived. But the 25% price advantage offered by the supplier of the bogus concentrate allowed the operations head to meet cost-control goals. Furthermore, the company lacked an effective quality control system, and a conclusive lab test for juice purity did not yet exist. When a member of the research department voiced concerns about the juice to operating management, he was accused of not being a team player and of acting like "Chicken Little." His judgment, his supervisor wrote in an annual performance review, was "colored by naïveté and impractical ideals." No one else seemed to have considered the company's obligations to its customers or to have thought about the potential harm of disclosure. No one considered the fact that the sale of adulterated or misbranded juice is a legal offense, putting the company and its top management at risk of criminal liability.

An FDA investigation taught Beech-Nut the hard way. In 1987, the company pleaded guilty to selling adulterated and misbranded juice. Two years and two criminal trials later, the CEO pleaded guilty to ten counts of mislabeling. The total cost to the company—including fines, legal expenses, and lost sales—was an estimated $25 million.

Acknowledging the importance of organizational context in ethics does not imply forgiving individual wrongdoers.

Such errors of judgment rarely reflect an organizational culture and management philosophy that sets out to harm or deceive. More often, they reveal a culture that is insensitive or indifferent to ethical considerations or one that lacks effective organizational systems. By the same token, exemplary conduct usually reflects an organizational culture and philosophy that is infused with a sense of responsibility.

For example, Johnson & Johnson's handling of the Tylenol crisis is sometimes attributed to the singular personality of then-CEO James Burke. However the decision to do a nationwide recall of Tylenol capsules in order to avoid further loss of life from product tampering was in reality not one decision but thousands of decisions made by individuals at all levels of the organization. The "Tylenol decision," then, is best understood not as an isolated incident, the achievement of a lone individual, but as the reflection of an organization's culture. Without a shared set of values and guiding principles deeply ingrained throughout the organi-

Corporate Fines Under the Federal Sentencing Guidelines

What size fine is a corporation likely to pay if convicted of a crime? It depends on a number of factors, some of which are beyond a CEO's control, such as the existence of a prior record of similar misconduct. But it also depends on more controllable factors. The most important of these are reporting and accepting responsibility for the crime, cooperating with authorities, and having an effective program in place to prevent and detect unlawful behavior.

The following example, based on a case studied by the United States Sentencing Commission, shows how the 1991 Federal Sentencing Guidelines have affected overall fine levels and how managers' actions influence organizational fines.

Acme Corporation was charged and convicted of mail fraud. The company systematically charged customers who damaged rented automobiles more than the actual cost of repairs. Acme also billed some customers for the cost of repairs to vehicles for which they were not responsible. Prior to the criminal adjudication, Acme paid $13.7 million in restitution to the customers who had been overcharged.

Deciding before the enactment of the sentencing guidelines, the judge in the criminal case imposed a fine of $6.85 million, roughly half the pecuniary loss suffered by Acme's customers. Under the sentencing guidelines, however, the results could have been dramatically different. Acme could have been fined anywhere from 5% to 200% the loss suffered by customers, depending on whether or not it had an effective program to prevent and detect violations of law and on whether or not it reported the crime, cooperated with authorities, and accepted responsibility for the unlawful conduct. If a high ranking official at Acme were found to have been involved, the maximum fine could have been as large as $54,800,000 or four times the loss to Acme customers. The following chart shows a possible range of fines for each situation:

What Fine Can Acme Expect?

	Maximum	Minimum
Program, reporting, cooperation, responsibility	$2,740,000	$685,000
Program only	10,960,000	5,480,000
No program, no reporting, no cooperation, no responsibility	27,400,000	13,700,000
No program, no reporting, no cooperation, no responsibility, involvement of high-level personnel	54,800,000	27,400,000

Based on Case No.: 88-266, United States Sentencing Commission, *Supplementary Report on Sentencing Guidelines for Organizations.*

zation, it is doubtful that Johnson & Johnson's response would have been as rapid, cohesive and ethically sound.

Many people resist acknowledging the influence of organizational factors on individual behavior—especially on misconduct—for fear of diluting people's sense of personal moral responsibility. But this fear is based on a false dichotomy between holding individual transgressors accountable and holding "the system" accountable. Acknowledging the importance of organizational context need not imply exculpating individual wrongdoers. To understand all is not to forgive all.

The Limits of a Legal Compliance Program

The consequences of an ethical lapse can be serious and far-reaching. Organizations can quickly become entangled in an all-consuming web of legal proceedings. The risk of litigation and liability has increased in the past decade as lawmakers have legislated new civil and criminal offenses, stepped up penalties, and improved support for law enforcement. Equally—if not more—important is the damage an ethical lapse can do to an organization's reputation and relationships. Both Sears and Beech-Nut, for instance, struggled to regain consumer trust and market share long after legal proceedings had ended.

As more managers have become alerted to the importance of organizational ethics, many have asked their lawyers to develop corporate ethics programs to detect and prevent violations of the law. The 1991 Federal Sentencing Guidelines offer a compelling rationale. Sanctions such as fines and probation for organizations convicted of wrongdoing can vary dramatically depending both on the degree of management cooperation in reporting and investigating corporate misdeeds and on whether or not the company has implemented a legal compliance program. (See the insert "Corporate Fines Under the Federal Sentencing Guidelines.")

Such programs tend to emphasize the prevention of unlawful conduct, primarily by increasing surveillance and control and by imposing penalties for wrongdoers. While plans vary, the basic framework is outlined in the sentencing guidelines. Managers must establish compliance standards and procedures; designate high-level personnel to oversee compliance; avoid delegating discretionary authority to those likely to act unlawfully; effectively communicate the company's standards and procedures through training or publications; take reasonable steps to achieve compliance through audits, monitoring processes, and a system for employees to report criminal misconduct without fear of retribution; consistently enforce standards through appropriate disciplinary measures; respond appropriately when offenses are detected; and, finally, take reasonable steps to prevent the occurrence of similar offenses in the future.

There is no question of the necessity of a sound, well-articulated strategy for legal compliance in an organization. After all, employees can be frustrated and frightened by the complexity of today's legal environment. And even managers who claim to use the law as a guide to ethical behavior often lack more than a rudimentary understanding of complex legal issues.

Managers would be mistaken, however, to regard legal compliance as an adequate means for addressing the full range of ethical issues that arise every day. "If it's legal, it's ethical," is a frequently heard slogan. But conduct that is lawful may be highly problematic from an ethical point of view. Consider the sale in some countries of hazardous products without appropriate warnings or the purchase of goods from suppliers who operate inhumane sweatshops in developing countries. Companies engaged in international business often discover that conduct that infringes on recognized standards of human rights and decency is legally permissible in some jurisdictions.

Legal clearance does not certify the absence of ethical problems in the United States either, as a 1991 case at Salomon Brothers illustrates. Four top-level executives failed to take appropriate action when learning of unlawful activities on the government trading desk. Company lawyers found no law obligating the executives to disclose the improprieties. Nevertheless, the executives' delay in disclosing and failure to reveal their prior knowledge prompted a serious crisis of confidence among employees, creditors, shareholders, and customers. The executives were forced to resign, having lost the moral authority to lead. Their ethical lapse compounded the trading desk's legal offenses, and the company ended up suffering losses—including legal costs, increased funding costs, and lost business—estimated at nearly $1 billion.

A compliance approach to ethics also overemphasizes the threat of detection and punishment in order to channel behavior in lawful directions. The underlying model for this approach is deterrence theory, which envisions people as rational maximizers of self-interest, responsive to the personal costs and benefits of their choices, yet indifferent to the moral legitimacy of those choices. But a recent study reported in *Why People Obey the Law* by Tom R. Tyler shows that obedience to the law is strongly influenced by a belief in its legitimacy and its moral correctness. People generally feel that they have a strong obligation to obey the law. Education about the legal standards and a supportive environment may be all that's required to insure compliance.

Discipline is, of course, a necessary part of any ethical system. Justified penalties for the infringement of legitimate norms are fair and appropriate. Some people do need the threat of sanctions. However, an overemphasis on potential sanctions can be superfluous and even counterproductive. Employees may rebel against programs that stress penalties, particularly if they are designed and imposed without employee involvement or if the standards are vague or unrealistic. Management may talk of mutual trust when unveiling a compliance plan, but employees often receive the message as a warning from on high. Indeed, the more skeptical among them may view compliance programs as nothing more than liability insurance for senior management. This is not an unreasonable conclusion, considering that compliance programs rarely address the root causes of misconduct.

Even in the best cases, legal compliance is unlikely to unleash much moral imagination or commitment. The law does not generally seek to inspire human excellence or distinction. It is no guide for exemplary behavior—or even good practice. Those managers who define ethics as legal compliance are implicitly endorsing a code of moral mediocrity for their organizations. As Richard Breeden, former chairman of the Securities and Exchange Commission, noted, "It is not an adequate ethical standard to aspire to get through the day without being indicted."

Integrity as a Governing Ethic

A strategy based on integrity holds organizations to a more robust standard. While compliance is rooted in avoiding legal sanctions, organizational integrity is based on the concept of self-governance in accordance with a set of guiding principles. From the perspective of integrity, the task of ethics management is to define and give life to an organization's guiding values, to create an environment that supports ethically sound behavior, and to instill a sense of shared accountability among employees. The need to obey the law is viewed as a positive aspect of organizational life, rather than an unwelcome constraint imposed by external authorities.

Management may talk of mutual trust when unveiling a compliance plan, but employees often see a warning from on high.

An integrity strategy is characterized by a conception of ethics as a driving force of an enterprise. Ethical values shape the search for opportunities, the design of organizational systems, and the decision-making process used by individuals and groups. They provide a common frame of reference and serve as a unifying force across different functions, lines of business, and employee groups. Organizational ethics helps define what a company is and what it stands for.

Many integrity initiatives have structural features common to compliance-based initiatives: a code of conduct, training in relevant areas of law, mechanisms for reporting and investigating potential misconduct, and audits and controls to insure that laws and company standards are being met. In addition, if suitably designed, an integrity-based initiative can establish a foundation for seeking the legal benefits that are available under the sentencing guidelines should criminal wrongdoing occur. (See the insert "The Hallmarks of an Effective Integrity Strategy.")

But an integrity strategy is broader, deeper, and more demanding than a legal compliance initiative. Broader in that it seeks to enable responsible conduct. Deeper in that it cuts to the ethos and operating systems of the organization and its members, their guiding values and patterns of thought and action. And more demanding in that it requires

The Hallmarks of an Effective Integrity Strategy

There is no one right integrity strategy. Factors such as management personality, company history, culture, lines of business, and industry regulations must be taken into account when shaping an appropriate set of values and designing an implementation program. Still, several features are common to efforts that have achieved some success:

- *The guiding values and commitments make sense and are clearly communicated.* They reflect important organizational obligations and widely shared aspirations that appeal to the organization's members. Employees at all levels take them seriously, feel comfortable discussing them, and have a concrete understanding of their practical importance. This does not signal the absence of ambiguity and conflict but a willingness to seek solutions compatible with the framework of values.
- *Company leaders are personally committed, credible, and willing to take action on the values they espouse.* They are not mere mouthpieces. They are willing to scrutinize their own decisions. Consistency on the part of leadership is key. Waffling on values will lead to employee cynicism and a rejection of the program. At the same time, managers must assume responsibility for making tough calls when ethical obligations conflict.
- *The espoused values are integrated into the normal channels of management decision making and are reflected in the organization's critical activities*: the development of plans, the setting of goals, the search for opportunities, the allocation of resources, the gathering and communication of information, the measurement of performance, and the promotion and advancement of personnel.
- *The company's systems and structures support and reinforce its values.* Information systems, for example, are designed to provide timely and accurate information. Reporting relationships are structured to build in checks and balances to promote objective judgment. Performance appraisal is sensitive to means as well as ends.
- *Managers throughout the company have the decision-making skills, knowledge, and competencies needed to make ethically sound decisions on a day-to-day basis.* Ethical thinking and awareness must be part of every managers' mental equipment. Ethics education is usually part of the process.

Success in creating a climate for responsible and ethically sound behavior requires continuing effort and a considerable investment of time and resources. A glossy code of conduct, a high-ranking ethics officer, a training program, an annual ethics audit—these trappings of an ethics program do not necessarily add up to a responsible, law-abiding organization whose espoused values match its actions. A formal ethics program can serve as a catalyst and a support system, but organizational integrity depends on the integration of the company's values into its driving systems.

an active effort to define the responsibilities and aspirations that constitute an organization's ethical compass. Above all, organizational ethics is seen as the work of management. Corporate counsel may play a role in the design and implementation of integrity strategies, but managers at all levels and across all functions are involved in the process. (See the chart, "Strategies for Ethics Management.")

During the past decade, a number of companies have undertaken integrity initiatives. They vary according to the ethical values focused on and the implementation approaches used. Some companies focus on the core values of integrity that reflect basic social obligations, such as respect for the rights of others, honesty, fair dealing, and obedience to the law. Other companies emphasize aspirations—values that are ethically desirable but not necessarily morally obligatory—such as good service to customers, a commitment to diversity, and involvement in the community.

When it comes to implementation, some companies begin with behavior. Following Aristotle's view that one becomes courageous by acting as a courageous person, such companies develop codes of conduct specifying appropriate behavior, along with a system of incentives, audits, and controls. Other companies focus less on specific actions and more on developing attitudes, decision-making processes, and ways of thinking that reflect their values. The assumption is that personal commitment and appropriate decision processes will lead to right action.

Martin Marietta, NovaCare, and Wetherill Associates have implemented and lived with quite different integrity strategies. In each case, management has found that the initiative has made important and often unexpected contributions to competitiveness, work environment, and key relationships on which the company depends.

Martin Marietta: Emphasizing Core Values

Martin Marietta Corporation, the U.S. aerospace and defense contractor, opted for an integrity-based ethics program in 1985. At the time, the defense industry was under attack for fraud and mismanagement, and Martin Marietta was under investigation for improper travel billings. Managers knew they needed a better form of self-governance but were skeptical that an ethics program could influence behavior. "Back then people asked, 'Do you really need an ethics program to be ethical?'" recalls current President Thomas Young. "Ethics was something personal. Either you had it, or you didn't."

The corporate general counsel played a pivotal role in promoting the program, and legal compliance was a critical objective. But it was conceived of and implemented from the start as a companywide management initiative aimed at creating and maintaining a "do-it-right" climate. In its original conception, the program emphasized core values, such as honesty and fair play. Over time, it expanded to encompass quality and environmental responsibility as well.

Today the initiative consists of a code of conduct, an ethics training program, and procedures for reporting and investigating ethical concerns within the company. It also includes a system for disclosing violations of federal pro-

Strategies for Ethics Management

Characteristics of Compliance Strategy

Ethos	conformity with externally imposed standards
Objective	prevent criminal misconduct
Leadership	lawyer driven
Methods	education, reduced discretion, auditing and controls, penalties
Behavioral Assumptions	autonomous beings guided by material self-interest

Characteristics of Integrity Strategy

Ethos	self-governance according to chosen standards
Objective	enable responsible conduct
Leadership	management driven with aid of lawyers, HR, others
Methods	education, leadership, accountability, organizational systems and decision processes, auditing and controls, penalties
Behavioral Assumptions	social beings guided by material self-interest, values, ideals, peers

Implementation of Compliance Strategy

Standards	criminal and regulatory law
Staffing	lawyers
Activities	develop compliance standards train and communicate handle reports of misconduct conduct investigations oversee compliance audits enforce standards
Education	compliance standards and system

Implementation of Integrity Strategy

Standards	company values and aspirations social obligations, including law
Staffing	executives and managers with lawyers, others
Activities	lead development of company values and standards train and communicate integrate into company systems provide guidance and consultation assess values performance identify and resolve problems oversee compliance activities
Education	decision making and values compliance standards and system

curement law to the government. A corporate ethics office manages the program, and ethics representatives are stationed at major facilities. An ethics steering committee, made up of Martin Marietta's president, senior executives, and two rotating members selected from field operations, oversees the ethics office. The audit and ethics committee of the board of directors oversees the steering committee.

The ethics office is responsible for responding to questions and concerns from the company's employees. Its network of representatives serves as a sounding board, a source of guidance, and a channel for raising a range of issues, from allegations of wrongdoing to complaints about poor management, unfair supervision, and company policies and practices. Martin Marietta's ethics network, which accepts anonymous complaints, logged over 9,000 calls in 1991, when the company had about 60,000 employees. In 1992, it investigated 684 cases. The ethics office also works closely with the human resources, legal, audit, communications, and security functions to respond to employee concerns.

Shortly after establishing the program, the company began its first round of ethics training for the entire workforce, starting with the CEO and senior executives. Now in its third round, training for senior executives focuses on decision making, the challenges of balancing multiple responsibilities, and compliance with laws and regulations critical to the company. The incentive compensation plan for executives makes responsibility for promoting ethical conduct an explicit requirement for reward eligibility and requires that business and personal goals be achieved in accordance with the company's policy on ethics. Ethical conduct and support for the ethics program are also criteria in regular performance reviews.

Today top-level managers say the ethics program has helped the company avoid serious problems and become more responsive to its more than 90,000 employees. The ethics network, which tracks the number and types of cases and complaints, has served as an early warning system for poor management, quality and safety defects, racial and gender discrimination, environmental concerns, inaccurate and false records, and personnel grievances regarding salaries, promotions, and layoffs. By providing an alternative channel for raising such concerns, Martin Marietta is able to take corrective action more quickly and with a lot less pain. In many cases, potentially embarrassing problems have been identified and dealt with before becoming a management crisis, a lawsuit, or a criminal investigation. Among employees who brought complaints in 1993, 75% were satisfied with the results.

Company executives are also convinced that the program has helped reduce the incidence of misconduct. When allegations of misconduct do surface, the company says it deals with them more openly. On several occasions, for instance, Martin Marietta has voluntarily disclosed and made restitution to the government for misconduct involving potential violations of federal procurement laws. In addition, when an employee alleged that the company had retaliated against him for voicing safety concerns about his plant on CBS news, top management commissioned an investigation by an outside law firm. Although failing to support the allegations, the investigation found that employees at the plant feared retaliation when raising health, safety, or environmental complaints. The company redoubled its efforts to identify and discipline those employees taking retaliatory action and stressed the desirability of an open work environment in its ethics training and company communications.

Although the ethics program helps Martin Marietta avoid certain types of litigation, it has occasionally led to other kinds of legal action. In a few cases, employees dismissed for violating the code of ethics sued Martin Marietta, arguing that the company had violated its own code by imposing unfair and excessive discipline.

Still, the company believes that its attention to ethics has been worth it. The ethics program has led to better relationships with the government, as well as to new business opportunities. Along with prices and technology, Martin Marietta's record of integrity, quality, and reliability of estimates plays a role in the awarding of defense contracts, which account for some 75% of the company's revenues. Executives believe that the reputation they've earned through their ethics program has helped them build trust with government auditors, as well. By opening up communications, the company has reduced the time spent on redundant audits.

The program has also helped change employees' perceptions and priorities. Some managers compare their new ways of thinking about ethics to the way they understand quality. They consider more carefully how situations will be perceived by others, the possible long-term consequences of short-term thinking, and the need for continuous improvement. CEO Norman Augustine notes, "Ten years ago, people would have said that there were no ethical issues in business. Today employees think their number-one objective is to be thought of as decent people doing quality work."

NovaCare: Building Shared Aspirations

NovaCare Inc., one of the largest providers of rehabilitation services to nursing homes and hospitals in the United States, has oriented its ethics effort toward building a common core of shared aspirations. But in 1988, when the company was called InSpeech, the only sentiment shared was mutual mistrust.

Senior executives built the company from a series of aggressive acquisitions over a brief period of time to take advantage of the expanding market for therapeutic services. However, in 1988, the viability of the company was in question. Turnover among its frontline employees—the clinicians and therapists who care for patients in nursing homes and hospitals—escalated to 57% per year. The company's inability to retain therapists caused customers to defect and the stock price to languish in an extended slump.

At NovaCare, executives defined organizational values and introduced structural changes to support those values.

After months of soul-searching, InSpeech executives realized that the turnover rate was a symptom of a more basic problem: the lack of a common set of values and aspirations. There was, as one executive put it, a "huge disconnect" between the values of the therapists and clinicians and those of the managers who ran the company. The therapists and clinicians evaluated the company's success in terms of its delivery of high-quality health care. InSpeech management, led by executives with financial services and venture capital backgrounds, measured the company's worth exclusively in terms of financial success. Management's single-minded emphasis on increasing hours of reimbursable care turned clinicians off. They took management's performance orientation for indifference to patient care and left the company in droves.

CEO John Foster recognized the need for a common frame of reference and a common language to unify the diverse groups. So he brought in consultants to conduct interviews and focus groups with the company's health care professionals, managers, and customers. Based on the results, an employee task force drafted a proposed vision statement for the company, and another 250 employees suggested revisions. Then Foster and several senior managers developed a succinct statement of the company's guiding purpose and fundamental beliefs that could be used as a framework for making decisions and setting goals, policies, and practices.

Unlike a code of conduct, which articulates specific behavioral standards, the statement of vision, purposes, and beliefs lays out in very simple terms the company's central purpose and core values. The purpose—meeting the rehabilitation needs of patients through clinical leadership—is supported by four key beliefs: respect for the individual, service to the customer, pursuit of excellence, and commitment to personal integrity. Each value is discussed with examples of how it is manifested in the day-to-day activities and policies of the company, such as how to measure the quality of care.

To support the newly defined values, the company changed its name to NovaCare and introduced a number of structural and operational changes. Field managers and clinicians were given greater decision-making authority; clinicians were provided with additional resources to assist in the delivery of effective therapy; and a new management structure integrated the various therapies offered by the company. The hiring of new corporate personnel with health care backgrounds reinforced the company's new clinical focus.

The introduction of the vision, purpose, and beliefs met with varied reactions from employees, ranging from cool skepticism to open enthusiasm. One employee remembered thinking the talk about values "much ado about nothing." Another recalled, "It was really wonderful. It gave us a goal that everyone aspired to, no matter what their place in the company." At first, some were baffled about how the vision, purpose, and beliefs were to be used. But, over time, managers became more adept at explaining and using them as a guide. When a customer tried to hire away a valued employee, for example, managers considered raiding the customer's company for employees. After reviewing the beliefs, the managers abandoned the idea.

NovaCare managers acknowledge and company surveys indicate that there is plenty of room for improvement. While the values are used as a firm reference point for decision making and evaluation in some areas of the company, they are still viewed with reservation in others. Some managers do not "walk the talk," employees complain. And recently acquired companies have yet to be fully integrated into the program. Nevertheless, many NovaCare employees say the values initiative played a critical role in the company's 1990 turnaround.

The values reorientation also helped the company deal with its most serious problem: turnover among health care providers. In 1990, the turnover rate stood at 32%, still above target but a significant improvement over the 1988 rate of 57%. By 1993, turnover had dropped to 27%. Moreover, recruiting new clinicians became easier. Barely able to hire 25 new clinicians each month in 1988, the company added 776 in 1990 and 2,546 in 1993. Indeed, one employee who left during the 1988 turmoil said that her decision to return in 1990 hinged on the company's adoption of the vision, purpose, and beliefs.

Wetherill Associates: Defining Right Action

Wetherill Associates, Inc.—a small, privately held supplier of electrical parts to the automotive market—has neither a conventional code of conduct nor a statement of values. Instead, WAI has a *Quality Assurance Manual*—a combination of philosophy text, conduct guide, technical manual, and company profile—that describes the company's commitment to honesty and its guiding principle of right action.

Creating an organization that encourages exemplary conduct may be the best way to prevent damaging misconduct.

WAI doesn't have a corporate ethics officer who reports to top management, because at WAI, the company's corporate ethics officer *is* top management. Marie Bothe, WAI's chief executive officer, sees her main function as keeping the 350-employee company on the path of right action and looking for opportunities to help the community. She delegates the "technical" aspects of the business—marketing, finance, personnel, operations—to other members of the organization.

Right action, the basis for all of WAI's decisions, is a well-developed approach that challenges most conventional management thinking. The company explicitly rejects the usual conceptual boundaries that separate morality and self-interest. Instead, they define right behavior as logically, expediently, and morally right. Managers teach employees to look at the needs of the customers, suppliers, and the community—in addition to those of the company and its employees—when making decisions.

WAI also has a unique approach to competition. One employee explains, "We are not 'in competition' with anybody. We just do what we have to do to serve the customer." Indeed, when occasionally unable to fill orders, WAI salespeople refer customers to competitors. Artificial incentives, such as sales contests, are never used to spur individual performance. Nor are sales results used in determining compensation. Instead, the focus is on teamwork and customer service. Managers tell all new recruits that absolute honesty, mutual courtesy, and respect are standard operating procedure.

Newcomers generally react positively to company philosophy, but not all are prepared for such a radical departure from the practices they have known elsewhere. Recalling her initial interview, one recruit described her response to being told that lying was not allowed, "What do you mean? No lying? I'm a buyer. I lie for a living!" Today she is persuaded that the policy makes sound business sense. WAI is known for informing suppliers of overshipments as well as undershipments and for scrupulous honesty in the sale of parts, even when deception cannot be readily detected.

Since its entry into the distribution business 13 years ago, WAI has seen its revenues climb steadily from just under $1 million to nearly $98 million in 1993, and this is an industry with little growth. Once seen as an upstart beset by naysayers and industry skeptics, WAI is now credited with entering and professionalizing an industry in which kickbacks, bribes, and "gratuities" were commonplace. Employees—equal numbers of men and women ranging in age from 17 to 92—praise the work environment as both productive and supportive.

WAI's approach could be difficult to introduce in a larger, more traditional organization. WAI is a small company founded by 34 people who shared a belief in right action; its ethical values were naturally built into the organization from the start. Those values are so deeply ingrained in the company's culture and operating systems that they have been largely self-sustaining. Still, the company has developed its own training program and takes special care to hire people willing to support right action. Ethics and job skills are considered equally important in determining an individual's competence and suitability for employment. For WAI, the challenge will be to sustain its vision as the company grows and taps into markets overseas.

At WAI, as at Martin Marietta and NovaCare, a management-led commitment to ethical values has contributed to competitiveness, positive workforce morale, as well as solid sustainable relationships with the company's key constituencies. In the end, creating a climate that encourages exemplary conduct may be the best way to discourage damaging misconduct. Only in such an environment do rogues really act alone.

Lynn Sharp Paine is associate professor at the Harvard Business School, specializing in management ethics. Her current research focuses on leadership and organizational integrity in a global environment.

a good start

NEW VENTURES CAN MAKE ETHICS PART OF THEIR BUSINESS PLAN.

BY KIRK O. HANSON

The entrepreneur has so many things on his or her mind: the "value proposition," the features of the product or service, financing, technology, building the team, getting the phones installed, just surviving from month to month. What role can and does ethics play in the critical first months and years of a company's existence? What can the entrepreneurial team do to *give* ethics a role in the start-up?

The study of how ethics works in companies—known as "organizational ethics"—has unfortunately focused primarily on larger enterprises. Starting in the mid-1980s, many larger companies established ethics programs staffed by ethics officers. These officers have encouraged others to study how they operate and to measure the effects of their programs. Those who study organizational ethics, fortunately, have been just as interested in how other enterprises—those without formal ethics programs—succeed in making their companies ethical and value-centered. These insights help us examine how start-ups deal with ethics.

It is obvious the start-up company is unlikely to establish a formal ethics program or appoint an ethics officer, though some start-up CEOs proudly declare that they are the new venture's "ethics officer." Even without a formal program, however, start-ups can create—and many have created—a very effective commitment to ethical practice. Examination of the best practices of these start-ups reveals several key steps new ventures can take to make ethics a distinguishing mark of the start-up's culture:

1. Ethical start-ups recognize the ethical dilemmas that surround them in the first few months.

The pressures to cut ethical corners are great in a start-up. How much puffery do you use in presenting your idea to venture capitalists? How do you divide stock ownership and options fairly among the founding team and later hires? How reliable does a product have to be before you ship it? How creative can you be in your accounting when the value of your stock is so sensitive to a stumble? When a deal falls through, how quickly do you tell your board and your funders? How generous can you afford to be in employee benefits in the early days?

2. Ethical start-ups make ethics a core value of the enterprise.

Start-up founders have discovered that they must explicitly embrace doing business ethically to counter the temptations to fudge various standards. Ethics should appear in business plans, in company mission statements, and in all other company documents.

3. The ethical entrepreneur finds early opportunities to make his or her ethical commitment real.

A Silicon Valley entrepreneur who took over a months-old company recently refused to send faulty financial data to the venture capitalists, over the objections of his new team. "You just don't do business that way," reflects the entrepreneur, who enjoys both financial success and a superb reputation today. He communicated clearly from that day the ethical standards he and the company would follow.

4. The ethical entrepreneur anticipates the ethical tensions in day-to-day decisions.

As business plans are written and product capabilities are described, the ethical tension between the truthful and the "hopeful" is inevitable. As a start-up tries to attract top talent, there is an unavoidable ethical tension in determining how rosy a picture to draw for the prospect. The ethically thoughtful entrepreneur anticipates these tensions and talks about them with the team before the situations are confronted. In later years of a company's life, this practice will become more formal ethics training.

5. The ethical entrepreneur welcomes ethical questions and debates.

Some situations cannot be anticipated, and the ethical entrepreneur must always keep an open door so that new ethical issues can be worked out. Even the willingness to take time to discuss and resolve tough ethical dilemmas gives the signal that ethics is important in the start-up.

6. The ethical entrepreneur is watchful about conflicts of interest.

It is hard to single out one area of particular ethical concern in start-ups because there are so many of importance. However, the world of high-tech start-ups emphasizes partnerships, strategic alliances, and "virtual relationships." These arrangements are rife with opportunities for conflicts of interest where an entrepreneur or start-up employee can line his or her own pockets to the detriment of the organization. An early and consistent stand against questionable conflicts of interest is an important dimension of a start-up ethics effort.

7. The ethical entrepreneur talks about the ethical values all the time.

The frantic pace of start-ups and their rapid growth create short memories and a staff that is often very new to the enterprise. Only by continually articulating the ethical commitment can the entrepreneur be sure the members of the organization—particularly new hires—understand the ethical commitment and know it is real.

8. The ethical entrepreneur weeds out employees who do not embrace the ethical values of the company.

Hiring is among the most important strategic steps a start-up takes. Inevitably, the venture will hire some individuals who believe financial success, perhaps just personal financial success, is the only value. The ethical entrepreneur is on the lookout for "teammates" who do not share the company's values and weeds them out before they can do damage to the reputation or culture of the firm.

9. The ethical entrepreneur looks for opportunities to engage the company in the community.

The start-up's preoccupation with meeting product and financial goals and with its own growth can lead to blindness about anything other than personal gain. Ethical entrepreneurs find ways to engage the team in community service and to emphasize the continuing importance of the team's family relationships.

10. The ethical entrepreneur takes stock occasionally.

Just as the entrepreneur must keep an eye on the start-up's cash flow and produce a balance sheet periodically, so he or she must also take stock of the company's commitment to its ethics and other values.

11. The ethical entrepreneur renews the commitment to ethical behavior.

Companies change as they grow. The most pressing ethical dilemmas of a $10 million or $100 million company differ from those of a fledgling start-up. Ethical values and the commitment to ethical behavior must be recast and re-communicated periodically, preparing the company and its employees to deal with the ethical dilemmas currently faced.

The rewards of being an ethical start-up are many. Personal and team satisfaction is the most prominent. Workers who feel free to act ethically and to deal with others ethically feel better about themselves. Greater personal satisfaction translates into higher productivity and to lower turnover.

For the individual entrepreneur, a reputation for ethical dealing can increase the opportunities for business partnerships and lower the "transaction costs" of managing an ongoing relationship. "The ability to trust the other party and to do business on a handshake speeds up the progress we can make," commented one entrepreneur. A reputation for ethical dealing can make it much easier to attract employees and financing to the current venture—or the next.

FURTHER READING

Alexander, Meredith. "Do You Need an Ethics Officer?" *The Standard*, July 3, 2000.
Global Business Responsibility Resource Center, www.bsr.org/resourcecenter/.
Ethics Resource Center, www.ethics.org.
Hanson, Kirk O. "Implementing Ethics Strategies in Organizations" (Monograph). Society of Management Accountants of Canada, 1998.
Nichols, Nancy A. "Profits with a Purpose: An Interview with Tom Chapman" (founder of Tom's of Maine, Inc.). *Harvard Business Review* (November–December 1992).
Paine, Lynn S. "Managing for Organizational Integrity." *Harvard Business Review* (March–April 1994).
Woodstock Theological Center. "Creating and Maintaining an Ethical Corporate Culture" (Monograph). Georgetown University Press, 1990.

Kirk O. Hanson has been appointed executive director of the Markkula Center for Applied Ethics; he assumes that post in August 2001. Currently, he is the director of the Sloan Program at Stanford University Graduate School of Business.

The 100 Best Corporate Citizens

America's most profitable and socially responsible major public companies

BY PHILIP JOHANSSON

Last year's national election debacle has certainly left more than one U.S. citizen wondering what citizenship is worth. In an era of faltering government leadership it is fortunate that a growing number of U.S. corporations are taking their own sense of "citizenship" more seriously. Many companies are going to unusual lengths to address the needs and concerns of their various stakeholders, groups that have a stake in or are impacted by a company's activities. The best among major public companies—as measured by service to seven stakeholder groups—have made this year's list of the 100 Best Corporate Citizens.

"We view corporate social responsibility as an asset we continue to nurture and grow."

— Douglas W. Leatherdale, chairman and CEO,

The St. Paul Companies

"Corporate social responsibility is a deeply rooted tradition in our company and an integral part of our character and reputation," said Douglas W. Leatherdale, chairman and CEO of **The St. Paul Companies** (No. 9), the Minnesota based insurer with more than $7.5 billion in revenues and total assets of $38.9 billion. "We view corporate social responsibility as an asset we continue to nurture and grow. It's a critical part of how we do business and balances the needs of all our constituents. In the long term, it will benefit our company and its shareholders."

Moving up from No. 85 last year to the top ten this year, the St. Paul gained the top score for "community," one of the seven stakeholder areas considered in this year's ranking of companies. The company's stellar score in the area of community stems from its firm commitment to the development of vital communities in the Twin Cities of St. Paul and Minneapolis. For instance, its Leadership Initiatives in Neighborhoods program, now in its 16th year, provides grants to current and emerging leaders to develop their leadership potential. Since 1998, The St. Paul has pledged more than $2.2 million to develop an ambitious vision to increase the number of teachers of color in Twin Cities urban schools, enhance the retention of talented educators, and better prepare teachers for urban classrooms. St. Paul employee committees are empowered to make grant making recommendations in the communities where they live and work. And The St. Paul's arts and diversity committee collaborates with United Arts, a local nonprofit organization, on local arts programming related to various cultures, perspectives, and diversity issues.

"Increasingly, companies and employees are caring about their communities and want to be part of a greater cause," said Leatherdale. "They want to do the right thing. As hard as that may be to define at times, the right thing usually involves making decisions and taking positive actions that make life better for everyone." In short, it means being a good corporate citizen.

Business Ethics first introduced a ranking of the 100 Best Corporate Citizens in 1996, using data gathered in-house by our own researchers. We returned to the list in the year 2000 with a new methodology, using the database compiled by the leading social research firm, Kinder, Lydenberg, Domini and Co. (KLD). Boston-based KLD collects and synthesizes data on a wide array of stakeholder related topics for over 650 top public U.S. companies, and provides the background research for the Domini 400 Social Index. KLD data was statistically analyzed by Sandra Waddock and Samuel Graves at Boston College.

"Societal and market forces will increasingly require companies to behave more responsibly, or risk failure, and we think that is a good thing."

—Andrew Lock, v.p. of human resources, Herman Miller

While last year's list incorporated data from four stakeholder groups, this year's ranking incorporates seven stakeholder groups into a single index. It includes a stockholder performance measure of total return for the three year period 1997–1999. The other six stakeholder groups are local communities, minorities, employees, global stakeholders, customers, and the environment.

High Five

This year's change in methodology, and of course a year's more data, resulted in a substantial reshuffling of companies. Thirty-one companies fell off the list altogether, including **Anheuser-Busch, Campbell Soup, Coca-Cola, Knight Ridder, Times Mirror, Washington Post Co.**, and **Wal-Mart**. Among the companies new to the list are **Freddie Mac** (No. 10), **Corning** (No. 31), **Apple Computer** (No. 32), **McDonald's** (No. 78), **Dow Jones** (No. 79), and **Eastman Kodak** (No. 82). Companies advancing included **Polaroid** (No. 8), moving up from No. 37 last year.

No. 1 for 2001 is **Procter and Gamble**, which moved up from No. 4 last year. P&G scored especially high in service to international stakeholders, where it tied for highest score with **State Street Corp.** (No. 12), **HB Fuller** (No. 15), **Avon Products** (No. 20), and **Starbucks** (No. 24).

P&G markets 300 brands to nearly 5 billion consumers in 140 countries, with approximately 50 percent of revenues coming from overseas. The consumer products giant has 93 manufacturing facilities in 44 countries outside the U.S., and has been generous in international grants and gifts in these communities, including earthquake relief in Turkey, community building projects in Japan, plus contributions for schools in China, school computers in Romania, special education in Malaysia, and shore protection in France.

P&G's Achilles heel is that the company has been a frequent target of animal rights activists for using animal testing in the development of products. In an effort to calm the criticism, in 1999 the company announced it would end the use of animal tests for all current beauty, fabric, and home care products, except where required by law. But animal rights advocates, such as People for the Ethical Treatment of Animals (PETA), remain concerned that raw ingredients and products being developed are exempt from the test ban. P&G will remain under their scrutiny until it adheres to animal alternatives such as cell cultures for all phases of product testing.

Coming in a strong second was **Hewlett-Packard**. Its stakeholder service included generous support of community development and education, amounting to $58 million in 1999, and an extremely employee-friendly work environment. HP offers employees profit sharing representing 12 percent of pretax profits, provides a stunning 52 weeks maternity leave, and was the only large computer company to avoid large-scale layoffs through the 1990s. But HP really shines in the area of diversity. Three women serve among the company's seven senior line executives, including Carly Fiorina, president and CEO of HP since 1999. The company has been commended for its high percentage of women in highly paid positions, the result of a program in which women and minorities in midlevel management are provided with special mentorship opportunities. Fiorina's eye-popping compensation package of $93.8 million in 1999, one of the highest in the country, is a concern. But the fact that she returned part of her bonus in 2000 after the company missed earnings goals provides some reassurance.

Third-ranked **Fannie Mae** may have an edge over other companies in the area of corporate citizenship, having been chartered by Congress to make homeownership available to a broader range of people. Since 1968, Fannie Mae has provided $2.9 trillion in mortgage financing for over 35 million families, many of them minorities or moderate-income families that could not otherwise have afforded a home. An inquiry by the U.S. Department of Housing and Urban Development (HUD) last year surprised many observers by suggesting Fannie Mae was not doing enough to promote homeownership of minorities in low-income neighborhoods. And some critics argue that government subsidies such as tax breaks give the company a competitive edge in the financial market, but the company insists these benefits are passed on to customers.

Fannie Mae scores high in the areas of community and diversity, and has been ranked near the top of everyone's "best" list, including *Fortune*'s "Best Companies for Minorities," *Working Mother*'s "Best Companies for Working Mothers," and The *American Benefactor*'s "America's Most Generous Companies." Franklin D. Raines, an African-American, is CEO, and there are two women and two minorities among the companies eight senior line executives.

Among the top five corporate citizens, **Motorola** (No. 4) was another company also coming in a top scorer in one stakeholder area, in this case customers. It tied for top score in this area with **Tellabs** (No. 35). With sales of $31 billion in 1999, Motorola spent $3.44 billion on research and development, or 11 percent of revenues, making it one of the largest R&D investors among U.S. corporations. This communications and embedded-electronics giant is known for making large, long-term bets on emerging technologies, such as its substantial investment in Iridium, a satellite communications project. The firm has had a total quality management program in place since the 1980s, and has often received product awards.

Recent lawsuits have alleged that Motorola's cellular phones caused or aggravated brain cancer, but some research casts doubt on these allegations. Also, like many other technology companies on the list, Motorola has some troubling involvement in military contracts, including nuclear weapon-related products such as missile guidance systems. In 1998, Motorola was the 52nd-largest defense contractor in the U.S., with $240 million in contracts with the Department of Defense. On the other hand, Motorola has been a leader among companies renouncing further activities related to antipersonnel mine production.

Top Dogs

While Motorola is the top contender in the area of product quality and innovation, **Herman Miller** (No. 7) brought in the top ranking for employee relations. The Zeeland, Michigan based furniture manufacturer gained high marks for its employee-friendly corporate culture, including employee ownership of a large fraction of the company (17 percent in 1998) and retire-

Business Ethics' 100 Best Corporate Citizens

Rank	Overall Score	Company	1999 Revenue (millions)	1999 Net Income (millions)	1997-99 Average Total Return to Shareholders	1997-99 Standardized values 3-year KLD averages					
						Community	Minorities & Women	Employees	Environment	Non-U.S. Stakeholders	Customers
1	1.404	Procter & Gamble	$38,125	$3,654	29.14%	1.442	1.743	1.261	0.114	3.749	1.099
2	1.384	Hewlett Packard	$42,370	$3,491	34.53%	0.968	3.158	1.659	1.576	0.175	1.541
3	1.261	Fannie Mae	$36,968	$3,834	23.97%	2.864	3.441	0.465	0.114	0.175	1.541
4	1.211	Motorola	$30,931	$817	48.06%	0.021	1.743	2.454	0.114	0.175	2.867
5	1.175	IBM	$87,548	$7,692	44.77%	2.864	3.158	-2.000	1.942	0.175	1.099
6	1.115	Sun Microsystems	$11,806	$1,030	143.91%	1.916	0.328	0.465	0.114	0.175	0.215
7	1.079	Herman Miller	$1,766	$142	26.44%	-0.453	1.743	3.249	2.307	0.175	0.215
8	1.049	Polaroid	$1,979	$9	-14.70%	3.811	1.460	-0.330	2.307	0.175	1.099
9	1.015	St Paul Cos	$7,569	$834	10.23%	5.232	1.177	0.465	0.114	0.175	0.215
10	1.003	Freddie Mac	$24,268	$2,0770	27.58%	2.390	1.177	1.261	0.114	0.175	1.541
11	1.000	Home Depot	$30,219	$1,614	84.76%	2.390	-0.520	-0.330	0.114	1.367	1.541
12	0.998	State Street	$4,692	$619	36.08%	0.968	1.602	-0.330	0.114	3.749	0.215
13	0.977	QRS	$125	$15	95.89%	0.968	0.328	0.863	0.114	0.175	1.541
14	0.962	Dime Bancorp	$1,987	$240	17.35%	1.679	1.177	2.056	0.114	0.175	1.541
15	0.921	HB Fuller	$1,364	$43	7.81%	0.968	0.328	1.659	1.210	3.749	-1.112
16	0.910	Cummins Engine	$6,639	$160	10.53%	2.864	0.046	1.659	0.479	1.367	0.215
17	0.890	Amgen	$3,340	$1,096	74.16%	1.916	0.894	0.863	0.114	0.175	0.215
18	0.884	Intel	$29,389	$7,314	38.52%	-0.453	0.611	2.056	1.942	0.175	1.099
19	0.877	Cisco Systems	$12,173	$2,023	104.00%	-0.453	0.894	2.056	0.114	0.175	0.215
20	0.871	Avon Products	$5,289	$302	10.81%	0.968	2.026	-0.728	0.114	3.749	0.215
21	0.855	JP Morgan Chase & Co.	$51,852	$7,395	13.46%	2.390	2.026	1.659	0.114	0.175	-0.227
22	0.842	Pitney Bowes	$4,433	$636	30.65%	0.968	0.894	0.863	2.307	0.175	0.215
23	0.842	Northern Trust	$2,804	$400	48.13%	0.968	2.451	0.863	0.114	0.175	0.215
24	0.833	Starbucks	$1,680	$102	22.24%	-0.453	1.177	0.863	0.114	3.749	0.215
25	0.832	Solectron	$9,669	$350	94.69%	-0.453	1.177	0.465	0.114	0.175	1.541
26	0.815	General Mills	$6,246	$535	7.53%	3.811	0.894	0.863	0.114	0.175	0.215
27	0.811	Brady	$471	$40	10.60%	0.968	1.177	0.863	1.210	0.175	1.541
28	0.808	Southwest Airlines	$4,736	$474	37.78%	-0.453	0.328	2.852	0.479	0.175	1.541
29	0.778	Time Warner	$27,333	$1,896	61.50%	1.442	2.309	-0.330	0.479	0.175	-0.227
30	0.773	Honeywell	$23,735	$1,541	24.53%	3.811	1.177	-0.330	0.114	0.175	0.215
31	0.758	Corning	4,368	$481	70.17%	-0.453	0.328	3.249	1.210	0.175	-1.112
32	0.754	Apple Computer	$6,134	$601	108.64%	0.021	0.894	-1.523	0.114	1.367	1.099
33	0.738	Whirlpool	$10,511	$347	14.77%	2.390	-0.237	0.863	2.307	0.175	-0.227
34	0.737	AT&T	$62,391	$5,450	27.25%	2.390	1.602	0.863	-0.434	0.175	0.215
35	0.730	Tellabs	$2,319	$559	52.48%	-0.453	-0.520	1.659	0.114	0.175	2.867
36	0.727	Adolph Coors	$2,057	$92	48.31%	1.442	2.026	-0.728	0.845	0.175	0.215
37	0.712	Medtronic	$5,015	$1,099	31.93%	1.442	0.328	0.863	0.114	0.175	1.541
38	0.711	New York Times	$3,131	$310	41.89%	0.968	2.026	-0.728	0.114	0.175	1.541
39	0.696	Computer Associates Int'l	$5,253	$626	34.97%	-0.453	3.724	0.465	0.114	0.175	0.215
40	0.678	Charles Schwab	$3,945	$589	78.57%	-0.453	1.177	0.863	0.114	0.175	0.657
41	0.676	Texas Instruments	$9,468	$1,406	86.53%	-0.453	1.177	-0.330	0.114	0.175	1.541
42	0.667	Dell Computer	$18,243	$1,460	168.04%	-0.453	-0.520	-0.330	0.114	0.175	0.215
43	0.667	Alza	$796	$91	18.71%	0.021	0.328	2.454	0.114	0.175	1.541
44	0.654	Gap	$9,054	$825	79.76%	0.968	1.177	-0.330	0.114	0.175	0.215
45	0.646	Nordstrom	$5,028	$207	21.60%	-0.453	1.743	1.261	0.114	0.175	1.541
46	0.646	Whole Foods Market	$1,493	$42	39.24%	0.495	1.177	0.465	1.210	0.175	0.215
47	0.640	Aetna	$22,110	$717	-8.86	%5.232	2.026	-0.330	0.114	0.175	-1.775
48	0.636	Ecolab	$2,080	$176	30.34%	1.916	-0.520	-0.330	1.210	0.175	1.541
49	0.624	Oneok	$2,652	$92	1.59%	0.968	0.328	2.056	1.210	0.175	0.215
50	0.616	Applied Materials	$5,096	$748	102.04%	-0.453	0.328	0.863	0.114	0.175	0.215

Business Ethics' 100 Best Corporate Citizens (continued)

51	0.612	Quaker Oats	$4,725	$451	23.07%	2.390	0.328	0.863	0.114	0.175	0.215
52	0.598	Target	$30,662	$915	57.51%	2.390	2.592	-1.921	0.479	-1.016	0.215
53	0.583	Timberland	$917	$75	54.46%	2.390	-0.520	-0.728	1.210	0.175	0.215
54	0.579	Novell	$1,273	$191	80.86%	-0.453	0.046	1.659	0.114	0.175	0.215
55	0.579	Clorox	$4,003	$246	32.66%	2.390	0.046	0.068	1.942	0.175	-1.112
56	0.563	Gillette	$9,897	$1,256	4.58%	-0.453	0.046	0.068	3.038	0.175	1.541
57	0.561	Kroger Company	$45,352	$237	28.36%	1.442	0.328	1.261	0.114	0.175	0.215
58	0.546	Compaq	$38,525	$569	34.55%	0.021	-0.237	0.863	0.845	0.175	1.541
59	0.543	EMC	$6,716	$1,011	144.17%	-0.453	-0.520	-0.330	0.114	0.175	0.215
60	0.533	Golden West Financial	$2,969	$480	20.10%	0.968	1.177	-0.330	0.114	0.175	1.541
61	0.532	Dollar General	$3,221	$179	33.71%	0.968	-0.520	0.863	0.114	0.175	1.541
62	0.525	Merck & Co	$32,714	$5,891	23.09%	2.390	1.743	1.261	-0.983	0.175	-1.112
63	0.520	USA Education	$3,259	$499	21.06%	-0.453	0.611	2.852	0.114	0.175	0.215
64	0.518	Tennant Company	$429	$20	10.34%	0.021	1.177	0.863	0.114	0.175	1.541
65	0.512	American Express	$21,278	$2,475	46.26%	0.968	2.592	-0.330	0.114	-1.016	0.215
66	0.509	EliLilly	$10,003	$2,721	32.80%	1.442	2.026	2.056	-0.252	0.175	-2.438
67	0.503	Deere	$11,751	$239	12.88%	-0.453	0.328	1.261	0.845	0.175	1.541
68	0.502	Nucor	$4,009	$245	4.69%	-0.453	-1.369	3.249	0.845	0.175	1.541
69	0.483	Xilinx	$662	$103	86.75%	-0.453	-1.369	0.863	0.114	0.175	1.541
70	0.483	Northwest Natural Gas	$456	$43	3.98%	-0.453	-0.52	03.249	1.210	0.175	0.215
71	0.479	3COM	$5,202	$404	-6.41%	0.495	1.177	2.056	0.114	0.175	0.215
72	0.476	3M	$15,659	$1,763	10.47%	0.968	0.328	0.465	0.114	0.175	1.541
73	0.474	Baxter International	$6,380	$797	18.49%	-0.453	1.743	-0.330	1.942	0.175	0.215
74	0.473	Avery Dennison	$3,768	$215	31.88%	0.968	0.328	-0.330	0.114	0.175	1.541
75	0.464	Oracle	$8,827	$1,290	121.08%	-0.453	-0.237	-0.330	0.114	0.175	0.215
76	0.458	Cigna	$18,781	$1,774	23.72%	3.811	0.328	-0.330	0.114	0.175	-1.112
77	0.455	Bellsouth	$25,224	$3,448	39.95%	1.442	0.894	0.863	0.114	0.175	-1.112
78	0.455	McDonalds	$13,259	$1,948	24.40%	0.968	2.026	-0.330	1.210	0.175	-1.112
79	0.451	Dow Jones	$2,002	$272	32.48%	-0.453	1.177	0.068	0.114	0.175	1.541
80	0.441	Sonoco Products	$2,547	$188	4.17%	-0.453	-0.520	1.261	1.576	0.175	1.541
81	0.433	Analog Devices	$1,450	$197	72.90%	-0.453	-1.086	2.056	0.114	0.175	0.215
82	0.431	Eastman Kodak	$14,089	$1,392	-2.14%	0.495	2.875	2.056	-2.079	0.175	0.215
83	0.427	MBNA	$6,470	$1,010	32.80%	2.390	-0.520	0.068	0.114	0.175	0.215
84	0.413	Scholastic	$1,166	$37	4.91%	-0.453	2.309	-0.330	0.114	0.175	1.541
85	0.413	DeVry	$421	$39	29.67%	-0.453	0.611	0.465	0.114	0.175	1.541
86	0.412	Lillian Vernon	$255	$3	2.88%	0.495	2.026	-0.330	0.845	0.175	0.215
87	0.412	Crown Cork & Seal	$7,732	$166	-22.52%	1.442	-0.520	0.863	0.845	0.175	1.541
88	0.412	Guidant	$2,352	$341	60.32%	-0.453	0.328	0.068	0.114	0.175	1.099
89	0.405	Modine Manufacturing	$1,111	$74	3.57%	-0.453	-1.086	0.863	2.307	0.175	1.541
90	0.390	Harman Int'l Industries	$1,500	$12	4.90%	-0.453	-0.237	2.056	0.114	0.175	1.541
91	0.387	Alaska Airgroup	$2,082	$134	26.03%	0.021	-0.520	0.863	1.210	0.175	0.657
92	0.386	Fifth Third Bancorp	$3,616	$668	44.85%	0.021	0.328	0.863	0.114	0.175	0.215
93	0.386	Lincoln National	$6,804	$460	20.37%	0.968	1.460	-0.330	0.114	0.175	0.215
94	0.376	Tribune Company	$3,222	$1,461	45.17%	0.968	0.046	-0.330	0.114	0.175	0.657
95	0.375	Biomet	$828	$125	42.60%	-0.453	-0.520	0.863	0.114	0.175	1.541
96	0.375	LSI Logic	$2,089	$67	91.38%	-0.453	-1.369	1.261	0.114	0.175	0.215
97	0.373	Walt Disney	$23,402	$1,300	10.84%	1.442	2.309	-1.125	1.210	-3.399	2.425
98	0.369	Sara Lee	$17,270	$1,179	11.93%	0.968	2.026	0.465	-0.617	0.175	-0.227
99	0.366	Nordson Corp	$700	$48	-5.73%	2.864	0.055	-0.728	0.845	0.175	0.215
100	0.356	Graco Inc	$442	$59	32.71%	0.968	-0.520	-0.330	0.114	0.175	1.541

Source: Morningstar for 1999 sales & net income, CRSP for total return to shareholders.

This year's ranking includes KLD data for six stakeholder groups in addition to owners: community, members of minority groups (KLD's diversity measure), employees, global suppliers and sources (KLD's non-U.S. operations measure), customers (KLD's product measure), and environment.

ment benefits worth waiting around for. Herman Miller's tradition of participative management and employee appreciation can be traced back to the company's founder, D.J. DePree, who pioneered an innovative corporate culture in 1923.

"We've led the way in creating policies described by others as 'progressive,'" said Andrew Lock, v.p. of human resources, "including employee recognition programs, gainsharing, employee stock ownership, adoption benefits, health facilities, stock options, and more. Those kinds of programs reflect our belief in the dignity and value of each individual and their right and responsibility to participate fully in the success and growth of the business."

Herman Miller also scored high in the environment area, making significant gains in materials recycling in the production process and conserving energy. In 1998 the company introduced an office chair made from 70 percent recycled materials and itself 100 percent recyclable. Herman Miller hosts an annual environmental conference for employees, customers, and the public, as well as a supplier conference where best environmental practices are shared.

At the top of the list in the diversity category is **Computer Associates International** (No. 39), a leading provider of e business software, which does all the right things in terms of hiring and promoting minorities and women. Founder and chairman Charles Wang, a Chinese-American, recently handed over the job of CEO to Sanjay Kumar, a Sri Lankan-American. In 1999 six of the company's 25 highest-paid officers were minorities, as were 14 of its officials and managers. One woman and two minorities sit on the board of directors. The company has generous family benefits and has extended all spousal benefits to domestic partners of gay and lesbian employees for the past five years. In 1998 *Computerworld* magazine named Computer Associates the top-ranked place for women and minorities to work in information systems.

The **Gillette Company** (No. 56) makes a splash in the area of the environment, where it earned the highest score for its proactive approach to environmental restoration. "Protecting the environment is part of Gillette's mission and values," said Dr. A. Wallace Hayes, v.p. corporate product integrity. "In 2000, we extended our environmental commitment beyond our facilities with an innovative public-private program to restore America's valuable wetlands, the Corporate Wetlands Restoration Partnership (CWRP)."

Gillette founded the CWRP in Massachusetts in 1999, in partnership with state and federal agencies, to help restore vital wetlands damaged by development and pollution. To date, more than 20 companies have contributed over $1 million in funds and services to the Massachusetts partnership, which has nearly completed the restoration of the Sagamore Salt Marsh. The expansion of the partnership to a nationwide initiative, with Gillette as national corporate chair, stands to make a significant impact. The company is also a participant in the pilot EPA Environmental Leadership Program, still another sign of the company's willingness to go beyond its own impact in addressing environmental problems.

A special mention goes to **Dell Computer Corporation** (No. 42) for the highest score in the area of financial returns for stockholders. Vying for domination in the lucrative computer market, with a healthy $33 billion in annual revenues, Dell averaged a mouth-watering 168 percent return over the three years 1997-1999. The company also scored high in the area of community, where its philanthropic efforts in Texas and Tennessee are legendary, though a compensation package for CEO Michael Dell valued at approximately $109 million in 1999 leaves one wondering if they couldn't contribute even more.

Missing or Wounded

This year's booby prize goes to **IBM** (No. 5), which dropped from its top position last year largely due to its mishandling of the change from a defined benefit to a cash balance pension plan, which drew widespread employee outrage. The switch cost some older employees as much as 50 percent of their pension, while it saved the company an estimated $200 million. The company did agree to offer more employees a choice of plan, but the unpopular move is still a blot upon IBM's otherwise positive leadership in the area of employee relations.

Perhaps as telling as the companies that topped the 100 Best Corporate Citizens are the ones that don't show up on the list at all. While the list is rife with financial companies, high-tech icons, and consumer products, there is nary one auto manufacturer or petroleum company. Transportation companies are represented only by **Southwest Airlines** (No. 28), with its admirable employee relations efforts, and **Alaska Airgroup** (No. 91). It may go without saying, but the social and environmental impacts of some products are hard to overcome.

To many observers, "corporate responsibility" is an oxymoron, like "bittersweet" or "pretty ugly." Today's multinational corporations have such an overwhelming impact on our lives, our communities, and our environment, they are often portrayed as villains, with their only focus on the bottom line. Although some corporations may deserve that unsavory reputation, this year's list of the 100 Best Corporate Citizens leaves significant room for optimism.

Andrew Lock at Herman Miller said it well. "Societal and market forces will increasingly require companies to behave more responsibly, or risk failure, and we think that is a good thing."

UNIT 5

Developing the Future Ethos and Social Responsibility of Business

Unit Selections

Key Points to Consider

- In what areas should organizations become more ethically sensitive and socially responsible in the next five years? Be specific, and explain your choices.
- Obtain codes of ethics or conduct from several different professional associations (for example, doctors, lawyers, CPAs, etc.). What are the similarities and differences between them?
- How useful do you feel codes of ethics are to organizations? Why?

Links: www.dushkin.com/online/
These sites are annotated in the World Wide Web pages.

Sheffield University Management School
http://www.shef.ac.uk/uni/academic/I-M/mgt/research/research.html

Trinity College/Computer Science Course
http://www.cs.tcd.ie/courses/2ba6/best967/dukej/index.html

UNU/IAS Project on Global Ethos
http://www.ias.unu.edu/research_prog/governance/global_ethos.html

Business ethics should not be viewed as a short-term, "knee-jerk reaction" to recently revealed scandals and corruption. Instead, it should be viewed as a thread woven through the fabric of the entire business culture—one that ought to be integral to its design. Businesses are built on the foundation of trust in our free-enterprise system. When there are violations of this trust between competitors, between employer and employees, or between businesses and consumers, the system ceases to run smoothly.

From a pragmatic viewpoint, the alternative to self-regulated and voluntary ethical behavior and social responsibility on the part of business may be governmental and legislative intervention. From a moral viewpoint, ethical behavior should not exist because of economic pragmatism, governmental edict, or contemporary fashionability—it should exist because it is morally appropriate and right.

This last unit is composed of seven articles that provide some ideas, guidelines, and principles for developing the future ethos and social responsibility of business. In the first article, Archie Carroll discusses some of the ethical challenges we will face in the new millennium. The second selection, "Old Ethical Principles: The New Corporate Culture," analyzes 10 old ethical principles and applies them to the new corporate culture. In the third article, "Profits From Principle," Bennett Daviss reflects why corporations are finding that social responsibility pays off. "Learning IT Right From Wrong" scrutinizes the addition of a computer ethics course to the college curriculum. The last three articles take a look at how some tech executives are supporting environmental causes, provide an example of ways an on-site child care center can be beneficial, and reflect the rising cost and debilitating effect of depression at the workplace.

ETHICAL CHALLENGES FOR BUSINESS IN THE NEW MILLENNIUM: CORPORATE SOCIAL RESPONSIBILITY AND MODELS OF MANAGEMENT MORALITY

Abstract: As we transition to the 21st century, it is useful to think about some of the most important challenges business and other organizations will face as the new millennium begins. What will constitute "business as usual" in the business ethics arena as we start and move into the new century? My overall thought is that we will pulsate into the future on our current trajectory and that the new century will not cause cataclysmic changes, at least not immediately. Rather, the problems and challenges we face now we will face then. Undoubtedly, new issues will arise but they will more likely be extensions of the present than discontinuities with the past.

Archie B. Carroll

As we transition to the 21st century, it is useful to think about some of the most important challenges business and other organizations will face as the new millennium begins. As I write this essay, the public seems to be more concerned with the Y2K problem and whether their computers will keep working, their power will stay on, their investments will be secure, there will be food in the pantry, airplanes will still fly, and that life as we know it will continue as usual. Optimistically, by the time this is published we will all look back and conclude that technology is amazing, humans are survivors, and we will wonder why we got all worked up about Y2K bug in the first place. This is my hope and expectation, so I approach this writing with the optimism that the world will not end in a technological Armageddon but that the transition will be relatively smooth, though perhaps jerky, and that we will return to business as usual soon thereafter.

This raises the question in my mind as to what will constitute "business as usual" in the business ethics arena as we start and move into the new century. My overall thought is that we will pulsate into the future on our current trajectory and that the new century will not cause cataclysmic changes, at least not immediately. Rather, the problems and challenges we face now we will face then. Undoubtedly, new issues will arise but they will more likely be extensions of the present than discontinuities with the past.

Questions have been raised in the past about ethics in business and they will continue to be raised in the future. The public's perception of business ethics has not wavered much over the past 30 years or so and there is no reason to think this will dramatically change. When the Gallup Poll first asked the public to rate the honesty and ethical standards of business executives in 1977, only 19 percent of those surveyed ranked them as "very high" or "high." When the same question was asked again in October, 1998, the figure was 21 percent. This is slightly better but statistically insignificant over this period of two decades (*American Enterprise*, March/April 1999). To be sure, some groups of businesspeople rank lower, such as stockbrokers, contractors, real estate agents, insurance and car salesmen, and advertising practitioners, but their numbers are pretty stable over this 30-year period as well. There is not much happening to cause us to think this will change.

There are a number of different ways we could approach this task of thinking about ethical challenges in the new millennium. We could think of them in terms of what new issues will arise or what specific industries will be affected. Such an approach would likely cause us to speculate about the impact of technology—computers, the Internet and World Wide Web, electronic commerce, or genetic engineering and human cloning. *Time* magazine has already hailed the 21st century as the "biotech century" (*Time*, January 11, 1999), so we could easily speculate about the business and ethical implications of this new reality we will face. Alternatively, but related, we could think of specific industries that are likely to pose ethical challenges. This approach, of course, would likely take us into medicine and health care (we do have an aging population), insurance, financial services, and telemarketing, just to mention a few.

Another important point is that all issues and topics will become more global in concern. What were once regional and national concerns have quickly become global concerns. George Soros has outlined the "crisis of global capitalism" (Soros 1999) and this doubtless will carry further ethical implications than we have initially thought.

Another approach to this task would be to look at some enduring or generic management challenges that touch the business sector, business organizations, and managers, for that is an arena which will be vital to business ethics regardless of topic, issue, industry, level of global analysis, and so on. In this connection, I have written about two topics over the past twenty years that touch upon managers and organizations, and I would like to spend the balance of this essay reviewing them and thinking about changes, if any, we are likely to see with respect to them: corporate social responsibility (CSR) and models of management morality.

Trends in Corporate Social Responsibility

Twenty years ago I proposed a definition of corporate social responsibility that has been found useful in thinking about businesses' responsibilities to society and has served as a workable base point in theoretical development and research on this topic (Carroll 1979). The four-part definition held that corporations had four responsibilities to fulfill to society: economic, legal, ethical, and discretionary (later referred to as philanthropic). This definition sought to embrace businesses' legitimate economic or profit-making function with responsibilities that extended beyond the basic economic role of the firm. It sought to reconcile the idea that business could focus either on profits or social concerns, but not both. It sought to argue that businesses can not only be profitable and ethical, but that they should fulfill these obligations simultaneously. Though I have described previously each of these four responsibilities that comprise CSR (1991, 1995), it is useful to briefly recap each as we think about the future.

The *economic responsibility* refers to businesses' fundamental call to be a profit-making enterprise. Though profit making is not the purpose of business (from a societal perspective), it is essential as a motivation and reward for those individuals who take on commercial risk. Though it may seem odd to think of this as a "social" responsibility, this is, in effect what it is. The socio-capitalistic system calls for business to be an economic institution, and profit making is an essential ingredient in a free enterprise economy. While we may think of economics as one distinct element of the CSR definition, it is clearly infused or embedded with ethical assumptions, implications, and overtones.

As we transition to the new millennium, the economic responsibility of business remains very important and will become an ever more significant challenge due to global competitiveness. The new century poses an environment of global trade that is complex, fast-paced, and exponentially expanding into capital, enterprise, information, and technology markets (Kehoe 1998). Hamel and Prahalad (1994) have told us that "competing for the future" will be different. They pose the economic challenges of business as tantamount to a revolution in which existing industries—health care, transportation, banking, publishing, telecommunications, pharmaceuticals, retailing, and others—will be profoundly transformed (p. 30). In addition, these challenges will be global.

In addition to economic responsibilities, businesses have *legal responsibilities* as well, as part of their total corporate social responsibility. Just as our society has sanctioned our economic system by permitting business to assume the economic role of producing goods and services and selling them at a profit, it has also laid down certain ground rules—laws—under which business is expected to pursue its economic role. Law reflects a kind of "codified ethics" in society in the sense that it embodies basic notions of fairness or business righteousness, at least as agreed upon by our legislators. As Boatright has concurred, business activity takes place within an extensive framework of law, and all business decisions need to embrace both the legal and the economic though he agrees that the law is not enough (1993, p. 13). In the 21st century, as we usher in the millennium, we will likely see the continuing expansion of the legal system. There will be no relief in sight as the growing number of lawyers being produced annually in our nation's law schools will ensure that the supply will drive the demand. There is no diminishment in Congress of legislators with law degrees. As long as these individuals continue to be instrumental in controlling our legal system, things may well get more litigious rather than less so. Factors in the social environment such as affluence, education, and awareness will continue to produce rising expectations, an entitlement mentality, the rights movement, and a victimization way of thinking. All of these feed into and drive a litigious society (Carroll 1996, pp. 10–16). Many laws are good and valid and reflect appropriate ethical standards, however, and we will continue to see the legal responsibility of business as a robust sphere of activity.

In addition to fulfilling their economic and legal responsibilities, businesses are expected to fulfill ethical responsibilities as well (Carroll 1979). Ethical responsibilities embrace those activities, practices, policies, or behaviors that are expected (in a positive sense) or prohibited (in a negative sense) by societal members though they are not codified into laws. Ethical responsibilities embrace a range of norms, standards, or expectations of behavior that reflect a concern for what consumers, employees, shareholders, the community, and other stakeholders regard as fair, right, just, or in keeping with stakeholders' moral rights or legitimate expectations.

As we transition to the new millennium, this category of CSR will be more important than ever. Business has embraced the notion of business ethics with some conscious degree of enthusiasm over the past decade, and this trend is expected to continue. Organizations such as the Ethics Officers Association and Business for Social Responsibility provide testimony to the institutionalization of this quest. Another statistic is relevant and impressive: corporations now spend over $1 billion per year on ethics consultants (Morgan and Reynolds 1997). A major research firm, Walker Information of Indianapolis, Indiana, markets new and innovative products: business integrity assessments and stakeholder management assessments, side-by-side with more traditional products such as customer satisfaction studies. What was once relegated to writings in obscure academic journals has now made the transition into practitioner books by the dozens. One such example is *The Ethical Imperative* (1998) by consultant John Dalla Costa, wherein he argues that ethics is becoming the defining business issue of our time, affecting corporate profits and credibility, as well as personal security and the sustainability of a global economy. He argues that by conservative estimates yearly losses to corporations due to unethical behavior equal more than the profits of the top forty corporations in North America and that such economic waste and moral loss requires more than a PR Band-Aid.

But there is a possible down side to this obsession that we should be sensitive to as the ethics industry grows and matures and we move into the new century. Morgan and Reynolds (1997) have argued that for two decades now we have engaged in "a vast campaign to clean up our ethical act" in the workplace, politics, and communities. We have crafted mountains of regulations, created vast networks of consultants and committees, and have made terms such as "conflicts of interest" and "the appearance of impropriety" part of our everyday language. However, they argue, the public's confidence in business people and politicians to "do the right thing" has plummeted to an all-time low. They claim we have made legitimate ethical concerns into absurd standards and have wielded our moral whims like dangerous weapons. We have obscured core truths. Now, inflated misdemeanors are the stuff by which careers and reputations are ruined. In this climate, real integrity has been lost to this obsession with wrongdoing. In summary, they have argued that the ethics wars have "undermined American government, business, and society." As we move into the early 2000s, their concerns pose some serious problems for thought and reflection.

The fourth part of the CSR definition is the discretionary, or philanthropic, responsibility. Whereas the economic and legal accountabilities are required of business and ethical behaviors, policies, and practices are expected of business, philanthropy is both expected and desired. In this category we include the public's expectation that business will engage in social activities that are not mandated, not required by law, and not generally expected of business in an ethical sense, though some ethical underpinnings or justification may serve as the rationale for business being expected to be philanthropic. The subtle distinction between ethical and philanthropic responsibilities is that the latter are not expected with the same degree of moral force. In other words, if a firm did not engage in business giving to the extent that certain stakeholder groups expected, these stakeholders would not likely label the firm as unethical or immoral. Thus, the philanthropic expectation does not carry with it the same magnitude of moral mandates as does the ethical category. Examples of philanthropy might include business giving, community programs, executive loan programs, and employee voluntarism. I have depicted the normative prescription of philanthropy to "be a good corporate citizen." This, however, is a narrow view of corporate citizenship. On another occasion, I proposed a wider view by portraying all four of the CSR categories to constitute the "four faces of corporate citizenship" (Carroll 1998). Upon deeper reflection, I came to think that a wider view which included being profitable, obeying the law, being ethical, and "giving back" to the community, was more fully reflective of what corporate citizenship was all about.

As we transition to the 21st century, I expect the current trend toward "strategic philanthropy" to remain the guiding philosophy. Businesses will continue to strive to align their philanthropic interests with their economic mandates so that both of these objectives may be achieved at the same time. One of business's most significant ethical challenges will be to walk the fine line between conservative and liberal critics of its philanthropic giving. It is becoming increasingly difficult to direct corporate philanthropy without being offensive to some individual or group. Jennings and Cantoni (1998) provided several vivid illustrations of how this might happen. Apparently, retailer Dayton-Hudson made a contribution to Planned Parenthood only to find right-to-lifers outside its stores cutting their credit cards. They did an about-face and made contributions to right-to-life groups only to subject themselves to pro-choice protestors. In other illustrations, U.S. West gave money to the Boy Scouts of America and was flogged by gay-rights activists. Levi Strauss withdrew support from the Boy Scouts, and drew a backlash from religious leaders. This type of dilemma will pose significant and continuing problems for businesses in the future as our special-interest society flourishes.

In summary, as businesses, in their quest to be socially responsible, seek to concurrently (1) be profitable, (2) obey the law, (3) engage in ethical behavior, and (4) give back through philanthropy, they will face new and continuing ethical challenges in the new millennium. I have only touched on some of the relevant issues, but they will doubtless extend beyond what I have chosen to discuss here.

Models of Management Morality

In 1987, I embarked on a "search for the moral manager." Pertinent questions then and now included "are there any?" "where are they?" and "why are they so hard to find?" (Carroll 1987). The thesis of my discussion was that moral managers were so hard to find because the business landscape was so cluttered with immoral and amoral managers. At that time I articulated three models of management morality: Immoral Management, Moral Management, and Amoral Management. The purpose of describing these three moral types was to delineate, define, and emphasize the amoral category and to provide models of management morality that I thought would better convey to businesspeople the range of moral types in which managerial ethics might be classified. I believed that through description and example managers would be able to better assess their own ethical behaviors and motivations and that of other organizational members as well—their supervisors, subordinates, and colleagues. I was moved to emphasize the Amoral Management category by virtue of my observational world that did not seem to fit under the category of Immoral Management. As I recap each of these moral types, I will comment on their relevance as we transition into the 2000s. Immoral and Moral Management are easier to describe and are more traditional, so I will start with them.

Immoral Management (or Managers) is a good place to start, for without them we would have no field known as business ethics. Positing that unethical and immoral are synonymous in the organizational context, I defined Immoral Management as that which is not only devoid of ethical principles or precepts but also positively and actively opposed to what is right or just. In this model, management decisions, actions, and behavior imply a positive and active opposition to what is ethical or moral. Decisions here are discordant with ethical principles and the model implies an active negation of what is moral. Management motives are selfish. They are driven by self-interest wherein management cares only about itself or about the organization's gains. The goal is profitability and success at any price, and legal standards are seen as barriers that must be overcome. The Immoral Management strategy is to exploit opportunities and cut corners wherever it is helpful (Carroll 1987, 1991). In short, the Immoral Managers are the bad guys. It is doubtful that ethics education or more ethical organizational climates will change them.

As we enter the new millennium, I have no strong reason to argue that this group will change significantly. There are still immoral managers and they will likely always be with us. If the initiatives of business ethics scholars, teachers, and consultants have had any impact, combined with initiatives from the business community itself, it is logical to argue that they will be a diminishing if not a vanishing breed.

By contrast, *Moral Management (or Managers)* represents the exemplar toward which I could well argue our teaching and research is directed. That is, as educators and business leaders, we are striving to create Moral Managers. John Boatright, in his 1998 presidential address to the Society for Business Ethics, spoke of a Moral Manager Model, wherein the manager both acted and thought morally, and Boatright concurred that the goal of business ethics is to turn out moral managers. In Moral Management, business decisions, attitudes, actions, policies, and behavior conform to a high standard of ethical, or right, behavior. The goal is conformity to lofty professional standards of conduct. Ethical leadership is commonplace and represents a defining quality. The motives of Moral Managers are virtuous. The motives are directed toward success within the confines of the law and sound ethical precepts (e.g., fairness, justice, due process). The goal of Moral Management is success within the letter and spirit of the law. The law is regarded as a minimum and the Moral Manager prefers to operate well above what the law mandates. The strategy is to live by sound ethical standards and to assume ethical leadership. If Immoral Managers were the bad guys, Moral Managers are the good guys.

There seems to be an inclination toward emphasizing Moral Management as we move into the new century and millennium. Obviously, it is the underlying premise or implicit goal of the business ethics field and much of its literature. For example, Moral Management is similar to Paine's "integrity strategy" in which she argues that ethics should be the driving force of the organization (Paine 1994). The model fits well with Ciulla's and Gini's discussions of ethics as the heart of leadership (Ciulla 1998, Gini 1998), and it is consistent with Aguilar's recommendations for leadership in ethics programs that can contribute substantially to corporate excellence (Aguilar 1994). The Moral Management model follows logically with Wilson's "moral sense" (1993), and is the underlying model for ethical leadership in Hood's "heroic enterprise" (1996). Moral Management is harmonious with Badaracco's belief that executives can use defining moments as an opportunity to redefine their company's role in society (1998). Finally, it must be argued that the Moral Manager is the prototype for "understanding stakeholder thinking" (Nasi 1995) and for managing "the stakeholder organization" (Wheeler and Sillanpaa 1997). Like the other models, the trends here are global (Carroll and Meeks 1999). All of these writings, and many others, suggest a bright future for the Moral Management Model and its associated characteristics.

The third conceptual model is *Amoral Management (or Managers)*. I distinguish between two types of amoral managers—those that are intentional and those that are unintentional. *Intentional Amoral Management* is characterized by a belief that moral considerations have no relevance or applicability in business or other spheres or organizational life. Amoral management holds that management or business activity is outside of or beyond the sphere in which moral judgments apply. These managers think that the business world and the moral world are two separate spheres and never the twain should meet. Intentional Amoral Managers are a vanishing breed as we enter the new millennium. We seldom find anymore managers who think compartmentally in this way. There are a few left, but those who are left seem reluctant to admit that they believe in this way. I do not anticipate that they will be as much of a problem in the next century. Richard DeGeorge (1999) also has been concerned with this group in his discussions of the myth of amoral business in several editions of his *Business Ethics* textbook. As he points out, most people in business do not act unethically or maliciously; they think of themselves, in both their private and their business lives, as ethical people. They simply feel that business is not expected to be concerned with ethics. He describes them as amoral insofar as they feel that ethical considerations are inappropriate in business—after all, business is business (p. 5).

On the other hand, there is *Unintentional Amoral Management*, and it deserves closer scrutiny. These managers do not factor ethical considerations into their decision making, but for a different reason. These managers are well-intentioned but are self-centered in the sense that they do not possess the ethical perception, awareness, or discernment to realize that many of their decisions, actions, policies, and behaviors have an ethical facet or dimension that is being overlooked. These managers are ethically unconscious or insensitive; they are ethically ignorant. To the extent that their reasoning processes possess a moral dimension, it is disengaged. Unintentional Amoral Managers pursue profitability within the confines of the letter of the law, as they do not think about the spirit of the law. They do not perceive who might be hurt by their actions.

The field of managers to whom the Unintentional Amoral Management characteristics apply is large and perhaps growing as the new decade arrives. These managers are not hostile to morality, they just do not understand it. They have potential, but have not developed the key elements or capacities that Powers and Vogel (1980) argue are essential for developing moral judgment. Key among these capacities are a sense of moral obligation, moral imagination, moral identification and ordering, moral evaluation, and the integration of managerial and moral competence. The good news is that this is the group that should be most susceptible to learning, changing, and becoming Moral Managers. Of the three moral management models presented, I would maintain that the Unintentional Amoral Managers probably dominate the managerial landscape. An alternative view is that within each manager, each of the three models may be found at different points in time or in different circumstances, but that the Amoral Management model's characteristics are found most frequently. If these are correct assessments, this represents a huge challenge for business ethics educators, consultants, and organizations seeking to brink out the Moral Management model in the new millennium.

Conclusion

There will be many challenges facing the business community and organizational managers as we transition into the new millennium. Many industries and business sectors will be affected. Products and services as well as channels of distribution may be revolutionized and with these changes will come the usual kinds of ethical issues that commercial activity inevitably generates. Though it is impossible to predict all the arenas that will be affected, the safest conclusion is that many of the issues we have faced in the latter half of the twentieth century will endure for some time to come. Corporate social responsibility will continue to be a meaningful issue as it embraces core concerns that are necessary to the citizenry and business alike. Companies will be expected to be profitable, abide by the law, engage in ethical behavior, and give back to their communities through philanthropy, though the tensions between and among these responsibilities will become more challenging as information technology continues to push all enterprises toward a global-level frame of reference and functioning.

With respect to the three models of management morality, it is expected that Immoral Management will diminish somewhat as values and moral themes permeate and grow in the culture and the commercial sphere. Immoral Management will become an endangered species but will not disappear. Greed and human nature will ensure that Immoral Managers will always be with us. Our goal will be to minimize their number and the severity of their impact. The Moral Management model will grow in importance as an exemplar toward which business and organizational activity will be focused. The great opportunity will be in the vast realms of Unintentionally Amoral Managers. As the public and many private schools and educational systems continue to eliminate a concern for virtue and morals from classroom teaching, or alternatively, promote values clarification or ethical relativism, a ready supply of amoral young people entering business and organizational life will be guaranteed. In recent years, however, there have been the beginnings of a moral awakening in society, and I would like to believe that this optimistic paradigm will succeed, grow, and survive, but it will be facing major obstacles. At best, unintentional amorality will continue to be with us, and thus we ethics professors and consultants will continue to be employed and to have a challenging task ahead of us as the new millennium arrives.

Bibliography

Aguilar, Francis J. 1994. *Managing Corporate Ethics*. New York: Oxford University Press.

American Enterprise. 1999. "Opinion Pulse." May/June, p. 90.

Badaracco, Joseph L., Jr. 1998. "The Discipline of Building Character." *Harvard Business Review*, March–April, pp. 115–124.

Boatright, John R. 1993. *Ethics and the Conduct of Business*. Englewood Cliffs, N.J.: Prentice-Hall.

Boatright, John R. 1998. "Does Business Ethics Rest on a Mistake?" San Diego: Society for Business Ethics Presidential Address, August 6–9.

Carroll, Archie B. 1979. "A Three-Dimensional Conceptual Model of Corporate Social Performance." *Academy of Management Review* 4: 497–505.

_____. 1987. "In Search of the Moral Manager." *Business Horizons*, March–April. pp. 7–15.

_____. 1991. "The Pyramid of Corporate Social Responsibility: Toward the Moral Management of Organizational Stakeholders." *Business Horizons* 34: 39–48.

_____. 1995. "Stakeholder Thinking in Three Models of Management Morality: A Perspective with Strategic Implications." In *Understanding Stakeholder Thinking*, ed. Juha Nasi. Helsinki: LSR-Publications, pp. 47–74. Also in Clarkson 1998, pp. 139–172.

_____. 1996. *Business and Society: Ethics and Stakeholder Management*, 3rd ed. Cincinnati: South-Western College Publishing/International Thompson Publishing.

_____. 1998. "The Four Faces of Corporate Citizenship." *Business and Society Review* 100/101: 1–7.

_____ and Meeks, Michael D. 1999. "Models of Management Morality: European Applications and Implications." *Business Ethics: A European Review* 8, no. 2: 108–116.

Clarkson, Max B. E., ed. 1998. *The Corporation and its Stakeholders: Classic and Contemporary Readings*. Toronto: University of Toronto Press.

Ciulla, Joanne B. 1998. *Ethics, the Heart of Leadership*. Westport, Conn.: Praeger.

Costa, John Dalla. 1998. *The Ethical Imperative: Why Moral Leadership is Good Business*. Reading, Mass.: Addison-Wesley.

DeGeorge, Richard T. 1999. *Business Ethics*. 5th ed. Upper Saddle River, N.J.: Prentice-Hall.

Gini, Al. 1998. "Moral Leadership and Business Ethics." In *Ethics, the Heart of Leadership*, ed. Joanne Ciulla, pp. 27–45.

Hamel, Gary and Prahalad, C. K. 1994. *Competing for the Future*. Boston: Harvard Business School Press.

Hood, John M. 1996. *The Heroic Enterprise: Business and the Common Good*. New York: The Free Press.

Isaacson, Walter. 1999. "The Biotech Century." *Time*, January 11, pp. 42–43.

Jennings, Marianne and Cantoni, Craig. 1998. "An Uncharitable Look at Corporate Philanthropy." *Wall Street Journal*, December 22, p. A8.

Kehoe, William J. 1998. "GATT and WTO Facilitating Global Trade." *Journal of Global Business*, Spring, pp. 67–76.

Morgan, Peter W. and Reynolds, Glenn H. 1997. *The Appearance of Impropriety: How the Ethics Wars Have Undermined American Government, Business, and Society*. New York: The Free Press.

Nasi, Juha, ed. 1995. *Understanding Stakeholder Thinking*. Helsinki, Finland: LSR Publications.

Paine, Lynn Sharp. 1994. "Managing for Organizational Integrity." *Harvard Business Review*, March–April, pp. 106–117.

Powers, Charles W. and Vogel, David. 1980. *Ethics in the Education of Business Managers*. Hastings-on-Hudson, N.Y.: The Hastings Center, pp. 40–45.

Soros, George. 1998. *The Crisis of Global Capitalism*. New York: Public Affairs.

Wheeler, David and Sillanpaa, Maria. 1997. *The Stakeholder Corporation*. London: Pitman Publishing.

Wilson, James Q. 1993. *The Moral Sense*. New York: The Free Press.

Old Ethical Principles

THE NEW CORPORATE CULTURE

Address by WILLIAM J. BYRON, *S. J., Distinguished Professor of Management, McDonough School of Business, Georgetown University, Washington, D.C.*
Delivered to the Annual Luncheon of the Duquesne University NMA Students Association, Pittsburgh, Pennsylvania, April 21, 1999

It would be an interesting exercise if you attempted, right now as I begin to address the topic, "Old Ethical Principles for the New Corporate Culture," to jot down on a notepad (on a mental notepad, at least) what you would regard as old or "classic" ethical principles—the time-honored, enduring principles that should always be there to guide the business decision maker.

I've come up with ten and will attempt to apply them to the new corporate culture. Without waiting for you to give me yours, I'm going to proceed to list mine. Here they are: (I) the principle of human dignity; (II) the principle of participation; (III) the principle of integrity; (IV) the principle of fairness (justice); (V) the principle of veracity; (VI) the principle of keeping commitments; (VII) the principle of social responsibility; (VIII) the principle of subsidiarity; (IX) the principle of pursuit of the common good; and (X) the ethical principle of love.

Principles are initiating impulses—they are internalized convictions that produce action. Principles direct your actions and your choices. Your principles help to define who you are. Principles are beginnings, they lead to something.

How do the old ethical principles outlined above play themselves out today in the new corporate culture? First a word about both "culture" and what is new in the "new" corporate culture.

A culture is a set of shared meanings, principles, and values. Values define cultures. Where values are widely shared, you have an identifiable culture. There are as many different cultures as there are distinct sets of shared meanings, principles, and values. This is not to say that everyone in a given culture is the same. No, you have diversity of age, wealth, class, intelligence, education, and responsibility in a given culture where diverse people are unified by a shared belief system, a set of agreed-upon principles, a collection of common values. They literally have a lot in common and thus differ from other people in other settings who hold a lot of other things in common. You notice it in law firms, hospitals, colleges, corporations—wherever people comment on the special "culture" that characterizes the place.

The old corporate culture in America was characterized by values like freedom, individualism, competition, loyalty, thrift, fidelity to contract, efficiency, self-reliance, power, and profit. If not controlled by self, or by social norms, or by public law, pursuit of some of these values could be fueled by unworthy values like greed and the desire to dominate. You have to remember that for some people greed is a value (a supreme value!), so is revenge; the list of negative destructive values could run on.

The new (or newer, or most recent) corporate culture is defined by many, but not all, of these same values, although they are interpreted now somewhat differently. And there are some new values emerging in the new corporate context. Think of this new context in terms of what might be called the new corporate contract.

What was once presumed to be a long-term "relational contract" can no longer be relied upon to sustain an uninterrupted employment relationship over time. What brings employees, even managerial employees, and their employers together in corporate America is now more of a 3 transactional contract; the transaction and the concomitant employment may be short-lived. Both parties to the employment transaction (the new corporate contract) negotiate the arrangement in a new way. The middle manager, for example, wanting to be hired says, in effect,

"If you hold me contingent, I'll hold you contingent." He or she will settle in, but not too comfortably; other options will always be explored, front-end financial considerations will be more important than they were in more stable times, and severance packages will be filled and neatly wrapped before the job begins. Not only will other options be considered as the ink is drying on the new employment contract, but actual offers will be entertained at any time.

Another term for this approach is free-agent management. The free agent will not jump unless a safe landing is assured, and he or she is well aware that the best way to get a new job is to be effective, and appear to be content, in the old one. But contingency, not loyalty, is the thread that ties the contracting parties together today. Let me continue the comparison now with the way things used to be.

Whereas the old (say, fifty years ago) corporate culture would tolerate an employer's not looking much beyond the interests of a firm's shareholders, the new corporate culture is growing comfortable with the notion of "stakeholder" and sees an ethical connection between the firm and not only its shareholders, but all others who have a stake in what that firm does: Employees, suppliers, customers, the broader community, and the physical environment, to name just a few. The corporate outlook is more communitarian, more attentive to the dictates of the common good. There was some of this in the past, a "social compact" between employer and employee that was somewhat paternalistic and relatively free of both the deregulation and foreign competition that have caused much of the present economic dislocation in America, but the dominant value of the old corporate culture was individualism, not communitarianism. There is evidence now that individualism is again on the rise. As that happens, you have to begin to wonder about the fate of a few of those "old" ethical principles.

What is "new" in the new corporate culture is more easily examined these days through the lens of employment contracts (written or unwritten). People have been getting fired since hired hands were first employed to extend an owner's reach and productivity. But now there is something new in the old reality of layoff or separation from payroll. In that "something new" lies the difference between firing and downsizing. There is more to the difference than a simple distinction between blue and white collars. Today's wilted white collars were never so plentiful, and their wearers' hopes for quick and permanent reinstatement have never been so thin.

Typically, organizations are "downsized" at the end of a process that has come to be known as delayering, restructuring, or reengineering. The machine-tool metaphors veil the psychological pain felt by men and women who are set adrift. Not all that long ago, those who bounced back quickly were leaving organizations that were not shrinking, just experiencing turnover. This was before the days of what the Economist of London, in describing the contemporary American economy, called "corporate anorexia."

Multiplication of managerial positions was then taken for granted as technology developed, markets expanded, and the economy grew. Now technology keeps on expanding, many old markets (and lots of new ones) continue to grow along with the economy. But layers of management, like so many rugs, are being pulled out from under the well-shod feet that, until recently, walked with confidence along the corridors of corporate America. Now they are out and looking—many could be looking for quite awhile unless they understand themselves and the new corporate culture. As their organizations shrink, displaced managers themselves have to expand personally. They have to enlarge their outlook and their personal ensemble of employable skills.

Now with all of this said, I want to line up the old ethical principles over against the ethical challenges presented by this new corporate culture.

I. The Principle of Human Dignity.

This is the bedrock principle of both personal and social ethics. In the new corporate culture, human dignity is taking a beating. In some corporations, workers at all levels are being treated as if they were disposable parts. Although employees will, regrettably, but for sound economic reasons, continue to be separated from their jobs, they must never be viewed by those making the downsizing decisions as disposable parts.

II. The Principle of Participation.

Every human person in any workplace has a right to have some say in the decisions that affect his or her livelihood. To be shut out of all discussion is to be denied respect for one's human dignity. The ethical thing to do in this new corporate culture, in cases either of layoff or of career continuation in the same organization, is to involve the employee in planning and in the execution of the plan. This means preparation for separation, should that have to happen; it also means enhancing the "value added" potential and the productivity of employees who will remain.

III. The Principle of Integrity.

Honesty is always the best policy on both sides of the employer-employee hyphen; it is also the best policy to guide relations with all the organization's stockholders.

It is one thing to take severe measures to guarantee the survival of the enterprise, it is quite another to deceive others and even worse to reduce employment in order to improve a balance sheet or boost a stock price. After downsizing, some who remain and occupy positions of power at the top of the organization will benefit economically; they should be honest about the extent of that benefit and the uses they intend to make of what might well be regarded as a windfall.

IV. The Principle of Fairness (Justice).

Everyone knows what fairness is. At least we think we know, and we are usually convinced that we are absolutely right. We just know it! Sometimes, a few additional facts or the recognition of our own biases will prompt us to reset our fairness clock, but we have a way of just knowing when unfair treatment occurs.

A strong sense of justice will safeguard a person of integrity from violating any trust. If no trusts are violated, if no injustice is involved, a downsizing in response to economic necessity can be justified. But there is such a deep feeling of injustice, of unfair treatment, in so many downsized corners of our new corporate culture that those in control must examine their corporate conscience for evidence of injustice done to millions of separated employees in recent years.

V. The Principle of Veracity.

Why "veracity" when you've just noted that "integrity" belong on your list? Integrity means living truthfully, while veracity, of course, means speaking truthfully.

Veracity is truthfullness, and the truth will always set you free. There may be unpleasant consequences for you if you tell the truth. But, as the saying goes, "the truth will always out," and the truth teller will always have a place to stand, a soul to claim, and a peace of mind that can never be taken away. Truth not just when convenient, truth in all circumstances is the only compass that works in an age of ambiguity. Truth telling, as difficult as it may be at times, is the only way to preserve an ethical corporate culture.

VI. The Principle of Keeping Commitments.

Here again the issue of trust is in the foreground. Inevitably, when journalistic accounts of the new corporate culture touch upon the human side of downsizing, you will read that corporate loyalty is a thing of the past. Corporations no longer keep their commitments, the story usually goes. And often that is exactly the case.

Commitments are the cement of social relationships. If commitments are kept in the workplace, morale and a sense of security will be high. If a firm simply cannot make commitments to its employees, uncertainty, anxiety, and the individual's commitment to self-preservation will increase in the best of hearts and the best of workplaces. Since fewer and fewer firms are able in this new corporate culture to promise permanent employment, closer and completely honest communication is all the more necessary if trust is to be preserved in the workplace.

VII. The Principle of Corporate Social Responsibility.

This principle relates to the economic, the legal, the ethical, and the positive discretionary or philanthropic categories of a firm's behavior. The good corporate citizen will make a profit and abide by the law. Just to remain within the law, however, is not the sum and substance of corporate responsibility; not everything that is required by ethics is also required by law.

Corporate ethical responsibility stretches all the way from respect for individual human dignity (in employees, customers, suppliers, colleagues, competitors) all the way out to respect for the physical environment that is necessary to sustain life on this planet.

Countless ethical considerations come to mind in the context of downsizing and this new corporate culture of economic uncertainty and contingent employment. One that I see as crucial belongs in the category of "employability" and applies to both employer and employee. Keeping an employee employable is an ethical responsibility of both employer and employee in the new corporate culture.

In a knowledge economy (not simply an "information economy") like ours in this new corporate culture, the ethical imperative points not only to the care of casualities, but also to the advancement of education for the cultivation of new ideas, new creativity, new technology, new products, services, and eventually, jobs.

VIII. The Principle of Subsidiarity.

Those who say the care of economic casualties and the creation of jobs should be "left to government," risk violating the principle of subsidiarity, which would allow neither decisions nor actions at a higher level of organization that could be taken just as effectively and efficiently at a lower level. This principle would push decision making down to lower levels, but sometimes government must act in the interest of the common good. And there will be instances when only government can address an issue properly and effectively.

The principle of subsidiarity should also apply in private sector organizations, in ordinary workplaces. This ties in with the principle of participation and, as is so often the case, is reducible to the principle of human dignity. Individuals are not to be ground under by impersonal, anonymous decision makers at higher levels in the organization.

IX. The Principal of Pursuit of the Common Good

Is a basic principle of ethical behavior; it is a bedrock principle like the principle of human dignity. Without it, social chaos would prevail. The "Common Good" is a catch-all phrase that describes an environment that is supportive of the development of human potential while safeguarding the community against individual excesses.

It looks to the general good, to the good of the many over against the interests of the one.

It is important that there be agreement in the community that the common good should always prevail over individual, personal interests. To promote and protect the common good is the reason why governments exist—a point worth noting here just after a discussion of the principle of subsidiarity, the principle that has a way of keeping government in its proper place.

X. Love.

One reason why the old ethical principles have continuing relevance in this new corporate culture, is the fact that they are rooted in a human nature that does not change all that much from age to age. Underlying human nature in any circumstance is the law of love. The challenge today is not to find a replacement for the law of love, which is always applicable, of course, to God, self, family, neighbor, and workplace associates, the challenge is just to let love happen in this new, but still very human corporate culture. The challenge is also there to be clear about the meaning of love; it means sacrifice, the willingness to be and do for others.

Now go back to your mental notepad and compare the "old" ethical principles you listed there with the ones outlined in this presentation. It would be regrettable, wouldn't it, if all those old principles just grow older as newer and greater challenges appear in the corporate culture and in the other activity centers of contemporary American life. That could happen. It will certainly happen if those who still recognize the old principles do nothing to apply them.

Five Forces Redefining Business

Profits from Principle

Corporations are finding that social responsibility pays off. This realization will change the very nature of business.

By Bennett Daviss

Ray Anderson built Interface, Inc., a billion-dollar international carpet manufacturer based in Atlanta, on a simple precept: A corporation's purpose is to earn a good return for shareowners while complying with the law. Then, in 1994, during a struggle to regain lost market share and shore up his company's sagging stock price, Anderson read eco-entrepreneur Paul Hawken's book, *The Ecology of Commerce*, which documents industry's profligate squandering of natural resources and sketches a vision of environmentally sustainable business.

Anderson took it personally. His company was chewing up more than 500 million pounds of raw material each year and excreting more than 900 tons of air pollutants, 600 million gallons of wastewater, and 10,000 tons of trash.

Reading the book was Anderson's epiphany—"a spear in my chest"—the CEO recalls. It also put a spur in his backside: Anderson set out to make his corporation's 26 factories on four continents the world's first environmentally sustainable manufacturing enterprise, recycling everything possible, releasing no pollutants, and sending nothing to landfills. "We're treating all fossil fuel energy as waste to be eliminated through efficiencies and shifts to renewable energy," he says.

Idealistic? Definitely. Unbusinesslike? Definitely not.

"In just over two years, we've become 23% more efficient in converting raw stuff into sales dollars—and we've only scratched the surface," Anderson notes. That efficiency has cut not only waste, but also a cumulative $40 million in costs. The savings, which were projected to grow to $76 million by the end of 1998, helped Interface make the winning low bid in 1997 to carpet The Gap Inc.'s new world headquarters in San Francisco. The Gap invited Interface to bid specifically because of the carpet company's environmental initiatives.

"We've found a new way to win in the marketplace," Anderson believes, "one that doesn't come at the expense of our grandchildren or the earth, but at the expense of the inefficient competitor."

Anderson's crusade is one example among countless others proving a new rule in business: Profits and social responsibility are becoming inseparable.

Helping Workers Work

Just ask Donna Klein, director of work/life initiatives for Washington, D.C., based hotelier Marriott International. Her industry depends on the low-wage workers who change sheets and scrub tubs. They often live below the poverty line and spend less than a year on the job.

The company couldn't afford to simply hike wages in an effort to retain more of its approximately 150,000 low-wage workers. Casting about for a way to reduce turnover, and thereby the extra costs involved in training and supervising new employees, Klein discovered that the workers were usually driven from their jobs by personal prob-

INTERFACE, INC.

Ray Anderson of Interface saved his carpet manufacturing company $40 million through measures such as recycling and cutting waste.

lems: domestic violence, scrapes with immigration authorities, becoming homeless, or an inability to master English, among others. Supervisors reported spending as much as half their working time trying to help employees straighten out their personal lives.

In 1992, Klein set up a 24-hour, multilingual hotline staffed by trained social workers whom hotel employees could call for help and referrals to aid agencies. By 1997, the project had cut Marriott's turnover to 35%, compared with the hotel industry's average of 100% or more.

The hotline is handling more than 2,000 employee calls each year. "It costs well over $1 million a year to run it, but it saves us more than $3 million a year in hiring, training, and other costs," Klein says. In 1997, Klein's office documented 600 cases in which the hotline was the key factor that kept an employee from quitting, saving an estimated $750,000 for that year, she reports. "We've documented increases in productivity, morale, and better relations with managers and co-workers as a result of the hotline. But we're not able to quantify the gain in managers' time. The hotline frees them to focus on customer service instead of employees' problems."

Such examples are legion. After the Malden Mills factory in Lowell, Massachusetts, burned during the 1995 Christmas season, owner Aaron Feuerstein continued to pay workers' salaries and benefits until a new plant was built. In the new factory, worker productivity reportedly improved by 25% and quality defects have dropped by two-thirds. Although some of the gains are attributable to newer equipment, Feuerstein believes it's "a direct result of the good will of our people." San Francisco's Thanksgiving Coffee Company invests a share of its revenues in community development among the Central American villages that grow its beans, ensuring loyal suppliers and reasonable prices during times of small harvests. Mercedes-Benz has designed its new S-class sedans and 500/600SEC luxury coupes to be entirely recyclable, giving it and its dealers a new source of low-cost used parts.

The evidence that social responsibility swells profits appears in studies as well as stories. Returns for the Domini 400 Social Index—a roster of 400 publicly traded, socially responsible firms tracked by the Boston investment advisory firm of Kinder, Lydenberg, Domini & Co.—have outpaced those for the Standard & Poor's 500 for each of the last three years. In 1992, UCLA business professor David Lewin surveyed 188 companies and found that "companies that increased their community involvement were more likely to show an improved financial picture over a two-year time period." A 1995 Vanderbilt University analysis found that in eight of 10 cases low-polluting companies financially outperform their dirtier competitors. And the U.S. General Accounting Office reports that employee stock-

INTERFACE, INC.

Skylights supply daytime lighting at Interface's new plant.

option plans and participatory management schemes hike productivity an average of 52%.

"We're going through a mind-change," says Marjorie Kelly, editor of the Minneapolis-based *Business Ethics* magazine. "Most of us still carry around the subliminal idea that ruthless behavior beats the competition and good behavior is money out of pocket. But the data shows that the traditional idea is wrong. Social responsibility makes sense in purely capitalistic terms."

Five Forces Redefining Business

Conservative economists, most notably Nobel laureate Milton Friedman at the University of Chicago, have long argued that the sole mission of a corporation is to maximize profits for the benefit of shareholders and that spending on social causes violates that prime directive. But the new marketplace is proving that profits can best be maximized by embracing, rather than forswearing, social concerns. The idea that profitability and social awareness are not antagonistic but interdependent redefines the purpose of business.

Five forces are converging to shape business's new social imperative: consumer conscience, socially conscious investing, the global media, special-interest activism, and expectations of corporate leadership.

1 First, today's consumers have learned by experience that societies and economies—like nature—are closed systems. Automobile exhaust doesn't disappear into the sky; it transforms the atmosphere and consequently our climate. When employers don't make health insurance available to workers, the cost of health care for those workers isn't saved, but is shared among all of us in higher health-care costs and taxes that support public emergency rooms.

Two decades ago, if a company made cars with exploding gas tanks or marketed U.S.-banned pesticides in Third World countries, it could view these as purely financial issues. Then, as the flower children of the 1960s became the consumers of the 1980s, such issues were recast in a moral light. Those consumers began speaking out—with their voices, their votes, and their wallets.

The result: By 1992, a survey by the Public Relations Society of America identified social-issues marketing—that is, celebrating a company's commitment to public issues as well as to its products and customers—as the leader among the industry's 10 hottest trends. The same year, the quarterly *Business and Society Review* reported in its summer issue that "corporate social responsibility is now a tidal wave of the future."

"People judge corporations today by their social performance as much as by their financial performance—their impact on the environment, their role in aggravating or relieving social problems," explains Richard Torrenzano, president of the Torren-

Reflective surfaces on the outside of Interface's new plant minimize the need for air conditioning, thereby reducing the company's energy consumption.

INTERFACE, INC.

zano Group, a New York consulting firm. "People indicate by their purchases not just the value of a product or service, but how they view the company's role in their communities." Because ethical probity shapes consumer choices, a company's deportment has become a crucial bottom-line concern.

For example, a 1980s boycott of Burger King for its use of beef raised on pasture slashed from South American rain forests damaged sales enough to force the company to change its purchasing habits. On the other hand, New Hampshire's Stonyfield Farm yogurt company has been able to expand its share of the stagnant retail yogurt market by touting its steady financial support for organic and family farms.

2 Consumers' new conscience has complemented, and cultivated, the second factor—the rise of socially conscious investing. The movement gained momentum during the 1970s and 1980s as institutions and investment funds were pressured to shed their South African holdings to protest apartheid. According to the Social Investment Forum, a New York-based nonprofit information clearinghouse, in the last 10 years the value of U.S. socially aware investments has grown from $50 billion to more than $500 billion and is one of the financial industry's strongest growth areas.

"If I don't invest in companies with actual or potential social and environmental liabilities, I'm reducing my risk of owning a company that suddenly owes huge fines or settlements in damage suits," says Hugh Kelley, president of the Social Responsibility Investment Group, an Atlanta advisory firm. Neither will his companies be rocked by boycotts and bad publicity. "Those kinds of problems go right to the bottom line."

3 Those potential problems are exacerbated by the third factor: a competitive, unsparing, and technologically endowed media—especially television—that makes once-abstract concepts like global warming or sweatshop labor personal to consumers. Once discovered, a company's ethical lapse can now be flashed to news outlets and brokerage firms globally before a CEO can hurry back from lunch. "Journalists today are much more sophisticated," Torrenzano adds. "They ask tougher questions, and they give no slack when someone has a problem. It motivates companies."

> A company's deportment has become a crucial bottom-line concern.

4 Fourth, zealous special-interest groups have become deft at using the media to link corporate practices with social and environmental problems and solutions. Burger King's troubles began in 1986 when the upstart Rainforest Action Network called on the world to boycott the chain, claiming it used "rain-forest beef" grazed on pastures carved from South America's imperiled tropical forests. At first, the company ignored the allegation. Within two years, Whopper sales slumped—as much as 17% by some reports—and the burger giant capitulated with a statement forswearing ecologically incorrect meat. "Activists are becoming increasingly effective in forcing corporations to cooperate in their vision of social change," noted the late Rafael Pagán, a pioneering corporate social-policy adviser.

5 Fifth, the public is transferring its expectations of leadership in solving social problems from government to business. Over the past two decades, the failure of federal "Great Society" programs and increasing partisan gridlock has exacerbated public demand for action against society's lingering ills. As a result, while Congress dithers, commercial firms pressured by consumers' new concerns are enacting social policy ranging from environmental cleanup to flexible work policies, from Third World economic development to new product safety standards. By those actions, companies not only gain a competitive edge but also ratify a new moral compact between business and society.

Increasingly, companies are embracing that new compact deliberately. The San Francisco-based group Business for Social Responsibility has grown from 45 members in 1993 to more than 1,400 today. "The companies joining the group aren't just the Ben and Jerrys of the world," says charter member Gary Hirshberg, co-founder of Stonyfield Farm. "We're getting divisions of Kraft, the Fortune 500, and investment bankers out to make a killing who recognize that this is the way to success. We don't just have the oddball New Age companies any more. We've got the suits." BSR's members now include giants such as General Motors and Coca-Cola and boast combined annual sales of more than $1 trillion—a seventh of the entire U.S. economy.

"These companies aren't joining just to say they're members," says Cliff Feigenbaum, editor and publisher of the *Green Money Letter*, a quarterly newsletter tracking the new business conscience. "They're joining because they want help."

Drawing a New Balance

Companies that venture into this new territory are learning that profiting by principle demands an unequivocal commitment to both conscience and cash flow. But the new compact also is forcing companies to calibrate a new and delicate—even precarious—balance between the two. Consumers United Insurance Company and The Body Shop have provided object lessons.

Founded in 1969, Consumers United was a company ahead of its time. It offered unisex insurance rates and covered policyholders' unwed domestic partners before either became a public issue. Founder Jim Gibbons turned full ownership of the firm over to the employees, who controlled corporate policy and could overrule his decisions with a majority vote. The wage structure ensured that the lowest-paid worker would be able to support a family of four. This experiment in controlled chaos thrived, and by 1986 the company managed $47 million in invested assets.

Gibbons deployed his clients' funds with the same earnest idealism with which he managed the company. The firm bought 26 vacant acres in Washington, D.C., and built low-income housing. It funded a local youth group and promised each of the 70 children who joined that, if they stayed drug-free and didn't make babies, Consumers United would pay their way through college.

Such largesse drew the attention of insurance industry regulators in Delaware, the state in which Consumers had incorporated. The regulators weren't convinced that bighearted gestures such as paying poor kids' college bills guaranteed enough future cash to pay claims. Finally convinced that Gibbons wasn't being prudent enough with policyholders' money, the regulators felt they had no alternative but to seek a court order declaring Consumers insolvent. In 1993, the state seized control of its assets and shut the company down. "It provides a cautionary tale for any business that pays more attention to its social mission than to its bottom line," *Business Ethics* writer Bill Gifford noted in an obituary article.

If Consumers did too much of a good thing, The Body Shop did too little. In the 1980s, promotional materials for the British-based body-care products company featured photos of co-founder Anita Roddick sitting in rain-forest clearings dickering with natives to buy their renewable products. It avowed that none of its products were tested on animals. Body Shop catalog covers promoted progressive causes. Roddick and husband Gordon became celebrated symbols of business with a conscience.

Then, in 1994, a six-page expose in the pages of *Business Ethics* detailed evidence that native peoples supplied less than 1% of the company's raw materials, that many of its ingredients were being tested on animals (although not by The Body Shop itself), and that its "natural" products included generous amounts of petroleum. The article also hinted that the corporation's well-publicized concern for social betterment was prompted as much by greed as by conscience. After the public glimpsed the gap between rhetoric and reality, the company's stock prices plunged and sales slumped.

"They were making claims that didn't exactly match their practices, and it came back to bite them," says Dan McKenna, president of Principle Profits Asset Management in Amherst, Massachusetts, an investment advisory firm serving the socially conscious. "They saw their financial position suffer when the reality didn't live up to the image."

Shoe giant Nike is busy teaching itself a similar lesson. Widely accused of using child labor in Third World sweatshops to make its high-priced sneakers, the company has launched a number of initiatives to improve the lot of foreign workers. In October 1996, Nike tried to polish its image by releasing an independent study showing that its workers in Indonesia and Vietnam were buying VCRs and otherwise living well. Three weeks later, an audit by accounting firm Ernst & Young detailing unsafe working conditions in one of Nike's Vietnamese factories made the front page of the *New York Times*. According to one report, in 1996 Nike paid Michael Jordan more for his endorsement—at least $30 million—than it did its 19,000 non-U.S. factory workers combined.

"That can be read as a statement of the way Nike balances marketing with human dignity," McKenna says. "It seems that Nike hasn't yet committed to the full meaning of social responsibility."

Business Ethics editor Marjorie Kelly agrees. "Social responsibility can't follow the catalytic converter model," she admonishes. "In a car, you can leave the engine unchanged and just bolt on a new part to take out the pollutants. But in a business you can't just open an ethics office down the hall and leave the company's culture and practices unchanged. A genuine commitment to social responsibility transforms not just what a company does, but also how it thinks."

What's Ahead: Four Trends

That commitment will continue to be tested in the next decade. Today's demands and pressures for corporate social leadership are redrafting the tacit contract between business and society. Four trends are shaping the terms of the new covenant:

1. Good works and financial gain must balance. During the cash-rich 1980s, socially involved corporations and pressure groups coined the term "the double bottom line" to describe a company's attempts to better its profits and its community at the same time. But the '80s are over and the double bottom line still has to be derived from a single balance sheet. In the future, each company will define its social role in terms of self-interest and fund good works only to the extent that the company gains financially from them.

For those reasons, social and environmental initiatives will focus largely within companies themselves. For example, a corporation may be willing to underwrite an alternative-energy program, but only in its own factory and only if the scheme doesn't add to costs, compromise product quality, or lengthen delivery times. A proposal for an onsite day-care center, flextime program, or employee gym will win favor only by showing evidence that it will reduce turnover and absenteeism enough to pay its own way.

Privately owned companies will have more flexibility but still must align social programs to profits. Stonyfield Farm plants forests to offset its factory's carbon-dioxide emissions—an investment that also strengthens its brand identity and consumer loyalty in an increasingly competitive industry.

2. Activists gain leverage by becoming advisers, not adversaries. Because financial self-interest will circumscribe corporations' social initiatives, the role of the activist is expanding from adversary to adviser. As long as there are corporations, there will be a place for corporate watchdogs. But in the years ahead, activists will gain greatest leverage by working directly with companies to help executives make the links between profit and social and environmental probity—helping them see the connections between life-cycle product engineering and cost cutting, or between better treatment of workers and money saved from turnover, lawsuits, boycotts, government fines, and public-relations expense. Adversarial groups will still prod with sticks, but activist-advisers will entice companies by dangling the carrots of cost savings and competitive advantage.

3. Corporations will be audited socially just as they now are financially. Progressive companies have begun to hire specialized consultants to rate their social and environmental performance; in the future, shareholders and activists will place all corporations under greater pressure to open their doors to these outside consultants. The ISO 9000 standards for industrial quality management, promulgated by the International Organization for Standardization (ISO), sparked the ISO 14000 standards for environmental systems management. Recently, the Council on Economic Priorities promulgated the SA 8000 standards (for "social accountability"), setting forth criteria by which companies' treatment of domestic and foreign workers can be assessed, rated, and publicized. Look for outside social and environmental auditing to become a new norm as companies seek to ingratiate themselves with savvy and discerning consumers.

4. Corporate social identity will be as important as brand identity. As people come to expect corporations to take a larger social role, companies will develop a social identity that consumers respond to as strongly and readily as they do a brand identity.

That shift links a corporation's behavior to its product image and, therefore, to its profits. When Texaco's corporate culture was accused of racial prejudice, millions of people boycotted the firm's gas stations. After Johnson & Johnson's open, thorough, and cooperative response to deadly tamperings with its Tylenol tablets, the pain remedy actually increased its market share.

As these and other companies have learned, a corporation will not be able to choose whether to have a social identity; the public will fashion one for it based on a company's social and environmental actions—or lack thereof. Companies sculpt brand identities by manipulating images in the public mind, but businesses will find their social identity harder to control. There are too many prying journalists, activists, and shareholders to avoid.

As companies learn that social or environmental gaffes gnaw at profits, they also will realize that there is only one way to guard against the financial losses that these kinds of blunders can lead to. Companies must "walk the talk": From the boardroom to the loading dock, they must adopt policies and practices that enact the new, nobler norms of corporate conduct that corporate precedents and public expectations are imposing.

Traditionalists have long argued that business's only social obligation is to maximize profit. The new social contract between business and society inverts that principle: In the new century, companies will grow their profits only by embracing their new role as the engine of positive social and environmental change.

About the Author

Bennett Daviss is an independent journalist who writes, speaks, and consults on education reform, socially responsible business, and other issues of sustainability. His articles have appeared in more than 40 magazines on four continents. With Nobel physicist Kenneth Wilson, he is co-author of the book *Redesigning Education.* His address is Walpole Valley Road, Walpole, New Hampshire 03608.

Portions of this article first appeared in *Ambassador Magazine*. Reprinted courtesy of *Ambassador Magazine* and Trans World Airlines.

Learning IT right from wrong

As universities add computer ethics to the curriculum, observers want to know how the new ethically enriched computer science grads change the industry.

By Linda Pliagas

A SYSTEMS ANALYST becomes aware of illegal activity—fraud, money laundering, evasion of taxes—at his company. After a late night of work, the analyst breaks the network's security code and examines confidential files. A few days later, an envelope containing several thousand dollars appears on his desk.

Elsewhere a software developer spends months working on a new program. She devises a scheme to take vengeance upon those who illicitly copy her code. Her program's protection feature allows only one back-up copy. Attempts to make additional copies corrupt the source disks and wipe clean any accessible hard disks or floppies.

Scary? Computer science students are tackling these and other moral dilemmas in computer ethics courses on college campuses this fall. The problems cited above are from *Computer Ethics: Cautionary Tales and Ethical Dilemmas in Computing* by Tom Forester and Perry Morrison, published by Massachusetts Institute of Technology.

Universities have heard the ethics call. To earn the Computer Science Accreditation Board seal of approval, a university's computer science curriculum must include "sufficient coverage of social and ethical implications of computing"—a significant evolution since the first computer science curriculum taught in 1968.

Ethics go to work

Cynthia Esty took a computer ethics course in the late 1980s to fulfill the criteria for her degree in business administration. Esty, now director of strategic alliances at digitalESP, an e-business solutions provider, in Raleigh, N.C., had no idea how the principles of technological integrity would dictate her career.

Esty decides with which companies digitalESP will partner. Part of this process includes examining the morals and values found in the potential partner's organization. "We incorporate [ethics] in everything we do. It's woven into our corporate environment. We don't want to work with people we don't trust." If Esty feels a company's principles are not up to par, the business is downgraded to vendor.

On the other hand, Michael Cohen admits he has yet to face an ethical dilemma as a software architect at Roanoke Technology, an online procurement software leasing company, in Roanoke Rapids, N.C. This May, Cohen earned two bachelor's degrees: one in computer science, the other in mathematical sciences.

As part of his studies at Johns Hopkins University, in Baltimore, Cohen took a four-week computer ethics course. At the first class meeting, Cohen and the other students were building a philosophical framework from which to analyze issues of piracy, hacking, Internet privacy, and encryption regulations.

Despite addressing such high-profile problems, Cohen has yet to see how school and work intertwine on the ethics front. "I have only been working for a short time so I wouldn't say that the ethics coursework has come much into play in my professional life," he said.

Cohen's boss has a different take. The new breed of ethically enriched techies has left a mark at the office, CEO David L. Smith says.

After realizing the company needed to monitor e-mail habits, Smith says his first inclination was to simply read the e-mail of employees he suspected were goofing off on company time. But instead of stepping into a privacy and ethics quagmire, "two of our programmers put their heads together and came up with a way that made that unnecessary," Smith says.

The morally driven solution led to the company installing a system to warn management when an employee sends or receives a certain amount of e-mail to or from the same address. This gives the manager, Smith says, an opportunity to counsel the employee without having to read the e-mail.

Many business owners, computer and software experts, and academics agree that having high ethical standards is important for future IT professionals to possess. "Today's students have incredibly powerful tools at their disposal—unprecedented technological advances empowering them to change our society, for better or worse. It is absolutely essential that they be schooled in the fundamentals of ethics to ensure their skills are applied appropriately," says Mark Bunting, host and executive producer of the nationally syndicated television series "The Computer Guy" and founder of Sky Television, a producer of technology-related television and in-flight programming.

Right and wrong, just in time

So just when did morality become entwined with the computer profession? C. Dianne Martin, Ph.D., a former computer ethics professor, recalls 1991 as the year professionals and others began to discuss the implications of not educating IT professionals about ethical and social responsibilities.

In the nine years since, the IT industry has changed dramatically and trust has become a real IT issue—and an industry within the industry. Martin works in the new "trust" field. She defines corporate policies and practices for GeoTrust, a Portland, Ore.-based company that provides buyers and sellers with access to an e-commerce participant's trust profile.

Martin is not alone in charging the industry with ethical responsibilities. Major players have entered into the discussion. Martin says a new computer science curriculum will be drawn up next year by the Association for Computing Machinery and the Institute of Electrical and Electronics Engineers.

George Mason University, in Fairfax, Va., isn't waiting for a new curriculum directive. The school requires all computer science students to take a computer ethics course.

Tamara Maddox, GMU computer ethics professor, says it's imperative for students to be aware of technical virtues. Undoubtedly, they will someday be faced with dilemmas that may redefine Information Age values. "They will not be aware of how to handle these issues if they have never thought of them before," she says.

"When you let the schedule change the quality of software you develop, that is an ethical issue."

—Don Gotterbarn, East Tennessee State University

Maddox, a lawyer and former software developer, wants her students to be prepared. Her Computer Ethics 105 students must participate in group discussions and projects and write research papers. Topics range from piracy to negligence in software testing, and Internet freedom of speech vs. pornography, which she describes as "an age-old issue with a new face."

Development of low quality software is a real ethical problem for the IT industry, says Don Gotterbarn, Ph.D., professor of computer and information science at East Tennessee State University, in Johnson City, Tenn. "When you let the schedule change the quality of software you develop, that is an ethical issue," he says. For example, says Gotterbarn, two years ago a computer expert did not program an incubator thermostat properly. The inaccuracy reportedly resulted in the death of two infants.

Although such a high profile example is emotionally charged, GeoTrust's Martin says you do not have to reach that far to find other examples of how ethics have played out in the industry. Think back to January of this year.

The Y2K bug is a classic lesson of the lack of social and ethical awareness among the computing industry professionals, Martin says. Years ago, says the former computer ethics professor, developers thought little about future implications of their work: Would airplanes be able to fly? What would the financial ramifications be? This lack of foresight brought problems of global significance.

Martin's academic colleague, Gotterbarn, sees another important event in the ethical history of the IT industry—powerful and fast computers in the hands of nonprofessionals. This, Gotterbarn says, has made an enormous impact on how the discipline of computer science is now being taught. "We used to teach computing in only technical terms—devoid of humanity. But they [students] did not get an immediate sense that their computing affects people. Every decision a computer professional makes impacts other people, either colleagues or laymen," Gotterbarn says.

Classroom antics

Gotterbarn remembers that when computer ethics courses first hit campuses, stock fraud made up the majority of the classes' "wow stories." Now technological developments in computing have impacted where computing power can be applied, and this has led to an enormous change in the way ethics is discussed in classes, he adds.

Just a few years ago, professors would cover a single, neat issue every week—equity, hacking, and security. Today deeper levels are uncovered. "Now we go into a little bit of philosophy for the nonphilosopher," GeoTrust's Martin explains.

Often "values clarification" is first on the class agenda. Students must realize, Gotterbarn says, that they arrive in class holding their own standards and ethics. Then with the ethics lightbulb on, the computer professionals' code of ethics is introduced. Once students have grasped a framework, social scenarios are given. Then they can begin to uncover if something is "not quite right."

Preventing problems should be the focal point in computer ethics courses, Roanoke Technology's Smith says. With his e-mail dilemma, he realized that most managers do not want to monitor personal communications from work. But if productivity falls, they have a responsibility to find out why. He calls this work problem a "two-edged sword."

Ethics instruction in computer science departments will undoubtedly continue. Martin hopes professors will teach the course in a more integrative and robust way than in recent history. "Ethics should be taught in many classes instead of being solely focused as a separate course," Martin says. Experts agree that by having standards of conduct ingrained into the computer science students' minds, the wish of every professor, employer, and manager will come true. Errors will be self-caught before they develop into moral catastrophes.

Will an education in ethics bring an end to the computer industry's dilemmas? No, Sky Television's Bunting says. "There will always be an element of our society who crosses the line and disregards such boundaries."

Linda Pliagas is a free-lance writer in Los Angeles. Contact her at npliagas@aol.com.

Tech Executives Devote Energy To Green Causes

By Jim Carlton
Staff Reporter of THE WALL STREET JOURNAL

BERKELEY, Calif.—Bob Epstein's campaign to get technology executives like himself to save the environment starts at his home here, where he has just replaced all the lights with more efficient compact fluorescent bulbs.

In so doing, Mr. Epstein, who co-founded database giant Sybase Inc. and two other start-ups and has a personal net worth in the multimillions, figures he is saving an estimated 5% in household energy consumption. That frugality makes him something of an anomaly in California, where many residents continue to burn their Christmas lights at full blast, despite dwindling power reserves.

Mr. Epstein is among a growing number of high-tech titans using their green to go green. "I want to do my part, and then some," says Mr. Epstein, who preaches energy conservation not only for himself but for everybody as a way to lessen the pressure on natural resources. Seeking causes such as the environment to escape what Mr. Epstein calls the "tedium" of just making money, these techies are applying some of the same energy and intensity they used in creating businesses to attack problems ranging from global warming to deforestation. Along the way, they also are gaining substantial tax and public-relations benefits as well as networking opportunities.

Microsoft Corp. co-founder Paul Allen, for instance, has set up a foundation to preserve forests that last year helped buy 600 acres of virgin woods in Washington state, his home. Intel Corp. co-founder Gordon Moore and his wife, Betty, have committed more than $30 million to the Conservation International environmental group, which is based in Washington, D.C., and studies ways to preserve biodiversity in the Amazon and elsewhere. After selling his Aldus Corp. to Adobe Systems Inc., company founder Paul Brainerd has set up the Brainerd Foundation, which supports Western environmental causes including efforts to halt logging in Alaska's rain forests and to protect wild lands in the Rockies.

And like any good technology trend, the eco-movement has swept into the Silicon Valley party scene. In September, Robert F. Kennedy Jr., son of the late U.S. senator from New York, held court over what Mr. Epstein calls the first "EcoSalon" in Silicon Valley, a soiree at the Atherton, Calif., mansion of Silicon Valley attorney Alan Austin and his wife, Marianne. Mr. Kennedy is a senior attorney for the Natural Resources Defense Council, one of the biggest conservation groups in the U.S. He asked about 100 attendees for their time and money.

After pointing out that the tech business is among the cleanest of industries, Mr. Kennedy told the gathering of chief executives and financiers: "I have thought for years we should be coming to Silicon Valley and knocking on your doors." (While software manufacturers have long been considered to have more environmentally sound practices than older industries, chip producers have only recently gained credit for adopting cleaner manufacturing techniques.)

Mr. Epstein, who recently joined the board of the New York-based NRDC, put on the EcoSalon through a group he helped launch in June called Environmental Entrepreneurs, or E2. With about 100 members donating at least $1,000 each, E2's goal is to raise more than $1 million for the NRDC's environmental programs. Chapters of E2 have been formed in Silicon Valley and New York, with a third planned for next year in Los Angeles.

Sipping chardonnay and merlot and munching finger foods, tycoons in turtlenecks and loafers huddled under chandeliers in the Austin reception room and chatted about their common love of nature. "I hike in the Desolation Wilderness [near Lake Tahoe] every summer and grew up in Tennessee going to the lake, so this is a cause that I can support," said Gary Reback, chief executive of the Scotts Valley, Calif., Web telephony firm Voxeo Corp.

"A lot of us are looking at ways we can benefit mankind, and do something other than just spend money," adds Charles Berger, chairman of AdForce Inc., a Cupertino, Calif., Internet advertising firm.

Few of the executives have devoted as much energy to the environment as Mr. Epstein, a wiry 48-year-old who in 1980 co-founded his first start-up, a pioneering database-maker called Britton Lee while finishing his doctorate in electrical engineering and computer science at the University of California at Berkeley. In 1984, Mr. Epstein and a colleague, Mark Hoffman, started Sybase out of Mr. Epstein's previous home in Berkeley. My main insight "was that once networks start to happen, you have to have software to manage those networks," Mr. Epstein recalls.

Mr. Epstein rode Sybase's meteoric rise to about $1 billion in annual sales over the next 15 years, stepping down in 1999 to devote more time to another of his start-ups: Colorado Micro-Display Inc., a Boulder, Colo., concern he co-founded in 1996 to make chips for computer monitors.

Over the last 10 years, Mr. Epstein says he has become increasingly concerned about global warming and other environmental threats caused by world-wide industrialization. With two teenage sons, he says, I realize "life will be worse for my children if I don't do something."

Still, Mr. Epstein hasn't lost sight of the profit motive and believes it is important for environmental groups to think in business terms. He has invested in and advises two high-tech start-ups—LocusPocus Inc. and Telleo Inc.—that develop products aimed at environmental activism. LocusPocus, based in Berkeley, sells a program called "Get Active," which helps environmentalists conduct mass-mailing campaigns. Telleo, San Jose, Calif., makes a software program that helps nonprofit groups as well as small businesses more efficiently use the Internet.

Mr. Epstein became involved with both those companies through contacts he made setting up the E2 group in Silicon Valley. He hopes to persuade other executives to embrace the environment, while possibly making money at it, too. "All environmental policies," Mr. Epstein says, "are economic at their core."

Though he is in the company of greenies, he rarely strays far from his entrepreneurial roots.

Mr. Epstein used his business skills to pick an environmental organization to support. He considered joining the Sierra Club, for instance, but found it too driven by personalities. The team-based approach of the NRDC was more to his liking and more like Sybase, he adds. He joined the New York-based group's board of trustees last December, immersing himself in NRDC campaigns such as a drive for greater energy efficiency.

Earlier this fall, for example, he spent the morning assessing the NRDC's participation in scientific projects at the U.S. Energy Department's Lawrence Berkeley National Laboratory to reduce the amount of energy used in household appliances such as ceiling fans and lighting fixtures. He pulls up to the lab here in his new, silver Toyota Prius, a hybrid-fuel vehicle that runs on both electricity and gasoline. His was one of the first delivered in the San Francisco Bay area.

Two bearded scientists in jeans lead Mr. Epstein, wearing tennis shoes and khakis, on a swift tour of the lab. "You'll love this, Bob," Noah Horowitz, a senior scientist for the NRDC, says with a smile as he and Erik Page, his counterpart at the Berkeley lab, show off a prototype they've developed for light bulbs that instead of screwing in can be plugged in and freely adjusted and directed. That enables the bulbs to shine more light toward one location, such as a reading chair, and reduces the need to have several lights on in a room. Mr. Epstein nods approvingly.

Though he is in the company of greenies, he rarely strays far from his entrepreneurial roots. Admiring a machine the scientists have developed to measure how much light in fixtures is directed up or down, so the fixtures can be designed accordingly to minimize energy use, he pointedly asks: "So what do you get from this intellectual asset?" Messrs. Horowitz and Page look puzzled, before replying that any profit from a commercial use of the machine or anything else they might develop would go to the lab, not to them.

"We do this for the good of humanity," Mr. Page says with a smile.

Child Care Comes to Work

Irvine office demonstrates how an on-site center can be beneficial.

By BONNIE HARRIS
TIMES STAFF WRITER

On a recent workday at her Irvine office, Traci Renner held a staff meeting, e-mailed clients, met with her boss and prepared a public relations proposal—all between diaper changes, feedings and play time with her 9-month-old son, Lucas, who rolled around the floor by her desk.

"It's nice to know I don't have to panic when my child care falls through at the last minute, like today," said Renner, stuffing a teething ring into her son's waiting mouth.

"Besides, I just like having him here with me sometimes."

At a time more families are seeing both parents hold full-time jobs, the 40-employee Benjamin Group public relations agency where Renner works is addressing child care in a way that many companies wouldn't dare—and its efforts have drawn national attention. Sick child? Work the day from home. Nanny canceled? Bring the kids on in.

Even though a tight job market and booming economy have prompted scores of employers to expand worker benefits and strike better work-life balances, officials say such workplace improvements haven't applied as much to child-care support.

It's taken nearly 20 years, for example, for the number of on-site corporate day-care centers to reach 8,000 nationally; in 1982 there were 204, according to a dependent-care consulting group in Michigan.

Operating costs, liability concerns and reams of licensing applications and inspections have deterred companies from making the on-site child-care leap.

But at Benjamin Group's Irvine offices, it's not uncommon to see Renner and other parents toting their children around the office, plopping them in a beanbag chair during meetings or putting them down for a nap in one of several office cribs.

Not everyone sees such an arrangement as practical or beneficial to the workplace. But as a result of this casual kid-friendly attitude and other programs for employees, the Silicon Valley-based agency has been repeatedly recognized by Working Mother magazine as one of the country's best companies to work for.

"It's nice to know I don't have to panic when my child care falls through at the last minute," Traci Renner says of bringing her son, Lucas, to work at Benjamin Group in Irvine.

And by the end of this month, the company's employees in Irvine will be able to enroll their children in an on-site day-care center called Executive Sweet, making it the first on-site, corporate child-care center in Orange County, according to state officials. Los Angeles County has just a few such centers. The Bay Area has 11.

"I'm surprised there aren't more," said John Gordon, a spokesman for the state Department of Social Services, which oversees day-care licensing. "I would have expected at least to see some of the larger companies heading in that direction."

But Sheri Benjamin, chief executive of Benjamin Group, said she has an idea why such child-care efforts are so unusual.

It's been a two-year process to open her company's on-site center, even requiring the entire Orange County office to move from Santa Ana to a larger site in Irvine with enough square footage to accommodate 20 children and enough room for an enclosed, grassy outdoor play area.

"Do you know how difficult it is?" asked Benjamin, who also set up an on-site center at the agency's headquarters in the Silicon Valley. "It's exhausting. But we've seen the payoffs. We were committed to this."

After two years of code inspections, building changes and licensing approvals, Benjamin said, she is now waiting on final approval from fire officials so she can officially open the center at the Irvine offices.

The trend in corporate child-care centers began in the 1980s in the health-care industry, with hospitals—and their large numbers of shift workers—leading the way, officials said. Employees at Hoag Hospital in Newport Beach have access to a day-care center that operates on its campus, but the center is not considered a corporate, on-site center because it is also open to the public.

Law firms and financial companies later began adding child care to their list of benefits, and now officials said they are seeing it splash into the technology industry. Motorola Inc., for one, boasts 12 on-site child-care centers in the U.S. and two abroad.

Cisco Systems Inc. runs an on-site center for roughly 100 children in San Jose and Amgen Inc., a biotechnology company in Thousand Oaks, recently expanded its 8-year-old center to accommodate 300, ranging in age from 6 weeks to 5 years.

"Child-care benefits, especially on-site child-care centers, are worth more than any amount of money," said Ilene Hoffer, a spokeswoman for Bright Horizons, which provides employer-sponsored on-site child care for more than 325 clients worldwide. "It's a competitive recruitment and retention tool for companies. If one company in an industry does it, many others tend to follow suit. They'd be crazy not to in this market."

Sharman Stein, a senior editor for Working Mother magazine, said employers are often put off by the cost of providing on-site child care, which can exceed $ 100,000 a year. But with the number of working mothers now topping 26 million, Stein said, she expects to see more companies begin "testing the waters," perhaps by providing emergency backup child care first.

At least 30 companies in California (a dozen in Orange County) offer such off-site services, designed to give working parents a safety net should their regular day-care arrangements fall through.

Typically, officials say, a working family will experience six to eight child-care breakdowns every year.

"It's just a no-brainer for companies to do everything they can to keep their working parents happy," Stein said. "We've seen time and time again that in order for employees to be productive, they have to feel like home base is covered."

At Benjamin Group, the office sometimes turns *into* home base, with 5-year-olds raiding the staff refrigerator or cozying up with a video in the company lounge.

What some bosses may frown on as a distraction, though, has evolved into what employees said is an unusual perk. With a staff of more than 30 women and a handful of dads, there is never a shortage of hands to pitch in if a child needs tending when the parent needs to concentrate on work. There is a lounge with sofas and a VCR, and plenty of toys, they said.

"Half the time I bring her in here, I don't know where she is," said account manager Morag Rich, referring to her 6-month-old daughter, Brenna.

"I'll get busy on something and then I have to walk through the office going, 'Who has the baby?'"

Added associate Christine Eastman, who joined the firm six months ago: "I don't even have kids, and I'm telling you, coming into the office after lunch and seeing the receptionist bouncing a baby on her knee is just plain fun."

The arrangement has been practiced in the agency's Orange County office for years while the company searched for a location that would meet the host of building restrictions required to operate a day-care center, said Benjamin, the chief executive, whose own children "grew up" in the center she opened nine years ago at the company's headquarters.

"When we started this back then, people thought we were bonkers, especially being the small company that we were. But we strongly believed it was the right thing to do," she said. "Now it's an enviable benefit in the workplace. And the returns have far outweighed any investment we've made."

In Orange County, there is already a list of employees who plan to enroll their children on the first day, Benjamin said. The company offers day-care subsidies that vary depending on salaries, but average about $266 per child per month.

The agency's general manager, Lisa Zwick, who is expecting her first child next month, said the new day-care center "made a huge difference" in her decision to return to work after the baby is born.

"It is such a relief to know I can come back here and have the baby in day care, but still so close by, while I work," she said. "All my friends are jealous."

Mental Illness: A Rising Workplace Cost

One Form, Depression, Takes $70 Billion Toll Annually; Bank One Intervenes Early

By Elyse Tanouye
Staff Reporter of THE WALL STREET JOURNAL

IN A TYPICAL OFFICE of 20 people, chances are that four will suffer from a mental illness this year. Depression, one of the most common, primarily hits workers in their most productive years: the 20s through 40s. Its annual toll on U.S. businesses amounts to about $70 billion in medical expenditures, lost productivity and other costs.

And yet most employers don't have a clue.

Even though Prozac has become a household word, few individual companies know the true cost of depression to their business, says Paul Greenberg, a health care economist at the Cambridge, Mass., consulting firm Analysis Group/Economics. That's because many of the indirect costs—such as reduced productivity and related illnesses like alcoholism—aren't readily apparent. And unlike those with allergies or appendicitis, people with mental or emotional problems tend to hide their conditions for fear of stigmatizing their careers.

What companies do see are the ever-rising medical bills to treat psychiatric illnesses among employees. U.S. antidepressant sales alone have risen more than 800% to $10.2 billion, since 1990, according to IMS Health. Public awareness of depression has also increased, as have the cost of interventions such as hospital stays and psychiatrist visits.

Seventy percent of large employers said they were concerned about rising psychiatric claims in a survey conducted last year by consulting firm Watson Wyatt Worldwide and the Washington Business Group on Health, an employer group. And companies tend to respond to that rise by trying to control costs. "Companies view health care, and specifically psychiatric claims, as a cost to be minimized," Mr. Greenberg says.

But depression is a tough disease to manage because its symptoms are largely invisible and subjective—even as it affects a person's moods, thoughts and energy levels. While its symptoms and severity can vary widely, the disease is particularly debilitating for working people: It often causes them to lose interest in their jobs and other aspects of their lives, to withdraw from social contact and to be overcome by feelings of worthlessness, guilt and hopelessness.

Sometimes, depression is triggered by an event, such as a death or divorce, but it can also occur without warning. For many, the disease is mild and transient. But for others, it worsens over time and, left untreated, can lead to very serious symptoms, such as suicidal thoughts that require hospitalization—or actual suicides that may seem to coworkers to come out of the blue.

Even when businesses do acknowledge and try to manage employee depression, it can be a thorny task. Bank One Corp., a Chicago-based banking and credit-card company, conducted an unusually comprehensive computer analysis of employee health data in the mid-1980s to determine what was driving its health-care costs so high. To its surprise, treating depressive disorders cost the company's self-insured health plan $931,000 in 1991—nearly as much as the $1.2 million cost to treat heart disease. The actual costs might have been closer, but the pan reimbursed treatments for mental health at a lower rate than other medical claims.

"The prevalence stunned us," says Daniel J. Conti, a clinical psychologist and director of the company's employee assistance program.

Even more pronounced was depression's impact on indirect costs, such as productivity losses from absenteeism. Depressed employees stayed out on short-term disability longer than employees with other common illnesses, and they suffered a high relapse rate. Another analysis showed Bank One's employees lost a total of 10,859 workdays over a two-year period because of depressive illnesses. In con-

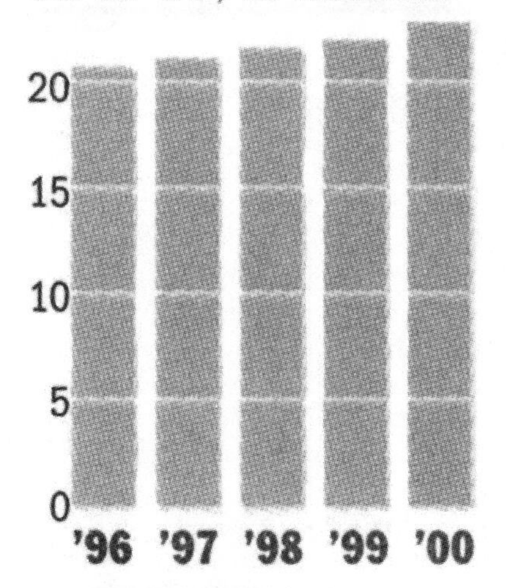

trast, high blood pressure resulted in 947 workdays lost and diabetes, 795 days. Depression also seemed to be insensitive to status, striking a cross-section of the company's staff, from clerical workers to executives.

Some reasons could be specific to the company: Two-thirds of Bank One's employees are women. Depression appears to strike women at about twice the rate it hits men, though it could be that women simply seek help more often than men. The company has also undergone a series of mergers, which can contribute to employee stress, according to studies.

Bank One decided to confront employee depression head on. In the belief that early intervention would mean fewer catastrophic claims later, the bank taught managers to recognize the signs of depression using the Depression Awareness, Recognition and Treatment program developed by the National Institutes of Health and the Washington Business Group on Health. It hired a staff psychologist to evaluate the treatment in each mental health disability case. It also mobilized its employee assistance program to help with employees' transition back to work. And it ran employee workshops on depression, stress management and managing relationships.

As it dug deeper, Bank One realized that many employees with mental illnesses weren't getting adequate treatment from its self-insured plan or from the several HMOs it offered. So in its self-insured plan, the company substantially reduced employee out-of-pocket costs for the first 12 therapy visits and stressed early intervention, which helps avoid hospital costs.

But less than 30% of its employees are in the self-insured plan, and Dr. Conti complains that HMO care is still a disappointment, despite pressure from Bank One. People treated under HMOs often receive drugs and short-term therapy, and while they return to work much faster, the relapse rate is much higher. The company figures it loses many more employee workdays because of the "revolving door" of employees leaving, then returning, only to leave again, Dr. Conti says.

Indeed, Bank One's effort to combat depression created a peculiar anomaly: The number of employees taking disability leaves for depression has ballooned, to 7.2 per 1,000 employees in 1999—four times the 1989 rate. Last year, about 500 employees went on short-term disability for depression, Dr. Conti says.

Is that figure abnormally high? It's hard to tell. Most businesses "have no idea what is driving their disability cost," Mr. Conti says, noting that Bank One's awareness programs probably spurred the jump by making more employees seek treatment and, ultimately, disability leave.

Still, there remains a deep-seated fear that admitting to mental illness, much less taking a leave for it, will hurt a career. Workers often ask whether getting treatment will make them uninsurable in the future, and Dr. Conti tells them they may encounter some difficulty. He also counsels those seeking treatment to be smart about whom they disclose information to.

The increased disability probably cost Bank One several million dollars in lost wages, as well as pay for temporary workers. But Dr. Conti believes the rise in disability is an initial blip that will decline in the future. "In the long run, it will pay off in lower numbers of serious cases and more productive workers," he says. "People will get help earlier and arrest the disease in earlier stages."

Knowing Your Rights and Responsibilities

The Americans With Disabilities Act helps protect workers with mental illness from employment discrimination. Some rights and responsibilities under the act:

Employees with a psychiatric disability

- Qualify for protection under the act only if their disability substantially limits a major life activity, such as sleeping or interacting with others
- Must disclose their disability to their employer to be eligible for protection under the act
- Can request reasonable accommodations, such as flexible work schedules, adjustments to their physical workspace, and adjustments to supervisory methods
- Can file a lawsuit or charges with state or federal agencies it they feel their rights are being violated

Employers

- Can't ask a job applicant about any mental disabilities before making a job offer
- Can require a pre-employment medical examination or inquiry after making a job offer, as long as it is required of all entering employees
- Can request an employee who is seeking accommodations to provide medical documentation of the disability
- Must keep all information concerning an employee's psychiatric condition or history confidential; the information must be kept separately from personnel records

Source: Equal Employment Opportunity Commission

New Medicines, Protective Laws Cut Dismissals

By Elyse Tanouye
Staff Reporter of THE WALL STREET JOURNAL

At age 34, Gerald Matusiewicz was riding high. He had a doctorate in metallurgical engineering, a budding career as an engineer at IBM, and a family. But his life began to unravel one day when a wave of intense anxiety swept over him. His mental illness was flaring up.

No one he worked with at International Business Machines Corp. knew he suffered from schizoaffective disorder, which falls somewhere between schizophrenia and bipolar disorder and causes him periods of overwhelming anxiety. He tried to keep working as if nothing were wrong. But then, uncharacteristically, he had an angry dispute with his immediate supervisor. When another manager, John Kelly, arrived to mediate, Mr. Matusiewicz told him he had suffered a psychiatric problem in the past and thought it was happening again.

Mr. Kelly gently suggested that Mr. Matusiewicz meet with the company's medical department for counseling. And the next day, after the medication his psychiatrist had prescribed made Mr. Matusiewicz drowsy, Mr. Kelly drove him home. During the 20-minute ride, Mr. Matusiewicz spoke openly about his problems. "It gets to a point where you can't hide it," says Mr. Matusiewicz, now 50 years old.

It was a crisis that could have derailed most careers. But sympathetic IBM managers and accommodating company policies helped him get back on track. Now, after nearly two decades with the company, the genial engineer works on some of IBM's most important computer-chip technologies.

More managers may find themselves in similar encounters as a confluence of legal, medical and social changes makes it possible for more people with serious mental illnesses to enter the workplace. Among these illnesses are schizophrenia, a psychotic disorder that can include symptoms such as delusions, hearing voices and difficulty focusing; and bipolar (or manic-depressive) disorder, which is characterized by periods of mania as well as episodes of depression.

The past decade has seen the introduction of powerful new antipsychotic medications that don't produce the muscle stiffness, shuffling gait and involuntary movements associated with earlier drugs. Because of this and other factors, many mental-health professionals often now urge patients to get back to work as soon as possible, a departure from longstanding views that holding a job might be too stressful.

All that puts new pressures on employers and can require special accommodations—allowing an employee time off to see a doctor, for example, or providing a private space to rest. Simultaneously, the individual's privacy must be preserved. Complicating things, the employer's legal liabilities are murky. And there are the lingering fears that mentally ill people will be unreliable or, worse, violent.

Workers have always struggled, if quietly, with mild forms of depression and anxiety, but medications such as Prozac and Zoloft as well as company mental-health benefits have enabled them to better manage—even conceal—their diseases on the job. But the five million to six million people with the more serious psychiatric illnesses in the U.S. have faced the greatest obstacles to working and, as a result, suffered sky-high unemployment rates.

Those companies that do hire and retain employees with serious mental disorders often find a payoff: Many workers with such illnesses have shown the strength to overcome great barriers and have acquired impressive credentials in the process. A study of 59 professionals and semiprofessionals with schizophrenia and schizoaffective disorder by Boston University researchers Zlatka Russinova and Marsha Ellison shows that about 60% of those surveyed have graduate degrees or have done some graduate work.

In some states, doctors and lawyers are asked to disclose mental illnesses during the licensing process. By and large, however, employers can't ask applicants if they have a psychiatric disability, and those seeking or holding jobs aren't required to disclose one. "There should be no [legal] way for an employer to obtain the insurance history or medical history of an applicant or new employee," says Claudia Center, an attorney at the Employment Law Center in San Francisco.

When a serious mental illness is disclosed, the Americans With Disabilities Act can protect employees with physical or mental disabilities against discrimination and requires that employers provide reasonable accommodations. Employers must also keep such disclosures confidential externally, but deciding who needs to know within the company is largely a matter of company policy, says Bruce Flynn, a senior consultant at Watson Wyatt Worldwide, a human-resources consulting firm.

Ms. Center warns, "There are certain legal rights you get if you disclose, but suddenly people will know something very personal about you, they might look at you differently, there may be discrimination."

Companies that hire and retain employees with serious mental disorders often find a payoff: Many of these workers have overcome great barriers and have acquired impressive credentials in the process.

If employees feel their rights have been violated, they can pursue legal measures, Ms. Center says. However, a study by researchers at the University of North Carolina, Chapel Hill, found that only 14% of charges filed by people with psychiatric illnesses under the disabilities law at the Equal Employment Opportunity Commission and state agencies had favorable outcomes for the employees.

In the very rare instance when an employer believes a mentally ill employee does pose a threat, it can bar the person from the workplace. In general, however, employees who use mental-health services aren't any more likely to become violent than the general public, mental-health professionals say. James Madero, a clinical psychologist in San Diego who helps companies prevent workplace violence, has been called in to assess about 500 incidents of employee threats, but only about 20 of them involved employees with serious mental illnesses.

But fears of prejudices keep some people under cover. As a young attorney and writer, Allen Wilkinson didn't tell his boss that depression was the reason he wanted to quit the firm. "I was afraid people would see me as a leper ... and would say, 'Don't listen to him, he's a loony.'" Later, when he was practicing in San Diego, his illness (diagnosed as a type of bipolar disorder) intensified. In 1995, he closed his office and put himself on inactive status without divulging the reason.

continued on next page

Mr. Wilkinson was in a deep depression for five years. At one point, he put a loaded pistol in his mouth "and just about ended it," he remembers. About a year ago, a psychiatrist prescribed him a newer antidepressant and antipsychotic that "turned my life around," he says. Mr. Wilkinson, 46, put himself back on active status as a lawyer, but mostly spends his time now writing books.

Research shows that stigma dissipates among employers who have experience managing mentally ill employees. Alan Bowler, 35, struggled with schizophrenia, and was hospitalized many times until he began taking one of a newer generation of antipsychotics. That helped him develop "a determination to get up and do something," he says. He attended a community college, where "I was top dog, with 16 A's," he says. "I was loving life." He then went to the rehabilitation center in Falls Church, Va., and was referred to Toyota of North Arlington in Virginia.

As an oil-change technician, Mr. Bowler proved a model employee. "It's a rarity that I would find someone like Alan," says Tom Ellmer, the parts and service director at the time he was hired.

Mr. Bowler has confided to co-worker Jason Wright, 33, that he sometimes hears voices. Mr. Wright says, "I've never felt uncomfortable," adding that Mr. Bowler told him he is doing well on medication. One day about two years ago, Mr. Bowler said he wasn't feeling well. "I knew he wasn't talking about an upset stomach," says Mr. Wright, who advised him to tell the service manager. "It has been a learning experience for me as well," Mr. Wright says.

Journal Link: See additional data from a report detailing the economic impact of mental illness on the workplace, in the online Journal at *WSJ.com/JournalLinks*

What Happens When It's the Boss Who's Suffering?

Paul Gottlieb's Story Shows Upper Ranks Get Hit Too; Screaming Atop the Cliffs

By Elyse Tanouye
Staff Reporter of THE WALL STREET JOURNAL

Paul Gottlieb was a 40-something rising star in the publishing world, sought after for top positions at major book publishers in New York City. In meetings with authors, business associates and employees, he was a take-charge executive. No one realized that sometimes at the end of the day, Mr. Gottlieb would sit at his desk, exhausted, and think about jumping out the window.

Mr. Gottlieb suffered from depression that deepened even as his career took off. "I slid from being myself to knowing how to play myself," he says. He knew what Paul Gottlieb's smile was like and so he put it on; he knew how he was supposed to act in business meetings and at cocktail parties. But shortly after being promoted to president and publisher of Harry N. Abrams Inc., he knew he couldn't go on. "I had to get better or I had to end my life," he says. He got up from his desk one day and walked across Central Park to his analyst, who called his wife and urged immediate hospitalization.

Coping with employee depression is increasingly on the minds of workplace managers. But what happens when the boss is the one with a mental illness? The repercussions on a business, its employees and stockholders can be enormous if the illness interferes with a leader's performance. The question may become more pressing as the economy puts executives under greater stress, and intensifies scrutiny of them.

"If this downturn continues, we will see much more of this problem because CEOs love control, and this is an environment in which you will have limited control," says Mortimer Feinberg, an organizational psychologist an chairman of BFS Psychological Associates, a New York executive-counseling firm.

It isn't clear how prevalent mental illnesses are in the corporate upper echelons. Executives rarely reveal having any impairment. Some people argue that mental illness isn't common in executive suites because managers with problems are weeded out at lower levels. Still, depression, anxiety, and other psychiatric conditions plague one in five people in the U.S., so it stands to reason that executives would be among the afflicted.

A few executives have disclosed or hinted at mental-health problems, including some of the most outgoing and vibrant business characters. In her autobiography, Katharine Graham, chairman of the Washington Post Co.'s executive committee, describes the pain in the workplace cause by the manic-depressive episodes of her late husband, Philip, when he was president and publisher of the Washington Post. He shot himself to death in 1963. Media mogul Ted Turner acknowledged in media accounts that he has taken lithium, a drug commonly prescribed to treat bipolar disorder. A spokeswoman for Mr. Turner now says he was misdiagnosed and has been off lithium for 10 years.

Securities laws require public companies to disclose anything that materially affects the company, and that can theoretically include serious health problems of key executives. "Invasion of privacy is one sacrifice one makes to lead a public corporation," says Jeffrey Sonnenfeld, head of the Chief Executive Leadership Institute in Atlanta. But even when the board knows of a problem, there is a "longstanding tendency to circle the wagons on boards and protect an out-of-control boss," he says.

When it becomes clear that the boss needs help, figuring out who should raise the issue can be tricky. A subordinate runs the risk of being ignored or punished for confronting the executive. Some experts say it should be a superior, the employee assistance program—or a trusted board member in the case of a problem CEO.

Often, companies turn to outsiders to handle uncomfortable encounters. Dr. Feinberg, chairman of BFS Psychological Associates, was hired by a board member of a large communications company to approach the president of an important division. The president was showing uncharacteristic mood swings. "Most guys don't want to admit needing help," Dr. Feinberg says, and this executive initially denied having a problem. But Dr. Feinberg had interviewed employees and recounted specific incidents in which he had lost his cool or been uncommunicative. The executive thanked him and got help. He recovered and eventually retired gracefully, Dr. Feinberg says.

In a different case Dr. Feinberg handled for a large food distributor in the Midwest, the executive denied having a problem. He argued that people were plotting against him, and refused help. Soon after, the board removed him, Dr. Feinberg says.

Tough economic times especially can take a toll on CEO psyches. Theodore John "Ted" Arneson founded a Minneapolis engineering firm, Professional Instruments Corp., in 1946 and built a successful enterprise that develops technical equipment. But the

continued on next page

turbulent economy of the late 1960s sent the company into chaos. As interest rates rose, banks called in loans with lower rates, and big clients cancelled contracts.

"I was simply overwhelmed by a string of circumstances," Mr. Arneson says. His first episode of depression struck in 1969, and he lost 40 pounds. But he kept his internal state to himself. "If my bank in 1969 had known that I had kinda lost it, for sure our company would have failed," he says.

As an entrepreneur, Mr. Arneson handled most of the top responsibilities, from sales to hiring to finance. He didn't have the deep reservoir of management to turn to that CEOs of large companies have. Neither could he step aside. He felt entirely responsible for livelihoods of 100 employees and their families.

He "toughed it out" for two years and eventually recovered. Other episodes and recoveries followed, each linked to tough business times. But in 1976 he attempted suicide, and ended up in a locked hospital ward for 2 1/2 months. "It got so damn bad, I was willing to kill myself, even though I knew what it would do to my family. It's a vortex that sucks you down," he says.

He was helped at various times by psychiatrists and electroshock therapy, for which he is a staunch advocate. Through it all, he steered his business through the economic turbulence. He is still the company's chairman, but a few years ago turned over the day-to-day operations to his three sons. Now devoting much of his time to suicide prevention, Mr. Arneson also sits on the board of the National Foundation for Depressive Illness, an advocacy group in New York.

Mr. Gottlieb, the New York publisher, says his illness didn't affect his business judgement but looking back, he says it may have affected some personal decisions, such as leaving three big publishing jobs.

'I slid from being myself to knowing how to play myself,' Mr. Gottlieb says. He knew what Paul Gottlieb's smile was like, and so he put it on; he knew how to act at meetings and cocktail parties, so he did.

Like many people, Mr. Gottlieb had been very intolerant of psychological problems and believed people should "pull up your socks and get on with it." Even as his internal turmoil grew in his 40s, he attributed it to a midlife crisis. But it was more than that. He felt a sense of worthlessness. He had a difficult time getting out of bed. Choosing a tie was "agony," he says.

One day, instead of going to the office, he took a drive and ended up in New Jersey at the sheer cliff overlooking the Hudson River and New York City. He walked to the edge and screamed. He thought about jumping. At other times, he walked through the streets, recklessly dodging traffic, "playing matador with the buses," he recalls.

Still, he remained a powerhouse executive of international stature. He was in meetings all day, attended social functions at night. "I truly believe my abilities as a manager continued at a pretty high level," he says, attributing it to an ability to compartmentalize his life. A year after joining Harry N. Abrams Inc., a major publisher of art books, he was promoted to president and publisher. Outside of the office, he was asked to become chairman of the board of the Dalton School, an exclusive Upper East Side private school. He turned down that request to avoid the added stress.

When he wasn't diverted by his work, he suffered great pain. "You feel you're operating on two levels... like tectonic plates that shift and move," he says.

All that ended within days of his leaving his desk and walking across Central Park to get help from his analyst. The next day, Mr. Gottlieb was examined by a psychopharmacologist—a specialist in drug therapy for psychiatric illnesses—who explained that his disease was physiological. In the hospital, Mr. Gottlieb took a cocktail of medications, which included different antidepressants, prescribed by the doctor. "Miraculously within 10 days, the plates came together," says Mr. Gottlieb, who returned to work, where people had been told that he had been out with a stomach ailment, diverticulitis.

Mr. Gottlieb resumed his life and a distinguished career at Abrams. He was soon named CEO and in his long reign there, pushed the company into new areas such as children's books, paperbacks, and international projects. Now 66, he gave up the CEO title at Abrams in January, after 21 years with the company, to become vice chairman of the parent company, Martiniere Groupe of France and remains a director of Abrams.

He says he hasn't felt depressed since his treatment, even through some trying times, such as a divorce. As bad as they were, he says, those difficulties were "nothing like what I survived in the illness. It is very useful to know you can survive."

Index

Test Your Knowledge Form

We encourage you to photocopy and use this page as a tool to assess how the articles in *Annual Editions* expand on the information in your textbook. By reflecting on the articles you will gain enhanced text information. You can also access this useful form on a product's book support Web site at *http://www.dushkin.com/online/*.

NAME: DATE:

TITLE AND NUMBER OF ARTICLE:

BRIEFLY STATE THE MAIN IDEA OF THIS ARTICLE:

LIST THREE IMPORTANT FACTS THAT THE AUTHOR USES TO SUPPORT THE MAIN IDEA:

WHAT INFORMATION OR IDEAS DISCUSSED IN THIS ARTICLE ARE ALSO DISCUSSED IN YOUR TEXTBOOK OR OTHER READINGS THAT YOU HAVE DONE? LIST THE TEXTBOOK CHAPTERS AND PAGE NUMBERS:

LIST ANY EXAMPLES OF BIAS OR FAULTY REASONING THAT YOU FOUND IN THE ARTICLE:

LIST ANY NEW TERMS/CONCEPTS THAT WERE DISCUSSED IN THE ARTICLE, AND WRITE A SHORT DEFINITION:

We Want Your Advice

ANNUAL EDITIONS revisions depend on two major opinion sources: one is our Advisory Board, listed in the front of this volume, which works with us in scanning the thousands of articles published in the public press each year; the other is you—the person actually using the book. Please help us and the users of the next edition by completing the prepaid article rating form on this page and returning it to us. Thank you for your help!

ANNUAL EDITIONS: Business Ethics 02/03

ARTICLE RATING FORM

Here is an opportunity for you to have direct input into the next revision of this volume. We would like you to rate each of the articles listed below, using the following scale:

1. **Excellent: should definitely be retained**
2. **Above average: should probably be retained**
3. **Below average: should probably be deleted**
4. **Poor: should definitely be deleted**

Your ratings will play a vital part in the next revision. Please mail this prepaid form to us as soon as possible. Thanks for your help!

RATING	ARTICLE
______	1. Thinking Ethically: A Framework for Moral Decision Making
______	2. Managing by Values
______	3. Defining Moments: When Managers Must Choose Between Right and Right
______	4. Doing Well by Doing Good
______	5. Doing the Right Thing
______	6. Crime in the Suites
______	7. When the Numbers Don't Add Up
______	8. Cut Loose
______	9. Electronic Communication in the Workplace—Something's Got to Give
______	10. Cyber Crime
______	11. Are You Teaching Your Employees to Steal?
______	12. Guerrilla Warfare
______	13. Harassment Grows More Complex
______	14. Wage Gap Continues to Vex Women
______	15. Racism in the Workplace
______	16. Older TV Writers Press Case
______	17. The Not-So-Fine Art of the Layoff
______	18. Termination With Dignity
______	19. Sorrow and Guilt: An Ethical Analysis of Layoffs
______	20. A Hero—and a Smoking-Gun Letter
______	21. Blowing Whistles, Blowing Smoke
______	22. Intentional Integrity
______	23. Excuses, Excuses: Moral Slippage in the Workplace
______	24. Gold Mine or Fool's Gold?
______	25. Leaders as Value Shapers
______	26. The Parable of the Sadhu
______	27. Trust in the Marketplace
______	28. Can Business Still Save the World?
______	29. As Leaders, Women Rule
______	30. Crimes and Misdeminors
______	31. Virtual Morality: A New Workplace Quandary
______	32. Mixed Signals
______	33. Diversity Worst Practices
______	34. Values in Tension: Ethics Away From Home
______	35. Global Standards, Local Problems
______	36. Privacy as Global Policy

RATING	ARTICLE
______	37. Companies Are Discovering the Value of Ethics
______	38. The Perils of Doing the Right Thing
______	39. Too Close for Comfort
______	40. Managing for Organizational Integrity
______	41. A Good Start
______	42. The 100 Best Corporate Citizens
______	43. Ethical Challenges for Business in the New Millennium: Corporate Social Responsibility and Models of Management Mor
______	44. Old Ethical Principles: The New Corporate Culture
______	45. Profits From Principle: Five Forces Redefining Business
______	46. Learning IT Right From Wrong
______	47. Tech Executives Devote Energy to Green Causes
______	48. Child Care Comes to Work
______	49. Mental Illness: A Rising Workplace Cost

(Continued on next page)

NO POSTAGE NECESSARY IF MAILED IN THE UNITED STATES

BUSINESS REPLY MAIL

FIRST-CLASS MAIL PERMIT NO. 84 GUILFORD CT

POSTAGE WILL BE PAID BY ADDRESSEE

McGraw-Hill/Dushkin
530 Old Whitfield Street
Guilford, Ct 06437-9989

ABOUT YOU

Name Date

Are you a teacher? ❒ A student? ❒
Your school's name

Department

Address City State Zip

School telephone #

YOUR COMMENTS ARE IMPORTANT TO US!

Please fill in the following information:
For which course did you use this book?

Did you use a text with this ANNUAL EDITION? ❒ yes ❒ no
What was the title of the text?

What are your general reactions to the *Annual Editions* concept?

Have you read any pertinent articles recently that you think should be included in the next edition? Explain.

Are there any articles that you feel should be replaced in the next edition? Why?

Are there any World Wide Web sites that you feel should be included in the next edition? Please annotate.

May we contact you for editorial input? ❒ yes ❒ no
May we quote your comments? ❒ yes ❒ no